"BACKSTAGE PASS TO THE FLIPSIDE 3"

Talking the Afterlife with Jennifer Shaffer Book 3

by Richard Martini

Medium Jennifer Shaffer
as I try to get in a word edge-wise

Backstage Pass to the Flipside 3, Talking to the Afterlife with Jennifer Shaffer Book Three by Richard Martini

Copyright © 2020 by Richard Martini. All Rights Reserved.

ISBN: 978-1-7324850-7-5

No part of this book may be reproduced by any mechanical, photographic, or electronic process, other than for "fair use" as brief quotations embodied in articles and review without prior written permission of the author and/or publisher.

The author of this book does not claim the individuals named in this book are the people themselves. There is no way to prove anyone is communicating from the afterlife, nor does author claim doing so. However, all of these interviews were filmed and/or recorded, and while the transcripts are edited for time and content, they reflect an accurate portrait of what was said (with personal information passed on to living relatives where possible or edited for propriety's sake). If anyone is offended by this material, I offer my sincere apologies, and like I do with all my books, suggest getting a refund for it, or returning it to whomever passed it along to the reader.

Also author does not claim to offer medical advice or prescribe the use of any technique as a form of treatment for physical or medical problems without the advice of a physician, either directly or indirectly. The intent of the author is only to offer information of a general nature to help you in your quest for emotional and spiritual well-being. In the event you use any of the information in this book for yourself, which is your constitutional right, the author and the publisher assume no responsibility for your actions.

Cover Art: "The Sistine Madonna" by Raphael 1514. Painted for the Benedictine Monastery in Piacenza, the painting depicts Pope Sixtus IV (who ordered the assassination of the Medici bros in Florence.) Raphael reportedly had a "heavenly vision" of the Virgin Mary and had this vision in mind when painting the portrait. Note the troubled looks both Mary and the baby Jesus give the audience from their side of the veil.

Homina Publishing PO Box 248 Santa Monica, CA 90406

CHAPTERS

Foreword - 7

Introduction – **Our Flipside Classroom** - 12

Chapter One – **Dancing with the Stars** – (TIM CONWAY, ROBERT EVANS, STEVE MCQUEEN) - 16

Chapter Two - **Maverick is in the House** (JOHN MCCAIN, ABRAHAM LINCOLN, ROBIN WILLIAMS, PRINCE) - 39

Chapter Three – **I Feel Good, I Knew that I Would** (ROBIN WILLIAMS, ELVIS and JAMES BROWN) - 53

Chapter Four – **Queen of Soul** (ARETHA, SYDNEY POLLACK) - 64

Chapter Five – **The Country is at Stake** (PRESIDENTS NIXON, KENNEDY AND AMELIA EARHART) - 77

Chapter Six – **The Frequency Is the Same** (LINCOLN, JEFFERSON, JFK JR, WILLIAM BLAKE, ROBIN WILLIAMS) - 88

Chapter Seven – **The Microsoft Guy and Curing CTE** (PAUL ALLEN, JUNIOR SEAU, DAVE DUERSON, KURT COBAIN, ABE LINCOLN, GEORGE WASHINGTON) - 99

Chapter Eight – **Very Thin, Very Metro** (ORSON WELLES ROBERT FROST THE MEDICI FAMILY) - 145

Chapter Nine – **Speaking of Frank** (SINATRA FREDDIE MERCURY BRENT TAYLOR) - 156

Chapter Ten – **It's All Frequency** (PRINCE ROGERS NELSON, JIM MORRISON) - 172

Chapter Eleven – **Sitting Shiva with Sitting Bull** (COUSIN MATT, SITTING BULL) - 185

Chapter Twelve – **We'll Be Right Back** (DICK CLARK, MERV GRIFFIN, HOWARD SCHULTZ, BLAKE EDWARDS, JOAN RIVERS) - 209

Chapter Thirteen – **Poppy** (GEORGE BUSH SR, JOHN MCCAIN, NANCY REAGAN) - 242

Chapter Fourteen – **Far Horizons** (JOAN OF ARC, CHRISTOPHER COLUMBUS) - 255

Chapter Fifteen – **He's Very Aware** (FDR, PENNY, GARRY MARSHALL, CLARENCE CLEMONS, DANNY FEDERICI) - 272

Chapter Sixteen – **We've Got This** (ALAN RICKMAN, MICK GOUGH, JOHN MCCAIN) - 294

Chapter Seventeen – **A Hell of a Trip** (MARTIN LUTHER KING, MARILYN MONROE, HOOVER, GANDHI) - 308

Chapter Eighteen – **The 13th Dalai Lama** - 322

Chapter Nineteen – **It's Not Something You Would Question** (TESLA, MARK TWAIN, SAM THE DOG) - 331

Chapter Twenty – **Healing and Helping Others** (MICHAEL JACKSON, HAWKING, SAGAN, EINSTEIN, TESLA) - 347

Chapter Twenty One – **Game Not Over Man** (BILL PAXTON, STEPHEN HAWKING, CARL SAGAN) - 360

Chapter Twenty Two – **They've Already Watched It** (NIPSEY HUSSLE, WILLIAM BUTLER YEATS, DAVID BOWIE) - 374

Chapter Twenty Three – **I Understand You're the Person** (CONVERSATION WITH ROBERT KENNEDY) - 380

Chapter Twenty Four – **It's Chinatown Jack** (ROBERT TOWNE, HIRA, ED TAYLOR) - 391

Chapter Twenty Five – **Night Tide** (HAWKING, LUANA, JESUS DENNIS HOPPER) - 415

Chapter Twenty Six – **Bunch of Hockey Pucks** DONALD J. RICKLES - 430

Chapter Twenty Seven – **Cub Fans Everywhere** – (FORMER CUB RON KUNDE, PRINCE, MICHAEL NEWTON, AN AKASHIC LIBRARIAN, NELSON MANDELA) - 439

Chapter Twenty Eight - **Gods of Rock and Roll Physics** (TOM PETTY AND FLIPSIDE TEACHER MA DURGA) - 464

Chapter Twenty Nine – **Planning Our Next Lifetime** CASS ELLIOT, JESUS - 474

Chapter Thirty – **They've Been Waiting** (ANTHONY BOURDAIN, BILL PAXTON, PRINCE, ANDY KAUFMAN, GARRY SHANDLING) - 489

Chapter Thirty One – **Not Gone, Just Not Here** (AMELIA, JESUS, DR. HELEN WAMBACH) - 501

Chapter Thirty Two - **Easy Riders** – (LUANA AND PETER FONDA) - 516

Chapter Thirty Three – **Our Librarian Luana** (LUANA ANDERS) - 537

Chapter Thirty Four - **Mamba Out** (KOBE, GIANNA BRYANT) - 550

Afterword – **"New Lange Syne"** (LUANA, PETER TOWNSEND) - 564

Acknowledgements and Author's Bios. - 579

Note: The above chapters represent conversations with a variety of people who show up in different sessions, answer questions asked weeks earlier, sometimes refer to conversations that were made in other chapters of "Backstage Pass to the Flipside." **No one, including me, can claim these people are the people that I'm claiming them to be**.

But in this construct, accessing people who used to be on the planet, I invite the people on the flipside to identify themselves to the best of their ability, I do the forensic research afterwards to see how accurate they were. (In the "Note" sections.) We "talked to" a number of folks, including "Aretha Franklin, Bill Paxton, Prince, Robin Williams, John Candy, John McCain, George Bush Sr, Abraham Lincoln, Richard Nixon, Paul Allen, Junior Seau, Dave Duerson, Orson Welles, Frank Sinatra, Anthony Bourdain, Sitting Bull, The 13th Dalai Lama, Nikola Tesla, Mark Twain, Robert and John Kennedy, Martin Luther King, Dennis Hopper, Don Rickles, Peter Fonda, Tim Conway, Amelia Earhart and the Alpha and Omega." **If you have any question as to *how that could be*, please start with the book or film "Flipside."** For the rest of you, the story continues on the next page.

FOREWORD

by Luana Anders and Jennifer Medlyn Shaffer

My two guides into the Flipside.

Jennifer today and Luana circa 1965.

(THIS FOREWORD IS REPRINTED FROM "BACKSTAGE PASS TO THE FLIPSIDE: TALKING TO THE AFTERLIFE WITH JENNIFER SHAFFER")

Forewords are an unusual introduction to the material inside a book. In "Flipside: A Tourist's Guide on How to Navigate the Afterlife" Harvard PhD Gary Schwartz offered to write the foreword, where he said that "self science" was something Einstein had done, and he felt my "journey into the Flipside" should be considered as part of that canon.

In "It's a Wonderful Afterlife volume one" Charles Grodin suggested in his foreword that he didn't quite know what to make of my forays into the afterlife but enjoyed my passion for them. In Volume two, Galen Stoller, a young man who passed away some years ago wrote an eloquent foreword from where he is now, detailing what he wanted to impart about the journey. *"It is a wonderful afterlife,"* he wrote (via a medium), *"but only because "it is wonderful to be alive."*

I suggested my pal and compatriot in this endeavor medium/intuitive Jennifer Shaffer should write the foreword, as she's the conduit for this research. But while we were discussing this, Luana Anders, my friend and inspiration for this journey (who passed in 1996 after our being best friends for 20 years), suggested (through Jennifer) that **she** wanted to write her own foreword to this book.

> *Note: Luana, besides being an actress who appeared in 30 features (including "Easy Rider") also appeared in 300 TV shows. Her film writing credits include "Fire On The Amazon" and "Limit Up" written with yours truly.) At some point in this book, she suggested I try "automatic writing." I sat in front of the keyboard, put my fingers on the keys and thought: "Type whatever comes to mind." I opened myself up to the possibility I could write something on her behalf:*

"First, let me be clear. Richard is not talking through me. I am talking to him through Jennifer (usually). She does her best to make it easy for him to understand what I'm trying to say, and I'm doing my best to make it easier for him to understand. But it is *leaning in* from both sides.

At the moment, Richard is typing this sentence and has put his mind on virtual hold (he claims it's a meditation technique) to allow "me" to take over his typing. Some people call this "automatic writing." **Doesn't mean it's any good. It just means it's automatic.** No brain stem involved.

First I'd would like to point out that chanting "Nam Myoho Renge Kyo"[1] saved my life. I know that Richard used to tease me about it, make fun of it – and I'm grateful for that because it allowed me to laugh about it as well.

> (Note: Luana would do her "daimoku" ("Nam-myoho-renge-kyo" prayer) in the car on the way to an event. She'd chant at lightning speed, decades of practice, which sounds a bit like "*homina homina munya homina.*" I would imitate her and she couldn't help but laugh. Chanting helped her navigate her *fear of parties*. Luana was an incredible listener, and on more than one occasion, I'd leave her for ten minutes at some tony event, come back to find a close friend sobbing, pouring out his/her life to her. She had incredible compassion, even as a listener.)

---

[1] SGI/NSA Buddhist chant. http://www.sgi.org/about-us/president-ikedas-writings/gongyo-and-daimoku.html

But it saved my life. I never would have made it as long as I did on the planet without being able to focus on something else so dear to me. **Saving humanity by chanting about it.** If you're not familiar with it, if you're suffering, I recommend it as a form of meditation and healing. You pray for someone else and you are healed. Simple as that.

I suggested that I write the foreword to this book because after all, much of it is about me – and I have little to say in the matter. Believe me, it was as shocking to me as it was to my class to have him (Richard) appear as he did – willy nilly – in front of my classroom over here.[2]

He just started speaking out loud as if was completely normal that some ghostly avatar would appear in front of our class and start blathering away about his "research."

But I applaud him for it. *He's got cojones this boy.* I can call him a boy – because I know him better than most. He's endearing... to me and to others. But at his core, he's that little boy that I've known for a long, long time.

It's important work that he is doing, important work that he and Jennifer are doing. To help us communicate with all of you back there on the planet, and to open up people's minds about the ability to do so. It's happened not because of any great cataclysmic event that's in the offing – it's happening because *it's time*. **It's time to shift consciousness, to shift gears to understand the nature of reality.**

It's going to upset some people, but we're on top of that as well. It's going to liberate most people. Help most people. And ultimately turn out to be completely accurate when others figure this process out.

Some may ask "Why now?" Some may ask "Is this a good thing to do to communicate with our elders and loved ones who've gone on?" **Well, we still have things to communicate to you, we still have thoughts, dreams, feelings and hope for humanity – because we**

---

[2] It was during my first deep hypnosis session where I found myself standing in her classroom, interrupting it. Everyone turned in shock as I appeared. She looked at me as if to say "WTF?" She looked about 20 years younger than when I knew her – at least 10 years before I met her. She looked embarrassed to see me standing in the class talking – but I continued to speak. (*Flipside*)

consider ourselves part of your journey as well. You may not think of us that way – but we think of you that way.

So please, allow me to offer this small token of appreciation for the fellow who is typing this sentence. Yes, you are a goofball Richard, you are someone that has vexed and frustrated me during my life, but also during other lifetimes.

But you also taught me how to laugh, how to let go, and how to be more of myself while I was on the planet. I know what my path was about, I know why I had to depart early – eventually you'll come to know these reasons as well. Suffice to say it's okay not to "know everything" or "why everything happens" but it is good to trust in the idea that they do "happen for a reason."

And let's focus on that for a moment – "focus on reason." What is reasoning? Taking the evidence presented in front of us, and trying to figure out what it means and how it can help *me* in my journey. We reason things out because that's what we do with our minds... we also can go "beyond reason" and allow things to happen to us, or for us... and that's how I want you to consider what you're about to read. That this goes "beyond reason." And there's a reason for that as well.

Okay, I'm telling Richard to stop now – and to let our mutual friend Jennifer go over this text and see what "resonates" or rings true for her. After all – it's those "feelings of resonance" when we get a shiver of truth, or when we get a feeling that we're actually learning or talking about something that's beyond our logic and thought, beyond our mind... that we truly are able to learn things... about the nature of reality and about the nature of ourselves. I'm fortunate because Richard can type at the speed of thought – I'm watching him do this as we speak, and I suggest a plethora of ideas and he's able to blast them onto the page.

One more thing about love. **I love you all.** I'm not just saying that as a phrase – but I want you to really feel what I'm saying. I LOVE YOU. I send my heart and soul and unconditional love to you who are reading this sentence. I hope and pray that you receive this love because love is what moves this universe, it is the giant engine of who we are, it's what or who God is, it's what or who *we are*. If you can wrap your mind around love – that's great – if you can't, that's okay too, just open your heart up to the idea of it.

Love yourself. Love your neighbor. Love your enemy. Love the idea of love, of creating love, or spreading love of being loved and giving it in return. That's about all I have to say on the topic except... "See you on the flipside." (To quote a corny phrase too often used by a close friend of both of ours.)

PS: (It's) Just a few days after my birthday – I would have been *xxx* age in your realm – but over here – not such a big deal. Which I prefer. Enjoy the cake.

Written *(as if channeled)* by Luana Anders

Luana and author on Via Veneto.

The photograph that James Van Praagh cited, when I was speaking live to Luana on the Charles Grodin Show circa 1996. When I put this photograph onto the fridge, I said "The essence of our relationship;" cappuccinos and cookies and unmitigated laughs.

When James was on the show, I called in from Santa Monica, and Van Praagh said "There's a photograph on your refrigerator that she says "Is the essence of your relationship." It was the first time I realized we could communicate, albeit through someone else, and we haven't stopped since.

INTRODUCTION
OUR FLIPSIDE CLASSROOM

Jennifer and Richard in our usual cafe.

Here we are again.

Welcome to the third book of interviews between myself, Jennifer Shaffer medium/intuitive, and Luana Anders actress/moderator and a cast of her friends on the flipside. Perhaps you've skipped the foreword, since it's also in book one and two. I include it for those who haven't read books one or two.

To bring you up to speed, Jennifer Shaffer and I have been utilizing the skills of my departed friend Luana Anders on the flipside to help facilitate conversations with loved ones no longer on the planet.

I've filmed more than one medium asking the same questions to the same individual (Bill Paxton for example) and learned that in general folks on the flipside may tailor their responses specifically to the person asking the question. So despite the fact that all three mediums said "the same things" in reply to my questions, someone else asking those same questions may get different answers, geared to them.

For example, if I ask questions of my father who is no longer on the planet, he may tailor his replies to his insight into me, or his ability to access me. One of his other children, or grandchildren might get a different answer to their questions based on his knowing their path and journey from his perspective.

A long way of saying "bring some salt with you" when you read these interviews. I film them and then transcribe them – sometimes I have not heard Jennifer correctly, sometimes she may have not heard the person on the other side correctly, sometimes they may show her a specific item which she translates into something and I may not be able to unpack the meaning behind it.

I won't pretend the process is science. I ask her leading questions because I can, because I already have proven beyond a shadow of doubt (to me anyway) that she is a cellphone to the flipside. If the dear reader is looking for verification, go back to the beginning, with "Flipside" and march their way through to the last two "Backstage Pass" books. This is an ongoing series.

When I get a piece of new information from the flipside, I try to hunt down confirmation via forensic research, then foot note it. When I get a contrary piece of information based on what a person still on the planet knows, I note that as well. But the purpose of filming these conversations, then transcribing them is to demonstrate it is possible to "converse" with people no longer on the planet; to demonstrate they are not "gone" – "they are just not here."

We all don't have the abilities that Jennifer or other mediums have. Based on the research, it appears each of us comes with "filters on the brain" that limit this information. Some are born without those filters (mediums) some don't have them in place until the age of 8 (some children) and some lose their filters due to some incident. (Note: See Dr. Bruce Greyson's YouTube talk "Is Consciousness Produced by the Brain?" for a discussion of medical data that indicates that the brain has filters that prevent us from accessing certain information.)

The ways filters can be disabled is most commonly reported as via a near death event, a drug induced consciousness altering event, via someone whose filters work differently (a talented medium) or via deep hypnosis (recommended.) People can see a hypnotherapist who is talented at guiding a person into another realm and speak directly with their loved ones no longer on the planet. Seeing a medium may yield the same result; a "confirmation that they still exist."

I've written extensively about hypnotherapy in "Flipside: A Tourist's Guide on How to Navigate the Afterlife" "It's a Wonderful Afterlife; Further Adventures on the Flipside," and "Hacking the Afterlife." I report on the 50 plus cases I've filmed of people under deep hypnosis saying the same things about the process; how we choose our lifetime, how we bring about a third of our conscious energy to that lifetime, how when we are here the filters on the brain keep us semiconscious about the experience, and when we return home we regain the conscious energy we left behind to be able to observe, process all of our previous lifetimes.

In the previous two "Backstage Pass" books, I point out that a medium like Jennifer is a bit like having an amazing smart phone to the flipside; if I ask the right questions in the right manner, I may get new information from someone no longer on the planet.

It's not my theory, belief or opinion people say these things; I've been filming our conversations for at least five years. I've compared our results with the results from the cases I've filmed and the cases from Dr. Helen Wambach and Michael Newton. They all say relatively the same things about the architecture of the afterlife. (Note: That's the name of the book that precedes this one.)

For the most part, I'm doing something a bit different than **"trying to prove that life goes on."** I spent the first books demonstrating life does go on; in this research, I'm demonstrating we can learn "new information" from people no longer on the planet.

People have asked me why there are "so many celebrities" in the "Backstage Pass" books. If you're familiar with "Flipside" you'll know that I was given the message to "annihilate vanity" ("Vanum populatum") by someone no longer on the planet. What people say on the flipside is that there is no such thing as celebrity, fame, or any of the hierarchy we pretend exists here. They "aren't famous over there."

Our moderator on the Flipside, Luana Anders, did over 300 TV shows and feature films, from "the Godfather" to "Easy Rider." She got to know and work with many people I never met – but if she knows them, or she knows people who know them, its easier to access their "frequency."

When someone shows up I'll ask why they did so. At some point, I moved from people I knew, or met, or who have shown up in sessions, to people I've never met, that existed centuries ago – just to see if I could ask questions. I started to "ask" Jennifer for certain people to show up – from religious avatars to political icons, to people who had fame and notoriety here on the planet. To my chagrin, they all seem happy to share whatever they can and their reports echo the other reports from people under deep hypnosis describing the afterlife.

The point of this exercise isn't to introduce the reader to famous folks, "dead celebrities;" it's to demonstrate how easy it is for someone to speak to people no longer on the planet. That being said, it's a complex form of communication. Imagine holding a Dixie cup up to one's ear that has a string that reaches over mountains. On the other end we have a friend or stranger trying to pass along information – sometimes they do so with humor, sometimes they do so with a desire to explore something they didn't get a chance to before leaving, sometimes it's my desire to know an answer that they may not know what that answer is. And sometimes they refer to conversations that Jennifer and I had with them years earlier.

Apologies for anyone I might offend with this research – I'm bound to offend someone. All I can say is, focus on your own ability to communicate with your loved ones. I suspect they were the person that brought this book to your attention in the first place. This is your LAST CHANCE to get a refund, return this book, without knowing how the play is going to end.

If you stop now you'll have consumed the blue pill instead of the red one... (or is it the other way around?) If you're confused as we jump into these sessions, please go back and look at "Backstage Pass to the Flipside" volumes one and two. This books begins where those left off.

Welcome to the Martini Zone.

CHAPTER ONE

DANCING WITH THE STARS

Tim Conway and Carol Burnett Photo: TheWrap.com

Tim Conway, Robert Evans, Steve McQueen, John Candy

As I recount in the previous two "Backstage Pass to the Flipside: Talking to the Afterlife with Jennifer Shaffer" we talk to people I knew who've crossed over that I can verify details with their families and friends. The person who helps us on the "flipside" is actress Luana Anders (*LuanaAnders.com*). Luana and I met in 1979 in a film class at USC and remained close pals until her passing in 1996.

Jennifer and I met five years ago, she works with law enforcement nationwide on missing person cases; I supply the questions (a number of interviews are in "Backstage Pass to the Flipside: Talking to the Afterlife with Jennifer Shaffer") Interviews include people I knew in life (Bill Paxton, Harry Dean Stanton, Rance Howard, Ray Charles, all people I'd worked with) and some I've never met.

The class member who raises his hand often is Robin Williams who never ceases to amaze us with his answers, or what he had to say to us from the flipside. When asked "What's one thing I can tell your friends that you want them to know?" He said "Love love."

We spent some time asking him what that meant, why he said it – but ultimately it means exactly that. Love the act of love, the giving of love, the presence of love, the journey of love – any and all aspects of love that you might bring into your life, or bring into the lives of others.

Have you ever had a dream where someone makes an appearance and you can't figure out why?

You didn't see them in a TV show, or in a paper, or no one was talking about them? We've all done it – and in my case, based on my research, I have to "allow the possibility" that their "higher selves" stopped by for a visit. The unique thing I have is this amazing medium, Jennifer Shaffer, whom I can bring in any dream, vision, idea or general conversation and get some answers from the flipside. As always, these answers are subject to interpretation – but because I'm open to helping her interpret them, we get to a place neither one of us would have on our own.

I'm *in italics,* and Jennifer is **in bold.**

Rich: I had a dream where someone stopped by to visit with me – don't know him from Adam. He is the actor Tim Conway – he seemed calm and measured, sitting at a table in a dream.

Jennifer: He's showing me like blueprint or a graph of some sort.

Of what? His life's path?

"No. How they all stack up." It feels that he's very smart the way he's coming through – it's not him, it's like... who's the guy in the wheelchair we spoke to?

Stephen Hawking?

Now he's talking about quantum physics.

So Tim is talking about that? How is consciousness related to quantum physics?

He's showing me consciousness going around - quantum physics - like circling. He says "It's much more complicated than quantum physics." He says "Particles have to go through everything, like a circular (or closed) solar system."

And within that is consciousness? Is that what you wanted me to express? Who was there to greet you when you crossed over?

I think it's a cat... (Jennifer aside) but I don't think he had cats.

We've heard that before, being greeted by someone you knew in a previous lifetime. Was that a surprise, shock or did you expect that?

Did he die of a heart attack? I'm getting it was a heart issue.

A friend of mine pointed out that all death is a heart issue – eventually the danged thing stops beating.

He says, "He was trying to take care of someone he didn't want to leave. I'm getting a daughter. His daughter." He's saying "The boys can take care of themselves."

I think Tim has 5 children. I looked him up prior to this; perhaps he wants to talk about his homeless son?

"That's his (son's) path," he says.

Okay, but that's it?

He says, "Homelessness isn't homeless over there. Technically everyone is homeless over there."

Okay, you're saying "they're all home now."

He's showing me the mind is like a computer that overtakes the (physical) body.

What do you want to tell your daughter?

He says, "There's some element of her worrying about the same health issues he had." He said "She's going to be fine and he loves her. Says he misses playing crossword puzzles with her and he loves her."

Anything for Carol Burnett?

He says (joking) "She can speak for herself." (Jennifer aside:) Is Carol here or over there?

No, she's here.

Now he's showing me something about dementia. Did he have that?

Well, Tim had it and that's what he officially died of.

(Note: "Conway died in a long-term-care facility after suffering complications of hydrocephalus... He also had dementia. "I'm heartbroken," Carol Burnett told The Times in a statement Tuesday. "He was one in a million, not only as a brilliant comedian but as a loving human being," she said. (May 14th, 2019)"

I just know Tim and Carol were close and I had dinner with her once with Charles Grodin. She was and is hilarious.

He's telling me they were closer than "friends." Like "The very best of friends."

Tim, you showed up in a dream I was curious if you wanted to come to speak to us?

I'm getting from Luana – he's comparing his journey to yours... He says people need to hear you more, because you are funny – they directed him to you, they're doing a lot of .. (Jennifer aside) Say again? Oh. He's saying "What it is - about all the layers of consciousness and humanity and everything... and he shows you putting it here and here and making it easier for someone to understand."

You think I should focus on that kind of conversation?

He says "He's not a comedian over there..." and he says "It's acting too." (Jennifer aside:) I don't know which part is acting.

Are you familiar with what we're doing?

(Nods) It's like there are millions of lights over there aware of what we're doing.

Tim, I think your son is in radio.

He showed me his son is thicker than this table. (Meaning not open to reports from the flipside).

You think I need to get this message out, is that what you're trying to tell me Tim?

He says, "Yes. Yeah; and to have fun with it."

Okay, I can do that. Thank you!

Halloween

Jennifer and I in our usual spot in Manhattan Beach. I'm in italics, and Jennifer is in bold.

Rich: Happy Halloween. Any ghosts from our class want to show up today? Luana?

Jennifer: Prince.

What's up Prince?

He showed me an African American girl he's helped.

I know who she is. We talked about her once before.

(Note: It's Jonelle Monae, the actress, singer who he says he's been helping with her dancing. I saw her on television talking about an act or routine that she was doing that was "inspired by Prince." Monáe told BBC Radio 1 that the Purple One collaborated with her on her new album, Dirty Computer, before passing away in 2016. "Prince actually was working on the album with me before he passed on to another frequency, and helped me come up with sounds," Monáe said. "And I really miss him, you know, it's hard for me to talk about him. But I do miss him, and his spirit will never leave me."
https://www.spin.com/2018/02/janelle-monae-prince-dirty-computer/)

He just said "you would know." I can never remember anything we say here ... whatever was said before, I feel like she's doing really well, I may not be getting all of it. But I think she got herself out of some trouble. I don't know what it's related to, if it's a personal thing, or health issue.

I will add this as an addendum to the chapter.

He says "Good."

I did invite some people today.

"There's a long line," Luana says. The guys that are involved with brain trauma (CTE) showed up. He brought up – that quarterback... Fran Tarkenton?

Yes, I know who they're referring to. Do you even know who Fran Tarkenton is?

Did he play for the Cowboys?

The Vikings.

Clearly I know nothing about football.

Well, he is a Quarterback; but is it Paul Allen, Dave Duerson or Junior Seau who who wants to mention Joe Namath?

It's Paul. I'm getting an image of a boxer who committed suicide.

Could be.

It has to do with the whole brain injury thing.

I was talking about it the other day – Jennifer has learned that many sports have CTE damage.

I didn't know I said that.

I should mention is not just in terms of football?

That's what they're saying – there are a lot of young athletes in high school getting it.

You mentioned a surfer... of course a boxer makes sense.

(Note: It's important to note that Paul Allen is coming from the flipside to remind us that Joe Namath's foray into hyperbaric oxygen to treat his CTE is a groundbreaking development and it's people on the flipside who are insisting we talk about it.)

I also saw a tennis player.

Well, one of the people I asked to speak with played some tennis; not professionally but had his own court.

Someone who played tennis with Jack Nicholson?

He could have. I know he played with his kids.

Robert Evans playing tennis in his court.

I know who you mean; I was just shown the Hollywood guy who died – but I don't know his name. He says "He was good at tennis, even though he didn't win."

Put in Jennifer's mind who you are.

This is the guy who knows Robert Towne – the Chinatown guy. I don't know his name. E something.

Evans. Is it the right time to interview him Luana?

She says "Yeah, they've been prepping him. He's ready."

Robert Evans with the "love of his life" Ali McGraw

Bob, I'm going to ask you the same specific questions I ask everyone.

You mean "Who greeted him on the flipside?" I'm seeing that he had a dog too by the way. Hold on – I just saw a giraffe and I have no idea what that means. We went from a dog to a giraffe.

Let's back up a second, take a look at him, what's he look like to you? Young, old?

I just saw – you remember the movie Austin Powers? He's showing me like a hat – looks like he's around 70. He's handsome. (Jennifer laughs) I asked if he did a lot of work on his face? And he laughed. Then he showed me Joan Rivers.

(A still from "Austin Powers" and from Bob Evans photos)

(Note: Not common knowledge, but indeed Bob had "work done." He went "on vacation" for a month prior to filming "The Two Jakes" (replaced at the last second) to have his face "lifted.")

I need him to focus.

He says "I have focus."

Who was there to greet you on the flipside?

He's laughing. He showed me a bunch of angels, big angels. I asked him, "Did you believe in the afterlife?" And he has this enormous angel with him – it is someone he loved so much.

With wings?

With wings.

Let's focus on this person for a second. What's this angel's name?

He's says, "It's his mother." He showed me something with him as a little boy, telling me "his mother is his guardian angel."

You saw your mom when you crossed over, as an angel?

He says, "Yes." She must have been Catholic or very religious.

When did you realize you were in the afterlife?

He says, "When people came forward - like Luana."

You remembered her? How did you recall her?

He says, "Through you. He showed me you playing the piano."

(Note: No one knows that I played piano at Bob's house when I was his acting coach, but Bob. Also when he hosted Robert Towne's wedding he asked me to play, be the music. I did.)

(Ding!) Yes, I played his grand piano at Robert Towne's wedding which was held at Bob's house, out in his giant patio. Show Jennifer our relationship, what kind of work we did together.

He showed me large graph – (waves her arm up and down) He says "He always loved seeing you, thought you were super funny, always calmed him down and you took care of him," he says. On some level.

(Ding! I spent two months as his acting coach prior to the filming of the Two Jakes. He was nervous and pensive about acting again – we worked an hour or so a day on a variety of exercises. The exercises were tongue twisters, making him sing a song, etc. I asked Robert Towne, "why are you asking him to do those?" He said "Because he talks too fast." I told Evans that he needed to slow down his cadence. He said *"Why-who-thinks-I-talk-fast?"* I found a video of him being interviewed, so I could show him how fast he talked. The interviewer asked about his relationship to ex wife Ali McGraw and, for fear of saying the wrong thing – he slowed d o w n and spoke normally. I pointed out that speed talking made him sound nervous, but slow talking gave him the power, the way Jack Nicholson always speaks slower than the people around him. By the time we were going to begin shooting, he would have made a fine second Jake. Alas, not meant to be.)

There was a moment when you came to me on the set of the film you were going to act in – the director hired me to be your acting coach, then at the last minute had second thoughts, wanted to fire you, I was in the middle of that. Bob, I know it broke your heart to not play that part, but later, we did work together - you appeared in my film "Cannes Man" playing yourself. You want to show Jennifer your book, "The kid stays in the picture?"

He shows me like riding in a car – when you asked about the book, he showed me someone riding in a car.

(Note: That's correct. A number of scenes in the film documentary of "The Kid Stays In the Picture" are variations of Robert in a car, while his voice over intones. Norma Shearer was a movie star whom he met at the Beverly Hills hotel and she took him home with her. He eventually bought that home and he lived in it for the rest of his life.)

Have you run into Norma?

Norma Jean?

No, another Norma.

He said "Yes, (I've run into) all the Normas, including Jean." (Jennifer aside:) Who broke his heart? That's who he ran into; someone who broke his heart. Hold on. He showed me this androgynous angel and said "That person broke his heart."

Was that your mom who broke your heart?

No, his mom was a guardian; it was someone else. A kinship; when he was younger. Someone in New York feels like. Something to do with a hairdresser.

He worked with his brother Charles at Evan-Piccone. He was in LA when he was discovered by silent film star Norma Shearer. That relationship propelled you into the highest levels of Hollywood. Do you want to show Jennifer where you wound up?

I saw a lion at first, but he said "Paramount."

You want to show her the other movies you were involved with? Our class can help us with this – (to Jennifer) Do you know who Ali McGraw is?

Sounds familiar.

They had a child together.

Felt like two – like one passed away.

(Note: No idea if this is accurate, but Ali did lose a child with husband Steve McQueen.)

He produced many iconic films, including "Love Story" that she starred in.

He went like this – (rubbing knuckles on his chest) and blew on them.

All right, but Bob, what's impressive about that?

He's saying, "He's proud of all the people he employed," he showed me all the lives involved – the love connected with that.

There are some women I know who you know.

"Three," he said.

(Ding! I have had three friends who for reasons only they could explain, wound up living in Evan's guest house. None of them ever had a bad thing to say about him – and praised him as being a benefactor, mentor and all around good guy.)

That's right.

He said "They took care of him." He said "It wasn't a sexual thing, having them live with him." He said "He wasn't interested in women necessarily; he loved them, but that wasn't his focus."

You want to show Jennifer your house?

He showed me like the film about Elton John- that palace, overlooking the balcony where the pool was. He collected things, glasses..

Yes, many things, including a wall of glasses, all smudged. He had an amazing guest house with a screening room.

Was it like the Playboy mansion? That's what it felt like.

A bit like that I imagine. Less tacky perhaps (I've been to both.) People would come from all over and be part of his orbit.

"He protected their secrets," he said, and that "You protected him."

(Note: "Protected" isn't the right word. Every day after our acting class, two young coeds (a boy and a girl) would show up at his place to frolic for pay. I got the impression they were putting on a show for Bob; I didn't stick around. Bob, from what I know of him, was always loathed by people like Francis Coppola and loved by people like Robert

Towne. To me he was always the consummate gentleman and fan. The only person who called me after a screening (of "Point of Betrayal") to congratulate me for "knocking it out of the park." If he had still been the head of Paramount when he saw it, I wouldn't be writing this sentence. He had a lot of women in his life and I've heard a number of unmentionable stories about his parties, but like anything, I judge people for how they behave towards people.)

You discovered many careers, or helped many people – look around the group that we've gathered here, you know some of them Bob.

He says "22." He says there are "22 people in the class that he knows."

Okay. So tell us, how did Luana help you to communicate with us?

She came to him before – I'm getting – before he crossed – and he's expressing gratitude for that, and a love for her because of you. He says "He was aware of her through Jack... (Nicholson). He's saying, "They just brought him to Luana."

(Note: Meaning that when he got to the flipside, as we've heard before, some of his friends invited him to join our group, "bringing him to Luana." As Tom Petty has dubbed her, the keeper of the backstage passes that allows people on the other side to talk to people over here.")

How did she help you prepare for today's conversation?

She told him to "Go easy on Jennifer."

Bob, you were a born flirt.

(Jennifer aside) He has beautiful eyelashes.

I spent 2 months as your acting coach.

He said, "You brought everyone out of him."

We found a video of him talking, I noticed that when he spoke of Ali McGraw he spoke slowly – otherwise he talked fast, but when talking about something you were afraid of, it was then you could connect emotionally to it.

He's mentioning something with a Frankie?

I don't know – tell us who that is.

Guy that used to do that ... movies with Elvis, surf movies.

Frankie Avalon?

He says, "Yeah."

Someone you knew?

He's saying something with him – see if there's a connection.

(Note: Frankie Avalon was considered for the part of the singer Johnny Fontaine in the Francis Coppola Evans production of The Godfather. This is one of those "hard to find" connections, but will continue to look for one.)

What do you want me to tell Robert Towne?

He says, "Don't be afraid of death, that everyone is all right over there."

What about his son, Josh? We're old friends.

"Josh can't hear it," he says. "It's going to take awhile."

Bob, this is going to be a chapter in the book...

Not the last one, it should be a beginning chapter – and there is no ending. "There is no last chapter," he says.

You're the only producer who ever called me after a screening to congratulate me.

He says, "He was intuitive. That Ebert and Siskel sucked."

(Note: That's a funny side note. Ebert and Siskel gave me a "thumbs way down" on the film "Limit Up." After screening my film "Point of Betrayal" at his home for Jack Nicholson (it starred the mother of Jack's two kids, Rebecca Broussard) Bob called me and left a long message saying he had screened the film for Jack Nicholson and they both thought I had "knocked it out of the park." He was effusive and very complimentary. Like I say; the only call I've ever had like it.)

Very funny. Well they're in our class now as well. I'm sorry I missed that call. Let's do a quick round-robin – before we get to the next guest. I'm going to say a name what do you want to say to them? Roman Polanski?

He says "To get out of his head, he's got a documentary he should be doing."

Francis?

He showed me Francis walking away... He says "We have him when he gets here."

Josh? He'll eventually read this.

He said "He wishes he had more time."

Ali McGraw?

He laughs. At first I asked "Thank her for loving me no matter what?" And he said "No. Thank you for putting up with my shit."

Alan the butler?

He gets the purple star – "Thank you for cleaning up all the messes, literally and figuratively."

Fans and friends or enemies?

He says "Tell everyone I'm amazed at how much work is being done on the flipside to help people (back there)." He showed me angel wings, to cover people.

Thank you Bob. Speaking of Ali, I'd like to get her ex husband to come in.

Hold on a second, they don't want them in the same room.

(Note: This is a pretty wild thing to say. I have invited Steve McQueen to visit us, but did not tell Jennifer who I was inviting – only Ali's ex husband. She doesn't know that Ali was married to Steve McQueen, who "stole her from Evans." The idea that they would insist Evans "leave" before McQueen came forward is hilarious and something Jennifer would not be aware of.)

Okay, so Bob step out please.

(Jennifer aside) Really? I don't believe him. He's saying, "He has to leave before the other one will come in." Then McCain just stepped in.

John McCain? What's he want to say?

He's talking about his daughter.

(Note: As noted, John asked us to pass along a message to Meghan, which I did through the producer of "Coast to Coast AM radio." I don't know if she got the message or not.)

Did she get the message?

I got the chills when you asked that: I feel like she has. He says "Thank you, and this is very interesting work... and eventually I'll talk to her." (Meaning Jennifer will speak to Meghan)

Okay, thanks John. Okay, I have this other guy I'd like to speak with, let's bring him in.

I got a T.

(Note: For the record, Steve McQueen's name was Terence McQueen.)

Tom?

This is Ali McGraw's ex husband.

Is he like Mike Tyson? I saw Mike Tyson.

Well, he was a tough guy, yes. Famous for a number of things. Put him in her mind's eye.

They're trying to show me... his name. Mc something.

Like McCain – but McQ...

McQueen. They showed me an old cult movie, I can't remember the name of it.

(Note: Steve's career began with an old cult movie "The Blob.")

Yes. Steve. Do you want to talk to us?

(Jennifer hesitates) "Sure." He says... "He died way too early."

(Ding!) That's correct. Jennifer probably doesn't know much about you.

I'm sorry; I don't.

Luana, I asked you to bring him in today, because of his connection to you, to Evans, because Steve stole Ali from Evans.

Oh wow. So that's why they couldn't be in the same room! That's very interesting.

Can I ask you some questions?

He says, "Yes."

Who brought you to this class?

He said, "Luana."

Who was there to greet you when you crossed over?

I feel like it's a daughter – someone younger than him.

(Note: Steve's daughter Terrie died 18 years after him. But when someone is "greeted on the flipside" it can be by the "higher self" of the person they're referring to.)

Let's talk about your youth. I wasn't aware that you had a very difficult relationship with...

He says, "His father. He was abusive." He said "He forgave him before he left. But yes, he was very abusive."

Steve McQueen. Wikimedia

But, if I may, was that part of the reason you turned into who you became?

"Yes. He had to be somebody different," he said.

How did racing come to factor in your life?

(Jennifer aside) He was a racer? I saw tons or cars racing by earlier and had no idea why. Before even Evans showed up.

He starred in the film "LeMans."

He's telling me there's a movie that's out where they portray him.

(Note: Ding! "Once Upon A Time in Hollywood." I forgot until she mentioned it.)

Steve McQueen and Ali McGraw during "The Getaway" Wikipedia.

Tell Jennifer about your journey.

He says, "He followed someone out here to LA..."

I think it was his mother.

He says "He loved his mom very much." But they put him in a detention center.

(Ding!) Correct, and then the military.

It felt like he went to auto shop or worked on cars during the juvenile detention center. It feels like he was kicked out of the military, or that he was never there.

(Ding!) That's right – he was often kicked out, until he became a Marine.

"He was a good Marine," he said.

Who are you hanging our with on the flipside?

He says "John Lennon." I get the impression he knew John in life, but he's hanging out with him now.

Luana told me about a conversation that you and she had?

Was he on acid or something when he talked to her? He said something about "making a move" on her.

That is what she told me; that you had "hit on her" somewhere, at a party perhaps and that she rebuffed you. Can you tell Jennifer what kind of cancer you had Steve?

He's showing me "Lung." I feel like his lungs hurt.

Correct. (Ding!) So was it caused by asbestos as you had feared?

"Yes, from his early childhood. It was compounded," he said – "Lead poisoning too."

Luana told me years later, that you had run into her on the Warner's lot and said something like "You were right, I'm glad you rebuffed me." Is that correct Luana?

She says, "Yes." Then she showed me a vault – like "Richard, you're a vault of information!"

It's weird that I can access that memory.

Time doesn't exist in your world – that's how it happens to me because I don't focus on it.

Steve is there anything you want to say to your fans?

He says, "Be fearless. Within reason, but be fearless." He says "live life in a way that contributes to others, (to) their wellbeing; if you're only focused on yourself all that energy makes it worse. If you focus on others, all the giving and receiving makes the world go around. Get out of your head." That's what he says.

Anything for Ali McGraw?

He showed me kissing her on her neck. I think her ex-husband wants to kill him.

Okay Steve, thanks; I've got one more today, it's this guy's birthday. I met him once.

A comedy improv guy. Belushi.

I met him, but I'm thinking of someone else.

Who's the one who scared me at the Chateau Marmont?

Belushi.

That was nerve wracking.

I think we chatted with him briefly before – but got distracted by the film director John Hughes, who showed up. But it's the comedian John Candy; his 69th birthday today.

He just kissed you on your forehead. Did you know him?

I met him once, he walked into the Coronet Pub on La Cienega, we were with our comedy improv class, and I led a standing ovation. Got everyone in the bar to applaud him and Eugene Levy. It was funny as he was in the midst of trying to stop drinking and we all wanted to buy him a drink.

That's why he kissed you. (Jennifer aside:) That's so cool.

You're 69 years young today...

John Candy; YouTube tribute page.

He says he checked off the planet 25 years ago.

(Note: He was 44 when he passed in 94.)

(Ding!) That's about right. Who was there to greet you on the other side?

I was shown Richard Pryor and all these other comedians. He says, "He stayed here for a while, didn't want to go. He was hanging out with this buddies, knew how sad they were."

You mean your buddies from SCTV?

Also Saturday Night Live. Billy Crystal came to mind.

Well, they may have been friends. I met Catherine O'Hara backstage one night and proposed.

"And she said no and you lived happily every after."

That's right. I was kidding. John who are you hanging out with?

He says he wants to tell his friends "Drugs are not the answer!" He says he's hanging out with Richard Pryor. He said he's "Making a band." He says he wants to be a musician next time (around).

What instrument are you going to play?

He says, "Bongos." He's very funny; feels like it's a routine.

Maybe as Johnny Larue? (His show biz character from SCTV.)

He said, "He wouldn't trade his life for anything," and "Thanks to Luana," he says "He's come to you a number of times."

Well, he popped into my head the other day. John, if you're hanging out with Richard Pryor, what do you guys do?

He says "They party all night long!" (Jennifer laughs, listens) Um. He says "We try to make sure that we keep you guys over there. We don't want anyone crashing the party (over here).

What do you mean by that? Who would you and Richard try to keep on the planet?

John Belushi is here – He's saying "It's that actor, the guy that was engaged to Ariana Grande for a minute."

Pete Davidson? So how do you keep him on the planet?

He says "We just follow him around and make him feel like he can't do the things he wants to do."

Do you talk to him, move things in his path? Butt dial his phone?

He says, "All of it." I'm reminded of someone (client) who came to me after the Vegas shootings. Her dad was a policeman who had died, and tried to protect her during the shooting. He tried to get her to leave – at first he made her desperately want to go to the bathroom, but she didn't leave, then he made her incredibly hungry, but she didn't leave – and it was finally through the intervention of her boyfriend who grabbed her hand, that they ran and survived. So that's what they're doing. (Everything)

So give us an example, Pete is at a party or a club; how do you stop someone from offering him drugs?

He says, "We screw with his phone, make him not see the incoming call..."

How successful are you?

He said, "About 80%."

Does Pete want to check out?

He said, "He doesn't. He doesn't realize how close he is, or that he's playing with that."

He talked about it once... like an attempt. He toyed with it.

He said, "It's not that he's toying with it" They're saying "No, that by his actions, his actions are making it easier for him to check off the planet."

Do you guys hang out with his higher self? How does that work?

He says, "Yeah." I think that's what they're doing – his higher self gives the self here subliminal messages.

Do you guys help him with comedy?

He says, "No. They think he's better than them (as a comedian)." They appreciate his humor, don't want him to think of them, because that'll make him think of the other side – leaving early – so they block it off." (Jennifer aside) That's so interesting.

So John, you want me to write something about this, a message from you to Pete?

He said, "He can't hear it; he won't hear it."

His friends might.

They're saying (then) "To tell him to stop doing whatever he's doing. They're trying to help him stay on his journey."

Very different advice, very good. One more thing. John anything you want to say?

He said, "He's going as a unicorn for Halloween. He wanted you to know."

Evans what are you going as?

He said, "You."

That's funny. Steve?

Steve thinks his costume is funny – He says "I'm going as a drag queen – Steve McDrag-Queen.

Ouch. How about you Luana? What are you going as?

She said, "Invisible."

Very good. Any last words?

Oh Robert's cat wants to come through.

Leo? Last words? Meow?

Hold on. "Tell Robert to stop worrying."

Will do. So Evans are you impressed by this class at all?

He says "A thousand percent. It's over the top. He says he wishes he had it before." Hang on. Your buddy just came through. The guy that you did a past life regression with?

Howard Schultz?

He said, "Yes." And he says something about Amelia Earhart; you have to get to the right place. Find Amelia first." (Then the success will appear).

Are you saying that as advice, or sarcastically Howard?

"Both."

(Note: I posted something online about Howard a few days earlier).

Howard is that okay I posted what I did about you?

"Yeah." (Jennifer aside) I don't know what you're talking about.

Really?

(Jennifer smiles) I promise you.

Someone asked me about a posting a full deep hypnosis session. I rarely do, because people don't want their secrets out. However, Howard used to show his past life regression to people in his office. He passed five years ago - when did we do that session Howard?

"2011," he says.

I posted it so this guy could watch the 3 hour version of Howard's session. Do you appreciate that?

He said, "He does."

We didn't make a movie together but we did this video together.

He blessed something. Someone came forward and "blessed the beads."

(Note: We do that when we drive in our car – I have a set of prayer beads given from Kutenla, the Oracle of Tibet, and every time I drive, my wife says "Don't forget to say "safe trip." It's something we do whenever we drive.)

Luana, did you make Sally Kellerman call me this morning?

"Yes, 100%, she did. She said, "She's leaving soon." Okay, bye.

CHAPTER TWO:

MAVERICK IS IN THE HOUSE

CLASS DISCUSSION WITH JOHN MCCAIN, ABRAHAM LINCOLN, ROBIN WILLIAMS, PRINCE

The night before our next session, in my upstairs bathroom, I heard the voice of Senator John McCain say (in my head) "I heard you're the person I need to speak to." I've had this happen a couple of times – and there's no mistaking the voice of John McCain. But I'm not a medium, so I said to him "John, happy to talk to you, but you need to get a backstage pass from Luana and show up in our meeting with Jennifer."

Senator McCain had passed a couple of weeks earlier, prior to our meeting, and I was curious if it was possible to talk to someone I had zero connection with. Generally we focus on people we have met, or people that on the flipside that we interview have met during their lifetime. My only connection to the Senator was interviewing his chief of staff as background for my script "Three For the Road" in the 1980's. (She spoke highly of him even then.)

I thought it odd to suddenly "hear" his voice in my head. The following is from the transcript. Jennifer's replies are **bold**, my questions are in *italics*.

Richard: Hello class.

Jennifer: I just got an image of John McCain.

(Ding!) Okay that was a person I invited today. Should we talk to John or (the other person I had in mind) first?

John.

Okay. Well, John, I heard your voice in my head two weeks ago, after you passed. "I understand you're the guy I need to speak with." I recognized your voice before I could figure out it was you. So at that time I just said "Reach out to Luana, and you can join us in our class."

"I'm the host," Luana just said. "Yeah."

John, who told you I was the guy to speak with? Or were they talking about our class over there on the flipside?

They're talking to me about New York, one of your relatives – feels like a guy.

Someone in my family who was in the Navy? I'm curious, because my grandfather was assistant to the Secretary of the Navy during World War II; maybe he knew John's father.

"It's your father."

Oh, okay. Well, my dad was a Navy Officer who went to school at Columbia University in New York City during World War II. John what do you know about our class so far?

"I know that we can talk to you this way."

Who was there to greet you when you crossed over?

He said "his first love." He's showing me a woman around 30; she had a bouffant; her hair is blonde...

Someone who crossed over before him?

It felt like a grandmother at first... maybe his first love was his mom... (His mother had an identical blonde twin sister Rowena who passed away in 2011. His mother is still alive at 106.) Was John close to Ronald Reagan? I just felt Ronald Reagan...

So Ronnie was there to greet you?

It's like they're *all* over there... He says "There's a time limit in terms of our ability to help our country, to help what's going on with (the current administration)."

Well, I prefer to not focus on (the current administration) right now; we'll get there, but I want to be specific about your journey. Who was there to greet you? This blonde woman and Ron?

Reagan was later. (Then) He was greeted by his regiment... I see the number 51 – number on his plane, or something?

(Note: When this was recorded, it was 51 years since he had been shot down over Vietnam).

He was shot down as a pilot a couple of times.

(Jennifer aside) I didn't know that.

That's why I'm here for odd confirmation. Are some of these people you were greeted by... where they people you...

"Helped."

People that you were in prison with? He spent 5 years in prison in Hanoi... I'm asking if some of those people are with you now?

"Yeah."

Are some of your captors with you now?

"Not yet."

Why not?

"They're learning... it's a process of learning, they're still learning... about the whole process."

You were a warrior and some of the people you killed were part of your journey as well. And your victims, people you killed in Vietnam also participated in your journey or path... as I understand it. Are any of your victims there that you've met? Luana help me with this, please, or is that a tough question?

"It's not a tough question." He showed me his life review – the people he killed were part of that life review; like he didn't party at first... When he went back (home), the life review for him happened instantly.

Did you recognize the people in your life review? Who was your guide?

I'm seeing a picture of Abraham Lincoln.

Somebody like Abraham Lincoln? Or is that a joke? He does have a sense of humor. John are you joking about Abe Lincoln being one of your guides?

"It is true, yes, I'm joking but it's true."

You mean "Yes it's funny, but it's accurate?"

Jennifer taps her nose.

(Note: As I've reported in these books, part of our work together is not judging whatever "comes forward." In that vein, the following should be filtered though that *"possibility that it's accurate."*)

So, hey, can you bring Abe forward?

Jennifer shakes her head in wonder... – "Yes." (Jennifer aside) I'm trying to not judge it; I read something about the White House being haunted today.

It is haunted... Especially the Lincoln bedroom. I've heard many of those stories... so John, before you invite Abe to join us, do you recognize anyone here in our class?

He showed me... Tom Petty.

Did you know Tom? You knew him from before?

"Yes." There's got to be a song or something connecting them.

(Note: The song is "I Won't Back Down" which Senator McCain used during the 2008 campaign, but Tom stopped Bush from using in the 2004 campaign.)

So John, the funeral for you was pretty dramatic; two Presidents spoke.

"Yes." (Jennifer: aside) I loved how his daughter said "*America has always been great.*" I was trying to follow all of her words, it was like ... I'm asking him; "Was it fun planning your funeral?" John said "I like to have control of everything."

Did you like their rendition of "Danny Boy?"

"It was off key."

That's funny. I read that you used to play that for people on your ranch.

Jennifer taps her nose. He says "That person (at the funeral) was very nervous."

Anything you want us to pass along to your family?

"My daughter's going to be fine," he says. "They're so much alike..." He says he's worried about his wife.

John you weren't able to lift your arms or comb your hair... I know you got through that, but is there anything you want to say about that?

"It made me stronger."

A diamond in the rough; a piece of coal that turned into a diamond later?

He says "He wanted to help people on a bigger playing field."

The rest of his life he fought torture and helped the reconciliation in Vietnam... and helped people worldwide. Speaking of torture, what do you want to say about the current president? From your current perspective?

He just left. He walked away... and Luana came in.

What does that mean Lu? It's ok if he doesn't want to talk about it.

He does – he went back and brought back a contract, or a scroll.

From his Akashic library?

Okay, I'm getting a lot of information, I have to make sure I'm not...

Don't worry, just say it and I'll ask questions about it.

Wow.

Is this a scroll from John's lives?

He showed me that he needed to feel the pain and torture and he needed to feel the bonding... so when I say he has the same energetic pattern (as someone who suffered for compassion) he

showed me Gandhi – it wasn't that he was Gandhi – but the end point would be the same for both of them.

So your choice for choosing a difficult lifetime... that choice was about him choosing a difficult lifetime to learn those lessons – so he could turn those coals into diamonds?

He just showed me the same stripe or medal that Tony Stockwell showed you... the star medal.

(Note: It's in "Architecture of the Afterlife." During an interview with the medium Tony Stockwell, we visited his council (a group of guides or teachers that help evaluate lifetimes). In Tony's case, I asked if his guide was wearing anything; he said a "star." I asked if he meant a badge, but he said "It's a literal star, made of light." Tony had earned this honor for experiencing a difficult previous lifetime, details of which I was later able to verify.)

The medal he earned; the star?

John says "He has three of them now..."

So what do the other two represent, different lifetimes? Or did they all come from this life?

They all came from this lifetime. Because he felt the torture, he then tried to correct it, and then he tried to stop it. Three different medals.

Anyone in class want to comment about what John is saying?

They all started clapping. I think they're clapping because I got it, or because we understand it.

So John, you've had other lifetimes where you were a soldier in war?

A general.

Were you part of that energy of wartime?

(Jennifer aside: We're all "lights" right?) He showed me – when you said "that energy" – all the lights lit up – so they can find each other.

So they find the frequencies. Okay, thanks for explaining that!

****

PART TWO: (Another day, another session. My questions in italics, Jennifer's answers in bold.)

Hi class, how are ya? Here's Jennifer, your friend and tour guide.

I'm seeing Abraham Lincoln. It's so funny; he wants to come through.

Okay. He wasn't invited today, but he can jump the line. Do me a favor Mr. President, stand up so she can see you. What's his outfit look like?

He actually... he's says he wears that stovepipe hat just to identify himself to most – but at the moment he's wearing this beret with a wool jacket almost looks like he's going to go for a horseback ride.

Have you reincarnated since your time here on the planet?

"Five times."

Is this outfit you're wearing related to one of those lives?

"Yes." He showed me being on the stage and watching the stage... In Scotland.

Did you go riding, hunting fox and stuff like that in this lifetime?

He had a pipe too.

What was your name in Scotland?

Alfred.

Last name?

Townsend. Feels like 1918. Lived from 1890 to 1918.

How did you die in that lifetime? In World War I?

No. It felt like he had cancer. His last name was Townes or Townsend. Is Wales in England?

(Note: Odd, just realized that a Peter Townsend shows up later in this research.)

Yes. Were you a Scotsman or a Welsh?

Welsh.

Would I be able to find your name if I looked you up?

Yes. Almost feels like Townes. Right by the water. I'm being shown a lighthouse.

What was it like, returning here for you? I'll guess you weren't consciously aware of coming back, but you had this lifetime where everyone was talking about you and you were likely really a big deal.. and now you come back and you're not famous at all.

"You're not famous over here."

Not on the flipside... was that your choice to return and have a life where it was not a big deal?

He says "He wanted a lifetime off. And then he showed me Maverick." (John McCain) I don't know why.

Let's ask him – would you like to bring John forward with you? Tell us why did John pop into your mind?

Did I associate these two before?

Yes.

I felt like he went from that Scottish life to a life with John McCain... I think John knew him or experienced him or was aware of him.. at some point.

Well let's ask John now that you're here. Abraham were you aware of John's lifetime that he lived and struggled and the struggles he had during this life?

"Yes."

What was your assessment of John McCain's struggles? How would paraphrase it?

"He felt it. He wanted to know what the pinnacle of the understanding of the suffering, that's the Buddhist part that comes in, like he wanted to know... like he showed me what starts the suffering or what makes someone suffer.. I'm being shown that by being tortured –... (Jennifer listens; "What is it?") Between lives he remembered the previous lives, and in this he felt that torture. And both of them tried to free themselves or get over the feelings of torture. Not get over... but.."

To process? We talked about John's previous lives of torture earlier.

I don't remember anything we talk about.

Let's ask Abraham about that – your feelings about the African American experience with slavery, he was so eloquent on the topic of slavery. Was that something that came from your education of this life? Or a previous one?

He says "From all of his lifetimes. He was being educated from his future self, and what they might require."

I have a fun question, there was a soldier you wrote about you used to sleep with. Back in the days when traveling across country, you would share a bed, you had a very close companion... were you guys closer than we imagine?

He's smiling; he's not showing me.

We're not trying to out anyone here – If you prefer not to answer that question, it's fine.

I felt that he cared for him deeply, but it felt like he was – he respected him so much like a son... he didn't treat him like a son, but he wasn't closer than a friend.

Okay. We did ask about your wife. Mary Todd.

"Ball buster," he said.

Okay. I know she had some stress during her lifetime.

"She lost her children."

Are you guys friends now? She had her own path and journey.

He just showed me Amelia Earhart, so whatever that means.

(Note: I'd guess that means she has her own path with or without him.)

Why did Ronald Reagan stop by?

Let's talk to him.

And Nancy is here as well. (Listens) What did Nancy call him?

Ronnie. I think he came forward because earlier we were taking to John McCain, you were one of the people who greeted him when he crossed over. Let me ask; how does Ron look now – old or young?

Young, he looks like a cross between – like when he was an actor; there's a photo with smoke in the room from a black and white photograph.

I know you and Nancy got married in the little brown chapel in Studio City near to where Luana lived.

"It was so simple, just very few people, a lot of people on her side but not on his," he says.

What's your opinion about what's going on in politics now?

He's having me look up (in the sky) – I'm trying to understand... I saw all of them, like a collective answering that question, about "what's going on now," or "what do they think about now?" I got "checks and balances" - I got the scales... that it will take years to rebalance. I asked if its "right or wrong"... (They're saying) "It will take years to rebalance."

Are you planning your next incarnation yet, Ronnie?

"No. Just taking it easy."

You had Alzheimer's, tell us, what you are doing now?

He loves horses; he's with horses.

He likes to ride around?

"It's a different kind of riding. It's safer."

What horse do you ride...

Her name is Delilah... sounds like.

Anything you want us to tell your kids Patty and Ron jr.?

"Thank you .. for taking care of the animals."

****

PART THREE Another day.... another session. My questions in italics, Jennifer's answers in bold.

Rich: Who wants to come through?

Jennifer: Maverick. I can't think of his name; I'm just going to call him Maverick.

John McCain?

Yeah.

(Note: This is 2 1/2 months after his passing.)

What does John want to tell us?

He just grabbed a chair and sat down. He says he "Won't waste his time talking even talking about (the current President); he's way beyond that." (She listens, laughs) He says, "It's waking up a lot of people (however), he's doing us a great service... People that never considered going into politics are now very involved, so he's done us a favor. But it should end soon." (Listens) He's talking about you Rich, he showed me you in my mind's eye. (Jennifer listens) He says, "You need to figure out a way to get these excerpts (of our conversation) to his daughter, she's having dreams or something with that as well.

His daughter Meghan?

The one on TV. He says "The one that likes Trump... but don't mention Trump."

Okay. I'm not a fan, but I'll do that. I'm happy to post these online, if it's the only way to try to reach out.

He says he likes me calling him "Maverick." You know me (Jennifer speaking), I'm not going to tell you to send it to her... But he's tried to butt-in a number of times (while you're speaking).

It's a good name for him... so Maverick... do you want me to reach out to Meghan, what do you want me to say to her? Give her a sign for her to observe, look for, to validate that you're there?

I'm talking to him at the same time as you're talking... he's showing me serious things. He says she's trying to decide if she's going into politics. (Pauses) He's encouraging her to go into politics.

How can we show her that it's you telling her to do that?

"She had a dream about him and wrote it down - information that seemed like it came from him and she wrote it down."

Okay, what's a way to tell her that?

"He's going to connect with her again."

So you want me to say "You're father came through and said the following..." But what's a code word so that she knows it's coming from you and not some nutball on the net? What did she call you?

"Dad." (Jennifer listens) Something with a teddy bear. I just got shown a little teddy bear, don't know if there's a connection there... it's light brown. Felt like it had pinkish overtones.

Something that you gave to her?

Either something he gave to her... I see her looking like a little kid. Feels like whenever he traveled, she had that around. Either a bear or a bunny.

Is it a bear or bunny? Pick one.

"A bear."

That's proof to her that you're still around?

"Yes."

She still has it?

"At least in her mind... I don't know if she still has it."

How about your favorite song you used to play off your balcony on your ranch?

I'm hearing "You've Lost that Loving Feeling." And then I'm hearing Neil Diamond too; "Coming to America." Hold on. Who's the one that um... who's the daughter that would sing the same song as her dad?

Natalie Cole. "Unforgettable?"

Look up "Unforgettable" for his daughter.

(Note: John McCain had eclectic tastes in music, he was a fan of Neil Diamond (who isn't?) but I couldn't find any specific reference to these tunes. However, if Meghan reads this at some point, perhaps she will.)

Okay, I will pass it along. Class was that okay for Maverick to butt in the way he did? Jump the line?

Luana is saying "He had special clearances." She's showing me it's very orchestrated over there.

Not sure how I can tell this to Meghan... what's she going to run for?

"Governor."

Of Arizona? Okay, well, from a flipside perspective Meghan might be a great politician.

She's struggling with giving up her freedom to do that (run for President).

I can't blame her. Okay, you heard it here first; John McCain says his daughter should run for Governor. Okay thanks everyone.

....

It's interesting to note; we know how much John McCain hated the current resident of the White House, we know that he loathed everything about him, but it's also accurate what he says about "how many people have responded and decided to run for office based on him." So that's worth noting. Sometimes the events that occur in front of us, are inspiration for us to change them.

I have no idea if Meghan McCain has any designs to run for office. I thought it was pretty interesting how specific he was about what office she should run for (Governor of Arizona). I have no way of knowing if that's something she should do – but I do know that it's important to realize that our loved ones are not gone; they just aren't here. She may find zero, nada, nothing about this report that is accurate – including the teddy bear that he cites and proof that it's him, and that "she'll understand that."

We were at the end of a two hour filming session, when she said that she saw "Maverick," and that he had something he wanted to say to us. And that was to "reach out to his daughter" to let her know that he wants her to run for office. And I've done that. This is not a theory, belief or opinion about the afterlife; I'm filming what people say under deep hypnosis and reporting that, in this case I'm filming an interview with a medium who has helped law enforcement with a number of missing person cases nationwide.

Mission accomplished Maverick.

CHAPTER THREE

"I FEEL GOOD. I KNEW THAT I WOULD."

Peter Coyote and Robin Williams. Courtesy Peter Coyote. (All Rights Reserved)

ROBIN WILLIAMS, ELVIS and JAMES BROWN

Robin began showing up in our book "Hacking the Afterlife." At some point, it felt as if the book was too long, and I was talking more about meeting him and his effect on me than what he actually wanted to say. So I took the chapter out. Then the next session, *apropos of nothing,* Jennifer said **"Robin is here and he wants you to put his chapter back in the book."** My mind swam a bit (was she in my computer too?) and then I said "Ok. Will do."

He shows up often in our sessions (as does Prince) and always has prescient things to say about mental health or about his path and journey or sometimes just silly, hilarious advice.

My questions are *in italics*, Jennifer's answers are **in bold.**

Richard: First let's say hi class; how are you doing?

Jennifer: Luana showed up and then Robin Williams.

So Robin; tell us - what's up?

He says "He's in New York." Some kind of an award or tribute is going on for him.

(There was a tribute for Robin in NYC on Sept. 19th, 2018 when this was recorded. https://donyc.com/events/2018/9/14/robin-the-ultimate-robin-williams-tribute-experience)

What's the formula for you to talk to us?

He just showed me like Hiroshima blowing up. Like this big cloud going up.

Like a nuclear reaction? I mean, is there a formula?

"Yeah there is."

Just for you and us or for everyone?

There is not really.. he showed me a 3D image of a body, then he showed me all the different planes (lines) coming in... kind of like Vitruvian man?

Vitruvian Man by Leonardo Da Vinci? Robin used this image with you before you're probably not aware of it.

Not at all.

Robin, how much do you slow yourself down to talk to us? If that's the right term.

He showed me everything pointing in, to the heart; he says "He has to slow his heart down to match the heart he wants to talk to."

But what's the formula to do so - half speed? One tenth?

"One third."

So the ratio is one third? In order for you to slow your frequency down to speak with us, you slow it down about a third?

He says "It makes sense because it's one third of the body." He just showed me that.

How about in terms of Jennifer elevating her frequency or energy? Does she have to move it up two thirds?

He said in my case, I just have to be.

Okay. That makes sense. She doesn't have to change her frequency at all because she's already tuned this way; is that correct?

"Yes." (Jennifer aside:) You must know I've never thought of this.

Is Jennifer more tuned than the rest of us – what percentage?

He says "75% more tuned."

Comparatively between me and her?

He says "50% for you... you're getting there .. you go up to 80 sometimes he says..."

I guess depending if I'm paying attention. Correct me if I'm wrong here.

He says "Caffeine affects it too... it helps you ask questions."

It allows you to bounce around or focus?

He just showed me marijuana..

Okay, and I'm sure Luana is helping as well (with this communication.)

Jennifer taps her finger on her nose. (Meaning "correct.")

So it's this idea of opening up channels to communicate with them, but also slowing down the frequency or the wave over there ... so it's not like we could create an app where everyone could tune in because each person is different?

He showed me a thumbprint.

Which makes sense. Everyone is unique – so the thumbprint is unique to each person. In order to communicate would it be like a ham radio operator who keeps dialing until they get a response?

"It's like something that... it's like being and nothingness going back to meditation. Opening your mind to slow your heart rate down."

I know it's not like folks could just dial that frequency in...

He said "Someday." (They'll figure out how to adjust the frequency.) Jennifer aside: Wouldn't that be cool? We just figured it out.

I know some scientists who are trying to do that – design a device to communicate, but if each person is unique...

He just showed me evolution, like the monkey, how much they can hear...

Based on all their lifetimes?

"Yes." Even people like me though, with all the fears I had before (with this work, speaking to spirit); once I got over it, it was like I was just ready to go. Once you get over it (the fear of being able to communicate) you're ready to go. He just showed *me* being a violin.

One that is out of tune, out of whack?

Not very much.

So all of your Jennifer lifetimes – from various forms of talking to spirit - you've been honing your ability to be able to do so in this manner in this lifetime. Now it's easier for you to play that violin of who you are?

Yes.

You're a Stradivarius.

I was shown that... in the form of a piano, like a Steinway... However, there's no hierarchy; it's just a tuned instrument.

Like I asked my concert pianist mom who is on the flipside about what kind of piano she is playing over there, and she responded "All of them she ever played," then you saw her as a young girl in front of the piano.

......

Well, let's unpack this if we can. Sometimes I'm in the heat of the moment, or in this case the heart of the moment, and I'm asking questions as fast as Jennifer can answer them. I know her well enough (and she clearly says so in this interview) that these are not topics she's invented, thought about or made up before.

It's what makes us a unique team to converse like this. She's open to whatever pops into her mind, I'm open to asking any form of follow up question. We hear in the previous book, from Luana, that if one thinks of "11:11" as a formula – we meet "at the decimals."

As explained, each 11 represents a hallway. One is ours; one is theirs. They need to "slow down" their "frequency" in order to be able to communicate with us, either through dreams, sounds, lights going on and off, or some other method of communication.

We've been told in our hallways, meditation, sleep can help increase our vibration (or block out the cacophony of the day) so that we can "meet at the decimals."

Robin is saying the same thing here. That he slows down his frequency about a third to communicate with us. In Jennifer's case, she doesn't need to "speed up" or increase her frequency to communicate, as she's already "built that way." (Meaning whatever filters she should have are not there, or were not in place like many others have.)

For a scientific discussion of "Filters on the brain" I recommend watching Dr. Greyson's "Is Consciousness Produced by the Brain?" on YouTube, or looking at the edited version in "It's a Wonderful Afterlife." There's a discussion of the medical cases that point to how frequencies appear to be blocked by our conscious mind while we are awake, perhaps to allow us to experience things fully.

However, some people don't have those filters, or have had them altered by a consciousness altering event – a near death experience, head trauma, or while under deep hypnosis, they are able to bypass those filters that prevent us from "hearing" or "accessing" this information.

Interesting to note that his reply to "So how can we build an app to help people do that?" he showed her a fingerprint. Each person has their own unique print (or frequency) and so that form of communication would have to be on a person by person basis – so that they could "tune themselves" to the frequency of their loved one on the flipside.

Also worth nothing, this description of how Jennifer's "many lifetimes" as a medium or someone similar have each contributed to her abilities now. That's a topic touched upon before – musicians, artists, doctors, etc, appear to choose lifetimes that will result in the qualities they seek further down the road. It might be on their tenth lifetime that they get to a point where they can use them the way they've wanted to.

I know this seems esoteric, and further if we consider the source; Robin is someone who is known for comedy, known for his lightning quick mind. However, Robin on the flipside is just another lightning quick mind who is observing the nature of reality from his new perspective, and whether he's "Robin Williams" of *Robin Williams fame*, or Robin Williams, the fellow who's had 22 different lifetimes prior to this (I'm making up a number) and in this one, he got a chance to experience using his wit at lightning speed in front of an audience – either way, I can't *not* quote him because "it's not something that sounds like he would say" – but rather, I've come to realize that we need to adjust our hearing.

We don't know much about what our loved ones sound like on the flipside, based on all their journeys, and our reactions to what they're saying are based on our own prejudices and limitations on this side.

*****

Another session. My questions in italics, Jennifer's replies in bold.

Okay, I'm curious; Robin anyone who wants to come forward, Luana anyone we haven't spoken to?

Bill Paxton is here.

Hi Billy; you want to say hello?

There was a person you talked to yesterday, he is giving me images of Ojai as you were talking... was this guy a biker ?

I think he is.

Bill wants you to talk to his friend, the bike rider. He needs your help.

Okay, Billy, but I think I scare people when I say Bill wants to say hello. So anything else you want to say?

He said thank you. He's saying "It's rough getting to the front of this class... then they make fun of you.. (when you're up here) " just because..."

Burt Reynolds showed up six weeks ago, but didn't say anything. Does he have something he wanted to say? If he doesn't want to talk it's okay.

He doesn't yet know how to communicate.

Well, you're welcome to chat with us – Burt, I think you met the film producer Jonathan Krane in our class. He can help you.

Did Jonathan have a heart attack?

(Note: Jonathan D. Krane was John Travolta's manager, produced a number of feature films and three of mine.)

Yes.

I didn't know this... but he's showing it to me – he showed me the arm hurting, fell over.

It was about a year ago that Jonathan checked out... I was thinking as weird as it is, out of all the people I've worked with, he was the only film producer, who took me seriously as a filmmaker. It's disconcerting to realize there was one guy and he's no longer on the planet.

But he can help you now... it's funny – he can help you now, and all of them went like this – (Jennifer shrugs.)

What does that mean?

Like they're embarrassed they didn't help you (career wise) before.

Sydney Pollack is part of our group, I met him through Jonathan. Sydney, I was talking to your daughter the other day. You know Phillip Noyce, just saw him recently.

They're talking about the filmmaker Michael Moore. They say they're giving him tons of information over there. Our buddy John McCain is helping Michael as well.

We had a wonderful conversation with John – very interesting, wide ranging, all kinds of info, mind boggling.

Who is the guy with big hair? He showed me Tina Turner.

Luana was friends with Tina, they joined Buddhism together.

The guy who sings "I feel good."

James Brown.

Is he there?

Yeah. Looks like it.

Slide on in James.

They're all laughing now. Prince did a lot of James Brown's dancing moves.

Prince just bowed and did the "I'm not worthy" bow to him.

He was the original. Everyone learned from him. Who was there to greet you when you crossed over James?

He says "His whole family." (Jennifer aside:) Did he know Luana? She was showing me Tina Turner... that was the connection – she's showing me that connection.

(Note: Six degrees of Luana. She knew Tina Turner, both joined Buddhism together (Nam Myoho Renge Kyo) and Jennifer is saying that James is showing her Tina, that's his connection to Luana.)

James, you led an unusual life, it was a bit all over the map. So why did you choose this lifetime?

"It was the simplest way to feed his family."

You were such a great dancer and great singer.

Elvis just stopped by.

That's nice, we can get to him at some point...

James wants to speak. He says "He chose this life to be an influencer, he influenced everyone to "knock it out of the park." He gave them that "by being African American, by breaking the boundaries to do whatever they wanted to do. By giving everyone else an easier path to do whatever they wanted to do."

That makes sense. Thank you. Does Elvis want to talk to us?

He does. He showed me Priscilla.

What about his daughter? Is he in touch with her?

He says "She's hard to reach because of her beliefs."

That's okay, it's allowed. Who was there to greet you when you crossed over?

His manager? (Jennifer aside) I don't know anything about him.

I know who he is. Did he appear young or old when he saw him?

Middle aged.

(Note: Colonel Tom Parker died January 21, 1997. Elvis died August 16, 1977 20 years earlier, but as noted "two thirds" of our conscious energy is always "back home.")

That must have been pretty unusual for you – you couldn't get away from the guy in life and there he was to greet you on the flipside.

"That's how he knew he was no longer here, because he was greeted by him."

Who else came to greet you?

He showed me five individuals.

Was you mother one of them? I know you were close; when did she come forward?

"She was right there with him." Was he tormented by the manager? I don't know anything about him.

In life, yeah, but I imagine, not over there.

He's showing me the man was like an equal with his mother...

Colonel Parker controlled his life...

I asked him if the manager apologized for his behavior and he said "No, but Elvis just understood why."

Does Elvis have any regrets about checking out early? Or was this an exit point as in "time to go home?"

(Note: We hear about "exit points" often – where people have a choice to "take the off ramp" but either don't or stay around for some other reason.)

He said "He had two exit points before but he didn't take them."

Do you have any regrets?

(Jennifer listens) Aw.. he loved Priscilla. Says "His heart broken over losing Priscilla... he was so heart broken over her."

(Note: When Jennifer says she doesn't know anything about Elvis, I know that to be accurate. Elvis and Priscilla separated on February 23, 1972, and filed for legal separation on July 26.)

So when you first met Priscilla did you recognize her?

"Yes. Instantly."

From a previous lifetime?

"Yes, but he didn't know it then."

Did you have a relationship with her in a previous life?

"Many." He's showing me... It's like they had opposite roles.

You mean like she a princess and you were a slave?

"Something like that."

What about your musical ability? Where did that come from? Did you have that before?

He's saying "Yes, a couple of times before. He wanted to understand what it was like to feel like everything was out of his control when he did music."

Okay. Who was the most surprising person for you to run into on the flipside? Who impressed you over there?

He's trying to show me ... someone in a surf movie... He's trying to show me a surf movie.

Someone you worked with in a surf movie? Someone who did a movie with you and you got to the flipside and you met this person and that impressed you? Okay, I'll look that one up.

(Note: I figured he'd done many, but I think he's referring to "Blue Hawaii" made in 1961. His close friend on that movie was Robert West an "American actor, film stuntman and songwriter... known for being a close confidant (of) Elvis Presley. (Wikipedia) West died in 2017, but according to these reports roughly two thirds of our conscious energy is always "back home" on the flipside. Sometimes people have a near death experience and see people who are still on the planet. So if Elvis ran into this friend, he would be surprised to see him as he was still alive when he crossed over.)

He says "This is a great class."

Thank you. Any any last words for us Elvis? Anyone in our class want to speak? Lu, anything you want to say?

Luana's voice is so calming and soothing, I love her voice... she's saying "Everyone just has to be more open, and interpretations come in so many ways...

Well, the fact that Colonel Parker controlled his life, wouldn't let him travel, go anywhere, for Elvis to meet him on the other side... is kind of funny.

He's saying "But he understood it."

Interesting that he said "he wanted a life where he was completely out of control." So that was perfect because the person who helped him get out of control was the guy who managed him – meaning he did a good job. Never thought I'd be rehabilitating Colonel Parker's image in a flipside session.

"Right," he's saying, "That was the role he played."

....

(Note: Luana didn't know Elvis, but she did know others that have shown up in our class. James Brown showed up because he does know members of our class, and "Elvis" swung by because all of these people "vibrate" or "exist" in a similar frequency. *But wait; there's more...*)

CHAPTER FOUR:

"THE QUEEN OF SOUL"

Aretha Franklin and Martin Luther King

Another day at Fishbar in Manhattan Beach. My questions are *in italics,* Jennifer's replies **in bold.**

Rich: Okay Luana, does anyone need to talk to us?

Jennifer: Prince is coming in...

(Note: Prince started talking to us during the writing of "Hacking the Afterlife." I met him while reviewing a concert for Variety, but did not know him. However, he told us enough things that I could verify what he was saying. He says he helps people back here on the planet when they need his help, with music, ideas or just remembering him. In this case, he's "escorting" Aretha into this classroom.)

Rich: Mr. Rogers Nelson, they just released the catalog with 10,000 new songs of yours, unreleased tunes. How do you feel about that?

He says "Amazing. It makes him feel good; it outweighs the sadness."

Prince, is Aretha over there with you?

She's having a blast! She's having so much fun... like *aiii!* (Jennifer listens) What? Ok. I feel like she's still learning how to heal herself... I felt her (healing process.)

We can talk to her now, if she wants to. But maybe it's too soon; it's okay if she doesn't want to.

She says *"Later. It's interesting though."* (Jennifer aside) Does she have a sister? She's up there with her... wait... no, two are up there with her... one is... down here?

(Note: Jennifer doesn't know anything about Aretha Franklin. After the session was over, I looked it up. Three of Aretha's sisters are with her, none are still "down here." So if that's enough to stop anyone from reading further, I call it a way to "get off this bus." She said "two are up there with her and one is down here." That's inaccurate. But as we'll find out she may be referring to someone she's close to.)

I'm aware that she didn't leave a will.

She says "She does have a will but they don't know where it is. It's not with an attorney."

Okay, please be more specific?

It's very old. Could be (in) an old mail. Did she have a lot of husbands? How many relationships did she have? I'm seeing five.

(Note: Wikipedia tells me she was married twice, but indeed, had five long relationships. Jennifer doesn't say she wrote the old email, but that it "could be in an old email" that someone else wrote, like an attached document, or the document itself.

I don't know, but whatever...

She's laughing... she's trying to give me a timeline.

The person you were married to will know where it was or his heirs?

"No, they won't know where it is. (It's) One of her sisters feels like..."

(Her sister) knows where it is?

"She won't know but she will know..." She's explaining that "She won't know.. but *should* know."

What's your sister's name?

(I'm getting) something with an S.

65

(Note: This is all accurate. I didn't know it at the time, but her niece is the executor of her estate, she did leave behind a handwritten will (a few apparently) and the niece eventually found it.)

Then we don't have to worry about (helping them find) it?

"So you'll know that when they find it, *you already knew* they'd find it."

Okay then, who's going to find it?

"Her sister, or someone related to her sister. She wants you to write about it..." (Jennifer listens, looks confused) I'm not saying she'd make it up, I'm saying it's hard to... – (aside to me, eyes wide) I can't believe I'm talking to Aretha right now! I just have to go with it.

She might want to talk about the song "Nessun Dorma." She sang it at the Grammys.

(Jennifer continuing) I've never heard her voice up close. She's putting me in a sweat... she wants to go back to the first thing (she said). Her sister (or someone related to her sister) has the will... feels like it's in a house in the 1980's...

In Aretha's house?

"Not in her house."

(Note: The will was found by her sister's daughter, Sabrina, whom Aretha was close enough to make her the executor of her estate. Sabrina later found the handwritten will in her home. AP News "Three Handwritten Wills Found in Aretha's Home" May 20, 2019 Nine months after this interview. AP News.)

They're all laughing.

Miss Franklin, look around who's here in (Luana's) class. Ray Charles is here – we've spoken to him. (Ray starred in my second feature film "Limit Up" playing God.)

She loved him. Luana's telling me she cut up that velvet rope and (Aretha) walked in.

(Note: It was Tom Petty who suggested our conversations were like "Luana has a clipboard behind a velvet rope and only those Luana deemed worthy could speak to us." He dubbed her the person with the VIP list of who gets "backstage;" hence the title of the books.)

Aretha who was there to greet you when you crossed over?

Prince says, "He was there and Ray Charles (as well.)"

Miss Franklin: anything you want me to tell your family?

"That I'm fine. I have no pain."

What was your favorite song?

She loved (the song) you said earlier – she's holding a flower... that thing you said before.

"Nessun dorma?" Okay, she substituted for Pavarotti at the Grammys, did an amazing version of this Italian aria.

She's saying "The lyrics are so amazing. They're super important."

They are? Well, it means "no one's asleep." I guess that's a metaphor that no one dies? "Nessuno dorma."

She said "She had a premonition before that... just the music."

(Note: I don't know if she meant a premonition about passing away, or about doing the song.)

Well, she stepped in for Luciano Pavarotti at the Grammy's. Can we ask; how's Luciano doing?

"He's here – he's mad about his death."

Luciano, you went up and down with your weight... so it wasn't unexpected.

So much anger. Um; he says "He was fat and happy – but he was up and down up and down."

Well, welcome to our group, Luciano – and say hello to your friend Aretha.

He says, "Six degrees of Aretha Franklin."

Luana, is this exciting for you to meet Aretha? The Queen of Soul?

She says "There's no hierarchy (here), but she adds spice to the class."

Anything else?

They say "come on back."

Okay, we soon will.

*****

PART TWO

The following session was filmed on Sept. 7TH, 2018 after Aretha's televised funeral. My questions in italics, Jennifer's responses in bold.

Richard: Hi class. I'll leap right in. Aretha, we're back, we met last week, can we talk to you?

Prince has her on his arm and he's walking her up the aisle.

Anything you want to say about your funeral Miss Franklin?

"Extravagant" she says. I just got an image of John McCain...

Okay, I invited him as well. Who wants to speak first? Aretha or John?

(Note: On my way to a session, I "invite" certain people to join us by saying their name aloud. Sometimes Jennifer identifies them immediately, sometimes I ask for them by name with her. In this case, prior to my arrival, I asked for Aretha and John to show up. After about a half hour of talking to him, (later in the book) Luana steered us back to Aretha.)

"Aretha. We cut her short (last week)."

I'm sorry Miss Franklin. When you crossed over, who was there to greet you?

She showed me dancing with this guy – he brought her into a memory.

(Note: He "brought her into a memory" refers to a method of "giving a person a "soft landing" on the flipside." At first they think that's the new state of things, inside a dream, but then begin to realize that they're in a new place and are not "gone." As we'll learn later, the person she was dancing with had an important role in her life John Hammond, iconic music man who had a hand in everyone's career from Robert Johnson to Bob Dylan.)

Someone we know?

Someone associated with her...

I read that Stevie Wonder came to see you (before she crossed).

"Two days before," she said.

(Note: I don't know if this is accurate. But when discussing time and dates, I'll defer to the person I'm speaking with.)

What did he say (to you)?

He said "It's okay (to pass); I've got a lot of friends up there."

Who have you been visiting with, Aretha?

"Everyone." She just showed me Marilyn as well – (Jennifer listens:) Let me try to say this as she said it; "I was the African-American Marilyn." The class is laughing along with her.

Aretha, there's a video of you playing "Nessun Dorma" for your granddaughter (on YouTube) – It popped into my head; were you an opera singer in a previous life?

"Yes."

In what era?

"16th century... Paris; somewhere in Paris. And she married somebody Italian."

Let me ask you a musical question, was the coloratura which you had in your voice, that you carried throughout this life – was that unique sound related to your previous lifetime?

"Yes, yep." (Jennifer aside:) She's showing me my brain (Jennifer's brain) and what I'm doing here (as a medium), and how my ability to use this (to speak to the afterlife) – is more accepted now. It wasn't accepted in all my lifetimes, but I can use it now

because it's carried through all of those lifetimes. I would have struggled with this ability if I hadn't figured it out.

(Note: It's an observation that we'll hear often in these sessions. That people carry their "talent" from life to life, and each time they hone it or work on it, or add something to it if it's possible in that era. Jennifer's memory of "being able to communicate with different realms has been reported in "Hacking the Afterlife." She's observing here that Aretha's answer to my question "Where did your singing talent come from?" by showing Jennifer it's like her talent to be a medium – the talent has been honed over many lifetimes.)

So then do most musicians carry their frequency of music from life to life?

"Yes."

What singer did you admire (during your life)?

She says "Sammy Davis Junior." (Jennifer aside:) I saw Sammy show up earlier... He was hanging out with Prince.

Silly question, but were you friends with Michael Jackson?

"Sure." She's like "Of course I was! That's such a *stupid question*. She loved him."

(Note: On another occasion we have a discussion with Michael about his path and journey, and he's very frank about it. But she's the first to call one of my questions *stupid*. It's allowed.)

Aretha, what do you want us to pass along to your friends and family?

She said "Tell them to breathe." She says "They're still looking for the will."

You said it was on a computer your sister had – (but I learned) all your sisters are gone.

There's someone like a sister to her (still here).

Okay, well, you did say it was going to be found in October. That's when I said "Then I guess I don't need to worry about it."

"They're still not looking in the right place."

Things could change... it may be that they're going to find something.

If they do then I think it's going to be contested...

(Note: Ding! It is being contested.)

So why were you born into Reverend Franklin's family?

"He wanted to change the world like Martin Luther King."

In terms of choosing the neighborhood to be born in?

"That's what she charted," she says. "That was her math."

(Note: In filming people under deep hypnosis, they often claim to be able to access their "life planning session." People plot out "mathematically" who they're going to be – sometimes with great precision, sometimes as improvisation. The "math" referred to was the path she "charted" like a musical score.)

Who was your biggest influence?

"God."

(Note: Not something I've heard before. People say it *here* often, but rarely during one of these sessions.)

I mean on the planet – who was it that you want to give a shout out to?

(Jennifer observing). He was white – trying to figure out who it is...

A singer?

"No."

A record producer?

"Yes." From New York. Feels like.

I can look it up.

"He believed in her and also he kind of saved her from her own family." (Jennifer looks at me) I don't know anything about her family. (It's).. her friend from New York. She met him when she was like 14."

(Note: John Hammond signed Aretha when she was a teen and took over her career. As noted, he was responsible for everyone from Robert Johnson to Bruce Springsteen becoming part of our musical songbook. This would make sense, even though I had to research this to see who it could have been.)

So what was your favorite song?

"Somewhere over the rainbow."

A fitting title for our discussion. Thank you Miss Franklin.

PART THREE

This ensuing session was recorded on March 26th, 2019.

Richard: Hi class. Hi Jennifer. So the other day, I had an entertaining class without you because I got to go see a movie and our class went to see it with me.

(Note: I went to a screening of "Amazing Grace." As I sat in the theater, I had an odd feeling our entire class was there. I have learned not to judge or dismiss a feeling like this; I can always ask Jennifer later "Was the class with me?" I felt Luana's friend Sydney Pollack sitting with us, (interviewed in "Backstage Pass to the Flipside") Aretha's friends James Brown, Prince, Ray Charles, MLK taking seats.)

Aretha what did you think of the movie that I saw about you this weekend?

She's saying "I was surprised. The lengths of it... – the lengths it took to get it out there."

Let me ask you Aretha, why did you not like this film so much that you didn't want it out there?

(Listens. Makes a face) "Body image issues." She just.. I'm asking her, "It was really about body image?" And she replied "You're one to talk."

Correct me if I'm wrong, but watching the film, I got the impression that you were ill during production.

"Absolutely." She says she **"had issues from diabetes"** – that **"her blood sugars were off."**

(Note: It is not public knowledge Aretha had diabetes or symptoms of diabetes; she died from pancreatic cancer, but I found an article where she revealed she suffered from those same symptoms. "...one thing that isn't widely known about this artist (AF) is that she is diabetic." https://www.diabetes.co.uk › celebrities › aretha-franklin)

I noticed you were coughing off camera; you looked like you were in pain.

"I was." She says **"Her whole body was in pain."** She said **"She was suffering from a number of things."**

Let me ask our pal Sydney Pollack, (who directed "Amazing Grace.") What did you think of the film?

(Note: There's an interview with Sydney in "Backstage Pass to the Flipside." I sent the private details he mentioned to one of his daughters, she reported the interview was "absolutely accurate.")

"There was something wrong with his hair," he said.

Ha, okay, your hair was bushy. I hate to be the critic Sydney, but part of the film was out of focus. While watching it I thought I "heard" Ray Charles say: "I could have filmed this better!"

"Ray is funny."

In the film, Reverend Franklin said Aretha had only called him the night before and said "C'mon down," which was interesting. Why didn't she ask her father to participate earlier?

She tells me that her father "took Aretha away from her mother," it felt like.

(Note: According to her bio, her mother died when she was younger.)

Aretha, we asked you earlier who you met when you crossed over, and you told Jennifer that you were were dancing with a man, who felt like a manager when you crossed over. Was it John Hammond, the famous record producer who signed you when you were 16 or 17 years old?

She's telling me "He took over for her father." (With her career).

He signed her to a record deal at Columbia. Sydney, what did you think of your movie?

"Love." He loved it. He just showed me hearts going up into the sky.. like there's love there.

As a director, what would you have done differently?

He said, "He would have put Aretha more on a pedestal."

For better angles I imagine. The film was as much sacred as it was revelatory.

"That's right," he says, "but that didn't make her look good." He says "There wasn't the money at the time."

Just to clarify, the main reasons you didn't want the movie to be released, Aretha, was how you looked?

"All of it." She felt "it wasn't optimal."

What did our class think of it?

They said "It was amazing. Even though she felt she could have done better as a performer."

There's a moment in the film that is otherworldly – it's during a call and response portion, where Reverend James Cleveland is calling out, Aretha has her eyes closed and is singing her responses, but the microphone isn't on her, and she isn't aware of it. It's an extreme close up, but you can see that she's in another place, transcendent.

"She was."

(Note: A reminder that Jennifer has not seen the film, and at this point, I didn't mention the name of the film either. So she's not giving me her opinion, but the opinion from those who've seen it.)

Then Reverend Cleveland moved the mic over to her so we could hear her.

Hold on. She keeps showing me Whitney Houston. (Listens) She says she had a great love for Whitney, felt like she felt a great responsibility for Whitney – I don't know why.

Okay, I'll look that up.

(Note: I did. Aretha was very close with Cissy Houston, Whitney's mom, and took care of Whitney often. They were very close, and her bio says they spent a lot of time together. Not something I knew, or that Jennifer could have known.)

But before we get off the film, I wanted to say the film shows what a profound instrument you have as a singer; it's on full display in that film.

She says "She realizes that now." (About the film)

It will be revelatory to those who see it...it comes out next month. It's called "Amazing Grace."

(Startled. Jennifer asks) It's called "Amazing Grace?" That's the song that Dave Chappelle told me she sang to him. I didn't know that! That's so cool.

May I ask what Martin Luther King thought of the film?

"Powerful."

I learned that Dr. King knew Aretha's father. Aretha, in a previous discussion you said a girl with the name S has your will. Who is that?

Did she have a daughter?

I don't know – I don't think so.

It feels like (the name is) a Shannon. Shaneen... or Shawna? (The name turns out to be Sabrina.)

I'm sorry, I didn't mean to interrupt Reverend King. I felt your presence in the theater, for whatever that's worth.

He said, "Thanks for inviting me."

After the film, I asked everyone to give me a one word review. I wish I'd written them down, as each reflected their persona.

(Jennifer aside) I asked the class, "If we should ask you guys to come to the movies with us?" and I heard an overwhelming "Yes." So I asked "Do you put that idea in our minds to go to the movies as well?" and I also heard a "Yes."

Like sneaking friends into the drive-in in the trunk of your car. Next time I'm in the theater I'll think of all the folks that may have suggested we attend this film.

Luana just said "Thank you."

For what?

"For filming this, for putting this out there."

*****

I looked up the executor of Aretha's estate and it turns out it is her sister's daughter, Sabrina. Sabrina replied to my email that included these comments verbatim, that while she feels connected to her mother on the other side, **"She did not believe the medium (Jennifer) was actually connected to her aunt."**

Which is fine. We're not here to prove that what Aretha might be saying – it's all subject to interpretation and trying to unpack imagery or sound. Then after it was revealed Aretha's handwritten wills had been found, I reached out to Sabrina. She was unmoved by that detail – she said she "always suspected a will would be found" and that Aretha "never used a computer, so it would be handwritten."

The point isn't to prove or disprove what people are saying on the flipside – handwritten wills aside - but to offer that they still exist and are available to speak to their loved ones. Aretha is still in touch with her niece, albeit through her sister – and that's good news either way.

The Queen of Soul remains the *Queen of Soul.*

CHAPTER FIVE:
THE COUNTRY IS AT STAKE

Pearl Bailey sings along with Richard Nixon (National Archives)

PRESIDENT NIXON, KENNEDY AND AMELIA EARHART

Rich: Hi class.

Jennifer: Amelia is here.

Hello Ms. Earhart. How is Amelia?

She showed me like Peter Pan – flying.

Did you fly in to see our class today?

Two days ago; she said she was in your head.

What were you doing there?

She said "There's lots of space." Now everyone is laughing, even Luana is laughing.

Very funny. There's an aircraft hangar of air in my head – what else is new? Let's ask Luana; how's everybody doing?

"They're learning."

About?

"About transmissions."

About how to communicate to our side? You mean about frequency?

"Morton" showed up to... (Michael Newton) He showed me Scott De Tamble (trained by Newton). Has Scott mentioned to him?

Could be. Michael, is there anything you want us to tell Scott?

"He needs to get out and talk (in public) more."

He's very good at it. When he speaks in public his events are always sold out. Let's go back to our buddy the pilot. I'm meeting with a former Federal agent who's been looking for her Amelia Earhart.

Does he have a connection to Obama? They're teasing you.

He's the guy who found the photo of Amelia on the docks. Let me ask you Amelia; what's he going to tell me?

He found something with numbers... something with numbers on it – could be an old document. I saw an old yellowed document.

(Note: I met former ATF Federal investigator and now friend Les Kinney a few hours after this, and only when transcribing this session did I realize that indeed, he had discovered an old yellowed document where a ham radio operator in Pennsylvania, a woman, had written down the radio transmissions she got from Amelia's Electra for three days after she landed the Electra on Mili Atoll. Amelia identified the island, and its terrain, and the numbers of where it was longitudinally. It's posted on EarhartOnSaipan.com)

He did find something; I don't know what it is. Did we discuss this before?

I know he went to the place on Saipan where she was initially buried. Correct me where if I'm wrong Amelia.

"He didn't find anything there," that's what they're telling me.

(Note: That's accurate).

I don't know if was the actual place that she and Fred were buried or not.

She's telling me "They were separate – (in) different places. I just got the sea with him..." Something in the sea. That's what I'm getting.

You mean he was buried at sea?

(Note: That could have been after his body was recovered and turned over to the Navy and buried at sea. In 1945, two GI's, Hanson and Burke were sent on a detail to dig up Amelia and Fred's body. (As detailed in Fred Goerner's book and mine "Hacking the Afterlife." When I first met Jennifer, she helped me to interview Amelia, and Amelia told us that her body was not recovered by the "two GI's" but had been moved. She said "They only found my arm." Ten minutes after the interview, I got a call from a retired NTSB investigator who said that everything I had told him about Amelia being arrested and taken to Saipan was true, as he had seen intelligence to that fact, but he added "When they dug up her body they only found an arm." It was six months before I could verify this detail, as Hanson and Burke were interviewed by the UPI in 1977 where they confirmed "they only found her arm and a partial ribcage." (Chicago Tribune, Jan 1977)

"Yes."

Did they rebury the rest of your body somewhere else?

She showed me a German shepherd – I don't know what that means - if the dogs took her.... or if German Shepherds represent some military version... or even the name shepherd...

Could be related to the Germans buried on Saipan; Germany turned Saipan over to Spain, then Japan. I understand two GI's dug you up and they found an arm and a partial rib cage – those pieces of you were probably buried at sea along with Fred Noonan. Is that correct?

"Yes."

And the rest of your body was moved...

To another location. Her body got moved twice.

To where?

I got that it is east from the place we originally talked about. She showed me horses.

(Note: This is described in "Hacking the Afterlife." Amelia had Jennifer draw me a map of Saipan, which was accurate, as I'd just returned from finding 15 new eyewitnesses who saw her there. She told me where I could find the "rest of her body" but I've yet to reveal that detail.)

If her actual burial place is east of this place we originally discussed; how many feet east?

Directly under the place we discussed.

(Note: I know where that is. If someone wants me to show them, let's go to Saipan together.)

So you're still there now? Your bones, teeth, skull?

Yes, there's something with the teeth that someone might have found.

Okay. With Amelia or Fred's teeth?

I don't know.

Okay, thank you Amelia. We'll dig into this at a later date. You said something about Obama?

Yes. I keep seeing a picture of Obama.

Who's holding a picture of Obama? McCain?

Nixon! He wants to talk to us.

Richard Nixon? Wow. My grandfather Edward Hayes helped get him into office. Holding a photo of...?

Barack Obama. He did that to show me a president who is still alive – and we were talking about that journalist killed by Saudi Arabians and how your dad built something over there.

How did you know that? What did he build over there?

Something to do with toilets? You may have told me.

That's correct.

(Note: My father built the largest university in the world; the King Saud in Riyadh. When he took over the project he discovered all the University toilets were facing Mecca... so he had them all adjusted a quarter turn so they were not facing Mecca. If you ever need to use the facilities at the University you now know why the toilets are crooked.)

So Mr. Nixon; we were talking about you knowing my grandfather Edward Hayes and how he helped in your election.

He says "He was a very big supporter."

To my eternal shame. Just kidding. So tell us, who was there to greet you when you crossed over?

He says "His mother." He's saying she had cancer and I'm getting that it was either his mom or she was someone who was like his mom.

I think his wife crossed over before him.

Is her name Pat?

Yes.

It felt like his mom when he saw her and then realized it was his wife, Pat.

(Note: Nixon died in 1994, his wife Pat in 1993.)

So Mr. President, you've had some time to hang out on the flipside.

He's mentioning something that happened in 1968?

That was the year when he was elected. What do you want to talk about?

He showed me the current administration. I asked if he wanted to comment on that and he said it was behaving the way it is for a higher purpose.

We've heard that before.

(Note: I try not to inject my own politics in these discussions – as we know on the flipside it doesn't matter. Everyone is equal. There is no hierarchy. But as we've learned, people behave in certain ways to help others to fulfill their potential, whether it's behaving badly (in the case of wars) or with noble intent.)

It is in the sense of us (over on Earth) being uncomfortable with what's going on, people are doing more for the country because (the current President) is the way he is...

Let me ask you about your path and journey, sir. I'm assuming you had a map; kind of what your journey would be.

It was all over the place – like a rumbling earthquake. He's showing me a fault line.

Did you feel like you succeeded in your path and journey?

(Jennifer reacts) Oh. He has bad breath... he showed me his kidneys; he had a physical ailment.

(Note: That is the first time Jennifer has mentioned something like this. Sometimes she'll "smell" a perfume, but the first halitosis report I've heard.)

Tell us Mr. Nixon, do you about any regrets? Do you regret Watergate?

He says "No. I regret getting caught." He says "The (energy of that) event - it opened up avenues for other people (to teach or learn lessons) – it's what Trump is doing for the US now (forcing people to confront what they care about) it's what he did (Nixon) for the US back then, and he never got credit for it. His was way more innocent, (but it's the) same thread of energy."

Let me ask you about Henry Kissinger? What's your impression of him?

He started laughing – he called him "an old fart." He showed me something very old – (Jennifer aside) I asked "is Kissinger still alive?" I had no idea. he showed me a photograph of a very very old man.

So, what was the happiest day of his life?

He just held up a photo of his daughter Tricia. At that moment, he knew something was greater than him in this life. Did someone in his family have polio?

He might be referring to FDR. Perhaps you're aware that other Presidents have spoken to us; is that why you're here?

(Note: Looking up any reference to Nixon and Polio, when he attended Duke law school, the Washington Post reported he carried a student with polio up the steps to school every day.
"Strange Career of Richard Nixon" 1989)

"Yes, its a frequency. Yes."

Anyone in our class you would like to speak with Mr. Nixon?

"Yes, Tom Petty."

Well, Tom seems to know a lot of people. Were you a fan of his music then or a fan of his music now?

He's a fan of it now.

In terms of my grandfather Ed Hayes who is also here, have you spoken to him in the past?

"Many times."

What do you talk about?

Golf. (to me: Did Nixon golf?)

(Note: I didn't know if Nixon golfed, but apparently he began when he was Eisenhower's vice President.)

I think he might have. Don't they all golf?

Hang on; what was it? He saying "It's how you come back, with more transparency." That's what he's talking to him about.

(Note: I'm not sure if he means to reincarnate but be more aware of a previous lifetime – more transparency.)

So this idea that politicians attract other politicians – my grandfather ran for office, the Senate in Illinois. Is it accurate that it's kind of a club? Like baseball players hanging out with other baseball players, it's a frequency issue?

"Yes."

In terms of your journey now, have you figured out who you're going to come back as?

Jennifer laughs. He said "Barack Obama." He says "He's going to come back and be a pilot."

Are you interested in politics again? Or have you done enough of that?

He said "I'm not going to come back." He says he's going to come back in something with his daughter, have a better life with his daughter.

Okay, this is unusual Mr. President; we didn't ask for you to come by – any parting words you'd like to pass along?

"Don't take Trump too seriously. Trump is making people come to terms with their belief systems; with politics. It's almost like a religious thing, everybody has to come to terms where they resonate – and Trump is doing that, forcing everyone into their own belief system." (Jennifer aside) I'm seeing President Kennedy.

Does he want to talk to us?

"Yes."

Welcome to our class, what do you want to tell us?

He says "Jackie is here as well."

He's not pissed at her for going off with Ari Onassis?

He says "They knew. They knew."

Their journey. I'm just kidding. They had an interesting path the two of them.

He says "He picked right..." and then Marilyn showed up. And then John Jr. He's saying something about him.

What about John Jr?

He's saying "He was stubborn, he shouldn't have flown (that day.)"

That's okay, that's a dad talking.

They all wanted to get back quicker so they could redo it or fix it up.

Well Mr. Kennedy, you had an unusual path and journey – I don't think we've talked before, have we talked to you before JFK?

No I don't think so... Also John McCain just showed up.

I would think they all generate the same frequency. Can I ask you some questions about your journey?

He said "Bay of Pigs" and then I'm being shown Trump and the Saudis. "It's similar," he's saying.

John you suffered while you were...

"Yeah," he's showing me his bad back.

If I can ask you, at some point when you took LSD, the CIA and the mafia were listening in, while you and a mistress were tripping in bed, and she was talking to you about world peace. Jackie you know this – and you told this girlfriend that you were going to become a peacenik – was that why the motivation for the CIA to assist in killing you?

A long pause. "Yes. They couldn't control him anymore. No one could." That's why his wife lived.

(Note: This was reported in the book "Brothers" by David Talbot. It covers the assassinations of both brothers, and is cited by JFK's brother later on in this book.)

I'm aware that you were taking huge doses of medication, "Dr. Feelgood" was giving you these shots – but once they realized you were dropping LSD they thought "We can't control him; we have to kill him." Is that what happened?

When you said that, I got Marilyn Monroe. Then he showed me his brother.

You're saying all three of you – part of the same group that was eliminated? The same guys involved in bumping you off?

He just looked the other way. He went like this – (looks away) he looked away. That means to me that no one looked at it (properly.) I'm getting there was something about a card found in a wallet.

Yes, a card found in car in Washington D.C., yes, I'm familiar with it – a card was found.

(Note: I have no idea how she could have – it's an obscure detail in Kennedy Assassination lore – that a card was found which pointed to evidence of why he was killed related to his relationship with Mary Pinochet Meyer, with whom he reportedly dropped LSD.)

I don't know any of this.

There was a whole thing with Bobby. According to the book "Brothers" it goes back to the Bay of Pigs story, and how they had actually planned a second invasion. It got to a certain point and then JFK was killed. RFK was reportedly forced to cover that up.

He says "Because the country and the presidency was at stake."

It's reported in "Brothers;" that people didn't want another Cuba event to happen, Bobby was persecuting the mafia so they had to eliminate him, but decided to help the CIA bump off JFK instead. Sam Giancana, reportedly involved, was tight with Sinatra, and by extension Marilyn, and they set the thing in play with rogue elements of the CIA – which is all in that book. So are you saying that Bobby's death was a result of that as well?

"Yes."

How is your brother Robert doing?

He says "They wanted to take out Bobby before JFK but he was too…"

Let's ask Bobby. Can we? Is he available?

Jennifer nods.

Is this accurate? And if so, did you feel bad about getting your brother killed on your behalf?

He says "No. He got *me* killed." He's smiling.

(Note: I sometimes ask challenging questions to see what kind of response I get. In this case, got him to smile and retort with something that certainly I did not expect.)

So you guys are all hanging out now?

"Well, Jackie O is hanging out with Marilyn Monroe!"

John what would you like to tell your family and friends?

"Liberty and justice for all... from the flipside." I asked him – how do people who resonate at the same frequency come together? He showed me branches of trees, and how those branches are the collectives; he showed me like the branches of an Indian tribe.

Each group generates their own frequency? Like actors, doctors, musicians, etc?

And then the group that I saw up here is connected to that.

Okay, Maverick, JFK, Bobby, Richard, what would be something you'd like to impart?

"To tell the truth no matter what. Speak truth to power, tell the truth at all times. Know that they're working with the ones that have open hearts. Liberty and justice for all for those on the flipside; always."

That's a good chapter.

All the presidents men on the flipside.

Who wants to talk to us next week?

I'm getting Lincoln and George Washington.

Okay, we'll see what we can do. Bye class!

CHAPTER SIX:
THE FREQUENCY IS THE SAME

The President: National Archives

LINCOLN AND JEFFERSON

Rich: Okay to shift gears; I saved this for the end, okay, so class... as we were talking last week at the end of our session talking to JFK, Nixon, Marilyn and Jackie O...

Jennifer: They're like the same... the frequency is the same.

In terms of Marilyn and Jackie – if I may, both created a persona that was very different than who they were as children. Almost like they pretended to be someone else.

I don't know how to put this, but I'm getting the sense that they both wished they were each other... or might have changed roles. There's something about having that frequency. Abraham Lincoln has joined us...

That's nice. Is that who wants to talk to us?

Bill Paxton and Tom Petty have come forward.

Bill and Tom are stepping in front of honest Abe? Oh my.

Yes. Hang on. Tom says he loves what you did last Friday night, wrote a composition or wrote a song?

Correct. I was working on a song, added music to it.. I appreciate the compliment...

It's the frequency... you bring people together.

Last week we talked about frequency on the flipside being like a tree. Different people in various places – you could see on one branch all the presidents, all the musicians...

They're still the same tree, the same emotion. The same frequency.

I've heard that musicians and doctors are on the same part of the tree.

They have the same frequency in how they express or get things.

Does Abe Lincoln want to talk to us? I was going to ask about about his favorite poem. I looked him up after we spoke last week briefly.

He's showing me being at the Ford theater.. what was the poem?

It was called "mortality." He loved to recite it from memory.

He says he knew a lot of poems by heart.

I also read Abraham was a big fan of William Shakespeare. Have you met anyone like him since you've been back home?

George Washington. George just came forward I just got showed the apple.

Can we ask George some questions, does Abraham want to help bring him forward?

He's already here.

What do you want to tell us from the flipside?

He said "Stop using the phrase the apple doesn't fall far from the tree" – it's the stupidest metaphor he's heard." He says "It's like Steve Jobs eating the apple." He's showing me that his teeth did hurt.

Duly noted and funny. So, who was there to greet you?

His mother was there to greet him. Then his dog. He had a lot of dogs. And then a pig. He said he couldn't kill this pig.

I know you had a farm on Mt. Vernon. Have you reincarnated since?

I just saw JFK and the Bay of Pigs.

A clever segue. Okay, let's ask President Kennedy a question, sorry to interrupt you George, but last week John said this Saudi assassination of a journalist was Trump's "Bay of Pigs." What did that mean?

"It is his cross to bear" – something that is right in his face... like he knew about it. "It's his... the difference is that he just lies about it, lies about everything."

His cross to bear emotionally?

He means personally, "Whatever happened he knew was going to happen... could have done something about it but did not."

This journalist being dismembered, he may feel responsible for that?

"He does." (Jennifer aside: it doesn't make me like him.)

Thank you. John. Anyone you want to talk to John?

Jackie and Marilyn and his son John... his son came in. I think his son loved... the model who was dressed as George Washington on the cover of his magazine. (Note: Cindy Crawford)

John, we have a mutual friend in Hollywood... Someone you dated.

He's showing me Daryl Hannah.

That's correct. (Ding!) I was going to USC film school with Daryl, put her in her first film. One day she told me she was going to marry Jackson Browne, and I asked if she'd met him. She had not, but she just "knew it." They were together for quite some time. Anything you want to say to Daryl?

"He says he and Daryl were more like brother and sister."
(Jennifer aside) Ron Howard's father just showed up.

(Note: We spoke to Rance, who starred in one of my films "Limit Up" after he passed. He's in "Backstage Pass to the Flipside" volume one.)

Rance, how are you doing?

He says "He's busy. Playing golf. He says he didn't golf much (in life) but he always wanted to."

Who are you playing with?

He's telling me "He's playing with the dad from happy days. Tom Bosley – a friend of Rance's. I think they're buried near each other."

How many holes do you guys play typically?

"One."

How long does the game last typically?

"24 hours."

That's funny. You guys are real duffers, aren't you?

"It's like the game goes around the world – it's kind of nutty. It's like a power or energy thing; they construct how to do it, where to do it, they hit like in barns in Kansas."

Does the ball drive further when you're hitting it etherically?

"Yes, but you have to be mentally strong to get that longer trajectory... you have to know where to send it to – you have to study it or learn it - in books, you have to have been to Kansas or to a golf course in Scotland to know how to get it there."

You have to know where it is going to land as well?

"There's like a walkie talkie, a device that helps you so you don't have to keep figuring it out."

Do you guys keep score?

"There's no need to. We play for energy." They're trying to show me gambling as well. They gamble over there.

That's funny – wow, Rance you blew my mind... cool. Originally, I got the impression you weren't happy about being in the first book... but I put you in anyway.

It was too early at the time, just after his passing.

But does he likes his chapter now?

He's giving you two thumbs up – and you're getting them from Siskel and Ebert too.

(Note: There's irony and comedy in this comment as well. The film Rance Howard and I did together got a "thumbs way down" from Siskel and Ebert, effectively killing it's theatrical release. In an earlier book, we spoke with Ebert and Siskel about their journey, and both expressed comic dismay at how they had "misunderstood" the film which had a "spiritual element" (Nancy Allen sells her soul to the "devil" to become a successful soybean trader, Ray Charles plays God.) So for them to be giving me a "thumbs up" with reference to Rance (who was in the film) is comically ironic.)

Okay, who wants to come forward since we pushed Abraham Lincoln aside, George? I had only asked who was there to greet you, let me ask you this, you owned slaves, when you went to the flipside, were any of those slaves there to greet you?

"Yes."

How did that feel about running into people in the afterlife that you had owned?

He says "Having a child makes you feel that way too." He showed me it's the same energy as owning a person.

Well, some might disagree with your assessment on that – but you're saying there's a form of unconditional love on some level?

"Yes. Because he had that kind of love for them." There were a couple of them that he knows that he was friends with. He is saying "They were friends."

George, are you friends with Jefferson?

"That asshole?"

Really? That's your assessment? Jefferson was an asshole?

"Yes." (Jennifer shrugs as if to say "that's what he's saying.") Now he's making fun of apple pie...

George?

They showed me his hair – it's very similar to Jefferson's.

The wig...?

I was being shown all of them - including Abraham Lincoln and their dorkiness.

Well, you guys hang out obviously.

He says, "It's the frequency."

What's an occasion that would bring you together?

"Trump."

So you sit around and talk about him?

He says "They don't waste their time. It's like a buffer. An excuse to get together."

People have talking about ghosts in the White House. Is that where you guys hang out?

He says it's them, "The secret service can't keep them out." He's saying that they go in there to warn people about what's going on.

Okay. So what kind of pranks do you pull?

Jennifer laughs. I kid you not – when you asked that I saw the photograph of toilet paper attached to Trump's shoe as he was walking up the steps of Air Force One.

You guys pulled that off?

They're showing me that they're all high fiving each other over that one.

Anything you want us to tell? What about you JFK?

He says "Not to give Trump that much power in our minds, let it go."

How about you Abraham? Anything you want to give us?

"Keep learning. And love who you are."

Abraham, you were a fan of someone we've chatted with before, Will Shakespeare. Have you met him since you got over here?

"Yeah."

What's he like?

He's showing me his mind, how every word effects every dimension and how everyone has tried to replicate that and it's very beautiful.

Can we talk to Will?

"Yes."

How old does he look?

In his 20's. Long hair, to his shoulders. Brown. Handsome.

Who was there to greet you when you crossed over?

I think two children of his.. initially I heard "His first wife."

I think I know what that means. Let me ask you a simple question, knowing that people have claimed this... I know your plays have been rewritten by others, but did you write the originals?

Someone helped him.

Who? A person here, or a higher self, like a guide?

William Blake.

(Note: We tend to be tied to time when talking to people on the flipside. Blake was born and lived after Shakespeare, however his higher self is always "back home." Reports are that a portion of our energy, about two thirds, is "always" back home. So when this reference comes up, if you just think of "the energy that one day became William Blake" it becomes easier to comprehend. It's shorthand in Jennifer's mind to see or hear the name William Blake – when she was likely referring to his higher self. Also noteworthy, Jennifer has a past life memory of knowing Blake as well.)

You mean like the essence of who Blake was, like his higher self?

I don't know.

We would know him as Blake, but you Will would know him as this person who was helping you to write?

He's saying "It is Blake."

(Note: We all have a portion of our higher consciousness "back home." So Blake's higher consciousness, before he was known as Blake indeed could have been helping Will to write (it's that frequency issue again.)

Will, what's your favorite play of yours?

(Jennifer aside) I'm asking was it "Romeo and Juliet" or "Hamlet?" and he's saying "I don't have a favorite; I like... I love stories, tragic love stories, with yourself, I like Socrates, Romeo and Juliet... he showed me a bunch of different stories.

But if you were forced to pick one – just because it's fun to ask... Julius Caesar... that Scottish play, Othello, Measure for Measure, the Merchant of Venice?

"By far it's "Romeo and Juliet."

By far, all right, very good, let me ask you, what do you regret about your lifetime if anything?

He says "I regret not loving who I was within it."

Within it? Why?

"I was tortured, which made it for good writing, but I couldn't enjoy it.. I got glimpses of enjoying it."

What do you miss about being on the planet?

Jennifer listens. He says "I don't miss it, I love hearing about it, so he showed me like the planet, with all the people thinking about Shakespeare and singing and dancing and doing his plays." That is the most... he misses.

Can you show up at any play that's being performed that you wrote? Because the frequency is there?

"Absolutely."

And do you do that often?

He says "No, no. He'd be quite bored" (with that.)

With what?

He's laughing; "If I have to hear another...!"

What, "To be or not to be?" because its...

"Boring!"

That's funny. Who is somebody who you appreciate as a storyteller?

"Beethoven."

Of course, musically he told epics.

"Absolutely."

We met him in class. We met his "Immortal beloved." How about you, Will you were married are reported?

"Couple of times."

Have you reincarnated?

"Many tentacles" he says.

So like a version of you – you only send a portion of you?

"Yes."

Have you done any other lifetimes as an artist or writer? I would think it was something you couldn't escape.

"Always," he says. He says "He likes the frequency of that."

Are you here now?

Yes, with me (Jennifer points to herself).

(Note: This is a funny answer that I can't let slip past. I've been interviewing Jennifer for over four years, and she knows the kinds of questions I ask. But in this instance, for the first time, the person I'm asking answers the question in a literal fashion. "Are you here now?" Yes, I'm with Jennifer." I'm asking if a portion of him has reincarnated. He's either trying to be funny or literal. "Yes, with Jennifer, pray tell, why do you ask Horatio?")

No, I mean is some part of you incarnated here now?

"No."

One last question to Will – what can we tell the planet you wanted to say to us? What do you want to tell us?

"**Love indecently.**"

Robin Williams told us to "love love." What does Robin think about that?

He showed up simultaneously as you asked that.

I think Robin should narrate everything we're doing.

"**Love love indecently.**"

I'm sorry Robin we can't improve on "love indecently;" it came from Will.

Jennifer aside: I've never heard anything like that...amazing! "Love indecently not correctly." Like love who you're supposed to love!

I understand.

I don't!

So Luana are you impressed we have these people here?

She says "Yes. You asked for them."

Okay, so where the hell are our lottery numbers?

We won the lottery right here. They're like "You don't win the lottery; you are the *freaking* lottery."

Or what does Bill Paxton say in Aliens? "Game not over man."

......

Okay – let's just stop here for a moment to take a deep breath. Are we talking to the people that I just quoted? As noted, I forge ahead and just allow whatever question to pop into my mind to do so. If I had prepared in advance, or could have a historian on hand, that would be fantastic.

I'm not trying to prove that George Washington said "this" and Abraham Lincoln said "that." What I'm demonstrating is that with a person who has a curiosity to ask questions, working with a talented medium, one can gain access to just about anyone.

There are controversial comments in here – including ones by the Kennedys about what happened to their family. At some point later, I include another interview where Bobby asked me to reach out to one of his family members.

Even though I know Daryl Hannah, and am fond of her as a person, I have no clue if their relationship was more "brother and sister." In fact it's an odd thing to say – they were dating, I've even seen footage taken from a paparazzo of them kissing. So it would have been much easier for Jennifer to say "Oh yeah, he loved her." But he didn't. He said "They were more like brother and sister."

Now – that could mean that she saw an image of a brother and sister – and translated it as that. Could mean he was trying to impart that he was her brother in a previous lifetime. Again – this is all interpretation of imagery and then syntax. Jennifer does her best to be open about whatever she sees, and I try to unpack whatever it might mean on a spiritual level. I'm often wrong, I'm sure.

People on the flipside talk openly about everything including sexuality (as Amelia Earhart does in "Hacking the Afterlife"). I think it's important to report verbatim, expand the record if I have information from multiple sources that may be the case. But in general; **what's said on the flipside stays on the flipside, unless I happen to be in the room; then all bets are off.**

CHAPTER SEVEN:
"THAT MICROSOFT GUY AND CURING CTE"

Two fellows who changed history. (Photo: The Guardian.com)

PAUL ALLEN, JUNIOR SEAU, DAVE DUERSON, KURT COBAIN, ABE LINCOLN, GEORGE WASHINGTON

(Note: on the way to class, I was thinking of interviewing Paul Allen, the founder of Microsoft. I thought of who might be able to assist in bringing him to class; I knew that Paul knew Julian Lennon. So I invited John Lennon to class to help us contact Paul Allen as he knew his son. I invited Anthony Bourdain to class as I thought he might have met Allen, and I invited Steve Jobs to help us facilitate a conversation because I assumed they had already met both here and on the flipside.)

Rich: Hi. How are you? Welcome back to class.

Jennifer: Yes. I've been looking forward to our class today.

So I've invited some people to join us today.

The first person who popped into my head was John Lennon.

(Ding!) I invited him to help us speak with this person that was friends with his son Julian.

Okay. So you really asked for John Lennon to be here?

Yes.

I'm being the skeptic on this one.

This guy that we want to speak with knows John's son so I asked him for help.

Someone who loved John's son.

I'll give you a hint – it's a male.

I'm hearing someone singing "Some Guys Have All the Luck." Is Rod Stewart still on the planet?

Yes, he is – but the song works. This guy was lucky; had "all the luck."

Anthony Bourdain came forward.

(Ding!) He was the second person I asked to help us today, as he would know him. I kid you not!

Was this guy a piano player?

A musician, played guitar, but not sure if he played piano.

Is he friends with Steve Jobs?

Yes. (Ding!) And that was the third person I asked to show up to introduce this guy to our class! Wow, three in a row. You are amazing. I asked Anthony because I guessed this guy would know Anthony, asked John because I know this guy knows his son, and I asked Steve because they were on the same level.

I get it. But I don't know his name, he's that Microsoft guy.

Bingo. Hi first name is Paul.

Paul.. I know who you're talking about. He owned a football team, a basketball team?

He did; he owned both. (Ding, ding!) His last name is Allen. Paul Allen. What do you get when I say his name?

"P.A." Jennifer laughs.

Is he here in our class?

Yeah. Got a couple of guys to round him up. It's funny – I don't know anything about him... it took me awhile to get it.

In terms of the flipside, it took a blink of an eye. Jennifer: you named three people I invited to help us – they were all right on the frickin' money. It's pretty ridiculous that you could nail that in three. So Steve, is Paul ready to talk to us?

He's kind of doing this. (Makes face of a guy leaning back.)

He's a little dubious?

He's not very... he's an inwardly spoken person.

Shy?

"Not shy, he likes to understand the mechanics of how this works." So I feel like he's watching. Like you would a game, I guess.

Luana can you push his chair forward?

Luana is going to talk for him.

I'm going to ask him some questions, we'll get into it. Why not? So Mr. Allen; who was there to greet you when you crossed over?

I just got a big football player.

Really? That's interesting.

I don't know... let me just go with it.

White or black?

Black – African American, or... he might be Polynesian – I wouldn't know – give me some more information.. It's like Luana is dragging it out of him.

He's reluctant?

I'm asking for some help - I'm (also) asking him that I need an algorithm for our app (one that allows law enforcement agencies to request help from mediums). Hello, can you do that please?

So the first person to greet you on the flipside was a football player?

"Yes."

Someone who played for the Seattle Seahawks and died...?

I feel like he didn't play for him, but somehow Paul tried to help him – he wanted him to play for him, but perhaps he died before he could play for him.

Paul wanted to help this football player... but the player died before he could?

"Yes."

Did he want to help him with an illness?

"Yes."

Did he have a brain problem?

That's what it feels like (waves finger in the air towards her ear) Like something to do with concussions. I don't know what that means.

(I think I do). That sounds about right. Paul you created an institute for brain science to help heal brains. You gave a 100 million dollars to help brain science.

(Note: It was 300 million. Dave Duerson came to mind - player for the Chicago Bears who left behind a suicide note that there was "something wrong with his brain." It was studied and helped recognize CTE. However, Junior Seau did the same thing a year after Duerson shot himself and his brain was donated to science. There's an interview with him and his widow later in this chapter, talking about this particular interview.)

Really? This is so fascinating and shows that I don't know anything... this is why it's so great because it shows I don't know what I'm talking about when I answer the questions. This guy was the start of it, it feels like, he was the one that... gave him (Paul) the idea (for the brain institute.)

That inspired Paul?

Yes. Paul was heartbroken over it (CTE). Here Paul owns a sports team and he feels like he was hurting them (the players)... – he even tried to create helmets that were stronger.

People said you created this brain institute because of your mom's Alzheimer's?

"Correct."

Is your mom still on the planet Paul?

It feels like she's here. (Note: She died at 90 in 2012.)

And your dad?

I think his dad is up there. (He died in 1983) Hold on a second, he's showing me this football player.

Let's talk to him - he's fine now isn't he?

"Yes," he said that "He (this player) was responsible for helping getting it out there" (into the public eye). He says "He's saving so many people (with this research) like if it wasn't for him – he's showing me how the energy of being the first, he showing me a huge part of it was...

This football player? Okay, there was a Chicago Bear named Dave Duerson who shot himself and donated his brain to science

Jennifer taps her nose. (Her quick way of saying "Yes.") That's it! (Rubs her arms) I have the chills.

(Note: Duerson's suicide was the test case for Boston University showing that in nearly every one of the cases they've studied, these players had CTE. The movie "Concussion" with Will Smith was about it. We speak to Dave in a later session.)

"He's saying that it wasn't his fault," I don't know, he's just going back to the...

Let's talk about brain science for a second; Paul, your institute has been studying this phenomena, and it's kind of an extension of what Jennifer and I are doing with Luana here. (Exploring consciousness).

He understands (what you are saying), he got the download (what we're doing) really fast. He still doesn't understand it completely. I asked him "Did you know you were going to die? He said "Yeah." But I ask "Did you know then?" He says he had this sense of urgency to do so much, so fast because he knew he was going to die. He lied about it (in public) to protect people.

(Note: Paul Allen had cancer, then recovered, but ultimately, died from the same cancer some years later.)

I know you got this cancer earlier in life – it went away and then it came back.

He says "He beat it the first time, (but) he wasn't done yet with his work. And it's not that he's done now, but he was able to create the foundation and to keep it going when he was gone.

What would you like to say to your sister?

(Jennifer draws a heart). He just showed me a big heart.

Jennifer are you aware of who his sister is at all?

(Jennifer aside) No. I just got the color red. I don't know what that means.

(Note: I looked up Paul's life before this session, knew that he had a sister Jody. I looked up to see if she was a Republican, perhaps that was the red part, both she and Paul had donated to parties on both sides of the spectrum.)

Paul if I was to contact your sister and give you a specific message from you what would that be, beyond a shadow of doubt make her realize you're still in existence. I know that's a tall order but Luana can help you.

Tell her that "She hears his voice." And there's something with the number 5 and 2. could be 52 or could be May 2nd. (Junior Seau, died on May 2nd, his number was 55. Dave Duerson's number was 22.) She has something with her hearing.

Something with her hearing?

(He means) She doesn't believe in this.... she can't hear him.

Funny; we have the guy who could most help us the most with our research into consciousness existing after life standing in front of us.

(Jennifer aside) That's a lot of pressure – thank god I don't know or remember anything during these sessions!

So Paul, something you want to say...

(Jennifer aside) How sweet was that football player showing up to tell him to say "thank you?"

Paul did you know this player or were you just aware of him?

He says, "He knew him."

Was there another athlete you knew who suffered from CTE?

He says "Many. Many. Many."

I'll ask some of our standard questions; Paul what do you regret?

"Time." (Jennifer asks) What about time? "I regret not loving more." He says "He regrets not being taught, if there was a way to be taught, how to of love unconditionally – he tried to do it so many different ways, I feel like he says he hurt the ones he loved the most."

Did you fall in love with anybody while you were here? Did you have that relationship with somebody?

Jennifer nods. Jennifer closes one eye.

You don't have to answer if you don't want us to know.

He's laughing.

Let me ask about your boat instead.

There's something significant about the name.

Can you put the name in Jennifer's mind – you had two big ones, but let's use the one known for music.

I feel like it was a lollapalooza kind of boat. I saw a jelly fish, I don't know what it is... okay, he showed me an octopus.

That's the name of the boat.(Ding!)

(Jennifer aside) He showed me the octopus at first, I cannot believe I didn't say "octopus."

You did say it. I didn't say it.

I'm such a skeptic; if they show me the first thing, I have to act like I have to interpret it "something else with tentacles..."

Luana is helping him communicate; assume he's communicating like he's (still) in kindergarten.

They're all laughing about the kindergarten comment.

So Paul, look around the class, can you see all the musicians that are here? Who's the person you most want to talk to or play with?

Prince. Jimi Hendrix showed up before, all the guitar players showed up before, I wasn't sure if it was because of when you said he played guitar (instead of piano). They were here to greet him.

So Jimi what's your opinion of Paul, what have you guys talked about on the flipside so far?

That he had a connection to Jimi while he was here, but he didn't trust it either.

Paul did something that's related to Jimi – both were from Seattle.

He showed me a huge building. He showed me like this huge foundation in front of different artwork and stuff... He showed me the Cleveland Hall of Fame thing.

Correct; it's like that. (Ding!) It used to be called the Jimi Hendrix museum; he created the west cost version of the Rock and Roll Hall of fame.

He's showing me all (Jimi's) his guitars, his shirts, the tie-dyed stuff. I love that.

Correct; (ding!) I've been there (Jennifer has not). They also feature things from Kurt Cobain. Paul have you run into Kurt?

Yeah. He's says he's worried about Courtney. What I'm seeing is that (Kurt) is planning for a return – I'm asking could you change the outcomes from there? He's showing us here – how (this research into the flipside) we are changing their outcomes.

Okay. So when we examine this stuff, we change our future because we become more aware of it?

We affect our future now by the work we're doing here (in this class). Whatever's happening elsewhere affects what's going to happen in the future. Kurt Cobain said that he saved Courtney by leaving... and that it also helped his daughter.

Kurt, anything you want to tell us or your friends and family?

He said "He's happy to have Paul Allen there."

Who greeted you on the Flipside, Kurt?

Kurt says "He was greeted by his dog."

What kind of dog?

"A little dog."

(Note: It's a common thing to meet a beloved pet on the flipside. It could be a pet from someone's youth, or in some cases, even from a previous lifetime.)

Kurt's plaque in his hometown of Aberdeen.

Okay Paul, how do we get people in your brain science foundation to consider what Jennifer and I are doing, so we can help them speak to you with this ongoing conversation?

He says "It will not take much – you need to write them."

What would you like to tell them in terms of opening up their research?

"Stop making everything science based. Open up.. to be open to (alternative) reasons... Tell them to be open to the way he left and why things happen."

Who is they? You mean the way people leave, the way they die?

"Yes and pay attention to that."

But can we put them in the right direction for that?

He says "You can't, not right away."

I asked Steve Jobs to help us with reaching out to Paul - what would...

They have a lot of words to say to each other, they both have nothing but mutual like... or love for each other.

What would you like to say to Bill Gates, Paul?

He says "Don't worry about the recent update." (Jennifer aside) There's something that crashed their computers? I don't know..

That's funny.

I asked Paul, "You mean you want to tell Bill "You got this? He's fine kind of thing?" He said "No, tell Bill to retire; to have fun."

When you first met Bill in high school did you...

In their garage.

(Note: They first worked together in a garage in Albuquerque)

My question is when you met Bill Gates did you know you were going to work together – was there a recognition of spirit?

"Yes, absolutely." (Jennifer listens) I don't think they liked each other at first, (it's like) they felt everything they were supposed to do (in the future) - felt like it was competitive and once they broke that – it feels like it was over a girl – (Jennifer laughs) I'm not even sure... what that means.

Well people would ask ... what about when Bill Gates reportedly had you removed during your cancer diagnosis?

(Note: Bill Gates' reported reaction to Paul's cancer was to have him removed from the company. I ask it that way to see what his response might be.)

"He's still bringing that up. Yeah."

How do you feel about that now?

(Jennifer shrugs) It's like "I couldn't care less." (Jennifer listens. After a pause) "I had the most toys. I won."

Very funny. Well that's a good question - you left with 20 Billion dollars left behind – what's going to happen to that 20 billion or do you care?

"It will be disbursed."

Do you care what happens to it?

Jennifer shrugs. He says "As long as it goes to causes the he was a part of."

People get so caught up in money – it's all they can think about - when they say your name, they often say "You mean even with 20 billion he couldn't cure himself from cancer?"

He says "Steve as well." (She gestures as if pointing at Steve.)

(Note: We interviewed Steve Jobs a couple of times. (His graduation speech is reprinted in "Hacking the Afterlife.") A friend who worked for both him and Gates did a deep hypnosis session, where he stopped by to talk about what he meant by his last words "oh wow.")

People are distressed because the world view is that making billions is a goal in life – that life is to accumulate money and it can't help you when you need it most – is that the point?

"Hell no," he says… and "pun intended."

By the way Anthony, could you step forward for a second?

(Jennifer pauses) He's smoking, waving away the cigarette smoke. He's (gesturing) like "she should have another drink." (Jennifer takes a sip of wine.)

Anthony, your old pal, punk rocker Lydia Lunch mentioned you today, said something like "When people die you celebrate their life and who they were and how they changed you."

(Note: She said "I'm not stressed over his death at all. I don't look at it as a loss. I look at it as what he's given us. We all go. It's what you leave behind, it's what you've given people. Yes, the absence and the hole is big when you have such a big personality. You have to focus on and you have to remember exactly what they gave you, which was somebody who did what they wanted to do, who enjoyed life, who was vivacious, who was generous, who was loving and just humorous.")

Anthony says "You turn it into nostalgia." Jennifer aside: Like my dad said.

(Note: We asked Jennifer's father for some advice on how to help people with grief. He said "Turn it into nostalgia." I asked what that meant. Jennifer said "He's saying when someone dies, memories are only sad. Nostalgia contains both sad and happy memories. If you can turn grief into nostalgia, you can begin to heal.")

So Paul look around anyone you want to talk to?

Prince.

Talk to or play with?

He said he wants to play (with him).

What would you want to ask Prince?

"How he wore those high heels."

Prince told us that dancing in high heels killed him.

(Note: When asked about why he was addicted to opioids and how that killed him, he said "No, dancing killed me." He said he was addicted to jumping off pianos in high heels. That led to ankle injuries which led to hip injuries which led to the pain pills.)

What kind of guitar do you have over there, Paul?

He showed me a Ukulele.

I see. Because that's as far as you've gotten (in terms of mentally creating it)?

He says "It's got a higher vibration. There's no hierarchy (including guitars). It's softer (in tone)."

And easier to play. George Harrison has spoken with our group, he's a huge fan of ukuleles.

Paul says "They're playing together."

George with Rainbow; photo Olivia Harrison (All Rights Reserved)

If you had one song to play... what would it be?

Something... sunshine?

You mean "Here Comes the Sun" or "Good Day Sunshine?"

Good Day Sunshine. (Jennifer aside: I don't know it.) They're showing me them tap dancing over there.

I think you had a recording studio on your yacht, you put out an album with your buddies. Anything you want to tell your friends or Julian Lennon?

Jennifer nods. "Yeah, he does have a lot of love for him."

A specific sentence for him?

He says "He loved him more than he knows." He's showing me two different kinds of feathers. (Jennifer aside:) I remember the story of how his father sent him the white feather, but also there's a black feather that got introduced. He says "Tell him to look for the

darker feather.. tell him to look for the darker feather, it's all one, it's the same."

A white feather with black feather? What's the metaphor; look for balance?

"Yes."

Like yin yang – balance. Does he need balance in his life?

"Yes, but who doesn't?"

(Note: I sent Julian this message from Paul about looking for darker feathers. He said that indeed, he has started to notice them. His reply was; "Yin yang.")

Dennis Hopper just showed up. Were they friends?

Well Dennis and Luana were... did a couple of movies together. What does Dennis want to say?

He says "It's a long line to get to talk to you."

I'm sorry. It's Luana's fault.

"Tell Rich...." hold on. He says "Tell you, don't be fearful about giving his family information."

Okay. I don't really know them well; I knew your ex wife.

He showed me all the connections.

Don't be afraid of mentioning it in public and having someone else pass it along?

"Yes."

So Dennis, what are you doing over there? Creating any kind of artistic endeavor?

He says "He's creating sounds. That's why he's part of that group."

We had people creating their environments; where do you hang out, or what kind of sounds do you create?

He says "He's recreating the sounds from earth.... exploring sound barriers."

For whom? Your self or pals?

Jennifer laughs. It's like "For our podcast up here."

(Note: I think he's joking that he's creating a background music track for our class.)

What kinds of sounds?

He showed me the movie with ... what's his name, the movie with the bear?

The revenant with Leonardo Di Caprio. You mentioned it last time – The Revenant.

Something connected to you about that, I don't know what it is.

Do you mean with the director or Leo?

Maybe Leo with this environmental work. The afterlife research - it's green because you're not wasting energy.

My question would be "Is anyone in this class aware of what Jennifer is talking about?" Or should we just keep doing what we're doing and they'll eventually figure out where we are?

You just have to put it out there, they'll find us.

Back to you Paul. Are you talking to anybody else up there?

"His sister."

You want me to tell Jody that she can hear you. What else do you want me to tell her?

"To get her health checked." He's saying that she's afraid of doctors.

Why? Something going on?

"No, she's fine. She just needs to get it checked to prove that she is. She's worried about (health issues); she won't believe it until she has them checked."

But I can't tell your sister "Hey your brother says to stop worrying about it from the flipside."

He says "A little more delicate. Tell her not to worry about it – her biggest thing is to worry about it; tell her not to worry about it, and the biggest thing is to get it confirmed."

In terms of us working with your brain science institute... should I reach out to them?

"Yes." Hang on. (listens) I feel you have to say "Be open to different realities and possibilities because he said that to them before he passed."

Anything I could say to convince them?

He just keeps saying that sentence - that "He told them before he passed, to expand what they were doing." And "Open up your research to different possibilities, open yourself up to consciousness and how to deal with that."

(Note: I have no idea if Paul Allen told that to members of the brain institute. But if he did, and you're reading this sentence, he's talking to you.)

If I may ask; who was with you in the room when you died?

Feels like it was his sister.

Was she by herself?

"Yes." But if feels like she left for a brief moment and then he passed. She left... it felt like she left... (the room). She feels bad... going to the restroom or something...

And you were met by Dave Duerson or someone like Dave? Was that unusual to see Dave? Was he wearing a uniform?

"Yes." (Jennifer aside:) Maybe that's the 52... that gave me a chill. 5 just keeps popping up as well. (Dave was 50 years old, word #22. Junior Seau died on 5-2-12 and wore #55.)

How are you occupying your time now?

He just showed me holding tons of paperwork, (she's) shuffling; getting things in order.

Are you doing any playing of music?

"That too; at night."

What kind of stuff you play? Blues, rock and roll?

"Everything. But right now he's focusing on the ukulele."

I would guess it's because it's hard to construct a Stratocaster or an amp – like what Prince can do – a ukulele is easier, has only four strings, there are only about ten chords...

I'm asking him "Is it a better frequency?" And he's like "No." It's like you said; "It's easier to construct."

Maybe one day we can tap into music on the flipside. That would be a great way to prove the flipside exists.

Does Paul know the guy who did the Titanic film?

Jim Cameron? Could be. Paul made a few films; most were money losers.

He says "It's just money."

I heard the other night, Questlove, the drummer for the Tonight show, was bereft about Paul's passing. He wrote that he's going to miss your encyclopedic mind of music – and Questlove his his own encyclopedic memory.

He says "He knows everything by its time period."

Well, take a look around; we have all these musical people in our group.

He says "He loves Aretha... and Whitney."

Thank you Paul. Catch you on the flipside class!

****

After this session, I saw the widow of Junior Seau on ESPN and contacted her through social media to tell her that her husband had showed up in our interview with Paul Allen.

She said she'd like to come up and meet with Jennifer and me and see if her husband might come through – and I suggested an experiment.

I didn't tell Jennifer that Gina was coming – it took about a month or two to make the appointment – but I only introduced Gina and Jennifer the day we filmed this interview. Gina had no idea what to expect, and Jennifer had no idea who she was.

The transcript was edited to leave out private personal information, but for the most part, you'll be able to get the idea of what occurred.

Junior Seau - Wikimedia

PART TWO – JUNIOR SEAU

Gina's comments are in normal font, my comments *are in italics,* and Jennifer's are **in bold.**

After I begin filming:

Jennifer: I literally got a whole line of people and a rope on both sides. (To Gina) How my process works is when I go into it, I look at the ground – and halfway thru a session, I was asked by someone "are they down there?" It's just how I process... you'll see me cock my head a little bit, they always come in on this side for me, it's different for everyone else – I get pictures, images, they may say names... they'll give names that might be associated to people here. I'm not trying to say, if I don't get something; I'm not going to get

every interpretation correct – you may have questions, ask them. I do work with names, that helps me with my connection; you may have brought a picture, I'm seeing it's on your cell phone.

(Gina nods)

They showed me like an old school photo, and you have something that is related to this person – on object. Um. Do you have four things in your purse?

Gina: Yes, including what's on the phone. (There are) Three things in (my purse), and then the 4th is on my phone.

Jennifer: They don't want me to use any of the items right now – (Aside, to herself) I wonder why are they testing me right now? Because I work on (criminal) cases, I get asked to go places, (to be close to where the crime occurred) but I won't – it's too much of distraction by being there. The truth is, if i go to Aspen it's to go skiing and not to find somebody – I know that sounds awful.

Gina: No, I get it.

Jennifer: I'm getting something... I'm getting a father. Is your father on the other side?

Gina: No.

(Jennifer nods, then continues) They were talking to you on the road up here, told you to put your phone down at one point, you were dealing with maps, they want you to know they were with you (on the trip here). I don't know your last name, and I didn't even know how to pronounce your first name!

(Gina nods as Jennifer is talking to her, wipes away a tear.) Gina: It's Gina.

Okay, there's someone you really love over there –... it's beautiful. Oh boy. Okay. I'm going to start asking questions – might not be the person ... but I feel like someone had a crash, could be an internal crash, that could be suicide possibly.

Rich: I'm going to let Jennifer know if something she says is correct; that is correct.

Gina nods.

Jennifer: I feel a lot coming through for her (Gina) – getting into your space. Um. Oh my god, this person has so much to say. He's on a knee actually.

Rich: Can you describe how he looks?

I'm seeing him as a bigger guy, but then he's showing me him as a little guy – like mini-me. Oh, he's like a bull in a china shop - yet to him, he's like this perfect (polite) British guy on one knee. I don't want to know his name actually, only because it might hinder what comes through... (Jennifer aside) I know that sounds like an easy cop out – (laughs) I'll have to use that (excuse) later. (Jennifer listens.) For him to be this magnetic of a personality... it's something else. He's showing me something on a wall, like art – I'm asking him, "Is she a piece of art and you're a piece of work?" (To Gina) Sorry – it was just funny... (Jennifer listens) He says you *are* a piece of art and he *is* a piece of work.

Gina: He does have a good sense of humor.

Jennifer: Does he? This is super fun for me. He tells me he cares about clothing or something like that – he knows my leather jacket, he liked it – (this morning) I went to put on my comfy thing and he's like "Don't wear that, wear the leather." (At the time) I didn't know that was him saying that. (Listens) Okay (he says) he was in the car with you... and last night you talked to him as well.

Gina: Yes.

There was a celebration a couple of days before... (Jennifer listens) Say again? (To Gina) He says "He can't stop staring at you – he keeps looking at you while I'm asking him questions."

Rich: Where were you a couple of days ago Gina?

Gina: I can't remember where I was yesterday.

Rich: I mean last week when we couldn't meet because your were on a trip? (To Jennifer) Is that the reason he's referring to?

He says "yeah."

Gina: I was with our son last week for his graduation.

Jennifer: There is something more – he is showing me Tiffany - ... like (a gift in) the blue box. He's also expressing how sorry he is; he's saying "He's so sorry and he wishes he could take it back." (Jennifer listens) He's swore didn't he?

Gina nods.

He's "I f*cked it up." (Jennifer aside:) He's been trying to swear for awhile... and I'm saying "No swearing!"

Gina: He did swear.

Jennifer: Okay, he says... "He fuuucked it up. I was a shit head, I shouldn't have done the shit I did – I didn't know..." (Jennifer aside:) This is interesting how he's trying to explain, the vast... (Listens, pauses) Luana (our class moderator) come help please... How would you say it? (Listens) He said "He didn't understand the vastness" – he's showing me with a picture, "the vastness of love he had for you and he knows you guys argued but you made up, you "*got*" him." He's showing me a "forget-me-not (indicates a string on a finger) or a promise – that's the tiffany thing, it was the bow.

Rich: Is that his way of saying forget-me-not?

Jennifer: Yes... he's saying "He would be buying you jewelry because he fucked up" kind of thing... he was laughing at that, like "Yeah, that was everything."

Rich: Can we ask to use his first name?

Jennifer: Yeah.

Rich: I don't think Jennifer will know who this is, based on your first name. I imagine you were born by another name?

He showed me something, was trying to make a sound... Is there a T?

Gina: (nods) mm-hmm.

He's showing me T... Tom?

Gina: Not Tom; it begins with T. It's his given name, he never went by it. I'll just say it; "Taina." He hated it.

Oh my friend shares that name. Hers is Tiana. I would never have gotten that.

Gina: He felt it was a girl's name – In his culture it's pronounced Taiyana... his teachers would say "Would she please stay up."

Rich: But you went by another name on the planet.

Gina: All of his life.

His original name is why he showed me the T. Then he showed me "Mr. T." (Listens) Oh, he really hated that name.. Mr. T was this big to him (makes a tiny gesture) – like he was this big. Is there an E in his name?

Gina: In his last name.

You're dealing with a family member who got sick..?

Gina: No. Not in my family.

In his family? He showed me it was something to do with Robin Williams. Was there something wrong with his brain?

Gina: Yes.

I asked him why he left the planet and he showed me Robin Williams. Which is so sad, I am so sorry.

Rich: But it's important to say he's on the right track; it has to do with that - the brain. Let's ask Junior. Oh, damn, I didn't mean to say his name.

Gina: That's why she kept saying she was seeing him as a small guy and he's a big guy. (The "Junior" version of him).

Jennifer: That's what he was showing me – I've given thousands of readings and I learn something new every time. Now, when I see a mini me – I'll know they're referring to the name "Junior." (Jennifer listens) He says "He's never left his family. He's never left her. He would have never done f*cking shit before he left. He says he caused you so much heartache, so many sleepless nights. He fucked up, he couldn't figure out what was going on with his own mind." He says "I couldn't get happy and it wasn't your fault. It wasn't your fault." He says "I know you don't believe me..." –

That's why he was on a knee begging for forgiveness; I didn't understand it (at first). My mind went to a proposal...

Gina: We were married. How does he feel about the kids?

Jennifer: You have three?

(Gina nods)

He told me "three." (To Junior, teasing) "What? You want credit for that?" He said he does. He's a dick! What a total dick; he's like "Me, me, me!" I said "Three," and he said "That came from me!" When I said (to him) "You're so frustrating," he showed me Gina as if to say "Imagine how frustrated she was (with me)!" Okay, let's calm down everyone. We are in a classroom setting, thank you Luana.

Rich: That's our class moderator. Luana. Who occasionally steps in to get everyone to sit down.

Jennifer: (To Junior) Do you want to say something? (Listens) He says "He was not in his right mind... He didn't have oxygen going to the brain; he was not in his right mind... or his heart... And I'm asking him about the kids, that's why Luana told him to sit down. (Jennifer pauses, listens. To Gina:) One of them is graduating?

Gina: Yes.

Jennifer: He says "he's so smart... (your son) – he's so sorry. (Junior) " He says one is jumping from middle school to high school?

Gina: From high school to college.

He's like "I almost made it to the finish line." (Jennifer pauses) He says, "He went and saw people privately... like doctors for (what ailed) his mind..." He says "Whatever he was taking made it worse."

Gina: He was on Ambien – lots of Ambien.

Jennifer: I took it once and saw so much shit it made me paralyzed. I couldn't breathe - I can only imagine taking that when you have that problem.

Gina: I don't think people understood.

Jennifer: He says "People covered it up."

Rich: Junior show Jennifer how you showed up in our research, if you don't mind.

Jennifer listens, sees something, shouts: "Ohh! Football!?!? He showed me the guy – the Microsoft guy! Their research they were doing!

Rich: That's correct.

Jennifer: For concussions! That's what he called all of this – I'm looking everywhere (to remember where she met him) and he's saying "Just relax." That's how he showed up. But I don't remember anything we say in these sessions...

Rich: You don't remember, but I knew who he was describing, it was when we asked the Microsoft guy who was there to greet him when he crossed over.

Jennifer: IT WAS HIM!? OH MY GOD! OH MY GOD!

Rich: Exactly. And this is what we are here for.

Jennifer: He greeted that Microsoft guy!

Rich: Let me ask Junior; what were you doing greeting Paul Allen. Did you know him?

Jennifer: He says "He did." He's showing me it wasn't like a meeting, but they were in the same room (at some point).

Rich: So you met him briefly but were there when he crossed over to thank him for that research his brain institute is doing? Obviously something you care deeply about.

Jennifer: "Yes."

Rich: So give us some advice on how can we help people with this problem?

(Jennifer laughs, aside) I'm sorry. He's so funny; I'm apologizing to him because I was telling him that he's so funny and that I was mad that he left the planet... but I didn't get it! But now I know –

(turns to Gina) He says "He wants you to understand without question; whatever happened; it wasn't him." He says "It felt like he couldn't catch up to whatever was happening and that's what was happening." He says "He never meant to hurt you and at the time he didn't understand even what he was doing..." (Listens) Okay... and then what?.. - He says, "It was like the last six weeks that (he) completely combusted, correct?"

Gina: Yes.

Jennifer: He says "Something triggered it; he didn't know what was going on..." (Jennifer aside:) I'm not calling him out for whatever he did, but I do feel that... He says "There's no words that will make up for it."

Rich: But Junior that's why we are here. There are words.

Jennifer: He says "He misses your perfume. He misses your pillow." You guys slept in different rooms sometimes?

Gina: Yeah, the kids, whatever.

Jennifer: I don't know if it's because he snored, or whatever... (Listens) He says "He didn't snore!"

Rich: Junior, show Jennifer what you did for a living.

Jennifer: It feels like it was philanthropy work; he raised money.

Gina: He did have a big foundation.

Jennifer: He's showing me the suits he wore; he remembers the feelings associated with the good works that he did. (To Gina) Do you have a hat of his?

Gina: Yes. (Pulls it from her purse) Here it is.

Jennifer: He says he was "Very passionate about children inner city kids..." Of course I should have mentioned football, because I knew that from how we met – the concussion thing - I knew it was football. But in terms of his vision of his being on the planet; it was to help kids.

Gina: It was the passionate thing that he most loved, helping those kids.

He showed me Michael Jordan – did they have things in common?

(Note: Jennifer later said she realized this referred to Michael's addiction to gambling. That was "something they had in common.")

Gina: I did see a medium after he passed, she came to my house, she didn't know anything about anything. She said "I got lost on the way here, and this man was telling me which way to turn how to get to your house and (said) he was your husband." And I started crying and she talked about him being sad and sorry and that he was "stuck."

Jennifer: No no no... they don't get stuck.

Rich: Junior explain that to Gina please.

Jennifer: He said I'm stuck talking through Jennifer – I don't know what's worse than talking through her! (Jennifer laughs, listens:) I'm sorry; he talks very fast here, he's projecting his thoughts all at once, and he wants me to figure it out.

Gina: I'm glad he's here; this is making my day.

Okay, now we have both Robin Williams, your husband Junior and... was it... Paul Allen?

Rich: Yes.

Jennifer: They're all there now, and they want to do something about this CTE – and what it is here – to really, really get it (that information) out there.

Gina: There was a friend of Junior's who did that a year earlier than him.

Jennifer: And left a note.

Rich: That's correct.

Jennifer: There are six of them (with him.)

Gina: Mike Webster.

Jennifer: Somebody who was a quarterback... I can't get the name. Was he with the Steelers?

(Note: We find out later who the quarterback is that he's trying to draw her attention to. A quarterback who has cured his CTE.)

Rich: Can we talk about Dave Duerson, the guy who left the note? Dave was the first person who said he's having trouble with his brain, he left it to science and they discovered that CTE was endemic in the league. What would you guys like to say?

Jennifer: He says "It's a different kind of cancer; it spreads." They're showing me the brain, and how it starts... like if you cracked an egg (gestures to the top of her head) and it starts leaking through."

Rich: Is it related to dementia in terms of plaque?

He says "No; it's about fluid and pressure."

Rich: How can we help people to effect change? To stop playing football altogether?

"There's too much money in it," he says. He says "They need more padding; more rules."

Rich: What do you want us to tell the league?

He's teasing me. "Can I have a different translator?" (Jennifer aside:) I'm afraid of getting this wrong. This is not to be taken lightly, I need some time to translate what he's saying. (Pauses, listens) He's showing me in the past, when kids were playing flag football; he's saying almost like trying to keep it like that, when they get the flag in flag football. Like that.

Rich: Okay. A Pop Warner kind of thing?

Jennifer: They need more awareness – they're showing me the neck, something to do with the upper spine, this part (taps the top of her neck) felt detached, they're saying they need protection here somehow and to still (be able to) move.

Rich: Like the neck armor that nights used to wear?

He showed me like Kobe getting a shot every time he got injured, they don't have any shots they can give for the brain. The game (of football) is still fun, they still love the game – but the game in and of itself, it's like an addiction, like gambling.

Gina: Some do end up with CTE and some don't.

(Jennifer listens:) You want me to tell her that? (To Gina) He says "I love your eyes." He keeps saying "I love your eyes." He says he has known you since you were little, but he knew that you could (handle) it. He says someone came into your life in November – a (new) relationship? He says he sent him to you.

Gina: Does he like him?

Jennifer (laughs): He says, "He's not a strong as good looking and can't dance as good as Junior does... and he's not as tall... but he likes him." He's funny – he's saying to me "You think I'm not going to send her someone better looking than me?" He kissed his fingers and tapped his heart... something with the heart – (Listens) It's that "He knows he'll always be in your heart, but I won't be in the bad part of it." He wants you to know... He led two separate lives, the way he used to think and how it changed how he could think – he knows that the (Paul Allen Brain) institute is going to make a difference..

Gina: It's the biggest legacy he's left behind... to die from this illness has awakened our country about it.

Jennifer: Is this what the movie "Concussion" was about?

Rich: Yes. That's the exact thing.

Jennifer: And it was before that guy...

Gina: Mike Webster died before Junior; it was about that doctor who discovered it.

Jennifer: They're all so grateful for that doctor – I didn't see the movie myself.

Gina: That's why Junior didn't like the NFL Commissioner.

Jennifer: He just showed me "It's all about money..."

Rich: That doctor is still alive isn't he?

Gina: Dr. Omalu? Yes.

Rich: Does Junior want us to reach out to him?

Jennifer: "Yes."

Rich: What do you want me to say to him besides thank you? Something that will help him identify that it was really you talking to us.

He's showing me a map of the brain – that he had a different point in his brain, showed me his brain – then showed me it being so big it went out of the room – he's so funny, but he showed me this point in his brain. If I can translate – a different part of his brain - it was a different part of the brain, but that it helped fill in the map of the illness. The illness that someone else had – his brain helped the doctor create a larger map - it's a unique map.

By saying that to him, he'll understand this in Junior talking to him?

Yes, and he's talking to him in his sleep, but the map is complete because of Junior's brain.

What's his uniform's number?

Jennifer: 55.

Rich: I think it's hilarious that you showed up in a restaurant in Manhattan Beach a few months ago and now we're here talking to your wife – Junior, who greeted you when you crossed over?

He says "His puppy dog – he had a dog he loved when he was growing up..." it feels like.

Who was the first person you encountered?

His grandma.

Was that a surprise?

"No, because he asked her to be there before (he left)." I don't think he knew her that well.

Who are you hanging out with now?

They're playing football but there are no injuries.. It's kind of like golf - he's showing me.. he's showing me a famous quarterback from the Steelers – I can't think of his name.

Rich: Okay, my question is how do you create the football game?

He showed me this 3-D Madden (football) game – (Jennifer to Junior) Really? He says "Like Madden football, his games – the games they play. But that.. "on crack" over there (hyper reality) – they take all the different football fields...

Are they the fields that you've played on? Or do you create them?

"Each person has the memory of their home field."

Is it a full team, 2 squads?

"No, it's like quarterback against quarterback; seeing how far you can throw."

But are you playing with full squads?

"No. Just a few players. There's the energy of the football player..." He's saying "We keep in our energy because we're still trying to help people understand what happened to make sure it doesn't happen in the future."

Stay on the field for a second – what position do you play in this reality?

"In the front... defensive player."

Are you knocking people down but they don't get hurt?

"It's different..." (Listens) Wow. This is amazing .. I saw the grid, of how a football player creates the field. For example, pretend we're watching plays on a screen in 3D; but they don't get hurt when you go through them.

But there are points... not for the impact of how strong you are, you get points by showing your focus to be able to go through them entirely. If they just nick the other player, they don't get points, it's like sacred geometry... (To Junior) Say again?

He says "It's a quantum field." He's teasing me, saying "I thought you had it! You're not saying it (correctly.)" It's a quantum field. And your quantum players... (Jennifer to Junior) Why did you show me that? Interesting... so athletes are athletes over there, I saw him as a Roman warrior with a disc, throwing a disc (in a Roman uniform).

We get to choose who we are (in the game) we've had all our lifetimes as athletes, and that dictates how we played the game. For example, I'm seeing Arthur Ashe playing football...

What position was he playing?

Receiver; he's catching the ball.

How often do you play? A lot, a little, sometimes?

He says "There's no time (over here)." He showed me like race car driving; he just showed me you can look on a grid, and say "I want to do this right now, (and choose that game) and all the lights (appear) and you know those the beepers go off – a calling card to get everyone together and whoever's getting in, to the game, is in the game.

(Rich: to Jennifer) We've talked about this before –

Jennifer: We have?

Rich: Yeah, it's like a signal goes out and all the players show up instantaneously to play the game.

Gina: Is he going to come back in another life (soon)?

Jennifer: He's waiting for you. His job right now is to be your guardian angel. He showed me a crooked halo in a big toga outfit – like funny; a silly crooked halo. He says he brought you that person (you're seeing) and knows he's a good guy.

Gina: The one I'm seeing now?

"Yes."

Gina: I wondered if he approved of him.

Jennifer: He says "He has an amazing heart and he's super bright, and he won't give you any of the BS you had with me – you get a break; well deserved and forever. (Jennifer aside:) You're going away in August?

Next month to Paris.

You have a reservation at the Eiffel tower?

Yes.

You're going to have fun. You already told him what kind of ring you wanted. Did you say no?

I tried one on.. a very big one.

Yes, he showed me a very big one. He says "it looked nice on you." He said "She deserves it."

Rich: Junior you have any questions for us?

Jennifer: That's interesting, he's like "You're already here! Can you guys come and play football? That would be so cool!"

He says "To tell his story, contact the doctor – it's important..." (turns to Gina). He says "The most important thing was talking to you and telling you how much he loved you and that he just... that for the time he had here, you were not only the love of his life; you just "got" him – even if you didn't like it, you still got him – he loves you and your kids so much.

He will never let anything bad happen to you ... and I'm sorry. I'm a much better player over here than I was here." It's what he was trying to say from the get-go, I'm sorry I didn't get it.

Gina: You said there was a long line of people?

Jennifer: They're all his players.

Gina: I see him in dreams, all the time on a football field – and I saw this after he died. His brother Tony.

Did Tony get shot?

Yes, he was shot earlier, before he died.

Junior says "His brother shouldn't have died." He said "Out of all the people his brother was so good – he didn't act that way; he didn't want anyone to hurt either." What happened to him? Something with his head?

Gina: I think he died of an overdose – I don't know if he OD'd or killed himself.

Jennifer Shaffer with Gina Seau

Jennifer: They showed me him in a car with fumes, so that's probably a suicide. He had a huge breakup and financial issues as well – He has an aunt over there, right?

Yes.

And your mom is over there?

She was one of 11.

Rich: The odd thing is how we came to be here. I saw Gina talking on ESPN about CTE, and I said "Wait a minute, that's the wife of the guy who showed up during our session with Paul Allen." What was your reaction to seeing that note from me?

I read it and I had chills.

Rich: So Junior, did you give her those chills?

"Yes." He's showing me holding her from behind. He says "Your other guy was in the room (at the time.)"

Gina: I think he was. When we first started talking about him – there was a car crash, remember you said that he drove off a cliff? Junior had attempted suicide before, drove off a cliff, so there was a big crash that he survived.

He showed me a car going over a cliff – I felt it was an internal crash.

The crash occurred, and I knew he needed help.

Like a year before.

Yes. We got a call from the hospital. His head went thru the windshield.

He lived on the beach too, right?

Yes, when I walked in here I thought of that beach. (Jennifer's office overlooks the Pacific).

Rich: When we do this kind of interview, I ask people why they chose their lifetime.

Jennifer: He says because of her (Gina).

Gina: I wondered about that idea you've said about people choosing their lifetimes. Why would he choose to be a poor Samoan living in the street?

Rich: Because those circumstances turned him into the greatest defensive player of all time.

Jennifer: What's Junior's last name?

Gina: Seau – when you walked in with your blue blouse – it's Charger blue. Last night I told him I was going to wear red, and here you are wearing Charger blue.

Jennifer: It was my dad's favorite team.

So Junior you chose this lifetime to go through these obstacles, is that correct?

He says "It's more complicated than that." He showed me the grid of choosing this, or that...and how it effects...oh! I love what he's showing me; it makes sense. That we're not just choosing this life, one solitary experience because whatever we do in a lifetime effects all the other lifetimes.

It's is like a 3 dimensional game and everything drops into all the other lives, each life affects the others – being a poor Samoan in this life might help the daughter of that person who ends up being the person who gets the coach who gets him to do this or that – each one is like a game.

He's showing me that.. every life effects every single life – like it's math, how a pi or pi squared, the nth, nth degree affects everything else.

So everything is math?

"It's all math."

Rich: What's your favorite food, Gina?

Gina: Everything.

Jennifer: He's telling me "pineapple."

Gina: I used to call him "my big coconut."

Rich: What do you miss about being here, Junior?

Jennifer: He's showing me playing football with his kids. He also misses your hair, the smell of your hair.

Gina: That's so funny – I was going to have it straightened yesterday, but I didn't. So I said "Hey Junior I'm coming here to wear it the way you liked it..."

Rich: (Laughs) Gee, I wonder why....

Gina: Here's a picture of him.

(Gina opens up her cell phone to show an old photograph of the two of them.)

Jennifer: That's the picture I saw when I said you guys met when you were really young.

Gina: Oh my god.

Jennifer: He keeps talking... he's saying "You'll never find anybody as good looking as me."

Gina laughs.

That session ended with Gina showing Jennifer the photograph on her cell phone that she had brought with her, and Jennifer said it was the same photograph she saw in her mind's eye.

****

PART THREE

After the Gina session, a few weeks later, Jennifer called me on a day we normally don't meet. A slot had opened up and she got the "message" we should film an interview. *My question are in italics,* **Jennifer's answers are in bold.**

Rich: Hi class...

Jennifer: It's full moon and a lunar eclipse.

So, why are we doing this now? Is there somebody that wants to talk to us?

(Note: Normally we meet on Thursdays. Jennifer reached out on a Tuesday and suggested a late afternoon interview.)

"Yes."

Let's ask Luana who's here; she has the backstage passes - whoever she wants us to see. If you could put it in Jennifer's mind if it's someone she invited or someone I invited.

It's someone you invited a couple of weeks ago – someone we didn't "get to." I got shown the guy from Microsoft; Paul Allen.

Paul, what do you want to say?

He showed me being behind you when you're editing (our footage.)

I took the Junior footage – and then cut in our clip of you...

He said "There needs to be another clip, it hasn't been done yet."

Okay.

Junior and Gina. Personal photo.

They showed me Paul first because I wouldn't recognize Junior – "mini me." There's another clip to this; a third clip. It has to do with a third football player.

(Note: During our session with Gina Seau, when asked to reveal his first name, he kept using "miniatures" of people to denote "Junior." Jennifer uses her hand to indicate a "tiny" person.)

Because we didn't talk to the third person?

I got shown Tom Brady – I know he's here...

(Note: In all three sessions, Jennifer kept being shown a Quarterback – she could not remember his name, so this is now happening again, which we figure out later one who that is, and why they want to mention him. We'll soon find out.)

Let's break that down. Who wants to talk here?

Junior. Paul just brought him in.

First I want to ask Paul – are you happy with the latest edited version of these interviews?

He says "Fabulous."

I took out the references you asked me to.

He says "Thanks." (Jennifer aside:) I asked if you should leave it in – he's not saying one way or the other.

I'll leave it in the book version?

But in words that disguise it. Who's taken over Apple?

Whatever his name is.

(Note: The reference is to Tim Cook at Apple, someone that Jennifer obviously doesn't know about, but Paul Allen does, and the reference that is being cloaked is a reference about Cook's private life.)

He showed me that when we were talking about that...

I don't understand.

I don't either.

(Note: But Paul does. I had to look that up – searched for details about Tim Cook's private life and Paul's reference to it.)

Okay, Paul anything else you want to tell us before Junior steps in? Do you still want me to reach out to your sister, Jody?

Does his sister have cancer or has a scare of it?

Paul told us she has an ongoing fear of doctors and cancer, his suggestion in our interview last November was tell her to go in and get it checked to prove she doesn't have it. Is that correct?

"Yes, absolutely. Now; it has to be done."

How do I get that to her?

"Through this interview."

So Junior, do you want us to talk about Dave Duerson?

"Yes."

Can you bring him in?

"He's there. He has his story too."

Let me clarify something that wasn't clear – Paul when you passed away, Junior and Dave were there to greet you? Or were there other players with CTE? Or just those two?

They're showing me they were the "front line." They showed me them in their football outfits - like "No one can get past us..." – pretty funny.

So Jennifer saw an African American player, a Polynesian which I assume was Junior – the African American was Dave?

"It was." (Jennifer aside:) I don't know these people, but he (is showing me) that he has a distinct mark on his forehead. (Perhaps from an old forehead injury.)

Dave's number was 22, and Junior's was 55. During the interview you kept saying you were getting a 5 and a 2.

You broke that down.

So can we ask you some questions Dave?

That's why he's here. (reacts) As he sat down he broke the chair. He said "He's a big guy, but not as big as the fridge."

What? Do you know what that means?

(Jennifer aside) I don't know, but was "The Fridge" a player from Pittsburgh?

No, he's a Chicago Bear. Dave's teammate.

The Fridge – YouTube clip

Well, he showed me that he took a chair, sat in it and broke the chair and I said "What, you're so big you can't fit in a chair?" and he said "I'm not as big as The Fridge."

Either Jennifer is really up on her Chicago Bear history – or he made a joke only Bear fans would get. The Fridge is still alive.

He showed me "There's a big difference between us. The Fridge had huge arms."

That's accurate. Dave – who was there to greet you on the other side?

Aw, he's so sweet, hold on. It was somebody like his mother – someone who took care of him, felt like a grandmother or an aunt. I think he had a lot of those. Felt like his grandmother and then... his dog.

What kind of dog did you have?

Almost feels like a German Shephard.

A mix? big? or medium sized?

He said "It's a small dog compared to me," and I said "That's not helping." He said he had the dog for 22 years. It felt like the dog died of cancer the year before.

The year before he passed? Let's talk about your brain issues.

He showed me the brain tissues – he showed me it felt like they were being cut; I asked if it was the steroids, he said "No, they took steroids back in the 80's." He said that it (his thoughts) wouldn't connect – it almost hurt, it felt like...

Disjointed?

"And then some." The way he presents it is waking up and not being able to get up, like having a cap – you want to look at the sky but you can't look past the wall, something is blocking everything so it felt like being paralyzed – and that's why they started freaking out about it.

No one knew?

He kept it quiet. For the last three months of his life... he tried to keep it quiet – but he tried.. whoever he was with knew, his family knew, he would make jokes... he took (sleeping pills) to go to sleep... whatever he took made him feel more paralyzed, discombobulated..

At what point did you realize did you needed to take your life but leave a note advising people study your brain?

When he knew that everybody else would be okay.

Financially? Or emotionally?

All of it. It was a big mess after he left – he's showing me tons of paper, he said "I was in too much pain. It was like "Fuck it. Too much pain."

What did you write on your note? Or what did you want your note to clarify?

He said "To please, please help the future players." Something along those lines.

You mean it's content more than precisely - whatever the note said, this is what what you want to message to convey?

Correct. And he said "I just can't (couldn't) take it anymore." He said "This was not me."

Who were you surprised to see on the other side?

I don't know who this guy is (I'm seeing). Best way I can explain this guy is he looks like Neil Diamond... looks like he was a quarterback.

Dave is the guy she's talking about on the flipside? Or someone here suffering from it?

Named Joe! Hold on. Joe Joe Joe.. not Montana...

(Note: This is the third time Jennifer has brought up this "Joe the quarterback" – after the session I found that QUARTERBACK JOE NAMATH has done extensive research into CTE who has using hyperbaric oxygen treatment to cure his own CTE. http://www.espn.com/espn/feature/story/_/id/13186859/joe-namath-believes-found-cure-brain-damage-caused-football).

Okay, I'll look that up. So Dave, what do you want to say to your fans?

Joe Namath from his YouTube page

He says "He did the right thing to help future players, that was my path, and don't be upset about what I did – even though I hurt some people along the way." He told me it was paralyzing.

Are you hanging out with Bears on the Flipside?

"All of them. They have the best football teams over there."

Do they all have the same positions?

They learn new positions. "Because it's not fair to be me and then there's The Fridge. The Fridge has it too (CTE) – actually he gave it to a lot of people." (Jennifer laughs) Sorry.

I get the reference because Fridge would often knock people into kingdom come. What's your advice on how to fix CTE, Dave?

"Armor." He keeps saying "armor." And by making it a virtual game.

How do we do that?

I can't explain it – they showed me the film "Tron." You still would have to have people (playing the game.)

Are you saying that would they're going to do in the future Dave? Virtual football? You can play but never get hurt?

"Yeah. They will."

How far in...

"2050." We won't be here.

(Note: She answered the question before I could ask "when will they have virtual football?)

Well, we will be around in some form.

And I'll be saying "I got that right too!" (laughs). Does he have a son? "Spread the wealth," he said.

I don't know – I'll look it up. What do you want to tell him?

He's really funny. He's showing me he was really fun before this happened. Literally... Their deaths were really close together, right? Junior and Dave?

A year apart.

I don't think they spoke about it.

Dave's death helped people understand why Junior shot himself in the chest instead of the brain. By the way Junior, how's your wife Gina doing?

"It calmed her heart (to talk to him), he's showing me she's more at peace. Sometimes it gets in her head, but that is what happens..."

So what did we miss in your interview Junior?

"Dave. It was Dave." Also, he showed me this surfer... Jimmy Miller. He's showing me this surfer who died, who had brain trauma as well – he was someone else who was there to greet him on the other side. He's telling me that he had brain trauma as well.

(Note: Surf legend Jimmy Miller died in 2004 from a suicide. http://www.surfscience.com/topics/surfing-lifestyle/life-as-a-surfer/surfing-can-change-lives-the-jimmy-miller-foundation/)

So Dave, let me ask you some of the questions we ask everyone; what do you miss about being on the planet?

(Quietly) Smells. He misses smells. Like women's perfume.

Dave it was reported that your family was not happy with the film "Concussion."

"Absolutely."

Were you not happy with it?

"It was Will Smith (starring) – I was happy. But they left a lot out, a lot of turmoil because they were afraid of legal stuff so they left it out."

Anything you want to say to people who watched that film?

"Take the overall knowledge from it but know that it was superficial." (Jennifer aside) I haven't seen it, so I don't know.

I'm online, looking this up and it says that you have a son.

What's what I was getting too – look (Jennifer holds up her notepad with the word "son" circled repeatedly.

What do you want to say to him?

"Live healthy. Drink lots of water. Know that I'm always your first guardian." And he says "Please know that I knew that you'd have a better life without me even when you knew I was there."

What is your son doing?

He showed me Kevin Hart.

Like your son has carried on your sense of humor?

"Yes. He's very smart. He has plan – he works with an investment group but feels like he's also in entertainment." Felt like a commentator.

And what does he run, Dave?

Some kind of a foundation...

It says online that he runs "The Concussion Foundation." What do you want to say to him?

He says "He's proud of him. (Then a private issue that I passed along to his son.)

Is your son aware of that?

"No, he's not aware of it. He allows it by not being in(volved) it."

You want us to make him aware of it?

"Yes."

How? Reach out to him on social media?

"Yes."

I'll try. So Paul Allen, how can we help Dave? Can you help with his philanthropy thing? Is your brain institute working on mapping or are they working on CTE? Or are they leaving that research to Boston University?

"They're leaving it to B.U."

What else can we say on your behalf for your friends?

"Tell them to buckle up, wear a condom, any protection you can – people die every day in car crashes, and it's something for his industry (football).. and so, ask for help; ask god or buddha or whatever you believe in – ask the universe for protection – ask for them to be with you – of course everything happens as it's supposed to..."

But you should ask for help.

"Correct."

Was this a life you'd planned or experience before? Helping people with brain issues?

"**Many (life) times before – this time around he made sure people would learn something about it.**"

This time your sacrifice will help science.

"**Yes; if they're awake.**" **He showed me everyone asleep and waking up.**

Thanks Dave.

Icon, legend; Dave Duerson. Private photo.

****

After this session, I did reach out to Dave's son. As of this writing I have no idea what he thought of this session, or his reaction to it. But what did Dave Duerson say? "Please please help the future players." *Message delivered.*

Recently, Jennifer and I were doing a session and Junior came through with a personal private message for his wife and daughter. I reached out to his wife and passed it along. It was basically that he was "aware of everything that was happening in their lives" and that he was "super proud of his daughter." Gina thanked me for passing along his message.

This chapter is chock full of so many mind bending ideas, it's hard to unpack all of them. All I can say is reread it, as I have done. Each time through I learn something new. Can the NFL do more to protect players? Yes. Did Joe Namath cure his CTE? Yes. Are Junior Seau and Dave Duerson okay on the flipside? Yes. Do they want to spread the word that players need to be protected more and that people can cure CTE with hyperbaric oxygen therapy? Yes. Are our loved ones always with us no matter what physically happens to them? Yes.

Do we play in quantum fields on the flipside? Play sports and games and entertain ourselves? Does love go on, life go on? YES. YES. YES.

What more can I say?

CHAPTER EIGHT:
"VERY THIN, VERY METRO"

Orson Welles' star – Author's photo.

ORSON WELLES ROBERT FROST THE MEDICI FAMILY

And now for something a little different... Another day. Another session. Another class. My comments are *in italics*, Jennifer's replies are **in bold**.

Rich: Let's invite Orson Wells. We've never asked him to class before.

Jennifer: He's been kinda busy. He says "He's got a movie coming out..." (Jennifer looks at me with a question mark)

That is correct: "The Other Side of the Wind" produced by Frank Marshall... his movie took 40 years to release.

"Yes."

How does he look to you?

Very thin, very handsome, very metro. I don't know anything about him.

Well, this is the guy who Rita Hayworth reportedly threw herself at him. Well, let's ask; did Rita walk into his room with only a mink coat on, the night before marrying Aga Khan?

Jennifer laughs. He says "She did that many times."

Okay, so Luana introduced me to Henry Jaglom.

He showed me a tape recorder. In a briefcase.

Yes, he reportedly taped your lunches at Maxim's restaurant.

He says he "lost his shit over that."

Funny. Your housekeeper told me at Henry's house, that Orson never left his home after that incident. He was upset at being taped – In Henry's defense, Henry claims Orson knew he was being taped.

Well, that's what he said; he said "he lost his shit" over that.

Okay, but c'mon dude, can we talk about your weight at that time? You didn't leave the house because it was hard to.

He was around 340 pounds. It's what it felt like.

His housekeeper told me she used to push you out of your bed with her feet. Get behind you and use her legs to get you out.

He says "he liked it."

I don't mean any disrespect to you. I'm a fan. You made Citizen Kane at the age of 25 – Michelangelo did the David at the same age. Both made masterpieces at a young age. Who was there to greet you when you crossed over?

He's showing me his little poodle; his little dog.

What do you regret about this lifetime if anything?

"Not being able to create more; he's showing me the movie stars he knew but not being able to create more films."

Tell us what are you doing over there?

(Jennifer suddenly sneezes.) Someone is here trying to get my attention. Who's the guy trying to get my attention; the guy who had Lou Gehrig's disease?

Hawking. Stephen wants to talk?

Wait... Orson's still talking. Okay. He showed me painting and there's like a sound that came through... and I asked "Are you creating sound?" He said "No I'm painting with music; colors I've never seen before, that I don't have in my rolodex."

Orson, what do you miss about being here on the planet?

"The smells." He says "The smells."

Any specific message you want to give to someone still on the planet?

He says, "Tell them thank you." It looked like... I don't know if it's his estate, whatever it is, they weren't taking care of it.. and he was very particular about it.

What about Frank Marshall who produced "The Other side of The Wind?"

He showed me his nails...

Orson's or Franks?

Orson's. (Listens) Okay; what do you want to tell Frank? (to me) "Tell him… he'll figure it out" – he said, "Tell him not to be afraid to get his hands dirty."

Okay.

Jennifer shrugs.

I was going to ask you about Gary Graver, a friend of Luana's, and a cameraman I knew.

Did he have a picture book of Orson?

Likely, he shot much of the film, he's in the movie, are you hanging out with Gary? Or who do you hang out with?

He says "He's still helping people over here."

Who?

Gary says "He's helping people he knew over here. People he knew and loved."

Okay, thanks. How about you Orson – who are you helping out?

He says "He's hanging out with Michael Jackson."

Okay. Learning to dance?

He says "He's learning to moon walk." *That's funny.*

Orson, who have you been impressed to meet on the flipside?

He's showing me William Shakespeare.

Okay. Well, a few weeks ago Will said he had assistance from a higher spirit while writing. He said it was William Blake, of course he was a couple of hundred years before Blake.

He says "Time isn't the same over there."

Okay, so was the higher conscious energy of William Blake an influence on you... or were you an influence on him?

He says "They just took turns." *He just showed me something I saw in London... what's the other guy's name? Charles Dickens.*

Can we bring him forward?

He's already here.

Charles - out of all your books what was your favorite? Tale of Two Cities?

"Oliver Twist."

I understand that you grew up next door to a poorhouse – or what was called a workhouse back then.

"Many of them."

I can see from your historical writings that you were an inspired social justice kind of guy.

He says, "Back then when you could be put in prison for writing propaganda."

Tell me the genesis of your story, "A Christmas Carol." Who's who? Was there an actual Tiny Tim?

He's telling me it was a metaphor for a political group. That "Tiny Tim" was a little bit like Napoleon – he had a vague notion of Tiny Tim as a head of state. Someone – a politician in England at the time who was short.

You were using political characters?

"Yes."

(Note: I had no clue that Dickens was using the characters in place of people he knew in government, but apparently many critics did. Here's one account that details what he's suggesting through Jennifer. https://britlitsurvey2.wordpress.com/2014/05/03/a-christmas-carol-the-political-backstory/)

I wrote a script for Universal Studios about a Washington Irving short story... I know that you two met. Can we talk to Washington Irving?

"Yes."

You used to have these salons and everyone would go up to your house on the Hudson and have these partners... and Dickens showed up there and went to Boston.

"Yes."

Charles - was "A Christmas Carol" based on an event with the flipside when you were young?

It feels like it did – like he had polio in a previous lifetime and all the stories intermixed.

Had you ever been visited by a ghost in your life?

"All the time." He says he "felt like he was haunted."

Who was visiting you Mr. Dickens?

He said "It felt like it was everybody who had passed unjustly..."

People unjustly killed or died outside of justice visited you?

"Yes."

So specifically when you wrote about these characters..

It feels like his brother might have died from polio or starving and that sparked everything.

Was "The Ghost of Christmas past" not a person you knew but a memory?

It is much more complicated than what I can get. It's all of it – Oliver Twist, all of them are based on many characters he encountered.

Have you reincarnated since then?

They're all laughing. "No. He's waiting for an opening."

How does one get an opening? Someone you're connected to has to pass on?

He's saying "It's almost like a lottery."

Do your guides help you to decide who you're going to be next?

He's showing me he's got enough people out there who were versions of him – people still on the planet... "The ocean is the soul; each wave is a different spirit." He has enough waves of past, present and future.

Will Shakespeare said he was bored showing up at his plays. Are you bored with your books?

"No."

What did you think of the Jim Carrey version of "A Christmas Carol?"

He said "He did an amazing job." Hold on. Luana is saying you need to give me a break.

Sorry; I've been torturing you for an hour straight. I want to get the secrets of the nukes before they go off.

She just wants to give me a break. (After a break for lunch). I just saw the painting "The Birth of Venus."

I know it well, it's from the Uffizi gallery in Florence.

I'm so confused... but I just saw her, Venus pointing... she's naked on a shell?

Let's have some fun, I'm going to ask for someone completely random to come forward. Can Simonetta Vespucci talk to us?

She's here. (Jennifer doesn't know she's the model for "Venus")

What age were you when you died?

"20."

That's correct. (Ding!) You died of consumption. How'd you like your funeral? (It was massive, the entire city participated in it.)

"It was enormous, it was amazing, it was like a wedding but a funeral, it was like the wedding in "Scarface."

That's correct. (It was a big deal) She married an older man.

"He had a son."

She was in love with a young boy in the painting...

She's showing me the painting, "Primavera."

Oh Jesus. That's correct. (Ding!) The boy's name was Giuliano De Medici. He was in the painting with you. Can you bring him forward?

"Yes." (Jennifer aside) This is so weird.

Giuliano, thanks for coming. I've written about your family.

"It's crazy!"

What happened to you?

He says, "He was stabbed."

Correct. (Ding! This is mind bending as I know it is accurate.)

He says, "He didn't see it coming – they wanted to make sure he was dead, they didn't want him to suffer, there was a certain amount of wounds that has something to do with it."

Can you show her where?

He says, "Florence. A church in Florence..."

Correct. (Ding!) The Duomo in Florence many people were buried... it happened in 1478.

(Note: I've been researching this story for decades, and in this particular sentence, not many are aware of it, but there were two assassins in the Duomo the day the Medici brothers were attacked. One was a professional assassin who waited until the host was raised (the agreed upon signal) and as Giuliano lowered his head, was stabbed 29 times. (His shirt still exists from that day and is in a museum in Florence.) A priest from Volterra offered to take the place of the Pope's hired assassin (Pope Sixtus IV agreed and helped the plot) and that priest missed killing Lorenzo but grazed his neck. He survived but Giuliano did not. But here I am, having spent decades on the story, hearing it from the horse's mouth. I'm flabbergasted, but in a good way.)

Here's what I want to ask, who was there to greet you when you crossed over?

He says, "His mother." He died when he was young, didn't he?

Yes. Is this normal for you; this conversation Giuliano?

He says, "Professors sometimes ask."

Giuliano de Medici (painted by his uncle, Botticelli)

Let's talk to your brother. (Lorenzo)

Did he have reddish hair?

Could be. But I want to talk to your brother for a minute..

Why did he feel like he robbed him – did they fight?

They were brothers, they argued sometimes, perhaps fought.

Was it over a woman? Over Simonetta.

Okay.

He is the older brother, right?

Yes. He was a poet and leader of Florence, he was stabbed too but he survived, I wanted to ask your brother Lorenzo a question.

Bust of Lorenzo by Verrocchio – National Gallery Author's photo

He says, "They just made it look like that – he was stabbed, but that part was staged."

Okay, that's possible. I think they sucked the blood out of Lorenzo's neck because they were afraid it was a poisoned dagger – or maybe that was made up – but Lorenzo you eventually became..

"A saint."

(Note: She could be referring to another saint we've met in this time period, interviewed in "Architecture of the Afterlife.")

A patron saint of the arts; you were well known, you created the first library, you were patron to a young artist... can you bring him forward?

(Jennifer aside) This is so funny.

Can Michelangelo come forward?

Yes.

He was also a friend of Lorenzo's.

He says, "There was something where someone got credit for someone else's work."

That's correct. Michelangelo got his nose broken in an argument over who painted what.

"Okay, yes."

This is hilarious, we've never spoken to them before... Lorenzo's uncle Sandro Botticelli painted all these things... and all you did was mention the painting "Venus" and we spoke to all the people involved with the creation of that artwork. It's wild. If I didn't know it was accurate, I'd assume it was our creation entirely. Anyways, thanks to the Medici family for showing up today, Simonetta as well. We'll catch you on the flipside.

Simonetta Vespucci by Botticelli. Uffizi Gallery. Author's photo.

*****

I've been researching this family for over 30 years, and as noted in "Architecture of the Afterlife" I'm quite familiar with the events and the story and the names of these individuals. I won't go into why that is, one might have to take a look at that book to get some insight into how I know so much about this story – but it's uncanny by any stretch of the imagination.

CHAPTER NINE

SPEAKING OF FRANK

Chairman of the Board; Author's photo

SINATRA FREDDIE MERCURY BRENT TAYLOR

Typical afternoon, I turn on the camera and say:

Rich: Hi class, who's here today?

Jennifer: Jimi Hendrix and David Bowie just showed up.

Is that related to someone I asked to come today? Could you put in Jennifer's mind why that might be?

Okay, now John Belushi showed up.

On the drive over, he popped into my head, and I asked aloud why we hadn't seen him in awhile.

Shut the front door!

No, really.

I believe you. I'm seeing George Michael as well.

He's associated with one of the folks I asked to join us today. But let me ask George Michael. Do you still sing over there on the flipside?

He says he does. But now he's writing more.

How does that work? Are you singing old songs or writing new ones?

He showed me that Elton is channeling him – "he's putting tunes in his mind." (Jennifer aside) I'm not judging it; he just showed me projecting thoughts into his mind. (Pause) Frank Sinatra!

Correct. (Ding!)

It was who was in my head; I just couldn't think of his name.

Does he want to talk to us?

(Listens) He was just talking to Marlon Brando and then Anthony Bourdain.

Anthony's a great interviewer – Anthony, you want to help us with this one?

Anthony says, (he asked Frank) "He wanted to know how Frank made it through unscathed." "The mind," he said. Sinatra says "He had many people around him where Anthony felt more alone, Frank had a crowd, where Anthony had millions of people who watched him... but not a group to support him."

Frank, you gave something to Quincy Jones.

He comes through smoking a cigar. Was it a cigar cutter? He showed me something small... almost like a picture of a... (Jennifer flexes her hand.) He gave him a ring?

That's right. (Ding!) Quincy said he'll never take it off.

He says "He gave it to him from the heart."

Quincy was his arranger.

He says "That's what Anthony did not have. He had people to micromanage him." Frank says "I loved Quincy."

Frank, who was there to greet you when you crossed?

Did his wife die of chest cancer? Or maybe a girlfriend, one of his first loves who died of cancer or something along those lines... She's beautiful... a brunette that was like Marilyn Monroe.

Were you surprised when you saw her?

He says, "She was there before he crossed over so he wasn't surprised."

You saw her in your hospital before you left Frank?

He says, "In his home." (Jennifer aside) I don't know how he died, feels like he was battling cancer.

(Note: He died of bladder cancer and some other afflictions in 1998. The brunette Jennifer is seeing is likely his second wife Ava Gardner who died 8 years before him.)

So who did you seek out when you got to the flipside?

He says, "Rock Hudson." That's what he showed me first.

Did you work together in a movie or just friends?

I asked "Do you mean that kind of friend?" and he said "No, just friends. They "got" each other. They had walls up for different reasons."

Are you aware of any other lifetime you had on the planet?

"Yes." It was in Europe is what it felt like.

Someone poor or successful?

He says, "Successful."

So when you decided to come back were you aware you were going to pick a golden voice?

He says, "Not when he landed, but yes."

What do you regret?

He says, "He really doesn't have any regrets, but he does regret some heartbreaks with siblings or children. It feels like... someone committed suicide over him... he says "He could have been a better friend to Elvis."" (Jennifer listens;) Oh. He's such a mobster.

You want to go down that path with Frank?

He says, "Yeah."

So Frank, a lot of your friends were criminals.

He says, "It was different back then," he says. "They killed people for fun – he put a guy on a wheel and people shot at him..."

Who did that?

I don't know.. He's telling me Joe Pesci played that person in a movie.

We're not judging ... what do you want to tell people who loved you?

He said "Breathe." (Jennifer aside) That was interesting.

It helps you sing too.

He says, "To not do drugs. He's saying drugs can be brought down in a metaphoric or etheric way and it's why people connect or try to ..." hold on... He's saying "It's like I want them to love. If you love you'll be more afraid to hurt. You'll be more afraid to kill someone if you love someone. If you just connect you have to compartmentalize the hurt."

Do you feel you imparted that with your songs?

He says, "Yes. I made them think of other things, I got them out of their heads, yes."

There are people in our class whom you helped.

He's showing me Aretha, and Whitney Houston when she was a little girl. That's what he's showing me.

Whitney, can you come forward?

He says, "He's helping her daughter... from the flipside."

(Note: This was before Whitney's daughter passed.)

Okay. If I can ask you Whitney, who was there to greet you?

She says "Elizabeth Taylor." (Jennifer aside: I'm sorry to ask; is she still here?)

No, she's now part of the rat pack. Liz you want to talk to us? Who was there to greet you?

She says, "Her first of 5 husbands..." I have no idea about her life; she says, "She was there to greet Michael Jackson."

And you greeted Whitney; why did you greet Whitney?

She says, "To let her know it was ok."

Do you have any regrets?

She says "Many. She's working with her daughter up there."

(Note: Liz has three, two with Richard Burton, one adopted, and another with Mike Todd)

Whitney, what do you miss about being on the planet?

"I miss the lights." She showed me like the lights onstage. Performing lights.

What was your favorite performance?

She's showing me the Olympics... didn't she sing there?

(Note: She did. It was for the 1988 Seoul Olympics. "One Moment in Time" which she performed live. I could ask Jennifer if she watched those Olympics, I know I did not, was not aware of this event, nor that she sang there.)

What was your happiest moment singing?

(For the film) "The Bodyguard."

What about you Frank? Your happiest moments?

He says, "When somebody recognized him..."

What do you mean?

He says, "As a good singer."

How old was he when he was first recognized as a good singer?

He's saying "9 or 19..."

Who was this person who recognized him?

He's showing me he had a suitcase, I don't know.. Showing me a suitcase, traveling somewhere... dark suit; it was probably someone in the mafia.

I think his first contract was with the mafia.

I didn't know that – he's showing me...

Mafia means "my family" in Italian. Frank, what's your favorite song out of all your tunes?

He says something with sunshine.

You are the Sunshine of My Life?

He's showing me Elton John – something that they... they've been showing me Elton a couple of times... and George Michael.

Let's talk to this other singer I invited today; a friend of George Michael's.

Freddie Mercury!

Yes, who I asked to come by today. How does he appear to you?

A little big bigger than he was then. Short hair, with an earring, short short hair...

What do you think about this movie "Bohemian Rhapsody?"

He says "They got the ending wrong." He's telling me over and over again – "It just came from one person." (Meaning only one person helped create the scenes.)

How did you like Rami's performance?

"A plus" he says.

The film on a scale of one to ten?

He says "It was a five." Jennifer laughs.

Freddie was from Zanzibar. And Freddie's real name was...

Faruk?

That is it.

(Jennifer aside) Shut the front door!

No that's it. I think the film honored your journey – gay people have given it a thumbs up, you did fall in love (Jim) and they got that right.

He says "They shortened it, the (actual) timeline... they were together a much longer time."

Did you know him before this life?

He says, "Many lives. He showed me he was a female... before."

Was Freddie or Jim the female?

He says, "Jim."

Who greeted you when you crossed over?

He starting singing "Mama."

Any regrets about your life and this journey?

He says, "None."

Do you miss anything?

He says, "Feeling, smelling. Tightness of the outfits, the tactile of the piano, the guitar, the kiss, the lips..."

Are you playing instruments now?

He says, "Yes." He's showing me something like an organ, but it takes up the whole universe...

What was the genesis of the song Bohemian Rhapsody?

He's showing it was him as a kid... he was young...

But the lyric; "Mamma, I killed a man?"

He says, "Metaphor; a broken heart."

Okay. When you wrote that song it was about someone breaking a heart? When did you realize you were gay?

He showed me as a baby. "When he was born."

What do you want to share with us about your journey or path.

He says "Not to worry; I'm doing fine, I'm doing amazing, there are not words to describe it."

Did you know David Bowie?

Through the song "Under pressure." He says "It was an honor to sing it with him. Then he showed me the rocket.

Major Tom? David's last record, Dark Planet. David Bowie's journey into the flipside. So Freddie what should we tell your fans and friends?

Jennifer makes a peace sign... "Peace and love. To live your best in it, authentically don't let anybody tell you differently."

Thank you sir!

Luana just went whew! This is exhausting. She's showing me that they give you questions to ask... it's a flow, it something that is orchestrated, but it's improvised.

Okay, for our third guest, this guy died last week. I'm going to tell you who it is as you would not recognize him. However, your dad Jim may know him on the flipside. From Utah, a Mormon, his last name is Taylor, first name is Brent.

My dad says "They're on it." (Meaning: "Asking him to step forward to speak.")

Can we talk to this guy?

"Yes."

Officer Brent Taylor – Family photo

Jennifer smiles.

So Officer Taylor from Ogden Utah, tell us about your journey.

He is very handsome. He has blue eyes.

(Ding!) Couple of questions for you. Can I call you Brent?

"Sure."

You were on your fourth tour of duty, what were you thinking Brent? (said in a lighthearted fashion, as I've found being lighthearted can yield different kinds of information.)

He says "It was silly... it was..." I don't mean silly, he's joking around. He says he died, but it was something... He says "It's like you come back from skiing and hit your head ... something very routine, it felt like. It happened outside... it was an outside shooting. It was routine (mission) – nothing had ever happened before (like it, during a mission), it was like a lone star dad did it.

(Note: I don't know what this means; "A lone star dad." The lone star in the window has been the symbol of a family who lost a son or daughter to war. Wikipedia)

Was this your 4th tour?

He says, "Fourth and a half tour."

(Note: Ding! He's correcting me, and us. Not a detail Jennifer would know, but is accurate. Again, I have not told Jennifer we would speak with this fellow, she's reporting what she hears or sees verbatim.)

Who was there to greet you?

He says, "God."

Good, we'll get back to that.

(Note: For purposes of brevity, I set that aside to continue our questions about Brent's journey.)

What do you miss about being here?

He says, "His kids."

What would you like to tell your kids?

He says, "That I love them and they'll see me again."

Anything you want to tell your wife?

He said, "That I'm sorry for leaving."

Well you're not gone, really, are you?

He says, "No."

Tell us how she can talk and connect to you.

It feels like after her grief, it's going to take a long time. It feels like three years; they met when they were young, it felt like they knew instantly... felt like...

Have you had other lifetimes with her?

(Jennifer to me:) Give me a second. Give me his name again?

Brent Taylor.

I felt yeah, they knew each other before. But they met each other in school could have been in college.

Where or how did you first meet in school?

He says, "Through a friend."

Show it to Jennifer. Were you inside or outside? Was it at a party?

He showed me online almost...

So you saw a picture of her before you met her?

No, hold on – they knew about each other but they hadn't met.

So that first time....

I keep getting BYU.

Don't judge it. Brigham Young University in Ogden; is that you where you met?

(Note: I have no idea where or how he met his wife. Again, we're meeting him for the first time. When Jennifer gets a detail wrong, it's because she's misinterpreting what she's seeing or hearing. Sometimes she is shown things that are metaphors for what someone is trying to say. The only way to know how accurate this is to interview his family. I have since learned he taught at BYU.)

He says, "Yes. Outside of BYU – but almost there."

Jim, you can help us with this...

(Note: Jim is Jennifer's father who is on the flipside.)

My dad says, "I'll try."

Brent this is Jim, he's a former Mormon bishop.

He said "he helped him before he came in" (to class today.)

Jim what would you like to tell Brett?

He says, "Don't judge it." He showed (pointed to) my head... to not judge it that we can talk (to each other.)

Is that for Brent?

Yeah, he's showing him so he can learn how to do this (communicate) on his own. We're the number one class to learn how to talk to their loved ones.

I want to be clear that Jennifer's father Jim can help you Brent, to be aware of the nature of...

"He is." (Helping him.)

Okay. I'm suggesting this, because you're going to learn things about your upbringing that might be contrary to as you learned them.

That's what my dad is saying to him; "Don't judge it."

Brent is that stressful or weird to have to address it? (This new reality).

He says, "Yes. Everything is weird over here." It's like he can't help (thinking) .. he's thinking about his wife and kids who are crying... and showing me that the church is helping them because they're saying (to them) "they're going to see each other again." But there's like a big wall, and they can't hear it. (Or hear Brent).

Brent, we can help them hear it – help them talk to you. Would you like us to do that?

He says, "Yes, but after the new year. It's too soon."

The reason I'm offering that is my wife looked at a picture of your wife and heard the message that she needs help. Who sent my wife that message?

"It came from all of us."

All right, so I think helping your wife to understand that you still exist and can communicate, will help other people – I'm not going to take on the church, I'll let Jim do that.

He (Jim) says "He's doing that over there but says he's "one of a kind."

But let's allow that the Mormon church has already adapted to the times, including with the ideas about plural marriages, dropping the "Mark of Cain" idea... but if we can get them to address or accept that people in the Celestial Kingdom are accessible and you can talk to them; that would that be a thing of value, wouldn't it?

(Jennifer laughs.) My dad said "It's funny, if I was in the Celestial Kingdom you wouldn't be able to talk to me." Hold on. (Jennifer aside to me) It's like my higher self can talk to my dad, but he's a fraction of what he is there (energy or soul wise), just like we're a fraction of what we are here. So my self is talking to him the best way I can.

What I'm asking is, that when I address this with your wife, Brent, or other religious folks, when we discuss the idea that "in marriage you were sealed..."

"For all time."

Right. It's to point out that fact is not religious but it's because we are always connected, because it's the nature of reality – that we are always "sealed" or connected to our loved ones for all time anyway, is that correct?

"The Soul is."

I think it's an important distinction... to make. That religions are trying to explain what the research shows – when we're "back home" we experience a different reality. After your death, I read that a fellow soldier wrote a letter to your wife; this guy was a military man.

A close friend it feels like.

Yes, correct, he was from Afghanistan – Brent trained him... His initials are A. R. – He wrote a beautiful letter to Brent's wife, reporting that Brent taught him so much about...

"Family." That's what Brent said. And "How it inspired him to be better, what it did for his whole family... he's talking about it and it's like people converted too because of him."

In the letter, he said family isn't important...

"It's everything."

Yes, that is what he wrote.

He said, "So the Mormons do have it right about family."

You said that "God was there to greet you..." How did that occur? Was god a male, female or an object, a thing? How did you perceive God?

He says "God was energy, like a big enormous amount of energy of love." He said he felt like he... "he knew when he experienced that love, he knew he had served well."

Served what?

"The country, his family..."

Okay, but I mean when you're meeting God and you're getting that feeling of unconditional love...

"That's it." He said it was "Unconditional love." I know your question is what was that? "I felt it more than I saw it. It's like I felt it and I experienced it."

So he felt God, more than he saw God?

He saw God too.

This is what I want to examine.

(Jennifer pauses) Give me a second. I asked was it energy or a person? He said "It was neither. He said he saw an indescribable light."

Knowing that you're meeting me and Jennifer and Luana for the first time – there are many around you, here in this classroom, who know about this journey.

He's like "I'm very miniscule."

You're someone who has had a profound affect on many.

He's speaking about his family. He says "His child is having a birthday that is coming up." (This was November of 2018).

When you say it was a bright light... was it more of an experience than an object?

He says, "Yes. It was an experience."

We've heard this before that God is beyond...

"Right it comes all at once."

(Note: Answered before I could ask. In "It's a Wonderful Afterlife," a guide responds to the question "What or who is God?" "God is beyond the capacity of the human brain to comprehend. It's not physically possible. However you can experience God by opening your heart to everyone and all things." We often hear in this research "love is the engine of the universe" or "everything is sentient and composed of the same conscious energy which is unconditional love.")

What can we learn about that radiation of that energy?

He says, "Yes, you can learn it from everybody else that you come in contact with."

Everyone has it, (that source energy) is that correct?

"Yes, humans and animals."

If you don't mind me asking; have you been greeted by anyone that you've killed as a soldier?

"Yes."

What was that like?

He said "He felt love coming from them. The same God Cure... – it's like a cure."

Was that surprising for you?

He said "Yes. Not surprising, but yes, he knew (with regard to) the way he lived his life..." (as a soldier...).

But are you aware now of what people say: that you've had many lifetimes?

"Right."

From what we've learned, is it possible to see that these people you killed in battle are part of your journey and they signed up for a life that you ended?

"That is correct."

Any regrets about this journey you've taken?

He says "He has no regrets."

Anything you miss about the planet?

He says, "Everything. The air. The trees, the crisp... the crackling of walking on dried leaves and sand between your toes and the salt air of the Salt Lake (in his home state) and the sunset with his wife his kids... and their toothpaste... (Jennifer puts one hand over the other) The hands that go over... the kid's hand that goes over his... seeing his son play baseball... seeing his daughter figure skate and his youngest child singing, one of them is singing crazily. Missing my wife. (after a pause) But not missing her cooking." Jennifer laughs.

(Note: This exchange brought tears to my eyes; it's the first we've ever had someone speak so poetically about what they miss about being on the planet. And the punchline is about as funny as any I've heard from someone on the flipside. Not something Jennifer or I would ever say – in light of who we are talking to, or think was funny, unless we were reporting it verbatim. I have no way of knowing if this is accurate – only his family will. If it's not accurate, then it was said so that his family (and others) could dismiss this account entirely. If it is accurate, then it was a revelation *for them only*.)

What was the one dish you didn't like?

He's saying "Casserole. Stroganoff."

Well, what about the Marshmallows-in-Jell-O dish I see whenever I'm in the all-you-can-eat buffet in Utah?

"Yes. That too."

In terms of Afghanistan; you were there quite a bit. What if anything do you miss about it?

He says, "The people. The people trying to work things out, trying to give them responsibility... um. Seeing people come together and not be torn apart."

Anything you want to tell Abdul Rahman?

(Note: He's the fellow who wrote the letter to Brent's widow telling her how much he taught him in life and wanted to share that with her. I didn't say his name earlier for this reason.)

He says "He's grateful. He's grateful. He didn't know that he would say all those things, but I feel like he helped him." (To write it.)

Are you grateful for writing the letter or for the friendship?

"All of it."

That's very profound Brent. Thank you for coming to talk to us, we want you to be aware that Jennifer's dad can help you at any time.

"He is."

Thanks Major Brent Taylor.

"Brother Brent."

Very funny. I promise to reach out to your wife after the New Year.

And I will, with this book.

CHAPTER TEN
IT'S ALL FREQUENCY

Jim Morrison standing off stage in Per La Chaise Cemetery, Paris. Photo courtesy of Elizabeth Stanley. All Rights Reserved.

PRINCE JIM MORRISON

Jennifer: Billy is here.

Rich: Hello Mr. Paxton. What do you want to say bud?

Is there something like "100 with Prince?"

This guy I'm talking to on Tuesday, Coby Utterback; feels as if somehow Prince has been visiting him.

"Yes he is."

So he asked..

"The frequency."

Correct. (ding!) He asked Prince to show him a sign, if it was the case, and his girlfriend turned to him while watching a rock concert and said

"Did you hear that riff that guy played was a total Prince riff?" He said he was in tears. So how'd you do that?

"Frequency. He put her awareness towards the guitar player." Prince says "I have a crew that makes things happen."

Who helped you?

"Luana."

So Luana has been helping you to communicate. Okay. Well what do you want me to tell this fellow Coby?

"Just be open."

Open to the idea that you're guiding him?

Prince says "Hey, people follow Jesus!" He's laughing. That's just him being funny.

Would it be useful to tell this guy you are his guide?

You have to explain about the frequencies. He's tapping into Prince's frequency – it might not be so much that Prince is a guide, per se, but he shares a frequency that Prince has with his own past lives...

This guy is a musician.

I feel like Prince was a teacher in the spirit world with him before he came here.

Prince, is that accurate?

He says "Yes."

In between lives Prince has met this guy?

Like a 100 years ago, that's where the 100 came from; that's why its still so fresh.

I need to put it in a way so that I can parse it... and next thing he'll be jumping off pianos.

"Yeah."

Okay, thank you sir. How about you Luana, anyone you need to reach out to?

"Her mother."

Marina? Okay.

Is she still here?

No. But what about your mother. Are you getting along better?

"Yes. They talked about working on their abandonment issues in the next life, not having those issues with each other..." I don't know what that means.

Unfortunately, I do.

(Note: Luana was abandoned by her father, who came back with PTSD from World War II and left his wife Marina. Marina owned a dress shop in Culver City and when it became impossible to make ends meet put her only daughter in foster care. Luana was reportedly molested, traumatized, (something she never revealed to me directly, but in bits and pieces learned later) but then Luana moved back in with her mom. That was fraught with argument until Luana "ran away from home" at 17 to join a troupe of actors. But here in this discussion, we're learning this was part of their life plan; including father, mother and Luana.)

You're mentioning this to Jennifer. Why? Is it related to Jennifer?

"Yes. Being misunderstood."

The reason you were arguing in the past is that you were both working on abandonment issues you carried through from other lifetimes. Am I saying that correctly?

"Yes."

Wow. That's wild.

She said "It's easier to work on it here than it is there."

Ha! Of course. I would think so because over here you can't see it in perspective.

They can figure it out here...

But here in this theater is the fun. Here, if you don't have the connection and emotion... it can overwhelm you.

I said thank you Luana; I've got your back.

PART TWO:

The Louvre: Napoleon. Author's photo.

NAPOLEON STANLEY KUBRICK

Another day, another trip to the fieldhouse on the flipside. In this session, I decided to see if I could call upon a historical person, someone I knew that I had no possible connection to. The questions I asked him were related to questions posed to me by an Oscar award winning screenwriter.

Rich: I talked to somebody yesterday who we interviewed in your office. My old boss, the screenwriter Robert Towne; friend of Luana's.

Jennifer: He came to mind.

I told him what we were doing and I said if you could talk to anyone on the flipside who would you like to talk to?

His dad just came through but I know that's not who he wanted to talk to.

I told him "You can talk to anybody." I'll tell you this, it's a historical figure.

The first person that showed up was Abraham Lincoln, but I don't think it was him.

Well perhaps Abraham can help us. Luana knows who this is, because it was I was talking to.

Was he a soldier during the Civil War?

He was a soldier but not during our Civil War. I'll tell you that he wasn't from this country.

Winston Churchill?

No, longer ago. If I give you a hint, you'll get it.

Mohammed Ali just showed up as well.

He's got to talk to us at a later date. 200 years ago my dear. I have to think about this – we normally have someone in our class who knows someone who knows someone. Luana has to ask her friend.

When was Napoleon?

That's it. (Ding!) He was around 1820.

Napoleon! How many tries did that take?

It doesn't matter. (For those keeping score, it was five.)

It's frustrating. Finally they showed me Napoleon.

Who showed you Napoleon?

Luana.

Can we talk to him directly?

Um... He's a little bit of a shit. Give me a second. Yeah, I guess we can. Mmm-hmm.

What do you see in your minds' eye?

He's actually kind of handsome.

Can you see his face?

I see his lashes – he's actually quite handsome.

Can you touch his hand?

There's something on his hand, felt like there's a wound on his hand.

Lets ask him – how did you get this wound my friend?

It feels like psoriasis – everything was cracking.

Look around the class; is this unusual for you to be here?

Yes it is. He was here like 3 times before when we were talking to George Washington.

So you recognize a few people in this group?

"Yes."

So you guys in our class that know him, can you help?

They are.

Mr. Napoleon – I apologize for having to take time out of your day, but I have some questions for you.

I keep getting ... based upon the paintings I've seen of him – he had lighter eyes.

Let's ask him – what color are your eyes?

They're blue.

(Note: "His eyes, deep-set, were reportedly gray or gray-blue." Wikipedia.)

They're dark on the outer iris and blue inside.

Who was there to greet you when crossed over?

"His mother." He showed me there were 2 days he was going in and out of consciousness.

What were you ill from?

I want to say it was something around here (gestures) in the stomach.

Was that natural issue, or was that something given to you that you died from?

"I felt like it was... transmitted. I also got an image of the plague." I don't know what that means.

Who transmitted that into your body?

Felt like "It was in the water."

So let's talk about that – did someone administer that stuff in the water, or was it natural from the place you were?

"It was not natural," he says.

So somebody put it in your water or food?

"Yes; felt like a drink."

Tell Jennifer what it was.

"It was poison."

Someone in class, can you put it in her mind what kind of poison that was and who administered it?

"Someone very close to him – first I got a female, then I got someone who was trying to overrule him. Felt like somebody he trusted, like a captain or something."

A man?

"Yes, maybe it was the nurse that administered it."

I'm going to ask you about a woman who was there when you died.

He's telling me "Serafina." Sounds like Serafina.

I'd like to ask you Betsy Balcome.

"She was a child. It felt like there were three kids. It felt like there were three kids associated with Betsy. She was like 9 when she met him."

That's about right.

(Note: She was 12. She lived on St. Helena with her two siblings and befriended Napoleon at age 12.)

"She could actually see – she was clairvoyant."

What makes you say that?

I saw information coming from the heavens (waves her hand)

Napoleon, was Betsy giving you messages from the flipside? Or were you friends?

"Yes," he's saying "He protected her. He was like a mom to a child, brother and sister, he protected her."

It's reported your last words were you reporting for duty.

"Yes. He saw his horse."

(Note: Reportedly, Napoleon's last words were, *"France. L'armée. Tête d'armée. Joséphine*" ("France, the army, head of the army, Joséphine"). I noted in "Flipside" that it sounds like he's reporting for duty, and then sees the love of his life.)

There was a woman you had a long relationship with.

"16... like 16 years."

(Note: Napoleon married Josephine, the widow of a man killed during the reign of terror, they were together as lovers and then married for 16 years. She died in 1814, he died 7 years later in 1821.)

They said you called out her name. Her name was Josephine.

"Sara Josephine" – which is my sister's name – "Serafina." That's why I was hearing "Serafina."

Let's talk about your journey – have you incarnated since?

"No. I saw a picture of (current President) and started freaking out."

I suspect you are talking about these individuals in terms of the negative energy they represent. Were you part of that energy?

"Yes."

What was up with you and Russia? Is that the Trump connection?

"Yes."

Millions died while you tried to conquer Russia, what were you doing?

"Trying to take over the world."

What could you possibly gain?

He says "In his demented mind he thought it would bring more peace under one rule."

Who did you say thanks to?

He made a "poof" sound.

That's very French. (Italians say "Boh!" and the French say "Poof!") He did have a lot of ego, is he still carrying that around?

He says "No more than Prince."

Touche' - okay, what actor might represent you on the planet?

Joe Pesci.

Were you Etruscan? Like Danny DeVito, they were notoriously short.

They were well bred. No; it was like his father's father that was short. "Somebody ruined the gene pool," he said. Why is Joe Pesci showing up? He's showing me he had Joe Pesci's attitude as depicted in movies; killing people. Now he's showing me a screenwriter, how they try to take over the world with movies. He says "I had a lot of blood shed, more people died. It's easier to make movies where people die and they don't bleed."

I'm aware a couple of filmmakers have tried to make a film about you.

He knows that. Who was the guy that was in the "Ten Commandments?"

Charlton Heston?

"He's over there."

Have we talked to Stanley Kubrick yet?

I don't know who that is. We're not done with Napoleon!

It's okay, is Stanley around?

Yeah, he is. He says "He's a step ahead of you."

Stanley; this is Napoleon. You wrote a long movie about this fellow.

Native son.

I asked "Did you get the story right?" and he said "No... the ending was wrong. That's why there were blocks about getting it made.

The ending was wrong? You mean the truth about Napoleon being poisoned?

"Yes. They always wanted it to be an enemy but it was his best friend."

Okay, I think I know who that is – the guy who invited him to St. Helena.

"Yes."

Here you are talking to Stanley who wanted to make a movie about you – and Luana's friend Jack wanted to make a film about you...

Jack Nicholson.

Correct. And yet Jack appeared in another one of Stanley's films.

Was that the redrum movie?

Very good.

He just showed me Jack's head. "The Shining."

Who was there to greet you when you crossed over Stanley?

When did he pass?

Like ten years ago. After the Tom Cruise movie came out.

"Eyes Wide Shut" Stanley?

Yes, Clockwork Orange, The Shining... Who was there to greet you when you crossed over?

He's showing me his dog. Kind of grayish... first I saw something blond...

A hound?

It's bigger... really big. I'm not sure of the name – I don't know know breeds.

(Note: This is accurate in terms of Stanley's affection for his dogs. According to a recent documentary, he moved to a larger home specifically to make room for his dogs and left detailed instructions about each one and how they should be fed. "At home, children and animals would frequently come in and out of the room as he worked on a script or met with an actor. Kubrick's many dogs and cats, toward which he showed an extraordinary affection, were often brought onto film sets or editing rooms." Wikipedia)

What do you miss about being on the planet?

"The smells, the tastes, the frequency – I have to tell you more about that too."

You were famous for not flying... was that OCD?

He showed me having panic attacks, but now he knows it was a past life thing. Now he does. He's showing me how his mind works.

Who do you wish you could talk to?

Everyone's laughing because he said "Luana."

Why?

"Because it's like you have to take a number to talk to her. You have to take a number."

Who do you want me to reach out to?

Jack.

And say what?

"Stanley wants Jack to know that he's okay."

You want me to tell Jack that he's going to be okay?

"Yes." **He's showing me the letters that were found in the furniture at Jack's home.**

That was a copy of Marlon Brando's will that Jack found hidden in a chair. Marlon, do you want to weigh in on this?

"Yes."

Marlon's star

(Note: Brando's will was found in a chair in Jack Nicholson's home (he lived next door.) Jack didn't know how it got there, but made a copy and sent it off to Marlon's attorney. A friend of mine showed me a copy and it clearly was altered (Marlon's signature isn't his signature). I mentioned this when we interviewed him in "Backstage Pass to the Flipside." I won't belabor the point here but reportedly (from him) his heirs didn't get what he wanted them to get.)

You were very quiet the last time we talked to you.

"I don't say much anyway. I don't need to. I can feel it."

Well, Jennifer's got to run, sorry we have to let you go Marlon. Napoleon thanks for coming in to see us...

He says "He'll haunt you in your dreams."

Stanley we're all fans of yours.

Was he a Buddhist?

He may be now. Anything you want us to tell your friends?

He says "He loves Nicole and Keith (Urban)."

Were you a fan of Nicole?

"Huge."

Our pal Jan Sharp was close to her.

"Yeah."

Okay, next time! Thanks class.

It feels like we're bouncing around the playground, but I've found that by just filming and transcribing, it's the overall effect that makes these interviews notable. They consistently say the same things despite being years apart in some cases.

PART THREE
SPEAKING OF HAWKING

Stephen Hawking; Wikimedia

STEPHEN HAWKING, CARL SAGAN, JAMES BROWN, MUHAMMED ALI

Another trip to the flipside. This is from November 2018. I asked for three people out loud prior to arriving at Jennifer's office. That is – driving along the coast highway, looking out over the Pacific and these three individuals, I just say their names aloud.

Rich: OK, someone I have on my list. This person was famous for not being a believe in the flipside.

Jennifer: Stephen Hawking?

(Ding!) I asked Stephen to show up to help this other guy come forward. That's funny and freakin' uncanny. Luana you know who I'm talking about. I called out his name this morning as I drove here.

Is his name Carl?

Yes. Carl Sagan. Wow. You get more brilliant as we go along. Carl. Can we ask you some questions?

I saw him in a museum once.

Can we talk to him?

Yes. He showed me Hawking, and how he put him in his lap and they just went flying.

Stephen has spoken to us before.. Carl you were famous for being an atheist – anything you want to tell us about the flipside? What was it like for you crossing over?

He showed me walking by himself..

Where? By the beach? In the sky?

He's saying whatever he thought of it would magically appear; it's like having a green screen and you would walk and you think of the ocean or the woods – and they would appear. And he felt like he was there, walking beside a forest on near the ocean.

Was anyone there to greet you? Or where you by yourself?

Interesting. He said nobody could greet him until he came to terms with believing (he was on the flipside.)

How long did that take? Was it a long time before you could believe you were on the Flipside?

Yeah. I don't know how long he's been gone - could have been 9 months, 9 years, it wasn't instantaneous.

(Note: Carl Sagan died in 1996.)

Who was the first person you finally did communicate with or see over there.. was it a guide? Someone we know?

So why am I being shown Queen Elizabeth?

Don't judge it... that was your first... Carl?

Someone is either projecting their thoughts...

You mean she snuck in here? You mean Elizabeth the Queen of England? Carl is that who you saw?

Jennifer shakes her head.

We can unpack this - I get that it could be a joke. So the first person you saw was the Queen; was she wearing a crown?

No. She looked old.

What was she wearing?

Just a frumpy outfit.

Did you recognize her as the Queen? You probably met her before.

"Yes."

So did Hawking.

"Yes."

Were you talking to her higher self or someone in disguise?

"Her higher self."

We're familiar with that concept.

She actually took his hand and started walking with him.

How did she help you realize you were in the afterlife or that there was an afterlife?

Jennifer listens. Thank you.. she showed him that she was still down there – like an aerial view, "I'm here, but I'm still there."

Interesting. Talk to us about you about the space craft Voyager and the metal record you sent into space. Do you pay attention to it, or it doesn't affect you at all, you're busy?

He says "It's boring out there."

Wait, you're saying the concept of billions and billions of light years away is boring?

The way that we know it – yes. Present time; to feel things... in order to feel things you have to be present.

Here? Okay. In terms of being over there who have you met or seen since Queen Elizabeth?

She laughs. He said "Billy Idol."

Well, he's still on the planet.

I know... I guess the Queen's showing up didn't work so then he had to show up.

Carl what do you want to tell your friends and fans, still thinking about you?

He says "Tell them to stop wasting time doing what he did."

Arguing about the afterlife?

"It's so pointless."

Well how can we help them?

"It's paradise over here."

How can we help them know that?

We can't.

So these books are not helping? These books are a waste of time carl, Mr. Blue Dot?

They're all laughing. "No! The books are timeless, people can come or go and think what they'll think and they'll find them like if I had come across "Flipside" in my 20's I wouldn't have been ready for it, but coming across it at Thanksgiving (a few years back) was the perfect time for it.

By the way, I'd like to compliment you for the concept of a pale blue dot. The poetry of those words is now in the lexicon.

That's what he was showing me, like walking and having it be like on a green screen, whatever your imagination takes you is where you are, whatever you believe in is correct. And the universe can't interfere, and I was thinking "can you interfere?" and he said "You can interfere that's why Queen Elizabeth showed up.

Somebody that really impressed him that changed his perspective?

It's like the science idea that when a ship appears, people who've never seen a ship before can't see because they've can't comprehend it.

Can you give us any advice on how to save the planet?

Stop using all the water.

Stop polluting all the water?

"All of it; stop cutting down trees. Stop eliminating the Earth."

Anything else you want to impart to your fans and friends Carl? Because they're going to be very upset to hear me claim that you still exist; they are convinced that you can not still exist.

"Yes. Tell them that he still exists. Through the writings. Through the footage. Through his voice. It's like that movie "Coco." As long as you still remember him he still stays alive." Muhammed Ali is here.

Hello sir. Who are you hanging out with in terms of people who are in our class?

"Aretha."

Anything you want to say to your daughter Maryam?

Either she got too skinny.. or she's not eating properly. He said "I'm still sexy."

What?

"I still am sexy."

If I may ask, why did you choose to be a boxer?

"It helped him connect with his higher self." He showed me two words. Freedom and love. He said "Freedom is love." He showed me Martin Luther King about 5 minutes ago.

Dr. King; who was there to greet you when you crossed over?

He showed me a child running to him.

A child you had in this life, or a previous life?

Doesn't feel like one of his children – doesn't feel like a child from his wife. But a child of his.

What do you miss if anything about being on the planet?

He says "Rumbling." He says "I miss talking..." - he shows me fighting for peace, but not fighting – "rumbling for peace" but being peaceful with it.

Did you know you were going to pass away at a young age?

He showed me himself as a young boy and how he always knew he'd die early. And that knowledge, it's what made him live every single day as if knowing he was going to die young.

What do you want to tell your family and friends?

To not give up fighting for peace... and then showed me (the current administration.) To keep fighting.

Whenever I hear your voice speaking, it freezes me in its tracks.

"It was the frequency you'd recognize."

The frequency of compassion, unconditional love?

"A knowing that things were going to be okay; it was a frequency that gave people comfort."

What do you miss about being here?

He says "Being on separate busses? I don't miss that." He says "I miss music. I miss the innovation to stand up for yourself. You're doing that now."

What's it feel like to be an inspiration to folks?

He's showing me all the presidents – everybody was... they were all inspirations. He just showed me the other guy – the good foot guy... the guy with the big hair...

James Brown?

There he is... he showed me James Brown. They've having fun. That's what I got.

Well, thank you Dr. King, Muhammed Ali, James Brown, Jennifer's got to run but we'll catch you in a future meeting.

Again; Jennifer and I are chatting over lunch; I've got the camera on and I ask questions related to whatever pops into my mind. We're not sitting down and "trying to channel" anyone. And as one can see in this book, people stop by when they want to, or when Jennifer's mind (or frequency) shifts to theirs.

If I remember that they came by for a visit earlier and we didn't speak with them, I pick up the conversation later. I once asked Prince what it felt like to him – we spoke to him one afternoon and then two months later, we picked up the conversation again. We asked him "What that felt like in terms of time" for him to revisit a conversation.

"Like a comma," he said.

As if we were in the midst of a conversation and a comma paused us briefly – and we continued it later. I apologize for the rambling nature of this narrative, but I'm filming it, then transcribing it. I'll edit it if there's something that's too personal that is mentioned, or I'll try to combine it with other conversations. But in this case, it's pretty much "As the camera heard it." Onward and upward.

Rich: Okay, back to you Luana.

Jennifer: She's like "It's busy here!"

I have a question about a tweet from your old friend about David Crosby – you introduced me to him one day at Hugo's restaurant.

(Jennifer aside) Don't tell me. (Listens) She said "He's cuckoo crazy... he was like that back then too." (Back in the day with Crosby, Stills, Nash and Young). She said "She feels like he's missing the point to whatever he's tweeting."

Well, in his tweet, he said he thought Jim Morrison wasn't a great poet or a great singer; we talked to Jim briefly in "Backstage Pass." I was curious what he might think about that.

He says, "He totally misses the point."

Mr. Morrison, do you want to say something about this comment?

He says "Obviously, I don't say anything well." (Jennifer aside) He's being sarcastic.

How about this, anything you want me to tweet to David Crosby in response from the Flipside?

He says, "Tell David he should have said that when he was around."

Well, is there something more poetic to say to him?

He says "David wasn't any good either, singing (his) lullaby's..." He says "Let him stew in it. He obviously craves attention and that's how he's getting it." Jim Morrison is telling me "He loved to write, he loved poetry, he loved writing... and that's the irony. Like he didn't want to be a singer, just wanted to write."

So people should do what you love.

He says "He's writing now, making poetry in his mind." He's also saying "Don't criticize people who can't defend themselves."

Well you can defend yourself now, Jim.

"Right." Then they showed me Michael Newton. "We can give a response as long as it heals people, and a response to David's comment doesn't heal. If the response is a way to open horizons, we can get a response, but he's says that he doesn't care. Jim just brought in Will Shakespeare. I think it's his birthday.

Will, is it your birthday?

He says "Yeah."

Are you pals with Jim Morrison?

He showed me the both of them. He says "Their energies are similar, their mannerisms are similar."

Jim, what do you want to say to your fans or friends or family?

He says "Live life. Hold on to nothing. Give yourself an opening even if it's only to be confused with what has been given, what has been told to you. Find your own path. March at the beat of your own drum. Even if you've stolen the drums. Be different! And make a different path. Don't follow everyone else or the same path. The same is so ordinary.

Is that it?

He says "Oui."

That's funny – well you are living in France as we speak. That gorgeous Pere La Chaise cemetery. You're so French mon ami. Let's break this down – you and fellow poets, like Will Shakespeare are in the same relative frequency?

He says "Always."

And you share frequencies?

He says, "They all do!" Then Prince showed up, David Bowie showed up (to demonstrate.) He said "We all use the same frequencies."

For music and writing?

I'm hearing "Your solar plexus is the same color as gold – there are different energy centers." (Jennifer aside) He's showing me chakras...

I think it was the great sage Sponge Bob who said "My spirituality is so hard I broke my chakra."

They are saying, "Everyone can get information, there are melting pots in all kinds of different areas, it's whoever is open to allow that information to come through. If you allow that space to show up it's much easier..."

What are some of the ways for people to connect to their higher self?

They're saying "Through mediation or music... writing.. painting. Channeling music, allowing it to flow through you. Channeling writing.

How can we pass that along to people?

They say "Tell them to meditate and visualize where their happiness lies. Meditate on where is your happiness, what is your purpose, what you are passionate about, dive in deeper and you'll discover what is it that you want that to do.

So when complications arise to your dream, if you've already seen the end result, then conflicts become a speed bump?

They're saying "It's a hiccup. Just a hiccup. If you are in your truth, there are no roadblocks, just different ways to go around."

If I may paraphrase, they're saying "Meditation is a key?"

"Some people call it prayer."

True. So Jim, what's an effective prayer or meditation to help people?

(Jennifer aside) I just got this overwhelming sense of love... He says "putting love into everything that you do. Visualize what love looks like to you and then get that feeling of love within you."

Do you mean related to another person?

He says "No, could also be a project – if you want to do the thing you love – you can send love to your friends, family before you see them."

How do you picture love?

He says "You don't picture it, you feel it."

So can I love the lottery numbers into existence for example?

(Jennifer aside) They're laughing. He says "Just know that everyone can have money – if you love what money can do or the purpose of what it can do that can help others, and change your relationship to it, it will get you more money – things will show up.

Wealth of love.

"Yes."

What more can you want?

*****

Indeed. What more can we want?

CHAPTER ELEVEN:
SITTING SHIVA WITH SITTING BULL

Sitting Bull; National Archives

COUSIN MATT, SITTING BULL

Another day, another session at Fishbar in Manhattan Beach.

Jennifer: Last night I was dreaming that I was at UCLA with my cat, talking like a person telling me that she has cancer…

Rich: In your dream?

Yes. My black cat.

I'm sorry. Well my kids have also had dreams lately about talking to our pets. Our son had a dream where our parakeet that is in the cage next to his desk was saying to him "I'm trying to talk to you but you aren't listening." And then Sherry had a dream where our cat was talking to her, complaining that when she talks to Sherry she doesn't listen. "This is really annoying; I try to speak to you and you don't listen to me" she quoted the cat saying.

I was astral traveling and I was aware of leaving my body and looking at me from above and being able to see other people – I was like "Wait, where are you from?" It seemed so normal, but then they were waking me up and I had to say "I have to go back."

I have a question related to astral traveling (out of body experiences). Can you see the thin wire that connects you to your body?

There was (one).

You can see it now?

Yeah.

What color is it?

Hard to explain, if the sun was setting at a certain point you'd see it... if you're traveling you'd catch the image of it.

In terms of what you're looking at now – is it flat or a cord?

Best way to explain is a special effect, like when you see Captain America run in a film, there's a stream behind him. It's like that's the (only) part you see.

If you were holding it in your hand? What's it look like?

Very thin, but very strong.

Let's ask our class... What is this thin silvery threat made out of? I say silvery because I've heard that before... you didn't say that, but my brother did when he saw his.

That's what it looks like though – but when the light goes through it... I would think it would be etheric... but light bounces from the reflection.

What is the cord made out of?

Feels like electronic neurons... I have no idea what I'm talking about... I asked "positive or negative?" but I'm getting "Neither."

Ions or electrons? Which is the better term?

"Ions."

We've heard that before.

"Something that makes it where you have a place that remembers where you're supposed to be."

Like quantum entanglement?

"Yes." (Jennifer taps her nose.)

Quantum ions? But why is it connected to a human spirit or conscious energy? I understand the function so that they can always find their body like breadcrumbs.

"So they can always get back in time," is what I got.

Did someone create this and if so who?

I would want to say… but it's not .. you know, "the connectedness to all things." Like, it's "God but not God;" the universal energy. I just saw the eyes of everybody.

We've talked about this, God not being a person or thing, but like the medium, or conduit, or a universal box that connects everything. That we're connected to each other, so we're connected to our bodies... the question is, who created the ions?

"Black matter?" He just showed me like a hole. A black hole.

Who showed that to you?

Feels like a lot of people, including my dad.

Well we do have one person we can talk to about it.. Stefano Hawking; wheel on in buddy.

When you said that, Steve Jobs showed up.

You want to say something, sir?

I'm like are you trying to harness the cord to go into other dimensions or galaxies and he's like "no…" Hold on. It's a

capability – I asked "Are you creating an opening to make the ethernet better to get more information?"

Are people working on this silvery thread to make it function better or are we talking about something that already exists and we're understanding it better?

What I'm picking up is "They're making it better so we can go there and they can come here."

Who? Everyone? Certain people?

"It is everybody's awareness as people escalate being awake, that strengthens it."

Obviously it's helping us.

"We're already there – the portals that are there."

You're there I'm hanging onto the tail of the kite. Let's follow that for a second, I was talking to my cousin Mary; her son passed away. So what are you up to cousin nephew?

He says, "He's filming over there." I have no idea what that means.

My cousin's marker "Son and Brother."

(Note: We've heard people doing all kinds of unusual activities from playing virtual football to golfing. In this case, "virtual filmmaking." Sounds logical to me.)

Welcome to our class.. Luana knew your mom and dad..

He showed me 20… was that a date?

I don't now.. he was in his 20's I think he was pals with my mom; he was hilarious, a very funny kid.

He just showed me my son.

Became an attorney, so what would you like to tell your mom?

Tell her that she's couldn't have saved me from what happened. Not to have guilt about it. There's something about her perfume he's showing me.. he loves it. He's doing really well. He says he finished school."

You mean school over there?

"Yes."

What kind of classes are you taking over there?

He showed me being in a Jeep filming he terrain, then being outside a jeep, something that has to do with aerodynamics, capturing things in time on film.

You graduated that class or you're currently in that class?

He said, "He graduated and got honors."

In a class called "Movement of time and objects?"

He says it called "How you capture objects as a frequency." This is getting over my head.

If you were going to give this class a name would would you call it?

"Strip... velocity X."

Can you do us a favor, can Jennifer's dad Jim help us? Please show us your classroom – how many people in your class?

He showed me... all of North and South America.

Giant auditorium, physically?

You would transport yourself there, they can fit everybody because... (Jennifer makes a gesture of shrinking.)

You can shrink in size or you're a point of light?

"Both."

(Note: For those familiar with Flipside reports, many people report "classrooms in the afterlife." The classes are often related to the movement and focusing of energy. To create objects, move objects, etc. I asked for Jennifer's dad as he recounted his classroom in great detail for us.)

Who was in your class?

He showed me someone very sweet, I'm getting a girl from Beijing...

Was she tall or short?

5'6 and 118 human pounds.

Okay, that's pretty specific. Do you hang out with her outside of class? Are you friends with her now?

Yeah, felt like she was like someone who hosts people for school... there was a crash of some sort with her.. either she got in an accident or something.

She was in a car accident?

Something like that. Physical crash.

Anything you want to tell your mom?

"Don't discount those dreams she has. Make sure to tell her that they don't speak in dreams, you start thinking something's wrong – they just don't communicate that way... and she gave him a rose."

She gave him a rose or he gave her a rose?

"She needs to slow down, like stop and smell the roses. Slow down, enjoy your life. Know that I love you." He's putting his arms around her.. "He didn't leave on purpose, like there was nothing... um... No reason behind it." (Jennifer listens:) Miss out on her making fun of him? No.

Say that again.

He says "You mean missing out on my mom teasing and making fun of him? No way!" He's saying "Their banter, they were like brother and sister." He says, "Tell her I kissed her on the forehead."

You ever hang out with my mom over there, the way you did when she was on the planet? Aunt Anthy?

Yeah, they're playing the piano together. He just showed me Tom Cruise sliding into the room in that film... and singing that song that goes "You never close your eyes..."

(Note: The Righteous Brothers song – "You've lost that loving feeling.")

Thanks Matt...

Happy thanksgiving class!

Oh, speaking of Thanksgiving. Can we talk to Dennis Hopper for a second? I was talking to your son's sister at Thanksgiving ...

His wife has a 30 year old and a 4 year old?

The doctors did their magic.

He said "she's got better genes." He wants to say that what you're doing (talking to the flipside) is right, everything you're doing is right, it's coming together and people are feeling it and they're showing me how everyone is feeling it...

So Luana, how do you guys celebrate Thanksgiving?

She's showing me them smoking a joint before dinner.

Speaking of hemp, I'm going to ask Sitting Bull to stop by.

Who?

Sitting Bull.

(Jennifer aside:) I have no idea who that is.

It's okay. Luana should. Can you bring him in? He's a Lakota Indian.

(Note: Fans of the book "Flipside" may recall that I remembered a lifetime as a Lakota medicine man. It was before Sitting Bull's fame and journey, but since experiencing that memory, I've had an affinity for their people, and when I get a chance, stop by the Autry museum in Los Angeles to visit some of their ancient artifacts.)

He's getting off his horse. He's really strong, very handsome. I think he was old when he died. He's very tall, as he appears, he has rings around his arms, (gestures) right here, rope and paint... he has feather... he has this huge thing on his back, like a ceremonial cape filled with feathers, but on his head just this one.. or three I can't tell.. the white one is very significant.

Sitting Bull: National Archives

Can I say thanks for showing up? Can you answer some questions for us?

He's very comforting. Bill Paxton is a big fan.

He must be the one to put him in my head for today's class.

Did he die really old?

He looked old. Do you want to show Jennifer how you died?

I don't feel like he was killed in battle or scalped. He was starving. I feel a taste of poison – or poison was involved. It feels really cold.

It was cold and his people were starving. He was with his people when he died. A betrayal was involved.

That's where the poison came in. Might not be literal poison... A poisoned heart, it feels like.

A native American turned policeman was tasked with arresting him, there was a fight and this guy shot and killed him. It was supposed to be an accident, but may have been an execution. I don't want to dwell on that, but I am interested in who was there to greet you when you crossed over?

Feels like his horse and his mother. He had a young wife. Early on... And like two kids I think.

(Note: Sitting Bull had six wives in total, four alive when he died, and he did have two natural born children. He may be referring to his first wife "Light Hair" who died at a young age in 1857. Sitting Bull died in 1890. Indian Country News.)

Were they all there?

I feel like everyone was there.

In terms of... when you walked into this space saw your horse and your mother, what did that feel like?

He said "He was so elated they were together again. United again. And it was warm."

Do you communicate with people of your tribe today?

He says "They channel him." What year was this? I was getting the 1860's, I saw all the battles...

That's correct. He was a leader and a fighter; and took a lot of enemies in his life. He also joined a group of entertainers. Can you show her that?

That's really funny... Did he do something with throwing knives?

Could be – they traveled, toured, it was a wild west show.

"Gone with the Wind" came to mind, then I saw Tonto and what's his name... the "Lone Ranger."

Gone with the Wind was a historical drama. In the show they reenacted battles and dressed up in "Lone Ranger" type costumes. He toured as part of a "Wild West show that included sharpshooters Annie Oakley and Buffalo Bill Cody. He was reportedly very fond of the sharpshooter Annie Oakley.

Sitting Bull and Wild Bill. National Archives

He was famous for fighting one particular battle out west. Can you show Jennifer that battle you were famous for? Not the reenactment on stage, but the actual battle.

(Jennifer listens, looks into the distance.) Wow. They had a lot of opposition.

From?

Felt like soldiers.

Our friend Sitting Bull fought the battle that resulted in the death of one particular famous soldier.

(Jennifer shrugs:) I don't know. It's not coming to me.

George Armstrong Custer. You're not familiar with it?

He's telling me "His people were starving, they starved out his people. It was justified."

But after Custer was killed the U.S. military felt they had to wipe out the Sioux nation – chased them to Canada – then later on his people were starving so Sitting Bull surrendered. But then was later allowed to tour with Bill Cody.

Wow.

There's a famous cafe in Rome where there's a photograph of Cody sitting at the same table I've sat at.

Is it overlooking a fountain?

It is, yes, the fountain near...

I saw the Spanish steps.

Correct. Caffe Greco at the bottom of those steps – you go to the back of the café and there's a photo of Wild Bill sitting at that table with members of his troupe. But after the tour in Canada, Sitting Bull rejoined his people and he helped his people with a dance that relates to our work.

He said "Spirit dances."

Correct... known as the ghost dance. Soldiers were afraid he was agitated the natives so to speak. In your version of this dance, would you conjure the spirits of dead native Americans?

"Yes."

The soldiers thought you were going to start fighting again... Was your death deliberate or an accident?

Pause. He said "Yes it was." I asked "Was it deliberate and an accident?" and he said "Yes."

What do you want me to tell your people on your behalf?

"They're stronger together than apart... and to thrive."

How do they do that?

He's showing me "Holding hands, staying connected;" he says "The casino money has caused a lot of friction."

There's also a huge amount of money the Sioux nation has refused for the US theft of the Black Hills.

(Jennifer aside) Why haven't they accepted it?

It's their sacred property – however the Lakota people have had a hard time with...

"Alcoholism." That's what he's showing me. He's showing me the money and the problems they've had. He's showing me lots of money, fights over the money. Um... he said "They should take the money and find another piece of land."

But they aren't going to do that. And I can't tell them "Sitting Bull told me on the flipside "take the money and find another piece of land." It's like people who fight over any sacred spot on Earth. It's hard to say "Well, we don't own that sacred place either, because the Earth does." Gaining that money would cause more problems wouldn't it?

He says, "It already has. They need to go to learn new trades... and find different work to do."

Is there something I can tell them about the flipside, about your journey?

He says, "Tell them that the ancestors are there to help. It does go on and on."

My research shows that native Americans religions are more correct than any religion I'm aware of about the nature of reality – how everything is imbued with the great spirit. It's reported to be in everything. Is the Great Spirit another word for consciousness?

He says, "Absolutely; they always had it right."

I have a spiritual question. Have you seen any white buffalo since you've been there?

He says, "Three."

Okay, what was that like – did you ask to see them or run across them?

He says "They came to him. They were energy."

Were they ancestors of yours or creatures created by people's belief in them?

He says "They were creatures that were belief turned into reality."

(Note: It's an obscure question, but from what I've read of the Lakota spirituality, religion, and conversations I've had, the "White Buffalo realm" was considered sacred, seeing a white buffalo was something that would be considered auspicious.)

And I've seen a peace pipe... one of yours I was told.

In a museum right?

Correct. (Ding!) The Autry museum in Burbank.

"Someone wants to buy it."

I haven't seen it in awhile – I saw it in a case.

(Note: Based on this comment, I reached out to the curator of the Autry, who said the Pipe was no longer on display as they decided to put it "out of circulation" but had no intention of selling the object.)

Let me ask you a questions about the use of the peace pipe. What was in it?

He showing me different plants.

Hemp or tobacco?

He said, "Both." Felt like it was both.

So the oil of hemp, the cbd oil which is in hemp - it caused the peace that was in the ceremony of the peace pipe?

He says, "Yes."

Are you planning on reincarnating soon?

He walked away when you asked that. So funny. "Too soon" he said.

Who would you like to talk to in our class?

He smiled and looked at Luana.

Well she is our spirit who speaks without a forked tongue... Sorry, couldn't resist. Can you give Jennifer a symbol or sign language that I can look up that would mean something in your language?

Jennifer points two fingers skyward, then two fingers down on a hand... then a fist in the hand, then turned and pounded twice. (Jennifer aside:) The class is chuckling.

Hey, you guys don't mock our asking about sign language. Tell us what that means while she's doing that.

"Two fingers is peace on the ground – hands crossed, something with a bird… He's showing me an ear with a feather."

What does that mean? There's a native American saying, there's a left and right wing but you need both to fly – for peace on the ground you need to think like a bird or be like a bird?

He says, "Be like a bird. But have the prowess of a wolf."

What does a wolf represent?

He says, "It's quiet but gets where it needs to go."

Okay, thank you – let me ask again, do you have one or two feathers in your hair?

He says, "One."

Behind you, on your ceremonial cape there are bigger feathers which represent what?

He said, "Killing people."

That's what I've heard. Another way to put it would be "victories in battle." How many feathers are the big ones?

"120" is the number that came to me.

So why just one feather – is that the spiritual thing?

He says, "Yes. He's supposed to remind you of…" (Pause)

Me of what?

"It's supposed to remind them of where they came from – their initial lifetime," he said.

I remember being a Lakota medicine man … did we ever meet?

He says "We did." I feel like he was a child when you were a medicine man.

Um.. okay. Luana; that was pretty unusual isn't it?

As opposed to…?

Bye class!

CHAPTER TWELVE
"WE'LL BE RIGHT BACK"

The Author on Merv Griffin with Charles Grodin. Private photo

DICK CLARK, MERV GRIFFIN, HOWARD SCHULTZ, BLAKE EDWARDS, JOAN RIVERS

It's another Thursday in Manhattan Beach. I've driven to Jennifer's office; on the way I've thought of a couple of people who might want to come forward in our class. But I wanted to leave space for someone on the flipside who wanted to speak with us – someone I may not know. I start the conversation, the same way.

Richard: Hello Class!

Jennifer: Hello.

Richard: I was thinking how when we work together we create something else when together, because I know my questions aren't the same as you normally get in your day to day practice – people come in to see you with their grief... the loss of a loved one, and I'm here saying things like "Hey, lets talk to Picasso."

I've only had two out of thousands of my sessions ask me questions like that... and it's only because they've read your books.

We're like Lewis and Clark here exploring the unexplored territory - not knowing what we're going to find and walking upriver and oh my god! There's Sitting Bull. (Who we spoke with a week earlier) By the way I wrote the curator and said "I heard that someone wants to sell Sitting Bull's pipe" – the curator wrote back and said "We took it out of circulation because we want to preserve it out of the light, but we have no intention of selling it..." Which is probably accurate, but perhaps Sitting Bull's comment will prevent them from selling it in the future...! Anyways, now that Sitting Bull is a member of our class, if he wants to talk to anybody here, he can. Luana anyone want to speak to us first?

Did you mention Dick Clark to anyone? Is he still here (alive)?

No. What does he want to say?

I just got shown a photograph of Dick Clark.

Who showed that to you?

Luana.

Okay Luana, bring him on in, we're open to you.

I know it's not the person you asked or requested to speak with (and I have not told her that yet either.)

Well, Dick Clark is somewhat related to the person I want to talk to... You see a pic of Dick Clark? What's it look like?

It's a photo in black and white of him.

In his era, doing American bandstand?

"Yes."

Luana are you giving Jennifer a genre?

"Yes." (She taps her nose, Luana's way of saying "correct you are sir.")

That you have a music person for us to speak with?

Like Elvis...

Are you being clever, instead of just showing Jennifer the face of who I wanted to speak with, does having Dick Clark's photo in her mind's eye help you or Jennifer to focus?

"It helps all of us."

What does that mean?

"It's supposed to help you and all of us to focus on him."

Okay, this person passed away a number of years ago, so people are talking about him and we've talked to this person before...

Are you talking about David Bowie?

(Note: I leave in most of the times we get the "wrong" name, so that people who are focused on that sort of thing, can get off the "afterlife bus" return the book for a refund, etc. In most cases she gets the name in between one and six tries.)

No, but he's welcome to join us. Someone said to me "You're out of time" last night. I thought to myself is that a warning? Or a pun? Because "You're out of time when you're outside of time."

Whenever you're in that matrix, you're outside of time.

It's a way of singing or writing a song I think – allowing yourself to be outside of time... I don't know who was singing to me. It seemed like a male voice. We're talking about someone from our class.. somebody who was of Tom Petty's era, who performed with Tom who is no longer on the planet.

I'm drawing a blank.

Don't worry about it.. park that thought. Luana, lets look around the room, who needs to speak up.

George Martin...

Okay, he's related to this fellow.

George Harrison.

Correcto-mundo. (ding!) Today's the day he died 17 years ago. He didn't want to show up to you?

He says, "He's busy."

That's fine. What's he busy doing? He doesn't have to talk to us.

"He's talking to other people in the class."

Two Georges. From the archive at Beatles.com

So George people are talking about you cause it's the anniversary of the day you checked off the planet. The new white album came out. You said George Martin... can we talk to George Martin?

Sure, I don't know who he is.

Luana do you know who that is? Can you bring him forward?

"Yes. Yeah."

Mr. Martin, can I ask you some questions, do you mind?

He says, "He got them this morning."

Okay, because I was talking to George Harrison this morning to prepare for our questions... So, Mr. Martin...

Did he die two years before George?

I don't know.. I think after... I know one of your sons.

He says "It was five years after."

(Note: That's correct. Ding! George Harrison died in 2001, George in 2006)

I met one of your sons in Cannes.

"Was he a little bit of an asshole."

He was funny... he's odd, a bit unusual. But you have two sons.

Do they have a big age range? And personality range?

I think so – yes. But the second son, show Jennifer what he's doing.

"Producing." I saw records flying.

Yes, correct, mixing records that George worked on. Show Jennifer who you worked with?

Freddie Mercury came through.

That is correct. (Ding!) He produced one of their records. But...

Did he produce "The Beatles?"

Yes, correct. (Ding!) He did.

He showed me that right away but I got confused.

Yes, but when Freddie Mercury jumps in what can you do? But tell her about your background George.

Does this go back to Dick Clark?

Let's see...

I just saw Johnny Carson as well.

George, you used to produce some comedy records with comedians, one of them I'm going to ask to come forward. Can you put him in Jennifer's mind? She'll know him as a movie star.

David Bowie came through again.

Sorry David, I don't mean to put you on a waiting list... I'm the encyclopedia of useless info. Some of the people you worked with included Peter Sellers.

I loved the Pink Panther.

The Beatles liked those early comedy records, George Harrison was a fan of those records that George Martin produced. Have you talked to Peter since you've been on the flipside?

Yes. He's hanging out with Robin Williams.

Okay, can we talk to Peter?

Yeah.

Who greeted you when you crossed over?

He says, "His animals." Um.. then it felt like a sister... but he's laughing. "It was his wife!" Jennifer laughs.

So your first wife?

Something like a second wife.

Was it her physically or higher self greeting you?

"It was not her higher self," he says. (Jennifer aside) I know nothing about his personal life.

(Note: Peter had four wives, the first three are alive, the fourth has died and is interred with him (he died in 1980.)

Peter, you were friends with our friend Hal Ashby who is also in class. Movie called "Being There." One of the best performances ever given in a film. What do you miss about being on the planet?

He misses the ocean... I asked "Can't you just go to the ocean?" He like "It's not the same. The salt."

The water on your feet or the salt air in your lungs?

He says "The feel of freedom." He's just breathing in.

What do you regret if anything?

He's so funny... he showed me like these big clown shoes that he couldn't fill... He says, "It was not taking enough risks."

Before we let George Martin go, I forgot to ask, who was there to greet you when you crossed over?

He says, "It was his mum."

What do you miss about being on the planet?

He says, "I miss the parties, the laughter, the perfume."

Do you regret anything?

I can almost smell a woman walking by with Chanel. It's interesting... um. He says "Not really; but if I did have one regret he wishes he spent more time with his kids."

You have two sons, Gregory and Giles – I met Gregory, and Giles is the one doing all the Beatle records ... a message for Gregory?

He showed me like him on a cliff hanging on really tight. "Hold on... never to give up on your dreams.

Gregory sounds beset by people complaining about him or his wife.

On Facebook?

Correct, (ding!) he was posting these things...

About Trump.

Correct. Anything you want me to tell Greg beside "hang on, follow your dreams?"

He's laughing. He says "Don't be a d*ck... and he needs to bring down his heart rate."

How does George appear to you? Hip, well dressed?

Old school.

What about your son Giles, what would you like me to tell Giles?

"Something about the third song."

You mean The White Album?

"Something about the 4th album," then he said "White Album."

He's saying there was a 4th cd? Is he talking about that?

"Yeah, it was a 3 cd set, he says, but there was a longer version on the 4th cd. It needs some undoing."

You mean it needs some work? I don't think they'll work on it.

He says, "I know that, I totally know that. You asked for specifics. It's the 4th album the 3rd song..." He says, "His son already knows what he's talking about as he considered it."

He considered it but he didn't do it?

"He cut it too short."

The third song on the 4th CD, you think he should revisit that?

"Yes."

Giles did the "Love" CD for the Vegas show and put that together.

(Jennifer aside) Wow.

A monumental piece of work... Giles is talking about doing another one.

Are they thinking of doing something like what "Mama Mia" did? A movie with all the songs?

Could be. There was a movie that did that "Across the universe" - it had all the Beatles songs...

(Jennifer) I never saw it.

They did a re-release recently... a Broadway musical director directed it.

He said, "I think she needed to be kicked out."

You didn't care for that?

He says, "Not at all. It was a piece of crap."

(Note: Nothing quite like a review from the Flipside – No offense to Julie Taymor. It's just one man's opinion, and for what it's worth, I enjoyed the film. Jennifer has never seen it and isn't her language anyway.)

What do you think Giles should work on?

He said "He just wanted to focus on this album..."

But any advice for him?

"He needs to be outside and focus on getting outside. Traveling."

John Lennon anything you want us to tell Yoko as we didn't ask before?

(Pause.) "She talks to him every day."

Okay, lets go back to George Harrison again – who was there to greet you when you crossed over? I know what you said before, but now I'm asking again just to see if it's the same answer. Who was there to greet you when you crossed over?

I see a horse. I see a woman on a horse.

That is exactly what you said before. Thanks. So what do you miss about being on the planet?

(Jennifer aside) That (horse image) makes sense to you?

Totally. What do you miss?

"Richard Branson."

You liked him?

(Note: I had no idea George Harrison and Richard Branson knew each other. Apparently they were good pals. https://www.virgin.com/richard-branson/my-memories-sir-george-martin)

"Not really" he said.

Ever the comic. Then why do you miss him?

He says, "He misses having fun with him."

Goofing around. Getting your weird sense of humor.

"Very weird," he said.

Do you think it's odd that I ask you questions like this?

He said, "No, I'm kind of used to it." (Jennifer aside:) You talked to him at night, he showed you laying down and talking to him.

Was that you singing to me last night? (I heard someone sing the words "Out of time.")

"Yeah. He's showing me your face while you're talking I always think that's weird..." hold on.

I'm out of time?

"Yes, because you're able to talk to them."

Or do you think I should write a song called "out of time?"

"Yes."

Did you like my new stab at a tune I put on YouTube "To be or not to be?"

"Yeah, it was kinda groovy," says John. Will (Shakespeare) just said "The title was fantastic." I forgot that it was already written.

"The title is fantastic?" (Obviously mocking me from the flipside. It's allowed) Well, your name is on it Will. (When I posted the song, I put Will's name for the lyrics). Sorry, Will there are no residuals.

He said "I'm going to sue you and show up at your door. Or in your dreams."

"Knock knock." "Who is it?" "It's some dude dressed in 16th century duds saying "What dreams may come? They've arrived."

He said (the song) "It's brilliant."

(Note: Okay, I'm flattered. I just got a flipside compliment from John and George and Will Shakespeare, or at least in my egocentric mind, I'm allowing that to be the case. They could have been totally mocking me, I have no clue. I know Jennifer has not heard the song – but I took "To be or not to be" and set it to music and put it online. Why not? Either way, NO ONE WILL EVER BELIEVE that these fellows are complimenting me, nor would I design to claim so (or put them on the album cover.) It's just flat out funny to me. I don't know how else to put it. Compliments from the flipside. Priceless.)

What do you want us to tell your pal Russ Titelman, George?

He just got a chair and sat down.... "Way back in the day." (Like I'm droning on.)

It was after your Beatle years that you knew our mutual friend.

Jennifer: Did he (Russ) do something with writing, editing of his music? A Producer?

Sweet picture of a sweet man by a good pal (Russ Titelman.) Russ and George by Massimo Milano. Used with permission, All Rights Reserved.

That's correct. (Ding!) Russ produced a number of Grammy winning records, including one of yours. He also is an excellent photographer and let me use one of you he took in our last book.

"He's one hell of a producer, one hell of a chap." (Jennifer said this in an English accent. Jennifer listens:) "Thank you," he said, "You have a nice accent."

Okay. So what about Russ Titelman, what do you want to tell him?

He showed me taking a volume knob and turning it up.

What does that mean?

(to George) Really? (to me) That's what he's doing.

His hearing isn't so good so maybe that's related to it?

Yes. (taps her nose) Tell him to "Turn up the volume..."

It's a pun, "turn up the volume Russ, it's also a way to hear George." What's a good way for Russ to reach out to you George, or for you to reach out to Russ?

"Through his guitar." I'm seeing him playing a guitar...

So while he plays guitar think of George?

I hate to ask this, did George play guitar?

Yes, it's funny because it shows how much you don't know about the folks we're talking to.

"He (Russ) should channel him (George.)"

Russ took some great pix you... one is in our book.

"That was really cool."

I know we asked your permission to use that pic...

"There are better ones he said, someone's arm is over somebody and looking off in the distance, 70's..."

There's one in the street.

Is there another one when they first met up in LA or saw the beach together?

A photo of you that Russ took at the beach?

He's just showing me the beach again.

(Note: I asked Russ about this, and he can't remember taking any pictures of George by the beach, but confirmed he has some things of George's.)

(To me) Did you know the woman on the horse?

No, I didn't. I knew your wife's sister - your sister in law, George.

When you pushed her away (meaning "ignored her") she said "Tell him to knock it off."

I think you said that it was your wife's higher self who greeted him on the horse.

Which wife died from cancer?

One of his earlier wives, its possible... his current wife, her sister went out with my brother. I didn't know George's wife Olivia, but I new her sister –

"She's still here on the planet."

Yes, correct. I'm sorry they didn't marry (as we've discussed before, when George said he remembered my brother hitting a home run during a softball game at his house.) I'm just trying to give Russ a message from you George. Anything other than "turn up the volume?"

Hang on. "He needs a haircut." Is he losing his hair? He's joking, showing me like trying to do the combover. Wow, he's a ballbuster George is.

So he's busting Russ' chops about his hair and his hearing? Russ has a fine assortment of cool hats. Maybe he's just being silly.

Hold on, "Something to do with a pick." It feels like there's a pick he has that could have been George's.

George may know this story – as I've mentioned it before, but I was there when Eric played that song for his son; "Tears in Heaven." I had the guitar pick from that session.

"And you lost the pick."

That's correct. (Ding!) Russ sent me another one with Eric's name on it.. are you referring to that pick?

"No."

So Russ has a George Harrison guitar pick?

Might be on the wall. "Framed."

You're saying use that pick to talk to George?

"No." Who has the artwork? You know about George's artwork?

I don't know – Russ has artwork of George's? He may have at one point. I know he had one of his statues of Buddha.

"Russ needs to listen and not to doubt, he's been trying to show him signs all the time.. 11:11 is appearing, like he's trying to contact him."

(Note: There's a chapter on the recurrence of "11:11" in a previous book where we talk about each 11 representing a hallway, and they have to slow down their frequency, we have to "speed up" ours so we can "meet at the decimals.")

Does Russ have a guitar or instrument of yours?

He says "He had or has 3 instruments of his." I'm seeing a harmonica.

I don't know – at one point he may have had his piano.. are you saying that if he takes the pick out, that he can communicate with you?

"He's just giving you a brash."

A brash?

"Yes, he's teasing you."

So I'm saying he should use the pick, open his mind and heart and play the guitar and he'll hear from you George is that right?

"Yes."

Thank you George, Mr. While-My-Guitar-Gently-Weeps. Perhaps George does listen in as well, I guess. Kind of like "Alexa" always listening. What did I hear this morning? Oh yeah, your song "All Things Must Pass..."

"Gas." (Jennifer makes a face, as if saying something to George.) Seriously?

All things must pass gas? Okay, that's a little sophomoric.

(Jennifer aside) It's not coming from me.

I heard that song this morning...

(Jennifer aside) That's a song?

Yes, "All Things Must Pass" - a beautiful song by George. Let me ask how you see him; is his hair long or short?

Shorter.

Can you see his face?

Yeah. Smiling.

So, can we talk to Peter Sellers? He's a friend of George Harrison's.

It's a Brit invasion! (laughs)

I know!

"Yes." He's here.

Hello Peter. Mike Myers is a huge fan of yours. Peter what do you want to tell Mike or your fans?

Laughs. He showed me the Pink Panther... (listens, seriously, then laughs.) Just now, I thought he was asking me something serious, and he said very seriously "Please watch the Pink Panther movies, so you'll prefer to go outside."

What do you miss about being on the planet?

"A lot of things, not just one thing." He says he misses the sense of smell.

Who do you hang out with on the flipside? Stanley Kubrick came by our class.

I keep getting Robin Williams.

Perfect, well, that's a logical person for you to hang out with. You guys make each other laugh?

"All the time – they try not to think (when together), because if they think they will make each other laugh."

There's a fellow that I met years ago, the man who directed The Pink Panther, he was a client of my pal and producer Jonathan Krane, who we've spoken with before, Luana knows him from "Group" (we spoke earlier to Sydney Pollack who reminded us that he was in group with Luana). I've met his daughter Jennifer a few times... whose mother is the first wife of this fellow. Luana can you put this fellow's name in Jennifer's mind?

Blake? I saw my son, Blake.

Correct. (Ding!) Blake Edwards. Directed Peter in The Pink Panther. Can we bring Blake Edwards in?

Sure... he's a tall guy. Was he a tall guy?

He can be tall over there. It's allowed. (People appear on the flipside, as they prefer to appear. Even though he might not have been tall here, that's how he's appearing to Jennifer) How does he look to you?

I see him with brown hair, looks like he's from the 70's; he has on wide collars and he looks really thin.

Hello Blake. Do you recognize the people in our class?

"All of them. It's a special club" he says.

I don't think you worked with Luana...

He says, "Not then, but since. Twice through you."

How did you cross over, who greeted you when you got there?

Felt like his heart gave out – from whatever complications he was having. Sometimes I'm shown that for other reason. I'm seeing that it was like was in his lungs, and he's correcting me; "No it was my heart." (For the record, he died from pneumonia according to wikipedia)

Who was there to greet you when you crossed over?

Why is Tom Petty coming in? (Listens) Okay. Got it. He says "A guy named Tom was there to greet him."

That's why you saw Tom? Close friend or a soul group member? (Often the case)

From his soul group. (Everyone has them, they're the people you normally incarnate with).

Did you know Tom in this lifetime?

He says, "Yes, in this lifetime," he did.

Were you surprised to see Tom waiting for you?

"Yeah." He was really happy.

What's Tom's last name?

Something like Tom's son... not Tomason ... I don't know.

Sounds like Tom's son?

Look for the Tom part...

(Note: Blake Edward's daughter told me it was likely Tom Waldman, who wrote a number of the Pink Panther scripts, an American who was a close friend who died 25 years before Blake. https://en.wikipedia.org/wiki/Tom_Waldman)

Was this someone you served in the military with?

Was he a pilot? He's showing me someone in a plane... a WWII plane.

What was Tom's occupation in this life? You guys worked together in England or Hollywood?

He says, "Everywhere."

Primarily – where was Tom living?

"England."

Did he work with you on your films?

He says, "You can say that."

(Note: If it was Tom Waldman, that is accurate.)

Blake, what do you miss about being on the planet?

He says, "The water and the breeze and the cold air." He doesn't miss the rain.

What do you regret if anything about your life here?

"More outings," he says. It was towards the end it felt he was like heartbroken.

Over not getting out?

"Over someone."

I'm sure Jennifer does not know who your second wife was, Blake, but if you could put her in Jennifer's mind so she does?

I'm seeing a singer... what was her name... I know that's not his wife... but she showed up. Liza Minelli.

Well, his wife was a singer, correct, also an actress but is mostly famous for appearing in other people's movies. Put a song in Jennifer's mind.

Jennifer smiles. (It's raining as we film this, she looks outside at the dark clouds over the ocean.) He says "The sun will come out tomorrow."

Okay, but what are songs where people sing them that are bigger than life?

Oh! (Seeing it) "The hills are alive!" He was trying to help me to get there. Julie Andrews. I know every song from that film.

She's still on the planet, she's still rocking, but is there anything you want me to tell your daughter Jennifer?

(Jennifer smiles) Did she have blue eyes? He said "Tell her I loved her from the moment I saw her blue eyes."

(Note: Jennifer, Blake's daughter, says her eyes were blue as a baby.)

So why'd you let her appear in Heidi?

Jennifer makes a face.

Don't judge it.

He's throwing it back at you. That's funny. He says he thought "She was mature enough." I don't know what he means.

Do you Jennifer know what I'm talking about?

(Jennifer aside) No!

So Blake, you let her appear in that movie that interrupted the Super Bowl... and she was chastised for decades, except now it's something people ask her to sign autographs about.

Was that in 67?

Could be... Anything you want us to pass along?

(Ding! Correct. Film was made in 1967, interrupted the Super Bowl in Nov. 1968)

He says, "Tell her she doesn't have to worry about cancer;" she's worried about cancer.

Stop worrying about cancer? Why?

He says, "She worries too much."

Does she have it?

He says, "No." She had a scare I think.

(Note: This is accurate)

She's got kids as well, anything you wanna tell your grandchildren, Gramps?

Jennifer makes a face.

If I can't poke fun at Blake I don't know who I can.

He says "Tell them to stop asking their mom for money." Laughs. He's kidding about that. That's a joke.

(Note: Blake Edwards was responsible for many laughs in his film career; all the Pink Panther films, Breakfast at Tiffany's and others.)

Who are you hanging out with on the flipside, Blake?

He showed me the brat pack.. he showed me Frank Sinatra.

You're hanging out with Frank? Do you hear him sing, or just watch him beat up mafia guys?

(Note: We interviewed Frank in another session, he was funny and sarcastic. I tend to be flippant when someone else mentions someone we spoke to in the past, just to see if that alters their answer.)

He says, "They play guitar together."

Did they play in life?

Blake played piano I think… Frank is learning (to play).

(Note: This is a common refrain so to speak. People can create "mental constructs" of instruments and then play them.)

So you're constructing the guitar to play it with each other? Is it 6 string guitar?

He says, "It's four."

That's a ukulele...

What's up with the ukuleles over there? (We've heard this before, Paul Allen said he's learning to play a ukulele.)

It's easier to play, three or four chords and you can sing almost any song. George Harrison used to hand them out like candy. Has Frank learned how to play the uke?

He says, "Yeah."

If I asked for a song to sing, what's the first thing that comes to mind?

Hold on. I can't understand this song.

Give me the lyrics. Frank, if you're going to sing a song with Blake what would you sing?

(Laughs. It's raining as we film this interview.) "The sun will come out tomorrow." At first it felt like "November Rain," but it was our peanut gallery throwing stuff out there.

Rich: Okay, so back to Dick Clark. So why did he show up?

Jennifer: "To say hi."

What do you want to say, Dick?

I asked him – he said "He got a lot of bands out there..."

He made many musical acts... later in life he told a couple of off color jokes and people filmed him doing that and people were like "oh my god! Dick Clark went blue!"

He's saying "I can't believe you're bringing this up."

I'm sorry, it was just in the zeitgeist.

(Note: It was a clip in Michael Moore's first film "Looking for Roger")

"I was better than soul train," he says.

I beg to disagree. Tell us who was there to greet you on the flipside?"

He says, "His cat. He had a little pushed up nose... an orange tabby."

Your cat?

He says, "Yes, it died 3 years before he did."

Was that surprising?

"Yeah."

Did you believe in an afterlife?

(Wags her hand) He says, "He wanted to."

Once your cat was there you realized you were somewhere else?

He says "It was a soft transition – like with Harry Dean." (Stanton – as reported in "Backstage Pass to the Flipside.")

I'm going on the radio Sunday night, what do you want me to tell people about you showing up in our class??

He says, "Tell them I didn't mean those off colored jokes and I'm sorry."

What else?

He says, "To keep making music, even though you might not think you're good at it, someone else might think you're great at... it... (Jennifer aside: he just showed me Kanye... "Another man's trash is another man's treasure.") "Don't give up based on what anybody thinks or tells you."

Does that apply to life or music?

He says, "Everything."

What do you miss about being on the planet?

He says, "He misses the interactions with people."

People you worked with or people in general?

He says, "Where you get to be surprised about answers... he misses... this is interesting – he's showing me how you don't really get to keep your thoughts on the other side. When thoughts come out, people see them. You can't hide your thoughts over there. Like he misses having a normal conversation, listening to someone else and being surprised what they're saying."

Like what we're doing. You were one of the consummate interviewers.

"Thank you."

And you integrated music on your show and rock and roll and the new years eve shows.. you were like the workingest man in show biz; what was that about?

"Not as many as Merv."

Why did you say that?

He showed me Merv Griffin. I did know Merv – he discovered my mentor, Lisa, and she showed me where Merv is buried.

Where is he buried?

In Westwood. Near Marilyn Monroe.

How far are you from Hefner, Merv?

"I was there before Hugh Hefner was there."

Okay, but how far are you from his tomb now?

He's showing me they're near each other.

Sorry Dick, I didn't mean to interrupt talking to you to talk to Merv.

(Jennifer laughs) You brought him in (meaning me)! This TV show filmed me leading to Marilyn's casket – it was the first time I'd ever been to that cemetery.

Very good, Marilyn we would love to talk to you, but right now we're talking to Merv. Who was there to greet you buddy?

(Listens) He was? What did he play in? (To me) You know the actor from Sanford and sons?

Redd Foxx was there?

No, the actor who played his son... I just saw the son's afro.

The guy who played Sanford's son? Him or someone who looked like him?

He says, "It was the guy who played the son on the show."

(Note: Desmond Wilson played the son and he's very much alive. However, as the research reports, "a third of our conscious energy is here, and two thirds is always back home." So Desmond's higher self could be what he's referring to. But he is accurate about this show: https://www.tvguide.com/tvshows/sanford-and-son/episode-1-season-5/earthquake-ii/100384/.)

How did you die Merv?

He's showing me his chest area...

Cancer?

"Yes."

(Note: It was cancer, prostate cancer, officially in 2007)

Desmond could still be alive... we don't know. What's he saying?

He's saying "It was the actor who played the son."

Was he a long time friend from this or other lifetimes?

He says, "Many lifetimes."

(Note: This is filmed and transcribed. I looked up Desmond and found that he had appeared on the Merv show.)

Show Jennifer where you met me, Merv, the first time.

On Merv's show? He's telling me "On his show."

Yes. (ding!)

I didn't know he had a show. He had a show too? I know Johnny Carson had a talk show.

I am so much older than you! Wow. That's fun for me that you don't know. Can you show Jennifer why you had me on your show?

He says, "You made everybody laugh about meeting someone."

Correct. (Ding!) I did. I made everyone laugh about meeting you – on your show, I said how I was at Musso and Franks and saw this superstar signing autographs like a "regular person" and you sarcastically said "Oh, yeah? Who was that superstar?" And I said "It was you." He totally changed after that moment. (to Jennifer) You sure you don't know this story?

(Jennifer aside) I never heard this story.

Hilarious. I was brought on your show by a mutual friend... Charles Grodin. Thank you Merv, we appreciate that.

Another story is that I met my mentor, medium Lisa Williams, through Merv. She teaches what Merv taught her, "you never say no, sign as many autographs as you can." He loved her.

So Merv – why all the shows?

"Because people are talented." He says "He could recognize talent even when they couldn't."

You had so many shows.

"Like 52 shows or something like that by the end."

I stopped by to say hello to you once at your hotel.

He's showing me your friend, the one who passed away and came to visit us... who died. The guy who made "Naked Dating."

Howard Schultz? Why?

(Listens) Oh. They're collaborating on how they're going to do it next.

Howard Schultz – Lighthearted Entertainment

Describe the process please. Had you met before in life?

I don't think so.

Who sought who out?

He says, "It's just lights, whoever you know, whatever you are... people tend to hang together."

(Note: People who have vibrated on a particular frequency here on the planet – artists, musicians... and television producers apparently.)

How did you bump into each other?

He says, "It was both; then he showed me like a map of everyone in the U.S., people in different places, and how they find each other."

Clumps of different energy frequencies that tend to hang out together in the afterlife, artists, musicians? Wow, cool. So Howard, weigh in if you want my friend; how are you guys working this out? You're talking about the next incarnation on the planet?

"Yes."

You mean like you're working out the story points of your next journey here; "You grow up in Wisconsin, I'll grow up in Iowa, we'll meet under the Hollywood sign?"

"Yeah." (Jennifer taps her nose, her visual for "exactly.")

Does anybody else weigh in on that? Guides, teachers? Anybody help you with those story beats?

They're laughing "Because there are like hundreds, or thousands behind them, helping them to plan." They're all laughing.

Does everyone have to agree on the process? I'm aware there's free will. How does that work?

"Oh, eventually they'll screw things up. But they (just) get a feel for it."

Merv, are you doing this with a lot of people or just Howard?

Yes, but Howard says "He wants to be a key player." They both want it – they both think they're more powerful together.

Okay, Lighthearted Entertainment was the name of Howard's company here... What kind of programming are you two going to work on?

(Jennifer smiles (to them) Say it again?) Humor... Peter Sellers just came back in.. Robin Williams... "Global climate change..." (Jennifer asks; What kind of...?) He's saying "Like documentaries dealing with global climate effects with either um... all of it, like the news about the planet and what's going on... and to find a way to have that information be more cohesive."

But you're saying with a comedic bent?

He says, "No, that's separate, the comedic shows will have humor because as they just think that's great medicine."

So you're planning like a network together?

"Ding ding ding."

What's the network going to be called?

"La-Google."

Very funny. Well, Howard's company was called Lighthearted because he was lighthearted. So you're stealing the talents of our class to build your new empire?

He says, "Yeah, that's pretty much it."

Will I have to sue you in the future?

He says, "Have at it."

That's funny. Well Howard is still helping people here; he's got a number of his shows still on the air, some of them bringing people together; his "Next" is still on MTV.

He says, "Everything I couldn't have" (in life, he seems to be joking.)

Well, during your past life regression which I filmed (for "Flipside) you did remember a lifetime with her when you both were Apache. So Merv... Mr. "we'll be right back." It's what he used to say before a commercial break.

Wasn't Johnny Carson the original talk show guy?

Steve Allen, then Jack Paar, who I met at Charles Grodin's house – very erudite guy...

They said they like the work that Letterman's doing now.

Johnny Carson was the only guy for a long time, then others tried to get in there, including Joan Rivers. They tried to do competitive stuff.

She says "It's about f*cking time you called me name! Sheesh!"

(I'm startled.) Joan you can speak up at anytime. Who was there to greet you?

She rolled her eyes. Oh my God, she's so funny. Jennifer laughs while listening. (to me) Did she have like three husbands?

(Note: It was two, her first was annulled in 1955)

She had the one who killed himself.

She said like "My three dead husbands greeted me... and my yummie little dogs." I think one of her dogs just died last year.

Charles Grodin told me about the time he went to dinner at your house, a formal setting with servants, and when the butler served him a plate, he pulled a tuna sandwich out of his pocket. He preferred to know what he was eating at dinner and where it came from.

She said "That was hilarious."

Joan, what do you miss about being on the planet?

"TV."

Being on it or watching it?

(Jennifer listens) She's talking about Trump, oy. "Every minute of the day all day."

I guess you guys are doing a lot of comedy up there about our current politics. I think it's Garry's Shandling's birthday today.

She says, "They've been drinking all day."

Do you guys get high when you drink?

(Jennifer aside) That's so interesting. She says, "You just take like a memory stick from one of your memories, drunk or stoned and you just recreate it."

You've created the whiskey, the sipping and then recreate the high from it?

She says, "You recreate it, yes."

Joan what do you miss, what are your regrets or both?

She says, "Her daughter."

Have you made up with Johnny Carson? Are you hanging out?

She says, "No."

Why not?

She says, "He's an asshole." She's just kidding.

What do you want to tell your friends family? "Surgery's not a good idea?" Didn't you die having something fixed?

She says, "Yes. I didn't die because of the surgery, but because I had a stupid surgeon."

You could have let your face drop.

She says, "Easy for you to say." (Jennifer listens, laughs) She's looking at Luana as if to say – "Is he really doing this right now? Giving me grief from the other side? Do I really have to explain to him?" (Jennifer waves her hand to slap me.) She's like "tell them (friends and fans) to have fun. Stop worrying about Trump. Have fun."

What does Garry Shandling want to tell us on his birthday?

He says, "He wants everyone to know... That the birthdays continue."

Because people are thinking of you?

He's saying "From the time that they're passed to their birthday, it's like starting over again with numbers. If you died a month ago, you're a month old on your birthday."

That's funny. That would make George Harrison 17 today. So people here celebrate you and you celebrate there on those days?

He says, "People are having fun (on the flipside)."

Anything you want to tell your fans on your birthday Garry?

He says, "Tell them to lighten up." Did he smoke pot?

He could have. I don't know.

He's saying "The CBD oil is good for you. Helps for a lot of things. Even depression."

*Well my favorite flipside quote is when Anthony Bourdain said that people should meditate more and I asked "Did you meditate?" and he replied "If I knew how to f*cking meditate, I'd still be there."*

True enough.

Anthony. How's things? We haven't heard from you.

He says, "Everyone should lighten up and f*cking have fun."

What about the last season of your show on CNN? Thoughts?

The last episode was just shown. He says "It sucked because it wasn't finished."

I saw an article about you complaining to your crew who forget to set up a shot, "proper planning prohibits piss poor performance." Which is fine, accurate – but I was thinking, you got your crew over to Hong Kong or wherever it was, you could have lightened up a bit.

He says, "But then that wouldn't be me." (Jennifer listens, by way of explanation) He was already feeling it… depressed.

A chef came out recently, Daniel Boulud and was quoted as saying you died from a broken heart and everyone related that to Asia Argento.

He says, "No."

What do you want to tell chef Daniel?

He says, "Tell him to stop projecting."

I don't know if he was saying Asia was involved, but online they started attacking her again… what do you want to tell people about that?

He says it wasn't why he killed himself.

You've told us that you weren't upset about her having other relationships.

He says, "It was allowed."

So that had nothing to do with you checking out, correct?

"Very little to do with it," he says.

Okay, that's a little different. So on a scale of 100, you're saying, your relationship with her had like 8% to do with your checking out, and 92%, you were already going to be checking out anyway.

"Yes, correct." He's saying she knew everything about what he did. It's not why he did it.

It was on reddit… I said I spoke to him last week – said I checked out because it was time to check out.

He says, "Yes."

So blaming Asia Argento would be like blaming the fact that you had a bathrobe? Wait a second, I'm writing dialog for you, can I get paid for this?

He's still telling you what to write... he's still telling you what to ask him.

So I can say "Blaming Asia is like blaming the bathrobe?" Or you want to rewrite that?

He says "Not the bathrobe, it's like.. it's like blaming the shoes he wore."

Bathrobe works though.

He says, "A little dramatic."

Talk to our friend Robin here. Everyone chastised Robin for his exit. If nobody knew what happened, he just died, or was hit by a bus, they'd be mourning – but because of the way he died, people get upset about that. I don't mean to bring up a sore point for y'all on the flipside. Anthony anyone you want to talk to?

He just showed me my friend who loves to cook, "Tell him to go easy on the pot cause that will make him depressed as well."

Anyone else need to come forward? Luana is that why you showed us Dick Clark?

"Yeah, to bring Merv in."

Dick did you know about our class? Have you heard about this class or have you been observing all along?

She says, "You're able to go in and download everything that's there (in previous sessions of our "class.")" So funny, it takes ten seconds over there to download everything all the classes.

Luana, this seemed like a convenient way – for you to show us who wanted to speak to us..

They had to show up (and a photo appeared of them) otherwise I wouldn't have known.

Luana holding up a photo is an effective way to bring that person forward? Was this helpful for Dick Clark?

"Yes, it helps them go to their people."

Just to clarify – someone joining our class – Dick Clark for example; he has his loved ones, family friends, and this kind of class exercise helps him to reach out to them?

"Yes."

Okay Dick, this will be a chapter in a book sometime in the future, what was your favorite band you introduced to America on "American bandstand?" Who were your favorite artists?

He showed me... Stevie Nicks, Fleetwood Mac, The Pointer Sisters, The Beatles, Elvis... (listens) "That shook up everybody," he said. He showed me something in black and white and then... he "likes Ryan Seacrest." He showed me Ryan looking up and said "Somehow he handles it all. He just deals with whatever, he has no life because of it."

Any tip you want to give him?

He says, "Don't make off color jokes." He laughed. "No. Ryan should give us tips."

Any last words?

I'm seeing Marie Osmond singing... "May tomorrow be a perfect day, may we find love and laughter along the way, may god keep you... until we meet again..."

(Note: One of the Osmond's signature tunes.)

Who put that in Jennifer's mind?

My dad. He showed me the time when he danced with Marie. She picked him out of a crowd – my dad carried that photo next to my mom's picture for the rest of his life. Let's ask my dad about the healing thing... when I asked him to give me a blessing.

Jim, you were a Mormon bishop; can you describe the blessing?

He showed me this pink energy coming in (from above her head)

What do you call it when you're asking for it?

Just "the prayer." (Jennifer aside; my side was so painful (from a pulled muscle). And you have to believe it in order for it to work.

He says, "I asked that Jennifer get healed and has no more pain or discomfort and that she will be able to resume her workouts, her daily activities, and not endure any pain."

Do you mentally think of the spot on her body that is in pain?

He says, "Yes." He can see where it's hurt; like I (Jennifer) can see people who are hurt… he's seeing it.

Are you generating the light or does it come from somewhere else and you're directing it?

He says, "It's from the universal source – like from God or Buddha."

Is that a physical place where that light is coming from?

He says, "Yes."

Where is that place? Deep space?

"It's from everywhere."

Except you didn't think of it as light, but as "God?"

He says, "Right. (It's) Love that has no name."

Wow, that's powerful. Were you in Luana's class?

"Yes, but not until now… until we (me, him and Jennifer) started working together. Not when I was here (still on the planet.)"

Thank you class, and see you next week!

CHAPTER THIRTEEN
"POPPY"

George Bush Senior from National Archives

GEORGE BUSH SR, JOHN MCCAIN, NANCY

Rich: I have a question regarding my appearance on Coast to Coast. Can we ask our group if I reported anything incorrectly?

Jennifer: They're showing me Abraham Lincoln. (Whom we had a conversation with previously) Did you say anything about him on the show?

No.

Ah, I see, I know what they're doing, that's their way of introducing me to President Bush.

Does he want to talk to us?

Later.

Later in our conversation today?

I don't know. I'm not going to look.

Okay, later.

Interesting. First they showed me President Lincoln, then showed me President Bush. (Aside) You know, I bought him soda once, they came through on this train and two FBI agents asked me if I would buy soda for him while the train was stopped. So I drove

them to a store and we bought him the soda. It was funny. I said "We're here to buy soda for the president."

Funny. How was he traveling?

He was on a train.

Okay, well, this is unusual. I know that Jennifer hasn't heard about you and that train since then and how you're connected today – but for her to remember that train ride is important... as it was named after you – the train is engine 4141...

(Jennifer shrugs) He says "Okay."

George, tell her about that train. Luana help him.

They all are helping him; he's just busy.

Busy?

(Jennifer smiles.) He says, "Well, not really."

I know you're busy dealing with a lot of mourning to go through. But can you spare two minutes for us?

He says "The clock is ticking."

That's funny. George tell her about the train, the train that you were on when she bought you soda, what's going on with that train today?

"It's being dressed up. He showed me the rails being brought up, and its all dressed up with the flag..."

He's taking a ride on that train; he's back on the train.

(Jennifer aside) Is that the same train?

It is... they named the engine after him for that whistle stop tour when he was running for President the second time, and they're taking him home to Texas in it. Now his body is on that train taking that trip. It's being dressed up as we speak.

Okay, he was describing himself as "Going away – leaving – he was trying to say that he was going on this ride I guess..." but he can't put a coffin in my head.

That's why I'm here, to translate that image. I asked him this morning to talk to us.

(Jennifer aside) Really? That's so crazy!

I did. I had this odd thought about him, and asked him to attend today. So George; who greeted you when you crossed over?

He showed me Marilyn Monroe... but he's kidding. "Barbara of course. Yeah. Barbara helped him; she couldn't wait."

What was that experience like? How did she look? Young or old?

"Like she did when they first got married." He said he was "Late getting there," I don't know if he meant late getting to the wedding, or getting back to her over there.

She crossed over, what, six months ago?

Um... did he have a child who passed away? I don't know.

Yes. Was that child there to greet him?

"Yes."

Show the child to Jennifer? How old is this child?

"It's his daughter. I'm getting the number four or forty eight... would she be forty eight now?"

I don't know. Could be. She was three when she passed.

Did she die from something in her heart or lungs? I felt her lungs not working.

(Note: This is correct; she died from leukemia)

How does she look now?

"Beautiful. She looks older; she looks playful, she has this curly winky-dink hair. It feels like auburn."

(Note: "Winky-dink not a word I've heard Jennifer use, but can imagine George using.)

Can you give Jennifer your name?

"Barbara's middle name" I think.

Could be. I think it was a family name.

I'm sorry, I'm just overwhelmed by talking to President Bush.

(Note: Pauline "Robin" Bush was named after Barbara's mother Pauline Robinson. Robinson was Barbara's middle name. At the age of 3, Robin was diagnosed with leukemia, her parents flew her to New York City for treatment but she died two months before her fourth birthday." Wikipedia)

George, I had the impression you appeared in my apt two nights ago.

"That's true;" he did.

You were with a friend, who brought you forward?

"John McCain."

Wow. (Ding!) Yes, that's the impression I had. Thank you.

He showed me John right away when you said he stopped by.

John, step in for a second, we're not going to take time away from talking to George; how did that work? Why did you bring him over to my place?

(After a pause) "Because we were going to talk to him two days later – prepping him."

So what does George need to tell us? I know he can speak for himself, but what is it you think he needs to tell us?

(Jennifer aside) I'm asking him something for myself... I saw something this morning, his grandson speak at a funeral, I wanted to tell him I was so grateful for him for being our president, all the missions he went on, I was telling him that.

Okay. But John why did you bring him to my place; to prep him? But you feel like this is important to participate in?

He's showing me his son, George – "W."

Let's ask some questions about W. He spoke eloquently at your funeral, what would you like to tell him?

Jennifer listens. (Jennifer aside) "Why?" (Jennifer shrugs) He says "to hang his hat." I don't know what that means.

Do you mean he needs to relax?

I'll share with you the feelings I had when he said that – to "hang his hat" means ... to not think that he can do something about what's going on in Washington now. Like "hang up your hat" – it's twofold, meaning "don't worry about it" because "he can't change it."

And everything's going to work out okay?

"Yes." John McCain is saying I remind him of... "I look like his daughter."

If you squint. (Just kidding) You kind of do look like his daughter Meghan McCain. So John, you've had the benefit of being off planet longer, this is new for him; everything is going to work out, no matter what's going on in Washington, D.C.?

Why is he showing me a fighter pilot or fighter pilots?

That was my next question. Who are these people? Are you seeing fighter pilots or just him?

He's showing me they were going to take a ride in a fighter plane... Was it a past thing? Like in the war?

Yes, George, show her what happened. The dramatic incident during your service.

(Jennifer gasps) Oh, he got shot down.

There were two guys with you. Can you bring those guys forward?

(Looks in the distance) "They were so young."

They were. Can you bring them forward, these two friends of yours? Have you talked to them over there?

"Yeah." They're laughing. (Jennifer pauses) They both died?

Yes.

I'm hearing they both died, and George lived, "he had terrible survivor's guilt," he said. "It was horrific for him and that's why he threw himself into his work."

So what was it like seeing these guys for the first time when you crossed over?

"Bittersweet." He said to them; "thank you." I felt like they gave up their lives for him.

Did you feel responsible for what happened?

"All of it. They shouldn't have gone out that day. They had a short time period (of rest), they shouldn't have gone out... there were winds." He's showing me. I don't know what this means.

I think it relates to wind conditions when they flew during this mission in World War II. George, do you want to bring the two fellows forward, to say hello to our class?

One of them had this curly hair... He looks like that actor; Rock Hudson? Did they make a movie about this?

I don't think so.

(Note: Except for the Angelina Jolie film, "Undaunted" none come to mind about this famous event: https://en.wikipedia.org/wiki/Chichijima_incident)

Can you guys share your names with Jennifer? They might give you a picture of someone we know associated with their first names.

He showed me Bill (Paxton)

Yes, that's right, his name was William White.

The second is Drew?

Delaney. John Delaney. So you two guys have been watching your friend live this unusual life – what do you think about that? Were you helping him? He said he thought about you all the time.

"Yes. They helped him a lot. They were very protective of him. Made sure he was safe." (Jennifer aside) Did we talk to Nancy Reagan?

I don't think so – what does Nancy want to say?

(Laughs) "Stop doing drugs."

Very funny. I know you were into astrology Nancy.

"She had her own psychic," she said... she said "I should be the first one to (be asked to) come."

Well, you'll have to get in line, ma'am, Luana's in charge of the guest list. Tell us, George what do you miss about being on the planet?

"The grandkids." (Jennifer laughs) I said "Do you miss Trump?" and he started laughing. He doesn't want to answer that question.

Well, I think it's best we don't ask about him, (As the answers often devolve into a "when will this end?") George, what else do you miss about being on the planet?

Was he a pilot?

Yes, he was.

"Well he gets to fly now."

At your funeral the minister described your last day on the planet, and when he mentioned James Baker massaged your feet, Baker burst into sobs. Do you have any message for your old pal "Bake?"

"Tell him to never give up." I wish I knew who you're referring to...

James spoke at his funeral; said the last thing he did was rub his feet.

He says "He felt it, but he was looking down at him from above." Baker is very religious correct?

Don't know. Baker was one of those responsible for ensuring that Al Gore didn't win the Presidency, but let me ask, what do you regret about your lifetime if anything?

He says "I don't have any regrets, but I'm going to miss seeing my family in this dimension as they grow up."

Well, I beg to differ; you will be able to see them as they grow up.

"Be quiet," he says. "This is all new to him," he says.

Okay. So let's ask our fellow classmate Anthony Bourdain – he's our go-to interviewer – do you have any questions for him, Anthony?

That's so weird - he kept coming in as you were speaking.

Well, I asked him to come along as well this morning. See if he wants to ask George a question.

He was jumping in and I was saying to him, "I'm sorry Anthony I didn't mean to overlook you." How did you know that?

He knows I'm not as good an interviewer as he is and he wants to ask George H. W. Bush a question! Go ahead Anthony.

(Listens) He's asking him about... Did George ever go to prison? Was he ever in...?

Don't judge it. What did Anthony ask him?

It has to do with being in a prison or a prisoner of war. He asked "How about the treatment...?" Either Anthony knew something about the country involved or the type of people that were involved in the prison.

Let's unpack this. You're saying Anthony's question is "What was it like in prison?" Is he talking about a war time prison? Is he asking about WWII, a Japanese prison which held guys that George was in the serviced with? Or are you talking about the first gulf war where people were put into Iraqi prisons. what war are you talking about?

"Japanese."

(Note: I didn't realize until I looked up this incident that it was George's friends who were reportedly eaten while being prisoners of war in the "Chichijima incident." I was aware that some pilots had crashed and been tortured on this island, but didn't know that George knew them. Anthony obviously does.
(https://en.wikipedia.org/wiki/Chichijima_incident.) I consider this "new information" as I did not know that George knew these soldiers, but Anthony did – and by asking him that question showed it was not a topic that could have come from me or Jennifer).

Anthony please clarify; are you asking about friends of George who served, when George went down some of the people that he knew went to those Japanese prisoner of war camps?

"Yes."

George, so did you know some of those guys who were tortured and eaten by the Japanese on that nearby island?

"Yes!" (Jennifer aside: "They ate them?")

Well, let's ask them – we can. The story goes that in this Japanese pow camp, they ate the livers of some of the soldiers as some kind of ritual humiliation... is that accurate? Was that a punishment? Or because they were starving? Is that one of those apocryphal stories people tell about prison camps?

She pauses. (Softly) It was because they didn't have enough food for themselves. (Jennifer makes a face; "Ew.")

I'm sorry to interrupt, but I think this is pretty unusual. We have Anthony Bourdain asking George Bush a question and you're trying to unpack it for us. Further, it's a question about food - an eating question – something you Jennifer had never heard of, don't know anything about where people were eaten in a pow camp in world war II by the Japanese. How weird is that? Anthony what was George's answer to that question?

"They did what they had to do."

Anything else you want to ask our buddy here, Anthony? Hopefully not a liver question.

"I didn't like food; He loved the places."

I quoted Anthony on Coast to Coast radio telling us "I didn't miss the food, but I miss the people." Was that close enough?

"Yes."

I hate to rewrite people talking from the flipside.

"Good job," he said.

So George, are you comfortable now with what we're doing?

Jennifer waves her hand "comme si comme ca" (little bit).

Well it's new for you, but I don't know if anyone else is going to be doing this with you, asking questions, because they're all just going to be talking about your accolades or failures.

He says "It is, it just takes some time getting used to it – getting used to the energy." He showed me getting used to the energy (waves her hand) and he said "He has lots of help."

So what are your favorite sox, dude?

White. (Jennifer makes a face. What kind of question is that?)

He used to wear funny socks; had socks with his pal Bill Clinton's face on them. Anything you want to tell our mutual pal Bill Clinton as a friend?

(Note: I met the future President when he was still governor, a friend of his produced one of my films, and he would call the set of "Limit Up" often.)

He said "They're building an alliance..." He's telling me that Bill is still really upset that Hillary didn't win, and it's like - it's eating him up inside.

I'm sorry to hear that.

"He needs to let it play out."

What about your kids?

"He says he had 5."

(Note: Six with the adopted Robin)

Anything you want to tell them?

"It feels like they adopted a couple two."

I don't think physically but he took care of other kids, like his friend Jim Baker's after his wife died young of cancer. Is that what you mean?

"Yes."

Why'd you move to Odessa Texas? What was that about?

"A higher elevation."

And trying to get away from the east coast?

"Yes. Washington."

Didn't do you any good, they pulled you back in. So we have a lot of people in this room who served in DC, including JFK, his son JFK Jr, I forgot to mention that on Coast to Coast, that he's hanging out with his son... anything you want to tell W, Jeb, anyone else?

Wow. He showed me a hurricane coming up, and more destruction on the Florida coast. Looks like a hurricane in January... when is hurricane season?

January. Not much you can do.

"Hunker down. Board everything up."

Anything else you want to tell us?

I told him that it was nice meeting him again, I asked him what soda I got him? I always thought it was grape, and he said it was Sprite.

Tell us about your daughter Robin – I know you were looking forward to seeing her, what was that like getting to see her?

He showed me Barbara standing next to her and he knew it was her even though she was much older in spirit, and there were just tears of joy and love, "So much love," he said.

Well what are you guys doing now? Are you busy with people doing memorials or hanging out with your family, connecting to them?

He says "Whoever calls him up, he's there." He says "It's a different kind of busy, he feels very... um... honored that so many people have thought of him this way."

Many people have giving you some tributes... it's interesting because the tributes are about your ability to bring people together and be their better selves as opposed to what policy you defended or did not. What do you ascribe that quality to...

"Patience."

Where did that come from?

"Barbara." She was his rock; she endured a lot.

Barbara, anything you want to say?

She says she likes your books – both her and Nancy too.

Laughs. Which books do you like the best?

She showed me "Hacking the afterlife. The last part."

Oh, okay, the Jesus part. That's funny. Maybe I can put that on the book cover, and endorsement from Barbara Bush and Nancy Reagan on the flipside.

(Laughs.) Hmm.

Let me ask; how do you access books over there? Does the whole think come to you altogether at once?

(Jennifer pauses.) I'm asking them how long it takes... She says "It kind of comes to you all at once. You can touch it and you access all the information inside..."

Anything you want to pass along Bar? – People knew you as a tough partner, smart, loyal and fun.

She says she "ruled it with an iron fist."

Who greeted you?

"Her daughter and then her mother..."

Who was there to greet you Robin, when you crossed over?

"A puppy dog."

Was this part of an agreement you had, to leave early and if so what was the lesson you wanted to learn or impart?

"Yes, there was a lesson." Wow. I get shown Barbara; it was for Barbara to learn how to... say it again? to live with pain because there was going to be future pain that would come and she had to be strong for it.. and I asked "Did everything happen for a reason?" and she said "No, but it did."

That's what we learned in our research.

Robin said "She should still be here!" and then Bill Paxton spoke up and said "And I should still be there too!"

True, Billy, but from the life perspective, the arc of your many lives, it seems to fit, doesn't it?

He says, "Yes."

I understand both Billy and Robin should still be here, but in terms of how her death taught lessons to Barbara and George, then that was a sacrifice she made and they made as well because before they came to the planet they were aware that she wasn't going to be there long.. is that correct Barbara?

"Yes." She thought about Robin the most, yes.

I know her father said that he thought about Robin all the time, but also his friends from the service, John and William. Say, did you guys ever show up in the White House or appear in dreams to him, how did that work?

He said, "He felt them at the ceremonies, when he was honoring other soldiers; he felt them. They were very important."

My father and grandfather were in the Navy in WWII. My dad was the same grade as you in the navy, Lt. JG, and my grandfather was a commander. Do you navy people hang out?

"Yes." Amelia Earhart is showing up...

Amelia; George – George meet the most famous pilot who ever lived.

It's a frequency they shared, even pilots get to hang out with each other on the other side. I have to wrap this up, I have an appointment.

Okay, thanks class. I appreciate you all coming through and everyone helping out with this interview.

George says "You're welcome."

CHAPTER FOURTEEN
FAR HORIZONS

On the way to meet Jennifer, I looked out at the ocean near Manhattan Beach and saw a ship, and said "Christopher Columbus!" as an idea to interview someone I could not have known, and no one I'm aware of would know him. Also Joan of Arc. I ask the questions, then look up the information to see how accurate they are.

JOAN OF ARC CHRISTOPHER COLUMBUS

Rich: Hi class, we're back in the Fishbar. We know you like it here. All right Luana, I asked for a couple of people to come today or do you want to bring your own people. Luana you're in charge of the class, behind the velvet rope...

Jennifer: I asked her if she's turned anyone away and she said "Yes."

Really. Who have you turned away?

She says, "Prince."

You mean because it was not his turn?

She said "Yes." (Listens) She wants to discuss you and her friend Fred.

(Note: That would be Fred Roos, film producer and old friend of Luana's. The way that Jennifer unpacks this information, since she doesn't know what Fred Roos looks like, is that she sees a photo of her own husband, "Fred" and then translates that into telling me that Luana wants to speak about my friend with the same name.)

Well, Luana, your script is with Fred, even though we haven't had any traction with it.

(Jennifer aside) You know I don't know about that stuff. Hold on. She showed me Jack Nicholson. Interesting.

Well that's what the film is about – her acting class with Jack, Robert Towne, Sally Kellerman, Dennis Hopper...Why refer to Fred?

She's showing me you in my mind's eye.

You want me to reach out to Fred? And say what?

He's going through something, tell him "Hey Luana says you're going through something and to chill out – everything is going to be okay."

Okay. Fred had a question about buying his old friend Harry Dean's home; we told him it was going to open a can of worms, that it was a good idea to open up the can of worms but Fred wouldn't get the house.

And did he?

I don't know.

She says "It took a lot of effort to get that (message) to you."

Duly noted. Anyone else want to speak to us?

I got someone playing the guitar... Prince wants to "Compliment what you did last week, last Tuesday or the week before." Something to do with music.

I was recording some tunes. You liked something I played the other day? That's flattering, but what's your advice on how to fix it?

"The ending." He says you end on a low note?

I did. I have a few clams in there. I can fix them.

(Jennifer aside) That's so funny.

I did ask for some other people to come through, I asked for a woman, historical figure, and a young girl.

Oh, Joan of Arc.

Jules Sebastian Lepage Jean D'arc. Metropolitan Museum.

Damn, you're good. Is she allowed in?

She's here. She likes my boots.

(Note: As you can tell, I don't judge what is said here. For the record, Jennifer is wearing high black boots, and prior to the session, driving to it, I said aloud the names of the people I wanted to chat with. Joan of Arc was one of them.)

What does Joan look like?

She has long hair, she's older... reddish brown hair; about 36.

Can I ask her some direct questions? Have you incarnated since?

She's showing me she was a nun in a subsequent life. She came back to live in Rome (in a subsequent lifetime.)

I read your diaries, I'm familiar with the inquisition. Can I ask you questions about that experience? Who were the voices talking to you? Higher self or somebody else?

It's like .. it felt like it was God but (also) like the Archangel Michael.

Was it Michael?

She says, "Yes."

Did you see him or just hear him?

She says, "She heard him; she didn't see him. She felt him."

Is this the same fellow, the same Michael that is associated with Jennifer's soul group or council?

She says, "Yes."

The same Michael we've been talking to in the past?

"Yes."

(Note: Under deep hypnosis, Jennifer spoke about her council and some of the avatars she was seeing on it. In follow up conversations (not under hypnosis) "the Archangel Michael" shows up. For Joan of Arc to say "Well, my guide is the Archangel Michael" isn't a claim that has hierarchy attached to it – Jennifer is reporting what she's hearing. She had no prior memory of knowing this prior to saying it – and later she says "I wonder if that's why I always dream about riding on horses" – with regard to it.

To date, I've met on various councils, council members "with wings" who claim to be the Archangels "Raphael" "Uriel" "Gabriel" "Ariel." (They're not coming from Jennifer – they're reported in "Architecture of the Afterlife." Only Michael has ever "appeared" during our conversations.)

So it was the Archangel Michael who showed up to speak to you in the woods?

She showed me those old pictures of people with halos, she showed me a halo on him.

Well, you've met him by this point, correct Jean? Is he a member of your council?

She also showed me a white wolf too – and she did say, "Yes, put that aside," then she showed me a white wolf. To answer your question, she says "Yes, he's part of her council."

Let's unpack this statement a bit. Are you saying that you saw a physical white wolf when you were in the woods? Did this visual precipitate your visions or hearing from the flipside?

"Yes."

Was it a real wolf or something put in your vision by someone else?

"It was put in her vision to make her feel protected."

Why did these occurrences happen, why did your guide Michael allow these events to happen ("hearing the voice of God to tell her to lead the French army") that would alter your life so dramatically? Were you eating rye bread (the mold on rye "ergot" makes LSD) and hallucinating (as we've heard other monks claim) or did something else precipitate this event?

(Jennifer listens, nods.) She says "It was berries."

(Note: I checked into this, there are some berries, (like elderberries) that cause hallucinations.)

So you were eating some berries, which allowed you to see your guide or this wolf?

She says, "It allowed me to relax to see it. Yeah."

And your guide said that you were going to go and lead France into battle?

She says, "Yes."

When you got to the palace and the king disguised himself to test your abilities; how did you recognize him?

She said, "By his nose, and his aura." She could see his aura.

(Note: The her to the throne (Charles VII) had heard of this young girl who was telling people she could speak to God, who was sent to lead

the French army into battle against the English. As a test, at their first meeting, the Prince had someone else dress up as him, and she identified the Dauphin immediately.
http://www.maidofheaven.com/joanofarc_charlesvii_firstmeet.asp)

So you were a medium weren't you? Gifted with sight?

She says, "Yes."

Had you anticipated what was going to happen to you in terms of your death?

She says, "No."

(Only known drawing of Jean D'Arc. National Archives, Paris.)

Jean D'Arc... I don't want to ask you to go through the death memory, but past it – once you're leaving your body who was there to greet you on the other side?

She said, "Jesus."

Dude gets around. Appropriate person to be there and for us to talk to. How did he look to you? Was he wearing a robe, sandals? How did he look?

She showed me him on the cross.

Because she had gone through the same sacrifice?

She said, "And then she saw his hands. And saw that he came off the cross." (Jennifer aside:) It was like how I see people when I see their whole journey.

At one point did you realize you were on the flipside?

She said, "From the first time that she felt pain, she was showing me she left her body..."

Your consciousness lifted out of you body?

She says, "Yeah."

What do you miss about the planet?

She says, "The horses."

Anything you regret about that life that you wish you'd done differently?

She says "She wishes she would have loved, to have had a love."

The guy who arrested you, an English soldier, his name was John Talbot.

She forgave him.

Are you aware of the connection between John Talbot and me?

Yes, I'm being shown ancestor.

My wife's ancestor.

I was shown "ancestor..."

(To Jennifer) What's the visual for ancestor?

(Jennifer aside:) I see a tree branching up and up and up.

(Note: My wife's family goes back to the Mayflower (Resolved White) on one side of her family, and back to the Earl of Shrewsbury on the other. John Talbot was given a royal title and property partially for his service to the crown and arresting Joan of Arc. Jennifer doesn't know this obscure detail, but Jean does.)

Well Jean, who are you hanging out with on the flipside? What are you doing?

She said "She's racing horses." She showed me Michael Jackson... she said she's learning how to sing. It's really funny, I'm getting this visual like it's "Night at the Museum." All these historical figures. There are a lot of historical women aren't there? It's funny I picked her.

I did ask her to come. Her name is Jean right? Jean D'Arc?

"Yes" she said.

Do you miss anything about that era or time or is that a distant echo now?

She laughs. "I miss the berries." (Pause) Then she showed me her feet in the ground, at first she said nothing, but then she said "My feet on the ground.... Also the candle lit rooms."

I'd like to mention your main accuser, the priest responsible for your death, when they put you on trial, where they asked you to argue for your life.

She's showing me there was something wrong with his eye... a creepy eye. Something happened later... like a spider bit him – he died a horrific death.

Was that your doing?

She says, "That was his doing."

So when he crossed over...

She said, "I kicked him back."

Was that startling for you?

She says, "No, they had an understanding. Like he was a father in the past life."

It's interesting you've been a symbol of resistance for centuries; what do you think about that?

"Not anymore" she says. "Now I'm going to be a diva." She showed me being a singer.

Next time around she's going to be a singer like Whitney Houston? When are you coming back or are you back?

She showed me Nancy Pelosi which is funny. She's an attorney - the justice thing will never go away from her; it feels like she's a lawyer.. or..

So a diva lawyer? That will be sometime in the future? Soon?

Part of her is already here. She's showing me Pelosi. Maybe a politician or someone like that. Or part Pelosi.

She's got a little Jean Dark in there. That's funny.

That's why she won't let it go – she (Pelosi) needs to retire.

What percentage of you is in Nancy? Five percent? Ten?

She said "Five." (Jennifer aside) Why'd you say five?

I don't know, just throwing out numbers. What do you want to tell your friends and fans? Are you accessible? Can people reach out to you?

(Jennifer aside) I didn't know it was her, every time I'm go into my own past life I think I'm on a horse, fighting in danger, in a castle... I may be accessing a memory of hers through my council members.

Can people access you?

She says, "Students and writers."

When you appear, how do you help them? In dreams?

"With their writing," she says. "With their power and their strength."

Are you a fan of any of the movies made about you?

"No." She shakes her head, no.

There was a black and white one... a Danish classic silent film.

She says, "They got the gist of it, but not everything."

Can we table this conversation and talk to Jesus for a moment? Ask him what he was doing showing up for Jean D'Arc. Are you available?

He says, "He thinks I'll cry if I see him."

He showed up with a friend of yours the other day. I asked him to change out of his traditional garb and put on a tee shirt and loafers so we didn't get hung up in how he looked. He did.

It was a specific outfit for her. He's saying "Don't get hung up on the shoe thing. Because I can walk on water."

That's funny.

He showed me something interesting; it's not that he walked on water, it's that everyone made people think he did.

So people just imagined that? Or did they make that story up?

What's it called when you're brainwashed? They brainwashed everyone.

He did that?

He says, "No. Whoever wrote the bible." (Jennifer listens:) "They were taking berries when they wrote that he walked on the water."

Very funny. They needed miracles to go with his story; Jesus couldn't just be a dude who helped people he had to pull off magic.

(Jennifer laughs) Water to wine! If only I could do that...

Luana? Anyone else? I did invite somebody else.

Did you invite someone on a boat?

Go with it.

Somebody at sea, almost like a cartoon. Who's the guy who took all the animals?

Noah. Does he want to come forward? It's not who I asked for, but Luana; you're in charge.

No, something else with the sea, this person feels like a captain of the sea. Feels like 500 years ago.

Okay, that's accurate. I asked for him – he's a famous guy.

Columbus?

(Ding!) Yes. I want to ask him some specific questions.

He said "He had a bad rap."

There was a priest who kept a diary aboard your ship.

He said "They were getting killed."

Okay, but you killed a lot of natives for gold; is that correct?

He says, "Yes."

*Those diaries paint you as a nasty motherf&*er.*

He says, "Yes, in the British Virgin Isles."

Let me ask this; were you Spanish? Italian?

It feels like both. Both Spanish and Italian. His grandmother was from... (listens.) Genoa. But his father was Spanish.

Were you a pirate? Before you went to Queen Isabella or were you just a sailor?

He says, "I was a survivor."

Good answer. But were you a merchant sailor from Italy?

He says "I was a pirate." He had a different name for it.

A black marketeer? Let's put it this way you were someone who operated outside the law – black market?

(Note: There are reports that Columbus was a black market trader (called a "pirate" in those days) who created a different persona to gain access to funds from the Queen of Spain. Documents show that he never wrote in Italian, and had no clear family ties to Italy, outside of the claim he was from Genoa. "In Italian he is known as Cristoforo Colombo, which was long thought to be his birth name, and in Spanish as Cristóbal Colón. ... There is even a theory that he adopted the name from a pirate named Colombo." Brittanica.com)

He says, "He was told that he should."

You never wrote in Italian; did you speak Italian? Did you know how?

Something he did not like about Italians; I don't know what it is.

Are you more Spanish than Italian?

He says, "Spanish. Close to France."

Eastern or Western side? Isabella is from the west.

He says, "He was from the east."

You were pretending to be Italian to gain favor from the Queen, but you were Spaniards?

He says, "His crew were Spaniards."

Did you pretend to be Italian to get money from Isabella?

He says, "Yes. He was in love with her, it was romantic."

Were they lovers? Or was it a crush?

There's something with that... "Too many clothes," he said.

(Note: That's an odd but accurate detail. Furtive love, or the kind where people are intimate outside of the prying eyes of courts and courtiers – required a lot of clothing in those days. Took hours to get dressed – not easy to get undressed. Still, an odd thing to hear.)

Where were you trying to get to?

He says, "India."

What were you trying to get? Were you after gold? Silver?

He says, "Silk. He showed me like drapes."

(Note: "A bolt of silk was worth its weight in gold" according to a biography of Henry Hudson, where the author pointed out "Pirates had granted Portuguese vessels safe passage, but not other Europeans. So they began to look for an alternate route to India." Henry Hudson: New World Voyager by Henry Butts. 2009. Dundurn Publishers. Pg 20.)

When you arrived, did you think you'd arrived in India?

He says, "It didn't make sense; it was too short of a trip."

(Note: Interesting observation. We tend to think of two months at sea as a long time, apparently he was assuming it would have been a lot longer.)

How was he dressed on the journey? How does he appear to you?

He says, "He was big – a foot taller than most, he was wide, no beard..." (Jennifer aside:) Where'd did he come across the Indians?

I think it was Hispaniola. Though that might have been the third trip.

(Note: He landed on San Salvador first, he had four trips to the Caribbean islands, never setting foot on North America. The third was to Hispaniola.)

He says, "It's the third one.. (trip) with the Indians. He showed me a native chief; big, tall - Like a foot taller and he had on that huge headdress."

Did you kidnap him; take him back to Europe or leave him alone?

He says, "Children. He took his children." (Jennifer aside:) Asshole...

The report I've read was that your men cut off people's hands for their gold – correct me if I'm wrong.

He's showing me everything was peaceful until they showed up.

You tortured people to find out where they got their gold. Because no one spoke the language.

He says, "He used kids for that."

(Note: In the People's History of the United States, Howard Zinn published a diary of a priest aboard the ships ((Bartolome de las Casas) who reported the wholesale slaughter and torture of these natives and their enslavement. His diary doesn't include Columbus using natives to hurt other natives; but that's what is being said.)

When you died who was there to greet you?

He says, "His mother."

The Italian mom?

He said, "Yes."

Was she from Genoa?

He says, "No, a city on the southeast of Genoa... Genoa."

What do you miss about being on the planet?

"The seas" he said.

What do you regret about your journey here? If anything?

He says he regrets not understanding language.

Or other humans?

(Jennifer nods.) He says, "I know."

Have you had a lifetime since then where you suffered?

(Jennifer listens) He says, "I was a prisoner of war."

What century was that in?

He showed me as a Japanese prisoner of war.

In World War II? Okay, that must have been difficult. Do you think it's appropriate they have a holiday after you? Or should it be something else?

He said, "Indigenous people day."

Duly noted. Well, you're a man of compassion now; I'd think you'd want the record corrected.

He says, "Yes."

Luana; I said his name, and Jennifer picked him out of the blue, I was looking at the ocean as I drove to your office.

(Jennifer aside:) And I saw a pirate at first.

Well, apparently he was one. Chris, anything you want us to tell people on your behalf?

He says, "To be free." He just showed me chains, then Martin Luther King. "To protect the environment and don't do the dumb stuff like raping and pillaging."

Okay, raping and pillaging not so good. Do you want people to know you weren't Italian?

He says, "It doesn't matter." (Jennifer aside) The thing is I don't know if his dad *was* his dad.

Well he does now. Let's ask him. Your father was Spanish but nobody knew it. You were raised by your Italian mother?

He says, "It was like a half split. He spent his life mostly at sea... half the time on land... the rest of the time at sea." He was like "A son of the sea."

Okay, very good; we find out that Cristoforo Columbo is actually a Columbus..

He might be French. A quarter is what it feels like.

Not Basque?

Feels like half Basque. (Jennifer aside) What is Basque?

It's a culture on the border between Spain and France – no longer a country, but the language and people predate Spain.

He says, "He wanted to be part of that." I got Portugal in the beginning...

Well it's close to Portugal. Your were Basque or considered yourself Basque?

He says, "No. I'm a Spaniard."

Okay, he's a Spaniard. But his father was not from Spain. Was your father French?

That's what I'm feeling – there must be something obviously... something with that.

When he presented himself to Queen Isabella, it was as an Italian?

He says, "He lied about that; she wouldn't have trusted him..."

Did you seduce her to give you a ship or just flirt with her?

He says, "She seduced him."

Queen Isabella. The Prado Museum

So you did have sex with her?

He says, "That's a little personal."

(Note: I wrote about this on my blog, and a friend who happens to be a hypnotherapist reached out to me and asked if I was aware that she had a past life memory as Isabella. I'm familiar with this hypnotherapist's work, she's top drawer, so if that's what she recalled, I don't doubt it for a moment. Looking at this portrait is also kind of eerie as it does indeed look like her. (Although carrying looks into different lifetimes isn't reported. Just noting it)

Dude, it's only been 400 years.

(Jennifer nods). I think he did.

Chris either you did or you didn't – it's not something that's an if, and, or but – did you do the nasty with Queen Isabella?

He says "Yes." And then "That's enough."

Okay, thanks everyone, thanks class, thanks Chris and thank you Luana.

An unusual chapter, I know. Rewriting history. But if I may observe, at the end of this roller coaster of history, from Joan of Arc, to Michael the Archangel, to Jesus, to Christopher Columbus... the point of this chapter is not to claim *"**We were talking to dead celebrities!**"*

I would also offer that what people are telling Jennifer (who is telling me, or more specifically, my camera) is based on her abilities to decipher visuals, sounds or sensations. When I ask the correct question – she often taps her nose as if to say "You got it" or "that's correct." I know Jennifer pretty well, her story, her journey, from a variety or perspectives.

So prior to this session, I had done some research into Columbus, research into Joan of Arc – not specifically for this meeting, but I had read the Howard Zinn "History of the United States" as well as the recounting of what happened to Joan on her last days, her trial, and what she said during it.

As noted, the information from Christopher Columbus was relative to what I had heard about him from Howard Zinn's "History" and the priest who recounted the horrors inflicted on the natives. However, the priest was also recalling his journey through the perspective of a man of peace, and we don't know that much about Christopher other than what's been written about him.

It's also why I asked if he'd suffered in another lifetime as he had made people suffer - and according to this account; he claims he did. Jennifer and I are at a stage in our conversations that she allows a visual to come forward and reports what she sees without judging it. According to previous sessions, people on the flipside can't "lie" or "make up" stories - as they won't come through. However, any medium will admit that they may mistranslate or get a message wrong. In this case, pretty specific answer to my pointed question.

To hear that he and Isabella may have had a liaison sounds fanciful – but again, Jennifer is only reporting. It's not her desire to create something that didn't occur – and perhaps that's how Chris remembered it. If we asked Isabella, she may recall it in a completely different fashion. People recounting their story from the flipside isn't that different than asking people about what they did 20 years ago. They may misremember, conflate, mix up dates and stories – but in general, from their new perspective they've had time to go over what happened "back then."

It's as mind bending to me typing up this chapter as it is for anyone to read it. I apologize for the bending of minds, but again, I'm just the reporter here. Perhaps in 20 years, someone will come along with another method of accessing the holographic memories of events, or in 100 years, we'll be able to access these events without mediums.

We'll see, won't we?

CHAPTER FIFTEEN
"HE'S VERY AWARE"

FDR: National Archives

FDR PENNY MARSHALL CLARENCE, DANNY

Rich: Hi class. All right Luana, I called for some people.

Jennifer: She showed me President Washington...

It's related. George... what was that thing you said about Jefferson; you called him an asshole?

He said, "Because he was."

Okay, what President have I asked to show up today?

(Note: She guesses a couple of different ones, then says:)

He's smoking a cigar, in a wheelchair.

Franklin. Correct. (Ding!)

Yes, he's here. I wanted to apologize to him; he showed up but I blocked him because I didn't know his name.

F.D.R?

He tried to show me that.

Do you need the wheelchair anymore?

He says "No." He showed me Eleanor.

Can I ask you some questions directly?

He said "No." Hang on, I've never had anyone say "no" before. He says, "You have to be very articulate with the questions."

And specific?

I know you always are, so I'm not sure why he's saying that.

It's okay. It's the first time he's had a conversation with me.

When you were little however, there's something that you.. that brought your attention to him. I'm not sure what it was, he's showing me you at age 3 in Knickerbockers. Something you saw on TV and was focused on him... might have had to do with Germany... and your wonder.

(Note: I did wear Knickerbockers for a family portrait at age 3. I don't remember wearing them at any other time, but I have a photograph of me in them.)

In shorts circa 1959. Photo by dad with mom.

Franklin, I want you to be aware of the folks in our class, the number of Presidents that have spoken before you.

He says "He's very aware." He's calling it "All the President's men."

Who was there to greet you when you crossed over?

I asked him, "Was it Eleanor?" and he said "No." (Jennifer makes a face.) It feels like a cousin, it felt like he was in a war, or something with war.

A cousin who died in the first World War?

He says, "Yes. They didn't know any better."

What do you mean?

I don't know... He didn't know the ramifications of war.

(Note: There is one cousin of FDR's who died in World War I. Quentin Roosevelt (November 19, 1897 – July 14, 1918) was the youngest son of President Theodore Roosevelt and First Lady Edith Roosevelt. Inspired by his father and siblings, he joined the United States Army Air Service where he became a pursuit pilot during World War I. He was killed in aerial combat over France on Bastille Day (July 14), 1918.)

In terms of your crossing over, was that a shock to see your cousin? Surprise you?

He's showing me that he couldn't breathe. I don't know if that's how he died...

(Note: FDR died from an Intracerebral hemorrhage (ICH), also known as cerebral bleed. Symptoms can include headache, one-sided weakness, vomiting, seizures, decreased level of consciousness, and neck stiffness. (Wikipedia)

He says "It felt like it was a dream."

What do you miss about being in the planet?

He showed me Marilyn Monroe.

Women?

"Yes." Amelia Earhart is rolling her eyes now.

Well, let's bring Amelia into this conversation. Franklin you asked Amelia to do something for you what was it?

He's laughing. (Jennifer makes a face.) He said "I asked her to not get caught. It was very simple."

Was she a member of your kitchen cabinet, the way you had Julia Child spying for you?

He says "Amelia had a lot of help, but she was the person who had to make the flight."

She had a couple of aerial surveillance cameras aboard the Electra, according to the research.

He says, "Yes." He's showing me them floating on the water.

Are you familiar with what happened to her after that?

He says, "Yes. They were really tired, like so tired."

They were flying into a rainstorm and had to divert their flight?

He says, "Into territory they couldn't get out of."

When did you hear she had been captured?

He says "Years, like a lot later."

How did you come about to hear that? After her plane was found on Saipan?

"Yes." He says "He sent search parties for her."

I'm aware that he did.

He said "I did everything I could..." He's telling me "They were playing a game, like the war, like the Japanese on Saipan... they were playing a game."

But were you also playing a high stakes game?

He said "Yes."

I'm aware that there exists a secret cable that was decoded a month after her arrest that indicated she had been arrested by the Japanese. Were you aware of that?

He says, "No, he wasn't."

So that means ONI...

"Kept it from him; didn't tell him."

Why didn't they tell you?

He said, "They didn't think she was worth it."

When did you discover what happened? When her plane was found?

Hold on. (Jennifer makes a face. Jennifer aside). That's fucked up. What it feels like is... that the ONI didn't want her to be a certain... like it was men versus women.

(Note: My grandfather, Edward Hayes was assistant secretary of the Navy at that point in time, was serving under Secretary Frank Knox, and was with Chester Nimitz when her plane was found on Saipan. I'm familiar with the Office of Naval Intelligence, but I know that Jennifer is not. This is fairly revelatory – you must remember that Jennifer doesn't know the details of what happened between FDR and Amelia Earhart, but I do. And he's not only confirming what I've known, but how he felt about it at the time.)

Let me clarify – correct me if I'm wrong; Churchill discovered the enigma code, but couldn't reveal it as it would show the Germans they'd broken the code – he allowed innocent British citizens to die, to protect their secret. Is that what happened her?

He says, "Yes." (Jennifer taps her nose for "they're saying that's accurate.")

So it was an awful choice, but it was war. After you passed away did you agree with the way things happened when Truman dropped the atomic bombs on Japan?

He showed me my uncle. (Jennifer's uncle). He worked on the physics of the atomic bombs, was one of the last to die of cancer, they were on the boat that carried it. My dad went on a camping trip with him, accidentally broke his hip, but within 20 minutes, secret service people were there.

Let me ask my grandfather – because we can, and I've spoken to him before – did he see those coded messages that they have found Amelia's plane at Aslito airfield in July of 1944?

He says, "Yes. He panicked over it;" – it felt like he panicked.

How did he respond? Did he pass that up the chain of command?

He says, "What could he do? He got tired of all these people lying about it..."

Well, Franklin, you sent your friend on this trip; and she paid for it. Any comment on that?

He said, "It was the same scenario we've seen before," and he says "He had to think of the greater good." (Jennifer smiles). His wife just swatted him over that comment.

(Note: I know how controversial this sounds. If one has read "Hacking the Afterlife" there is a report from Amelia Earhart about her flight and how she felt being incarcerated and dying of dysentery on Saipan. But this is the first time I've been able to ask questions from another person involved. In this case, despite my pointed comments about him being partially responsible for Amelia's journey, it's interesting to note that he's putting this saga in the context of "history" as to the choices for the "greater good." Hard to argue with someone on the flipside about the "greater good.")

Franklin, what do you miss about being here?

He says, "Tactile things." He's showing me like blisters on his hand from rolling around in the wheelchair. He showed me his hand, the pain he felt... (Jennifer aside) I asked "But didn't people take you everywhere?" He says "Those callouses and blisters are from not being able to get to places." He says he actually misses that, and misses being in charge of that.

Oddly enough I've seen footage of this – in the archival newsreels of the 1930's at UCLA. The cameras were rolling when he was dragged out of car, propped up in front of a podium, one aide stood behind him and held him up before the news reels footage began. After the speech he dropped to the floor and used his hands to crawl across the stage, where he was dragged into the window of a car and off he went. It was amazing that wasn't public knowledge.

(Jennifer aside) I had no idea.

I appreciate you talking to us Mr. President. What would you like to tell people about your journey now, if anything?

He just showed me Peter Pan, like flying. He says "Go and stop procrastinating. Go and stop procrastinating. Live your life as if it was the last you'll ever have."

Was the polio something you chose knowing how much you would influence humans overall?

He says, "Yes." He said "Someone kind of pushed him into it."

Anything else? This is your chance.

He says "Eleanor knew way more than I did. We had different paths."

Eleanor Roosevelt, Library of Congress

Eleanor, if I may ask; who was there to greet you after you crossed over?

I'm seeing a cat. Feels like a lot of them.

And what do you miss about being on the planet?

She says "Perfume. The smells."

Anyone's perfume in particular?

She says that you know.

(Note: When Eleanor's secretary published the secret letters, it was revealed that she had a long love relationship with her.)

You miss the thing the perfume is often attached to. After your cats who was there to greet you? Who were you surprised to see?

She says, "Her mother.... and her father."

You and Franklin had an agreed upon relationship.

She says "Iron clad."

What do you regret about your journey if anything?

She said, "Not knowing the easiest way to make publications known to more people... Instead of through a simple typewriter."

You wish you were able to do reach more people directly? You regret to you didn't have a computer instead of typing?

"Yes." Jennifer taps her nose.

You were a prolific writer... beloved by many.

"All," she says. "And Amelia." She brought in Amelia.

Let's talk about Amelia; what was your relationship?

She said, "Love. She was in love with her. Not lover." She said "She said was a lot older, but it was a love more than what people know. She said she was the one who spearheaded the search for her, she said she was the one who wanted to find her, loved her, she went into depression after they couldn't find her."

What did Amelia teach you?

She taught her something playful. Like golf... or was it music?

Driving. But I've heard that Amelia also took you for a...

She said, "Flight."

A night flight around DC.

She says, "It was more of a photo op."

When you crossed over, how long did it take you to find Amelia Earhart?

She said, "Two seconds."

What was that like?

She said to her "I never stopped looking for you."

And you found her.

"Yes."

What does Amelia look like to you?

She says, "Like she was when she was a kid – it's her energy; she's showing me super excited."

I'm asking about the perception of people over there seeing their loved ones.

She says, "It's the energy that was the least complicated."

How does Amelia see you?

"As someone who took care of the President" she said.

Franklin, anything else you want to tell us?

"He says he's sorry about Amelia. And then he shows me the country.. not broken, but rattled and split. You know how you have a piece of wood with splinters, he's showing me a piece of wood that's riddled with splinters and says "That's our country now.""

True, but when you became President the country was rattled.

"But it was nothing like this." (Jennifer laughs). He says "I didn't lie about it."

Don't you feel like we're going to solve this?

"He's not predicting, (but) he's showing me defenses being down, what (the current administration) is doing, how we're becoming more of a target."

But this will sort itself out, won't it?

He said, "Yes. It's designed to ruffle everyone's feathers to get people accountable for everything."

Okay thank you folks.

Clarence Clemons Photo Wikipedia

Luana, who else did I invite today?

Is the other person you want to talk to in music?

Correct. Luana put in Jennifer's mind who the lead singer of the band was that we're asking to come...

I'm seeing an African American... played in a rock band that is famous... I don't think I know his name... (Ding!)

But you might recognize the instrument he played or the lead singer of his band. Let's focus on something else. I met this guy, can you put the place in Jennifer's mind?

Felt like a party or a bar. (Ding!)

Yes. It was a party in the Hamptons. I was at some event, saw him by himself and I spoke to him.

I'm getting a saxophone. (Ding!)

That's correct. He played with...

Springsteen. That guy! I don't know his name. (Ding!)

Clarence.

He was trying to tell me Terrence.

Clarence and I have someone in common, someone he used to date, lived with her years ago, a close friend of mine.

I'm getting Shaka... Shaka Khan?

Yes and no. Her name is Chacon. (Ding!) Lilia Chacon. That's correct. Clarence who was there to greet you when you crossed over?

He said, "His grandmother."

Your nephew is touring, how's he doing?

He said "Way better."

(Note: Clarence Clemmons nephew is playing saxophone with the E Street Band these days.)

Clarence anything you want to say to Bruce?

He says, "Tell him to slow down."

All right.

He says, "There's something going on with Bruce's ear... left ear... maybe he's losing hearing in it." (Sometimes she sees an ear because they're saying "I'm talking but he's not listening). He says, "He needs to write more."

Okay. Clarence can you bring your friend Danny Federici forward?

(Note: Danny Federici sat in with my band in LA one night, he was pals with our guitarist Bob Bernstein. I could not believe how he made my keyboard sound – he was amazing. He died after Clarence, was also a member of the E Street Band.)

Danny Federici, who sat in with my band. YouTube

Danny, who was there to greet you?

He said, "Clarence."

How'd that happen?

He said, "He saw him before he left."

(Note: This often means, "in the hospital." Like the way dementia patients begin to see their family or loved ones who've crossed over, it's because the filters on their brain have shut down.)

When you got over to the other side... what happened?

He says "I saw Clarence as younger... and Clarence said "We have to get going because we have to play." We went on stage and we played but I didn't have my instrument!

He was missing a keyboard?

It was from a memory that they both had.

Where was the show the memory came from?

He says "Chicago."

You're on stage, and are you standing in the place you normally stood?

He said, "No; there wasn't room for me."

Did you see the rest of the guys?

"Yes."

Did anyone recognize you?

"No."

What song were you singing?

(Jennifer aside) That one where the girl was pulled onto the stage.

"Dancing in the Dark?"

He said "Yes."

At what point did you realize you were in the afterlife?

He said when "He was put in the audience, was looking up and there was no one at the keyboards..." something weird like that...

Bruce mentions it in his show where he had a dream his dad was in the audience and he saw himself standing next to his dad and looking at himself singing on stage.

That's what he was showing me ... I know it wasn't him...

So Danny, you see the band playing without you... then what?

They all laugh, then Clarence and the rest of they all come to him and laugh and say "Dude, we're never going to let anyone else play your keyboards!"

Do you remember playing my keyboard?

He said, "Yes, twice."

(Note: My band "Imminent Disaster" played the House of Blues twice, and our guitar player Boo Bernstein has played with many session players. One day he asked if Danny could "sit in" and I was in awe of his playing. I forgot that he did two sets with us until he mentioned it.)

Wow. That's correct.

He says he "changed everything... (all the controls)."

You did! Anything you want to tell Bruce?

I was shown Eric Clapton, they need to do something together.

All right Luana, we have one more person to chat with, someone who just crossed over, someone we both knew. Luana put this woman in Jennifer's mind. G'head.

Penny Marshall; private photo.

Jennifer: (laughs). It doesn't work like that!

Luana, this morning on the way here, I said this person's name and her brother's name. She went to the flipside a few days ago.

(Listens) Laverne! Didn't I say early on about Fonzarelli earlier?

Yes, you did. (reference to Ron Howard) So Penny... "Carol Penny." Luana, is Penny available to talk to us?

She just cleared her throat.

Luana we need your help facilitating this... is Penny available to speak with us?

"It's Laverne."

Yes, but Penny Marshall is her real name... you remember her as Laverne, I'm familiar with her as a film director as well. I also want to see if your brother is available, I met him as well.

She just said "That was a long time ago."

Yes, that's correct, I first met him on the set of your show.

She said, "31 years ago."

That's possible.. (It was actually 36 years ago. "Star Peepers" episode of Laverne & Shirley)

(Jennifer aside) I don't know.

Rich: It's probably correct.

(Jennifer) Were you playing a waiter or driver or something?

Kind of; I was a guy who delivered a...

"Pizza." She showed me the pizza car arriving.

Right. I was a pizza delivery guy who showed up almost missing a few slices of pizza. I would arrive with pizza, wiping crumbs from my face and a story about where the missing piece was. Harry Dean Stanton was in that show. Enough about me. Penny who was there to greet you when you crossed over?

She showed me Shirley (Cindy Williams) at first.. is she still here?

Yes, she is, but it's possible for our higher selves to greet our loved ones... was it Shirley?

(Note: As we've heard before, sometimes, the "higher version" of ourselves is there to greet us on our "return." People under deep hypnosis claim that we only bring "about a third" of our conscious energy to any lifetime, and that two thirds, or some larger portion is always "back home" (their words.) I knew Penny from her pal Charles Grodin, had spent a number of fun evenings with her.)

Hold on, she's showing me a dog.

What kind of dog? A white dog, black dog?

Hold on, she's just getting used to it. (This form of communication). She's showing me a goldfish. All of her pets. (Jennifer laughs.)

The reason I ask that question to everyone we interview is because I can't know the answer to that, only you can, Penny. So your pets greeted you, who was the first person?

Garry Shandling?

(Note: We talked to Garry earlier, that is a chapter in book two of "Backstage Pass.")

Could be, maybe that was for you to recognize her brother who is also a Garry; a film director.

She says, "Her brother was the first person to greet her, but he was not the person she saw at first, its like she (had the impression she) was dreaming.." She saw her animals.. because her animals were her "soft cross over."

(Note: In the chapter about Harry Dean Stanton in "Backstage Pass to the Flipside" he told us that Luana had appeared in his hospital room first to greet him, and then when he crossed over he was in a car with her driving to the Monterey Pop Festival in 1967 with Fred Roos driving. Later, I spoke to Fred and confirmed the details.) Harry thought he had "fallen into a dream." Then at some point, he realized it wasn't a dream, that it was the "afterlife" and he said that Luana had given him "a soft landing.")

Her animals gave her a soft landing?

It's so interesting to me (what I'm seeing) and then later in a field, she sees her brother and then other people started appearing.

How did your brother Garry look to you? young or old?

"Young" she said.

What do you miss about being on the planet if anything?

Jennifer laughs.

What? Don't judge it.

(Jennifer aside) I didn't realize how funny she is. She says "I miss going to the bathroom." It's just cute, the way she said it (imitates Penny) *"I miss going to the bathroom!"*

Okay, that's a very Penny thing to say. Penny, can you show Jennifer where you and I performed together?

In a park?

No.

(Note: I leave in the mistakes, so people can see the process. Sometimes she sees things and misinterprets them, sometimes I misinterpret what she's saying. It was not in a park, so for those who want to get off the "is there an afterlife?" bus, they can.)

Was it on the boat? She showed me that earlier, she was showing me the boat. She showed me that scene.

Oh, you did say that. (earlier in our conversation). Yes, the Bob Shaye millennium cruise Penny and I were both on... (she the invited guest, me the piano player) I always do this when transcribing, I see that you said something five minutes earlier... Yes, it was on the boat – Penny, you had me play some music for you.

The Sound of Music? Show tunes?

It was "Hello Dolly" which you did as a parody for Bob and Eva Shaye. I played and she sang and danced for them. Hilarious.

(Jennifer aside) I would not know any of that. Was Penny good friends with the girl from Star Wars that we've talked to before? (In "Backstage Pass" I know that we have never talked about Penny, or that Carrie and Penny were friends, and it's not something Jennifer knew or could have known.)

Carrie Fisher? Yes. What makes you say that?

Because she showed up too. Carrie and her were talking.

Okay, so, Carrie? When did you show up to meet Penny?

She said, "As soon as she got off her ass."

What does that mean?

She said, "As soon as she knew she was in the afterlife."

What did you say to her?

She says, "Come on! whoo!"

How does Penny look to you?

She said, "About 40." (aside) Were they in love?

They were very close friends.

She says, "They loved, loved, loved each other."

(Note: Recently I heard that one day they got tired of their annual parties. I don't know the cause of their breakup, but on the flipside; everyone becomes pals again.)

I was at one of their infamous birthday parties, up at Gore Vidal's house. Charles Grodin brought me and Luana. Their parties were pretty notorious. Penny, what does Carrie look like to you?

Like Princess Leia.

C'mon. Really?

She showed me the buns. She did!

But that's how you're (Jennifer) seeing her, correct?

Yeah, she shows me in her 30's.

All right. So what are you girls up to?

She showed me like Thelma and Louise. Thelma and Louise in a hot rod. Cruising around.

Where do you guys cruise to? What have you shown Penny so far Carrie? I know it's only been a couple of days, but then time is different over there.

She says, "We're just catching up, so much to catch up on, but it happens FAST, so you just go (makes a gesture) and you know everything." (Jennifer aside) Wow!

Carrie, who was there to greet you? (We asked this earlier, but I like to repeat the questions.)

She says, "My mom Debbie... well her mom died two days later, but it was like the same time, by the time she came around."

What do you guys miss? Penny what do you miss?

She says "Smoking."

(Note: Big smoker. Ding!)

Carrie what do you miss?

She said, "Flowers.... and being awake." Jennifer aside: She's laughing.

Anything you want to mention to your pal Mark Hamill, Carrie? In a sentence?

"Get a divorce."

C'mon. I don't know him well enough to say that to him on his Instagram page... "Mark, I spoke to Carrie and she told me to tell you.." Something else please.

(Jennifer aside) I've never had someone so funny talking from over there... ask again?

What does Carrie want to say to Mark, Luke Skywalker that I can put on his Instagram page?

She said "Get a job." (listens) "Don't come up here."

How about "Don't be in a hurry to come here. You've got a long way to go?"

"Yes." And "You're not welcome up here..." ...that was tongue in cheek.

Penny anything you want me to tell Rob Reiner - your ex husband?

They're all laughing. "Is he out of the MeToo movement?" That's a joke. Wait, who's Rob Reiner?

I'll tell you in a minute. The joke is "thank god there is no #metoo movement on the flipside?"

She said, "Yes. God's a little prejudiced."

Funny. By the way, Luana was an acting coach for one of his girlfriends: Patrice from "Personal Best."

(Makes a face, in a Penny voice) "And how's that going for him?"

Touche' – He's doing fine now; he's happily married I think. Okay Penny, how about your brother Garry? Can we talk to him?

Penny and her brother Garry. Private photo.

"Yes." (He's here.)

Hi Garry. How are you?

He says, "Good."

How does he look to you, Jennifer?

Very crisp, very put together.

Let's ask Garry; who was there to greet you when you crossed over?

He says, "His grandfather."

What do you miss about being on the planet, if anything?

Hmm. He's showing me like a hot cup of coffee (gestures in her hands) and the wind, like if you go to an outdoor restaurant.

And who are you hanging out with over there?

"Marilyn."

Oh, that's funny – everyone wants to hang out with Marilyn when they get over there, very funny. (We've heard a number of people claim to be hanging out with her). There's someone from our class that you're probably hanging out with Garry. Who would that be?

I don't want to say... but Robin Williams. I'm seeing Robin.

Well, he discovered Robin. Cast Robin in his show.

I didn't know that.

He created... Mork and Mindy.

(Jennifer gasps) I didn't know that!

Now that Jennifer appreciates you Garry, anything you want to tell your friends and fans?

"Nanu nanu." (Listens) Hold on. "Keep dreaming. Keep getting those things growing." (listens) He says "It's not really like dreaming, just dream it. You're (actually) creating."

He helped start many careers.

He said "six."

Ha. Okay, I remember talking to you after a show at the Falcon theater – with Sally Kellerman.

Sally keeps coming up.

Okay, it was the time when you introduced me to Lorna Luft.

I don't know who that is.

Liza Minelli's sister. She thought I was Richard Martini the Broadway producer in NY. I said "You may have forgotten how he looks but I would never forget you, my dear." Garry laughed.

That's funny.

What about Sally?

She really misses her husband.

(Note: We had a conversation with Sally's husband Jonathan Krane and their daughter Hanna, who both checked off the planet a month apart.)

Penny anything you want to say to Cindy Williams?

I feel like they were estranged.

They were, but reconciled.

I'm getting that she's saying "Let it go. It was so stupid," she says. She says "People got in the way, managers, producers..."

Yeah, there was a lawsuit, they didn't talk for years. So Penny, you're apologizing to Cindy?

She says, "Not really."

Laughter. Okay, anything for your daughter Tracy?

(Listens, smiles). She says, "Tell her to stop crying! Tell her to stop worrying about trying to organize this huge event.." (aside;) Penny is calling it her "wake." Something about letting go of balloons.

Sending balloons up after the memorial? (Something we did at Jonathan Krane's memorial – a stack of white balloons.)

Feels as if her daughter is really heart-broken that her mom's gone. Like a little girl. Penny wants her to know that she's okay.

How can I help?

She says, "With the music."

(Note: As mentioned, Penny and I performed a musical onboard this Bob Shaye yacht, so I think she's referring to that.)

No, I mean what can I say to her that will be helpful?

I just got you playing the guitar.

That's not going to happen.

I know, but they don't waste thoughts. She says, "Tell her to stop fretting over the details of whatever it is," (she's saying) like "Everything's going to work out." Everything's going to work out and "If they can't make it they can't make it." And she should invite "Shirley" But she seems to be kidding about that.

Hang on, you're saying it should be more of a musical party than a wake? More of a party than a funeral? To celebrate her life?

She said, "Abso-f*cking-lutely."

Okay, I can pass that along.

"I had a great life," she said.

You had a great life... And you're having a great afterlife?

She said, "Starting to."

You're welcome. Take a look at our class, I bet half of your old boyfriends are in there.

"All of them." (she laughs)

Okay, thanks everyone, thanks Carrie, thanks Penny, thanks Garry, thanks Luana. You're always welcome in our class, and we'll catch y'all on the flipside.

******

Another example of a wild conversation that I film and then transcribe. A bit all over the map, but then if I edited the transcripts they would seem like I was making them up. Hard to make up something as chaotic and insane as this. I know, I've tried.

Onward and upward!

CHAPTER SIXTEEN
"WE GOT THIS"

Senator McCain. National Archives

ALAN RICKMAN MICK GOUGH JOHN MCCAIN

Another session at the Fishbar. I came armed with a couple of names I was looking to speak with. My questions are in italics, Jennifer's replies are in bold.

Rich: Hi class, all right Luana, who have we invited to class today?

Jennifer: Princess Diana?

No, but that's unusual. But let's not discount that image. Could be related in some fashion.

Is it about a car crash or somebody who died in a crash?

No, I don't think so. I invited someone whom I've never met personally, but who was brought up to me by a woman who sent me an email the other day.

And she's getting information or seeing someone no longer on the planet.

Yes, that's correct.

But she's never met this person.

Right. Should I give you some hints?

It's a male. British?

Yes.

Maybe someone who knew Princess Diana?

We talked to Diana in class before, maybe he's referring to meeting her in our class once he got here.

He's an actor.

Correct. An actor whose name you might not recall but you would know by face.

I got somebody from Harry Potter...

Yes. Correct. (ding!)

I got somebody wearing a white outfit in Harry Potter. Was he that wizard?

I don't know if he ever wore an all white outfit; but he played a teacher.

Oh, I know, it's... does he look like the lead singer of "The Cure?" I don't know his name.

(The young version of Robert Smith) Yes, enough so to tell you his name: Alan Rickman.

I loved him, but I never would know his name.

Welcome to our class Alan; I should ask Luana - is Alan allowed in class today?

She says she put the thought in your head today.

(Note: That makes sense to me because as I was driving to Jennifer's office, and I couldn't remember his last name, but remembered that I wanted to speak with him, so I said to Luana in my mind's eye; "What's Alan's last name?" and suddenly heard "Rickman." I said aloud "Thank you Lu.")

I also want to speak with another friend of Luana's who worked with Alan.

She showed me a cat.

(Note: Luana had a number of cats over the years. Robert, Mr. Bailey and Maggie I knew, not sure why she showed Jennifer this cat first.)

Okay, well he was an older cat. He visited me in Tibet while I was in a tent on Mt. Kailash. Alan worked with him in a number of shows. Alan are you familiar with whom I'm talking about?

He says "Yes. (That) He told him about it."

Okay, so Alan...

He's laughing; he thinks it's funny that you think it's your own thoughts (asking these questions.)

Well Alan; who was there to greet you when you crossed over?

Something about his.. "Mother, Father and step-dad."

(Note: Alan's father died when he was 8, but I have no record of whether his mum remarried or not. She passed in 1997.)

All three?

He says, "Yes."

Is this unusual for you to be having conversations like this with people back on this side?

He just showed me Harry Potter. (laughs) Like, (highlighting) just the concept of the witches and magic...

Well there you go. I get it. "Yes, I hear from folks on the flipside all the time" - but I don't want to put words in your mouth. Did you know Princess Di?

He was older than her, correct? (Yes, by 15 years) He says "As a

young chap, as a younger guy, they met." He said "He did meet her."

Duncan Clark with Prince Charles and Alan Rickman at a premiere.

(Note: What's mind bending is that when I searched the internet for an image of the actor "Alan Rickman" and "Princess Diana," up came a publicity photograph of a close friend, Duncan Clark, who I was on my way to have dinner with that night. Diana is not in the photograph, but her husband was (Charles). Duncan (far left) explained how the photo was taken, and why it was taken. Duncan is a firm disbeliever in all things flipside by the way.)

So Alan, what do you miss about being on the planet if anything?

He says, "The magic." (laughs)

What do you mean by that?

He says, "The magic of all the connectedness; the coincidences that are not coincidences - when they are so contrived (created) from the other side."

How'd you meet your wife Rima?

He's showing me a pool table, like in a bar or a pub somewhere... does she sing? He's showing me her red lipstick.

The red lips drew you in - had you known her before, in a previous lifetime?

He's showing me her eyes, something to do with her eyes; he discussed it with her. And he's showing me a computer, as if to say "If you look it up you'll find this information."

(Note: Alan Rickman met his wife, the professor Rima Horton, when they were students at the Chelsea School of Art; they were a couple for five decades but didn't marry until 2012. There are numerous photos of her with Alan, wearing red lipstick.)

Did you marry anyone else?

His only marriage was to her. "Ball and chain," he said. He's joking.

Nice to be so lucky to have the right ball and chain - since they keep you connected to the earth. So may I ask why you two did not have children? Or is that none of my business?

"That too," he says. But he said "He was too busy." I don't think she wanted to, either.

(Note: As to having a family, he's quoted as saying; "You should remember I am not the only one involved," he told the Guardian's Susie Mackenzie in 1998. I did not know much about Alan until I looked him up after this session.)

So Luana you might let him know this is how I ask my questions, a little too personal sometimes.

They're both laughing about it.

Who were you surprised to see on the flipside? We've got quite a few people in our class, who were you surprised to see from this group?

Bill Paxton. Didn't he meet his wife in London?

That's right.

He says he "Was surprised to see Abe Lincoln."

(Note: Whom we've also interviewed).

You did some work with a playwright who's appeared in our class. I'm thinking of our pal Will. You did a lot of Will's plays, we've had a conversation with him; I know it's cheeky for me to say "He's here," but have you seen him since you've been over there?

"Shakespeare... Yes."

(Ding!) What was that like?

He says, "Love." Just love.

Was it love for you or from him to you?

He says, "All of it," they were connected; and it's love for what seems like a philosophical discussion they had together.

Did he give you any notes, or were you corrected by him?

He said, "Many times."

You did a lot of his work.

(Before I can finish the sentence) "Studied it, intensely."

Any correcting going on?

He says it's just like with me (Jennifer) "It was all about interpretation..."

I just thought that would be funny, being back home and the playwright calling you out... saying that's not what I meant with "To be or not to be..." or "speak the speech I pray you!" Okay, no one wants to hear me do Shakespeare. Anything you regret about your path or journey?

Kind of little bit about not having children, but also he feared that he was going to die young. That was a huge fear. And he didn't want to leave that way, but then it was too late. Um... he says his regret was not producing his own Shakespearean works.... instead of just being an actor, being a director and all that other stuff.

I understand - It's like he let people cast him instead of casting his own fate.

He said, "Correct."

Why do you think you were often cast as a villain?

He says, "It was too easy." It was (because of) his voice.

What is it about the quality of your voice that influenced people?

(Laughs.) He said, "It's easily villainized."

You can throw in a dig about the audiences who think that anyone who speaks with clear diction must be a villain. But I don't want to put words in your mouth.

He says, "Yes, very much so. Like the American way of saying "I'm doing good" instead of "doing well.""

How does Will Shakespeare look to you Alan?

He said, "He's got dirty blond hair. I know that's not how he's seen normally. He's got long hair, a ponytail."

He wears it in a ponytail? What color are his eyes?

"Sea green" he says,

Does he have a strong nose?

He said, "Strong cheeks. High cheekbones."

If you were going to cast him, who would play him?

(Laughs) "Brad Pitt."

Is that coming from you Alan, or coming from Will?

"All of us."

Brad's a good choice. The actor who played him in Shakespeare in Love (Joseph Fiennes) was kind of fair.

He says, "He's trying to explore those concepts in a way for people to comprehend, and that it won't be just coming from the other side. It's like Shakespeare using words and ideas to transform humanity; to give people another version of what the universe is like."

A way of understanding what the universe is about?

"Ding ding." (She taps her nose)

"Reality is only light and transformation."

"Yeah." Hang on, I have a question for him... (Pauses) So funny. I asked "So when you guys meet up over there, do you guys look like you used to, or like we do?" (Like humans) And he says "We can, but then when we travel, we "energize." He showed me like the transporter room in Star Trek. He says, "It's too many headaches to look like we did as people remember us, over here." But he's showing me it's like a three dimensional hologram.

I understand. It's a mental construct. In order to appear as you once looked, you have to do so by creating the math that would accomplish that CGI. Jennifer, looking at Alan, what color is his hair?

Grey: it's short, falls over his ears. And he's making himself look sexy.

With his deep voice no doubt. We have a mutual pal... can you show Jennifer who that is, Alan?

Sting came to mind.

Okay, I've met Sting. What do you want to tell Sting?

He says, "Tell Sting to stop levitating."

What do you mean by that? Do you mean "be more in your boots?" Not so off the planet?

He said, "Yes, you'll have plenty of time to do that later."

He does that kind of stuff.. tantric meditation.

"Tantric sex. It's overrated," he said.

Okay, next time I run into Sting I'll tell him; "Hey, Alan Rickman told me to tell you to stop levitating bro." Okay, now please show Jennifer our mutual friend. She might not know his name.

James Brown just came through.

Sorry, James, you gotta get in line. We've got other folks to talk to. "Get on the good foot" and take a seat brother.

He crashed the party.

I'll tell you his name; Michael Gough, we called him "Mick." He was an actor who played Batman's butler in four of the films; I want Alan to bring him forward if he can.

He's been there the whole time and now he's being seen. I just saw him appear; like this whole Star Trek energizing thing is amazing.

Michael Gough Actor's Photo

How does he appear to you?

He's not tall, has brown hair; he has the energy of a 30 year old. Was he in love with Luana?

Could be. They did some plays together in New York in the 60's when she was like 19 years old, on her own for the first time in Manhattan. I have a photo of those two hugging back when they were young together... and then later in life when we ran into him on Broadway.

Luana and Mick Gough backstage "Breaking the Code."

Was he 50 then?

I don't know... but seeing him in the play "Breaking the Code," I convinced Luana to go backstage, she was reluctant at first, too shy. We sent a note we were waiting backstage, but no one gave it to him. We wandered into the pitch blackness of the stage, heading towards the actor's rooms... and we stumbled into him in the dark. He heard Luana before he saw her. She said "Mick?" and he said "Luana?" He was flabbergasted, it was dramatic; no one told him we were there, he had this moment of seeing Luana for the first time in decades in the dark. Fun to witness.

He says, "He gave her a big fat kiss."

He did; back in his dressing room I took a picture. Then some years later, in 2004, when I was in Tibet, I was in a tent on the north side of Mt. Kailash when I heard his voice, clear as a bell. Mick, do you want to tell Jennifer about that?

It felt like he was saying "Wake up, wake up!"

He did - by that point Luana had already passed away...

Yes, hold on a sec. Did he show you or tell you that "It was so much bigger than that?"

Something like that. I woke up to the sound of his voice, "Richard darling, I think what you're doing is...

"Amazing... even bigger than what you think."

That's right. I woke up and thought "Oh no, Mick must have passed away." I sensed Luana was near by. He said to me "Luana and I do this sometimes, we travel around the universe together..." Luana had passed a few years earlier, but I had yet to begin this research, so I had no clue how he could be traveling with her without having crossed over himself.

Taken a few days after I heard his voice on Mt. Kailash

He didn't pass for another 5 years, correct?

Something like that. (It was 7). Once I got off of Mt. Kailash, I emailed his wife Henrietta from an internet cafe in Darchen, Tibet. She told me he was alive and fine, but it took me a year to get him on the phone to ask him "Did you ever have any dreams about traveling around with Luana?" He said "No, darling but I find that absolutely..."

"Fascinating."

Yes, that's what he said. So Mick, who was there to greet you when you crossed over?

(Pauses, smiles) "His dog."

Which one?

He said, "Number two."

What do you miss about being on the planet?

He showed me grapes. I don't know if its wine or... He says, "Red wine."

Is there anything you regret?

He says, "Not going to the ocean more."

Who are you hanging out with over there, anyone from our class?

He said, "Prince, now."

Prince is everywhere! Are you and Luana still taking those trips around the universe together?

"No. Because the universe is them." He says, "The universe is us."

Okay, but what would be an example of a place that you were on your way to with Lu, when you stopped by to say hello to me in Tibet?

It felt like she wanted to go up there to figure out how to help them...

Help who?

The Tibetan people.

Let me ask, Luana, how did you pull Mick onto these trips?

She says "She paid his higher self to do it..." she's joking.

Like here's some cash, c'mon let's go for a spin?

She says, "His higher self knew they were buddies; when he was asleep he was open to everything she said."

Were you two boyfriend and girlfriend at some point? I didn't think so, but you never know.

"No, more like a teacher and student," she says. Whatever that means.

It makes sense. He was a brilliant actor, and Luana became one. I know he loved you beyond measure.

She says, "Yes."

He even liked me because he loved you.

He says, "He loved the way you played the piano."

(Note: I forgot that I played piano *for him* until she said this.)

Right, he did hear me play. There was a point where Luana and I were apart for six months, and I remember getting a lovely Christmas card from him, saying something like "Good friends are always good friends even when they're apart." He was such an adorable human being, and I was thrilled to visit him and Henrietta in their home in the English countryside where I scattered some of Luana's ashes in his garden. Mick what do you want me to tell your wife Henrietta?

He says, "Travel more, see the kids;" he showed me New York. He's showing me visiting Machu Picchu, bringing that in.

Can your wife reach out to you? Do you guys talk all the time or is she not aware of you?

He says, "It hurts too much... but he's around there, trying to scare her." He just went "Boo!"

Should I give her the 1, 2, 3 method of reaching out to a loved one that we've learned here?

"Yes." Hang on. There is something... like she smells him, his

cologne or some kind of soap. Sometimes it's around her or she can smell it. I can't interpret that.

Any message for your old pal Tim Burton?

He says, "Tell the chap to hurry up."

You mean stop being so slow between films?

Either that or to hurry up and acknowledge his pals on the flipside. He's showing me that he's holding on so tight.

Holding onto what tightly? To his reality? Or does that mean there's nothing I can say to him that might connect you two?

"There is... give him one of your books... the one with the chapter on Harry Dean Stanton...The one where he says to believe in the possibility of an afterlife."

Harry Dean is in our book "Backstage Pass. ("Backstage Pass to the Flipside: Talking to the Afterlife with Jennifer Shaffer Book One")

He says he loved the "ride in the car" story.

(Note: Harry Dean recounts how he realized he was "on the flipside" and not in a dream. He saw that Luana was driving a car up the coast of California, on their way to the Monterey Pop music festival in 1967. I asked Harry (on the Flipside, via Jennifer) when did he realize he wasn't in a dream, and he said "When we got a flat tire. While we were fixing the tire, I looked at Luana and said, "but we didn't get a flat tire on this trip. And she said "I know!" He said that was a "soft landing" for him to realize where he really was.)

It's a great one, thanks Harry Dean. Alan Rickman: anything else you want us to pass along to your friends and family?

"Tell them to write more; Because you bring in more of his essence when you do so."

Thanks class!

CHAPTER SEVENTEEN

"A HELL OF A TRIP"

Marilyn's star. Author's photo.

MARTIN LUTHER KING, MARILYN MONROE, HOOVER, GANDHI

Rich: Hi class, here we are with Jennifer. Luana, who is here in class that wants to talk to us in class today?

Jennifer: First person that came through is Prince. He's showing me you playing the guitar... that's his way of showing that you were playing music...

Well, I referenced him yesterday because the sky had gone "Prince."

It was gorgeous.

Purple.. but Prince, today is a national holiday for someone we've met in class.

Martin Luther King.

We've met him briefly. Prince, do want to bring your friend forward so we can talk to him?

He's talking about the government shutting down. There's a lot of people concerned about not being paid and abuse of power.

Can we talk to you for a couple of minutes?

"Yes." He's talking to the guy with big hair.

(Note: We've filmed enough of these interviews for me to understand what Jennifer is saying even when obscure.)

James Brown?

"Yes."

Martin we've spoken briefly before, we do share an alma mater.

He said, "Yes."

Why did you choose Boston University to go to college?

He said "He wanted to be closer to people who were going to change things... and there was family there." I think he brought his family.

He did. What do you remember about Boston?

He said, "It was cold. It was opening up he says, thinking wise... a different way of thinking. um. I don't think he felt he was going to have more support from Boston, but Boston needed his support."

I would offer that getting your Doctor of Theology in Boston gave people a different perspective of you.

He says, "Absolutely."

Who was there to greet you when you crossed over?

I think his younger brother... and his mother.

(Note: MLK's younger brother was Alfred Daniel Williams King, born 1930, died July 21st, 1969 from accidental drowning (His family wasn't sure how he died, but was found in the pool). Martin's mother was alive when he died, so I asked the following:)

Your brother and mother or someone like your mother?

He said, "It wasn't his mother; it was his grandmother." I got mother first, I'm asking Luana to help so I can hear him better... "It was somebody who raised him, felt like someone who raised him. I presume it was his grandmother." And now he says "Everybody raised me."

Who were you surprised to see on the other side if anyone?

He says, "He was surprised to see a lot of different people." I'm seeing President Kennedy.. it felt like he had... (Listens:) He says "Just the different multiracial people who were there – there wasn't color – there was no color."

Did you say JFK was one of the people who came to greet you?

(Jennifer aside) That was the first thing he said, but in my head I'm thinking "Did JFK die after him?"

Try not to judge it. What did you and John have to say to each other?

"Thank you... and... that was a hell of a trip."

We've spoken briefly to JFK; He died in 1963 and MLK in 1968.

I must look silly to not know these historical dates.

Well, it just shows that you're not trying to piece something together, you know? Martin can we go to the last day on the planet you were here?

"Yes."

Who was this guy who shot you? Was this just one angry guy or some overall group?

He says, "It was an overall group."

Can you point to one person in particular?

It looks like Ku Klux Klan... I'm seeing a hat.

Are you seeing a Klan hat? Was this a political thing?

He says, "It was a political thing."

So, you were very aware of the shortness of your lifespan, because you spoke of it often in your speeches "I may not get there with you." Let me ask, when it finally happened, what was the feeling? Some people say it's a relief?

He said, "Relief. Yes."

I don't mean that in a negative way, just observing that the last ten years of your life were under constant threat.

"Correct" he said.

Let me ask you to address something.. Hoover had a burr up his ass about you Martin... Martin, have you talked to him since you've been over there?

He says, "They do it every time they come to earth. They switch roles."

Luana, can you bring Hoover forward? Just briefly?

"All the President's Men." He's smoking. A lot of cigar smoke.

You were notoriously a cross dresser; what was that about?

He says "He just thought it was kind of fun." I feel like he did it since he was little.

No judgment here; was that just a crossdressing thing, or were you gay?

He says, "I was."

I want to ask you about a young Chicagoan – a guy named Fred Hampton. When he was he killed by the Chicago Police, were you involved?

He says, "They did it to protect him."

Who, Hoover?

"Yeah." He says "He didn't pull the trigger..."

Right, the Chicago Police pulled the trigger ... Did you order them to? Or did the Chicago PD just do it on their own, as they were trying to eliminate the Black Panthers?

He says, "Yeah. They blamed him (Hampton), that kid for something he didn't do." I don't know anything about this.

Can we bring Fred Hampton forward Lu?

Um. I'm not getting a yes or a no.

Okay, very good, at a later date. Let's table that for now. I've been working on a story about him, but I'd really like to get a thumbs up or down from him.

I'm getting a thumbs up.

(Note: I know that Jennifer knows nothing about the assassination of Fred Hampton, a young Chicagoan who fell into the job as the local head of the Black Panthers. He started free clinics for poor people and food banks, and the Chicago Police executed him as a result.)

J. Edgar, who was there to greet you on the other side?

His nanny or his care giver. He's telling me that Susan B Anthony was one of them.

What? Did you know Susan B Anthony?

He's showing me what feels like a mother son relationship.

(Note: Susan B Anthony, the famous suffragette, died when Hoover was 11. For Jennifer to pull a "Susan B Anthony" reference during an interview means there's likely *something* that connects them. (Perhaps he liked her clothes?) Sorry, couldn't resist.)

Listen, it's long been rumored, there may even be evidence of it, but you're assistant, Clyde Tolson, is that accurate to say he was your lover?

He says, "Yes. Abraham Lincoln had the same."

Wait a second, you're outing Abe? We've had that discussion already with Abe and he specifically said that while he did have a male adjutant that he slept with while traveling, the idea of crossing the sexual line wasn't something he would have done. He says he was honorable with the people he worked with.

"He's very honest, Abe is. Very honest."

Very funny J. Edgar. Although you were less so – what was your life review like?

He showed me – then he showed me his mind, how it wasn't normal.

While he was on the planet?

He's showing me that as a result of something being wrong with his mind, that's part of the reason he did the things he did.

I'm sorry Martin to interrupt our interview to Hoover, since he was responsible for so much stress during your lifetime. I understand that was his role, and part of his role – but let's go back to you Martin for a moment. What do you miss about being on the planet?

He said, "He missed grapes." He showed me wine, (Jennifer aside) I'm not saying he drank wine. "He misses the ability to taste and smell." He says "He misses the banter."

Between friends? Or adversaries?

He said, "Both, just knowing that you can do something about something horrible."

Out of all the people you met in life, who most impressed you? demeanor honesty stature?

He said, "His wife."

Good answer. Let me ask you, there's someone we've chatted with that you paid a lot of respect to; a particular person in our class.

Was it Muhammed Ali? It's what he showed me.

(Ding!) Could you bring him forward? What do you guys talk about?

He said, "Our next plot for our next "go round." Martin wants to be the boxer, and Ali might be taking on his role."

(Note: It's a small detail, but the only time I've heard "go round" mentioned before is in professional bull riding. In the film I shot 2nd unit, "Cowboy Up" they call the next bull ride, "the next "go round." It may be in other sports as well, but that's the only place I've heard it.)

Ali was quite the preacher.

He says, "They both had the same sarcastic love and loyalty to one another." (Jennifer listens:) Yes... They're saying "They would die for each other."

Why did you say "yes" just now?

He was just telling me how much he loved Martin, and how they'd die for each other...

This is a silly question, but which do you prefer, Muhammed Ali or Cassius Clay?

He says "It doesn't really matter."

Who was there to greet you when you crossed over?

I think it's his daughter. A daughter he lost in life. I think she was a baby when she died.

His daughter Myriam is alive, but we've heard that often – people are greeted by the child they lost. A child who was there to greet you when you crossed over?

He says, "Yes."

You spent the later years with Parkinson's. You were still pretty funny – punchlines were hilarious.

He said, "I always had it going on. Just do it was my motto."

Nike stole that from you?

He says, "Yes."

I remember your story of how that teacher told you you wouldn't amount to anything... and how you used that insult to fuel your boxing career.

"Hell yeah!" he said.

What are you doing over there? how do you entertain yourself?

He says he dances a lot – he's showing me when he was young and dancing. He talks to Prince... (Jennifer listens:) hold on... he hangs out with John Kennedy. They're all planning their next...

venture. They're showing me what they loved – they know what they loved, I'm sorry – he just showed me all the curves of women. ....James Dean showed up.

Can we talk to him?

"Yes."

Welcome to class – have you met Luana?

He said, "Yes."

Many other people here you know...

He says "It's like a brat pack." Thank you. (Jennifer aside:) He likes my jacket. That is so cool.

Who was there to greet you when you crossed over?

He said, "A puppy dog. A dog that looked like Lassie."

From your youth?

From his adult lifetime which was very short.

You had the dog in LA or NY?

He said, "NY."

What do you miss about being on the planet?

He said, "I miss the girls. And that too... his motorcycle."

Speaking of speed...

He said, "I loved going fast. Fast and the furious." (Jennifer aside) Why was I being shown that? He showed me (names an actor that I've met in the past that he references later.)

I know him.

(Jennifer joking) Of course you do.

Well, let's return to that. James, people are going to be interested in your journey. Did you know you were going to check out early?

He says, "Not really, he knew he was being reckless, he said he should have died 10,000 times over."

You're aware of how you influenced generations of actors.

He says, "Yes. But not as much as Shakespeare."

Luana...

She says she had a poster of him, she showed me she was a big fan.

Brando has shown up in our class, they're all big fans.

"Yeah."

Where did that energy come from for you to be an actor or be someone else? From this lifetime or many other lifetimes? Where did that come from?

He said, "Came from this lifetime."

Any particular teacher?

Why do you keep showing me (this actor)? Hold on.

Maybe he was the original "bad boy."

He said "He was the original outsider."

Show Jennifer where you went – where did you go after growing up in Indiana?

He's saying California. (Ding!)

When he was younger...

He also showed me Bakersfield.

He died near there. But he also lived in Santa Monica... is that accurate?

He says, "Yes." He's saying "Before NY. He went from California to NYC. He had a girlfriend there.

(Note: That's correct. Ding!)

Pier Angeli. Was there any fellow that influenced you in the path of bisexuality?

He said, "Rock Hudson."

He gets around; we've talked to him before. Anything you want to pass along to people?

He says, "Be yourself; that's all anybody needs."

Let's skip back to Martin, are you still here?

He's talking to James Brown, Muhammed Ali, Tom Petty.

There is someone we've spoken to who had a profound influence on you Martin. Someone who's life and journey...

Was it President Lincoln?

Like him, but someone else.

He's showing me – Gandhi.

(Ding!) Have you talked to Gandhi since you've been over there?

He says "He talked to him while he was still alive."

We spoke to you Gandiji – you told us the first words in the afterlife were "Hey Rama..."

He showed me all the lights that came towards him.

Can we ask you some questions on Martin Luther King day?

He says, "Yes."

What was it about nonviolence? Was it something you thought was effective or part of your journey?

He says, "All of it. Humans just shouldn't be abused. Humans... shouldn't be..." (Jennifer aside: show me that again... He's very charming by the way.)

How do you see him? Young or old?

Like in his 30's – he showed me a picture that my girlfriend has of him. His voice is just very peaceful.

Who was there to greet you when you crossed over?

He says, "It was everyone that he's ever helped. All the lights were coming towards him."

What do you miss about being on the planet if anything?

He's giving me the sense of walking in the dirt barefoot. Also hot, crisp air. He misses his mother's cooking. His mother was there to greet him – he's showing me she was there often, like he was going there and coming back. He's showing me something like rice and seashells and corn.. bread... I wanted to say like um... like jambalaya.

I've been to your home in Mumbai, walked around your place.

The back room – was it all white? It was his meditation room?

(Ding!) Yes, where he used to make cloth – it was all white.

He's showing it to me. "That was his favorite room," he says; "That and the kitchen."

Is there anything about that lifetime you regret that you didn't do or wish you had done?

He says, "He wishes he wouldn't have been idolized. He wishes he could have helped more."

You helped a lot of people.

He says, "I know."

From your perspective now, people have to go through things?

"Correct."

So those journeys of suffering...

He showed me Maverick again. (John McCain.)

(Note: As we've learned people can learn a lot about life through suffering, and McCain saw a lot of learning.)

By the way John, has anyone seen the post I wrote to report that you told us to tell your daughter to run for Governor?

He says, "Yes, someone related to her. Like a cousin. I think she might have seen it."

Did she pay attention to it?

He says, "It made her think, allowed her to have a moment so that he could come through."

Good, that's all we wanted. So Gandiji – have you reincarnated since, are you thinking about it?

He says, "No; they're getting a plan together."

Martin where do you want to be in your next life? who are you going to be in your next life?

I'm seeing North Korea. What he's trying to show me, he's going to remain the same kind of person, but he has to go through different...

To change it... If you're someone who loves to get into the battlefield, you choose the most difficult playing field.

"Yes." He's saying "It's difficult to get others to join him."

He chooses the most difficult places to reborn. What about you Muhammed Ali? Or do you prefer Cassius? It's a Roman name – wasn't he a gladiator?

He said, "Absolutely."

Let's ask James Dean who are you going to be in your next life? Are you back yet?

He says "Yes." He keeps showing me this same actor every single time. (Names the role this actor played in a film.)

You mean you're returned as that actor?

He says, "Yes."

Hang on... I know this actor. This is crazy, are you telling us you are actually him?

"Yes" he said.

I know him through his best friend. Are you telling us you're that actor?

He says, "Yes."

How much of your energy did you bring to this actor's life?

He said, "30 per cent."

(Note: I ask this question often, and I've heard it from many under deep hypnosis. That we bring between 20 and 40 percent of our conscious energy to any lifetime. Thirty would be the normal amount.)

Luana, please clarify. Is this actor aware of this on any level?

"Yes," she said. "He is."

You want me to make him more aware of it?

Jennifer nods.

How about you Marilyn? Who do you want to be on your next journey or are you back?

She said, "She wants to be JFK (this time around) so she can be with Jackie."

Well, you're friends now – you used to hang out with JFK at a local Santa Monica eatery, Chez Jay's.

She said, "Definitely, she misses it."

What did you eat at Chez Jays?

"Same thing over and over."

What do you want us to tell people about you?

She said, "That she's with an incredible group of friends and loved one and she's happy happy happy."

Gandhi are you back yet?

He said, "No." And he's pretty consistent about that. I've got to run.

Okay, bye class!

****

After this session, I texted my friend who is best friends with the actor who James Dean was telling us that he's reincarnated as.

I texted "Hey, has anyone ever told your friend that he was the reincarnation of someone?" He texted back JAMES DEAN. I called him and he said "Ever since he was a teen, people would come up to him, psychics, whatever and tell him that he was the reincarnation of Dean. Why?" I told him – and he was gob smacked. I suggested that we chat about it sometime – maybe drive him around to some of Dean's old haunts and see what comes to mind. My friend said he would – but later told me "You know, it's not something he's focused on at the moment."

Apparently he came back and didn't have the kind of fame he had before, but he also didn't have the stress or worries. I'd say all in all, he made a wonderful choice.

Then about six months later, I was talking to a "librarian" who was in an Akashic library. (In "Architecture of the Afterlife") During the session I asked him if there was any human being that he ever saw in his library that he was impressed with. He said "James Dean."

Mind you – I was doing a session with a woman over skype who lives back east. She was answering my questions fully consciously, and was getting a tour of her Akashic library from her guide. But I saw this as a moment to verify (or deny) what I had already heard from James. I said "Let me ask you a question about James – I had a conversation with him recently..." and the librarian interrupted me, "It was correct. You do know who he has reincarnated as."

I'm not really sure how to characterize how one feels when hearing that kind of confirmation. It's mind bending, if not blowing. But there you have it – wondering if James Dean is going to return? He's already back and loving it.

CHAPTER EIGHTEEN
THE 13TH DALAI LAMA

The 13th Dalai Lama (Photo: Charles Bell)

Another of my experiments. In this instance, I am aware that a person brings "about a third of their conscious energy to a lifetime." That was consistent in all of Michael Newton's cases, and is consistent in the over 50 deep hypnosis cases I've filmed. I've also found it to be accurate in terms of the work Jennifer and I are doing – someone will claim to be "greeting on the other side" by someone who is still on the planet, still "among the living." For someone not familiar with the process, that would instantly eliminate the answer – they tend to block it because they aren't aware of the possibility.

In the book "It's a Wonderful Afterlife" I interviewed author David Bennett ("Voyage of Purpose") where he reported during his near death event seeing a particular friend "in his soul group" during his accident (where he drowned for 12 minutes). A science officer aboard a ship, he was later tested and retested by scientists at UVA studying near death experiences. But the detail that I focused on was that he "saw his friend in his soul group (class of friends) on the flipside when this guy was still alive. However, as David reported, "he was translucent, like the outline of him was there – not all of him was."

Then later in life, David did a between life hypnosis session with a Newton Institute trained hypnotherapist and David told me in our interview, that he saw his friend again, only by this time he had died, so when he saw him in his "soul group" he was "fully there." In other words, not translucent, but fully in spirit form.

I've heard this often in the research – our loved ones may greet us on the other side (sometimes during a near death event) and we may be startled to see them. Sometimes they're individuals who actually have passed away (according to the research done by Dr. Greyson at UVA). But as we've reported in some of the cases in this book, someone might see or "run into' someone who is still on the planet.

Based on this consistent reporting, I thought it would be novel to attempt to speak to someone who is clearly on the planet, but access them in a particular time frame (the 13th Dalai Lama instead of the 14th, who is here.) I'm familiar with the lineage of the Dalai Lamas, have been to Tibet and visited a number of them (stupas) as well as have read the book "the 14 Dalai Lamas" which goes into detail about each of their lifetimes.

I'm familiar with the life and journey of the 13th Dalai Lama, when I was researching a screenplay "Younghusband" – I was focusing on the story of how the 13th had to deal with the British invasion of 1906 and how they responded to it. (Over 3000 unarmed Tibetans were mowed down by British Maxim guns in the plain of Gyantse, which I visited). But I was also familiar with the unusual relationship between the 13th Dalai Lama and Charles Bell, a British officer who was stationed in Darjeeling when the 13th Dalai Lama had to flee India during the Chinese invasion of that same time period. The Dalai Lama fled Tibet for the first time, ever (later repeating that flight in 1959)/

He got to Darjeeling where he was hosted by this young British officer Bell. The 13th had avoided the British when they invaded in 1906, so he was surprised at the generous and genteel nature of this young fellow. They became best friends, and the Dalai Lama invited Bell to live in Lhasa – the first Brit to do so, and he lived there for decades and wrote about it extensively in his books. They're a fascinating insight into a world gone by.

But based on my previous knowledge of this World Leader, I thought it might be a novel idea to see if we could access him in our little restaurant in Manhattan Beach.

Rich: Hi class. Who should we talk to? I asked some folks to swing by, but who do you want us to talk to?

Jennifer: I got the Dalai Lama, but I know he's still alive.

Don't judge it. Specifically let's talk to this Lama. Can you bring him forward?

He showed me the current one but it's a different one.

(Ding!) Can you see him?

He has darker skin.

Does he have any facial hair?

He has something twisted..

(Ding!) Yes... his moustache. I asked him to come today. I gave Luana a list people, and this is definitely the most obscure and different person we could invite. Can we talk to you directly? Let's allow that I know who you are. Jennifer does not.

Were you with him in Tibet?

Not physically. Perhaps spirit wise. I visited his tomb, but no, I've never met this fellow. Let's be precise... You're the Lama prior to the current one?

"Correct."

Who was there to greet you when you crossed over?

He's showing me many people. They are all chanting. Wearing robes.

Anyone in that group wearing yellow hats?

Two.

If they could come forward, could you introduce them to Jennifer?

It was his two predecessors. One of them was a teacher, and one was like a brother.

Was unusual for you to greet them as you crossed over? Was it different than what you had imagined?

It was much better – he was present for that process and he was aware of what was happening.

(Note: Buddhism doesn't consider people being fully conscious in the afterlife, it's thought that between lives, we're like "wisps of smoke" that move from one lifetime to the next. People in general are aware that Tibetans claim that the 14th Dalai Lama (Tenzin Gyatso whom I've met a few times) is the reincarnation of the 13th Dalai Lama.

But I'm aware that based on the research, we only bring a portion of our conscious energy to a lifetime. So indeed, while the 13th may have returned as the 14th, a portion of who he was "back then" is accessible and we can have a conversation with him. She described him precisely, darker skin with a twirly moustache. I've read some of Charles Bell's biographies of him – Bell being a British officer who lived in Lhasa for over a decade.)

You had an English friend... Charles Bell. Do you know who I'm speaking about? During your lifetime you made friends with this fellow.

Was he a writer?

Yes,(Ding!) Bell wrote a number of books about living in Lhasa, and about your life. So is it accurate for me to argue that a portion of your conscious energy is in Tenzin Gyatso, the 14th Dalai Lama?

He says "He has access to all the way back. He's saying that the 14th Dalai Lama has this access... all the way back to the 1st and beyond." (Jennifer aside:) I don't know what that means.

It's okay, I do. But I'd like you to clarify this please, how a certain part of your conscious energy came to your next life as the current Dalai Lama?

He showed me ocean waves; how the ocean and the waves are that same person, but all the energy and all the knowledge goes back.

So you have access to everything? All of those memories?

"Even more when you're aware."

(Note: I think he's referring to the idea that when you're aware of all your lifetimes, either through meditation or some other access, you are both the memory and the action at the same time.)

What percentage of your conscious energy is in this one?

He just laughed and walked away.

Why?

He came back. He said "All right. All of it."

You're saying that the 14th has access to the memories of all of them – but my question is about the percentage of that conscious energy that came to his lifetime. For example, the current Dalai Lama is not aware of this conversation we are currently having, so the 14th isn't completely aware – so that means he has less a percentage of awareness than you currently have because you are aware of it.

Part of him is aware of it.

(Note: We reportedly bring a smaller percentage of our conscious energy, but his point is that when someone has full access to it, it doesn't matter what that percentage might be because it is "all of it." But I'm debating him in the spirit of deeper comprehension.)

Aware of this conversation? Okay. Some part of the conscious energy of the Dalai Lama is aware of this conversation. That makes sense. By the way is the class impressed we have the 13th Dalai Lama visiting us?

They said "Yes, it's like having Jesus stop by."

Well, yes, we've chatted with him too; even had a conversation with Buddha... By the way, your Holiness the 13th, have you spoken to the Buddha Siddhartha since you're return?

"Yes."

What did you learn from him once you were on the other side?

He's laughing. He says "To just stay away."

From what?

"From earth!" – (meaning to not reincarnate again) He's laughing... He's saying "By allowing them to get into it again, and to call up to them (him and other lamas) to come back."

What do you think about the current situation in Tibet?

"Sad, very sad."

A lot of people have been setting themselves on fire.

He's saying "It is wrong."

You're recommendation is to not set yourself on fire in protest?

"Never. Treat your body like a temple..." He's showing me he understand, "They can't take it anymore because their insides are burning; there is no difference."

Let me ask you, is there a date you can give us in the future when this will be resolved: where China will no longer control Tibet?

It feels like 2200... like 170 years from now.

Sorry to hear that. Are you familiar with Robert Thurman?

That's what came to mind when you said Charles Bell.

This person we're calling the 13th thought of Thurman?

Yes, I don't know his name. He says there needs to be another movie about Tibet... there needs to be... I know you're talking about Robert the father of Uma Thurman. But he's talking about making more movies, is expressing that there is something with accountability that is not being spoken of...

With the Chinese government and what they're doing to Tibetans in Tibet?

"Yes."

Accountability with what the Chinese are doing in Tibet?

Yes, he just showed me it's like North Korea and Kim Jong Il.

Let me clarify, I've made a couple of films with Robert Thurman, documentaries.

Yes, and he's saying one was very peaceful.

One that I made about refugees in Dharamsala ("Tibetan Refugee") and one about Robert Thurman in Tibet "Journey into Tibet with Robert Thurman.")

"It was very beautiful he said, he loved the images."

Thank you – but Robert can't politicize his work about Tibet in order to be able to travel there again. But do you have a specific request? Something I should say to Robert that comes from you?

"Tell Robert not to wait." Something with a signature and a scroll?

Are you telling him he should write something?

"No, something he should translate."

He is a translator.

I didn't know that.. I'm seeing this language... looks Sanskrit.

Are you talking about the Notovitch document?

"Yes!" He just tapped his nose.

(Note: It's something I discussed in "Hacking the Afterlife" in great detail. For Jennifer to reference this is unusual, and again, try not to judge it. But he's referring to the document that the explorer Notovitch claimed to find in Hemis (a Tibetan monastery in Ladakh) where he claimed his Nepalese guide translated a Tibetan book for him – the "life of St. Issa." It's controversial because it claims an alternative story about the life of Jesus, including him studying with various esoteric religious sects along the silk route. I go into detail in it in "Hacking" but for him to mention that Robert Thurman has access to a copy of it (somewhere) and wants him to translate it is a bit odd. I spoke to Robert about it and he's not aware of any ancient document that he's aware of that might resemble the Kanjur of Hemis.)

Okay. Where can I find it?

I saw it up high somewhere.

In Tibet? In India?

He's showing me a picture of a monastery. On the backside of a hill.

Is it in Ladakh?

"Yes." (To the 13th) Show me again please. (To me) If you look at a map of India... I'm being drawn to this top corner...

Where Leh is?

"It's in Leh." I see Jesus walking with it.

Okay, well that's what the document is about. Jesus is walking with it? The 13th wants Thurman to translate it?

"Yes." It's in really really old Tibetan language.

How many copies exist?

"Three." He says "There's three." One is in the U.S.

Is Robert aware of it?

It feels like he is – but doesn't realize it. It's in something that's like a museum.

What's the document called? Will he be able to recognize it by the title?

I don't know. But whenever they show me Jesus and Buddha they show them like this – together – (makes a together gesture.)

I get what they're saying.

I don't.

So Jesus - what's up? Can he come forward? We've chatted with him before. Are you down with this? This idea of translating your document because this will help people in some fashion? Is that what you're saying?

He says "It will make them see through things, it's really interesting, not necessarily help them but help their awareness go – vrrom – like seeing through everything; like breaking all the borders and boundaries..

So Robert's translation of the Kanjur of Hemis – if that's what it's called, and within that this story about Issa living in Hemis, you're saying that would be a profound thing?

"It would be every great thing."

Okay, listen let's thank the 13th for showing up... Very kind of you. Taishe delek.

I can't begin to unwrap this session. Except to say that I'm an equal opportunity heretic. I've had people say "Oh yeah, right – like Robin Williams or Prince would stop by to talk to you. Please." I've had people say "are you insane? You're claiming that Jesus/Buddha/TsongKhapa/the13thDalaiLama stopped by for a chat?" "Abe Lincoln? John McCain?"

No – I'm not claiming anything. I'm just reporting. When they say the same things consistently – I report that. It's up to everyone else to claim they don't exist, they can't communicate with us, that the dead are dead, and to leave them alone. I had one person claim I was stealing people's grief... well, far be it from me to steal anyone's grief.

I can only point out that claiming their loved ones still exist shouldn't be a problem -- unless they don't want them to still exist, don't want them to "be hanging around" for whatever reason. They mourned them, they're done mourning and they've moved on.

As Jennifer's father put it so eloquently; when you can move grief to nostalgia, the healing process begins. I'm just dealing with nostalgia – both sad and happy memories – and pointing out that there's no set time period to move grief to nostalgia.

If you're like me and don't believe in death at all – that the actual role of playing death has been upended, circumvented, that Death himself has been fired... then claiming that I am not giving people the proper amount of time for grieving may be accurate. They can always read these books later on down the road.

But think of all the laughs they'll have missed.

CHAPTER NINETEEN
"IT'S NOT SOMETHING YOU WOULD QUESTION"

Tesla and Mark Twain from National Archives.

TESLA, MARK TWAIN, SAM THE DOG

Rich: Hi class. Hi Luana. I've invited some folks, but I'm leaving it up to you who should speak to us.

Jennifer: Robin Williams showed up.

Okay, I did have the impression that I talked to him earlier today.

He said "The answer to the question is yes." What were you thinking about?

I started to look at a Channeling Erik video – I had no specific question, really... but Robin, if the answer is yes, tell us the question.

He says "stay in the question constantly." Like, if you're constantly questioning, you will get information.

You mean answer for me or is that for everybody?

"For everybody."

So what is a good question?

So many he says, hold on. He's so cute – he says "Lets go see the stars" and I'm like "Okay." (Jennifer listens, laughs). He said the question is not something you question; it's something that is given to you so that you get the question. You know how we sometimes say we think we're asking these questions, but they're actually giving us the questions?

Okay. Oddly philosophical today Robin. Who stuck Jennifer in Dave Chapelle's life this weekend?

(Note: Jennifer was at the Chateau Marmont when Dave Chapelle said hello, and in a few minutes she was telling him about a trip to Tokyo he was about to take, but wasn't aware of. And when the trip to Tokyo occurred, his assistant texted her to say "You'll never guess where we are.")

Who's that guy? His name is Farrelly? The blonde?

You mean the guy who won the Oscar for Green Book?

No... It's Chris. Chris Farley.

So why did you do that Chris? Does he want to come forward and speak with us?

Apparently yeah, it was planned.

Chris, we ask the same questions to everyone.

"He was prepped," he said, by Luana.

Okay very good. We do that to help you access how to communicate with us. So who was there to greet you when you crossed over?

He's showing me his dog.

Describe it to us so people will know what kind of dog you had.

A German shepherd. A smaller dog though.

Wait - is this my dog or your dog?

(Jennifer aside:) What is your dog?

My dog was part German Shepard, part miniature Collie. And he was one of the people that I asked to speak to today.

Jennifer nods. "He's here."

All right... Sam, my dog can sit down while we talk to Chris. Sam, sit.

He acts like one of those dogs that herds sheep.

He looked a bit like one of those – an Australian cattle dog; blue heeler... a sheep herder. Does he want to talk to us first or does Chris? Luana?

She keeps putting you in my mind's eye – Like Martini's going to talk first. Sam is here; let's talk to Sam.

Okay, hi Sam.

Did you get him when you were 8?

Yes. (Ding!) That's about the age when he came to me.

Author with his pal. Circa 1965.

Did he leave when you were 21?

Yes. (Ding!) Describe how you departed from the planet to Jennifer because I don't know what happened.

He had a seizure, felt like a blood clot.

Was it an administered thing or were you out running free?

He was out running.

Oh god, I'm so glad to hear that. Can you show Jennifer where you were running?

He's showing me water... near the ocean? Or a lake.

Yes (Ding!) Lake Michigan.

Yes. What were the circumstances... who was with him? We all thought they had put him down.

No, no, it was from a blood clot, a seizure, he was running...

(Note: This is about as emotionally connected as I get to these sessions. I don't try to speak to my loved ones or relatives outside of Luana, because I'm trying to focus on the research, and ask cogent questions. But in this case – my closest, nearest friend on the planet, my dog Sam.)

Someone suggested that ... but let me ask you some questions Sam; who was it who took you home from Orphans of the Storm?

It felt like a little boy.

So right away you were adopted by this boy?

"Yes."

What was the little boy's name?

Curtis... I feel like. Could have been a fostering thing.

(Note: This is out of left field, but when typing this section, I thought of Bill Kurtis, the famed Chicago newscaster. At the time he had a son, Scott, who was around 5 years old at the time. Kurtis' home is not far from Lake Michigan, above Lake Forest in Mettawa, and is a famed garden estate. I don't know if this is where Sam wound up – I could ask – but it's just fun to imagine him here.)

The farm of Bill Curtis in Chicago that Sam is mentioning.

Were there other dogs there? Or were you by yourself?

It felt like he was by himself at first, but there were two other dogs... he was never left alone.

Let me ask you this – my brother Rob thought he saw you later in life, you may not be aware of that...

No, he was. Why am I being shown Boston?

Because that's where I went – back to school in Boston. My brother said he thought he saw Sam, with other dogs running around.

He was trying to find you.

(Note: If you want to hear a lump in my throat, have your dog who was your best friend for 12 years tell you that he had been "trying to find you.")

When you died, who was there to greet you on the other side?

His mom.

Did you understand our path and journey together?

"Yes. We've been together many times."

Can you put in Jennifer's mind another lifetime with us together?

He's showing me a lifetime in Italy.. with the both of us, me as well.

Who was Jennifer in that lifetime?

I was a little girl.

And Sam, were you a dog in that lifetime?

I'm getting a visual of a horse.

So we've been together before, and we found each other again?

"Yes."

What would you like me to pass along to people, people are so bereft when they lose a pet - are you able to go and visit them from the flipside?

"Yes."

How does that work? Is it a frequency thing?

He says "Yes, it's like a dream state – he says "They'll put an awareness towards them.. into their mind – people think they're thinking of them, but they're putting their awareness to them, letting you know "I'm here I'm here I'm here..." – but they often go to "Oh my god, I've lost my pet..." When people see them they go into the grieving... its just like when you lose someone over here.

So let me ask you Sam, when you're over on the other side – do you initiate the contact sometime, or is it the person back here?

He said "I do." It is something that has to do with um... it's the things that go in between... like like like..

Like quantum entanglement?

"Correct. String theory."

So once we've connected in a lifetime, we're entangled?

Connected forever.

What about me and my current pets? Are they aware of you?

Yes, but he's showing up as a horse.

Describe this horse, what's he look like?

He's all black.

What year was that in Italy?

1540.

What city was that in?

In Tuscany. Toscana.

What was my role in that life? Jennifer was a little girl, what role did I play?

You were in charge of everything; the vineyards.

Like a landowner? Sam, thank you – you've made my day and you're always welcome to join us. I apologize for not being there the for your last day on the planet.

You were – he wouldn't have known it any differently.

It's been a source of angst.

Heal that.

(Note: About a month after this session, I was doing an interview with a woman from Chicago who had a near death event (Steph Arnold – that interview is in another book, **"Architecture of the Afterlife"**) and when accessing her council, I asked if they were familiar with my work. The head council member said "Yes" and when I asked "How?" She showed Steph Arnold my dog; Sam. I said "Wait a minute – you're telling me you're familiar with me accessing councils in the afterlife while people are not under hypnosis through my dog who died 40 years ago?" Steph paused and nodded. "That's what she's showing me." I had only just met Ms. Arnold that morning on Skype – and there's no written account of Sam I'm aware of anywhere in the world; until now. And he showed her – a woman I've never met except on Skype – that he had been "talking to her council about this work I've been doing with the flipside." Mind went from bent to blown.)

Okay back to Chris Farley and his inspirational coach who "lives down by the river."

He just showed me Jim Carrey as the fire guy...

That character was Chris' tour de force – the motivational speaker. Chris you left behind a lot of really good friends,...

I'm seeing the woman who died from breast cancer ...

Gilda Radner? Are you hanging out with Gilda, Chris?

"Yes."

I'm sorry to interrupt you for that conversation with my dog Sam, but who greeted you when you crossed over? What was it, a drug thing?

A combination. And day's worth of the combination. He's showing me another person from SNL.

Who? John?

"Yes. John Belushi was coming through..."

Well that would make sense as well because where you met Dave Chappelle was the same place that John died; the Chateau Marmont.

(Jennifer aside) Oh my gosh.

So John; we've talked to John had a wonderful conversation with him... – Chris, anything you want to say to your old pal David Spade? I don't actually know if he was your friend but you did some movies together.

He's saying like tell him to quit thinking about what he shouldn't do. Kind of like saying the same thing Dave Chappelle. They spend so much time thinking about what they shouldn't do, it's hindering what they should do.

In terms of life or comedy?

"Comedy."

Do you regret anything about your life or was it part of a contract to check out early?

He says "It's not like he got paid more money to check out early." (Jennifer laughs)

You mean, he didn't get any credit for coming home early?

But he's planning his next experience. Oh my gosh, they're having a field day, remember when Robin Williams was Mrs. Doubtfire? That's what they showed me Chris coming back as.

That would be hilarious. What do you miss about being on the planet?

Everything – he's making me smell peanuts. Peanuts on the floor of a bar, going to a bar. He says he misses his friends.

I know you grew up my home state.

He says "Depends on how you define growing up."

What do you want to tell your old SNL boss Lorne?

"Tell him to get a life."

As opposed to SNL?

"Tell him to stop judging what he puts on there – he holds back so much now; he can't help it... from what he puts on there."

He's afraid of what?

The public. He showed me a picture of the audience, the public.

I met Lorne at a friend's wedding, some kind of beef between them.

He thinks your friend stole information or something from him.

Probably told a story about Lorne off camera that he didn't want people to hear.

That sounds right. Some private information.

Chris, who are you hanging out with over there?

John and Aretha. (Jennifer aside:) I miss them when they're on the other side...

So Chris is hanging out with John and Aretha? Anything the Queen of Soul wants to say to Dave Chapelle?

He told me she was singing in his ear.

What was she singing?

She showed me you writing and playing something on the piano – one of her tunes... one of the songs that um..

You mean, like Amazing Grace?

Yes.

(Ding!) Okay, that's odd. I was recording a version of "Amazing Grace" the other day – to post on YouTube. I looked up the song, and then after that discovered that her movie "Amazing Grace" was coming out. She does a version of the song that is beyond amazing.

I had no idea about that.

So Aretha, you were singing Amazing Grace in Dave Chappelle's ear? Or he heard you singing in his ear?

He told me he heard her singing that song in his ear. And she's showing me that is accurate; she's showing me that it was on a subconscious level... and that her voice was infiltrating his energy field. (Jennifer aside:) I've never seen that before.

Can you do that with other people?

She does that with people who are asking for it.

Thank you Aretha. So are you hanging out with Chris?

They all intertwine with people that they meet here in this class... they're showing me it's like being at a stoplight – they're somebody they see walking across and they're instantly connected to that person.

Who orchestrated Jennifer meeting Dave Chapelle?

They put it in his awareness to look over at me, come over and say hi – He shook my hand, and I thought of John Belushi, but I didn't know he died there. I don't know if that opened it up, but they gave the opening.

John are you hanging about at the Chateau?

He says "Yes, it's too much fun not to."

Is that because people think of you when they're there?

"Yes, it's a church," he says.

Okay, the Church Marmont

"Think about all the people who've stayed there - it's like a church, it's like all the people who go into the Sistine Chapel. Their energy stays behind."

A lot of artists stayed there over the years, not that many died there.. but it's like a church for you? Or it's like a church for the people here?

"It's for everyone who wants to get inspired, you can't help but feel the energy of all the artists who've been there – that's what brings the church aspect back in."

Thank you. So Luana, let's turn back to you.

"It's about time," she says.

Who else can we talk to? I know we made people wait.

The guy in the wheelchair just showed up. Hawking.

I didn't ask for him but a colleague of his.

Who?

First name Nick.

Tesla.

(Ding!) Can we talk to him?

You get both.

How does Tesla look to you?

Short. Scruffy. Curly hair.

About how old?

30. I'm seeing that he was very OCD and very tailored.

He was.

(Jennifer aside:) I don't know. He showed me Orson Welles...

Orson made a movie about Tesla.

No, not him... it's so funny he's saying to me, "He wasn't showing me Orson Welles, but another film person who had OCD." What's his name?

Howard Hughes?

"Yes. That's him. He was fucked up with OCD."

Nikola, who greeted you when you crossed over?

His cat.

(Note: Tesla was notorious for adopting pigeons later in life, and witnessed the death of a dove, seeing a "light come out of her body" that was "brighter than any light he'd been able to create in a lab." (That would be pretty bright, as he worked with huge amounts of electricity.) So being greeted on the flipside by one of his pets would make sense.)

What do you miss about being on the planet?

(Laughs.) He shows me "Driving Teslas."

Did you appreciate that company named for you?

"Yes."

Do you appreciate Elon Musk?

He says "He's trying to help him (Musk) – although he doesn't really need it...

Okay, when you were a child you fell off a horse...

"Hit his head."

Correct.(Ding!) Did that contribute to your obsessive compulsive behavior?

"No. That happened later on, but he's saying that his head hit and everything was coming in all at once; that's what it felt like."

(Note: Tesla was a famed eccentric, when he dined ate the exact same dish, had stead and 18 peas on his plate, always served 18 napkins. He abhorred pearl earrings and would not shake hands.)

You were famous for being able to imagine an invention in your mind and then...

"Just create them. He was silenced for it."

Silenced? What does that mean?

What every happened when he was 57? It changed everything.

(Note: The age of 57 would have been 1916. JP Morgan cut off his funds; in 1915 the New York Times reported that the Nobel Prize in Science was to be given jointly to Tesla and Edison, but that Edison refused to share it with him; it was awarded to someone else. In 1916 Tesla had to declare bankruptcy, and declared he was penniless. The rest of his life he was hounded by creditors for his rent at various hotels in Manhattan, until 1934, when Westinghouse (which he had made billions for) agreed to pick up his hotel costs.)

Your opinion of J.P. Morgan?

He says "He was a liar."

Who was that who tried to silence you?

One of three.

(Note: Again, Jennifer doesn't know that J.P. Morgan first tried to hire Tesla, then when he discovered he was using the money Morgan gave him to work on "free electricity" rather than "wireless radio" or when Marconi lifted Tesla's patents after seeing him demonstrate wireless transmission at the Columbia Exposition, Marconi used Tesla's invention to send the first "wireless" transmission across the ocean. Later, Morgan paired Marconi with Edison, and Tesla was kicked to the curb so to speak, his name mostly forgotten until this century.)

Edison?

"Not so much."

Was it big money or the government trying to silence you?

"All of it."

Why?

"Because he wanted to give away electricity for free... they weren't going to have it."

(Note: This is mind bending. I know that Jennifer doesn't know the story of Tesla, but indeed, when he told J.P. Morgan that he was going to invent "free electricity" for the planet, Morgan notoriously said "Instead of oil wells I'm going to invest in antennas?" Tesla's lab was burned afterwards, both in Manhattan and Colorado. He never recovered financially from that, and it's pointed out that Tesla was never granted a patent for his "free electricity" invention – and that every head of the patent office since Morgan has been a former oil executive. His invention was about using the "electromagnetic properties" of the rotation of the earth to create electricity. All someone would have to do to access it was put up mile high antennas near their home.)

May I ask; is electricity for free a practical idea? Was your invention of putting giant antenna's behind people's homes a practical idea?

"No. It would have been used the wrong way."

What can you tell us about how we use electricity today? How we can help our planet?

He just took me to a visual of water again.

Is it about the conductivity of water?

"Yes." He showed me clouds and how they go up.

Condensation? Can you do the same with electricity?

He said "That's half the equation."

Allow me to try to clarify; are you saying an electrical particle of a water goes up and electrifies a cloud?

"Yes; they have to figure out the other end of it. The renewable part of it... they keep showing me it's like the filtration system. I can't figure it out.

We talked about this before, water going through Earth. Like a filtration system of water going through Earth, then evaporating into a cloud. Let's just open this door a little bit, Nick.

He said "Nicholas."

Okay, Nikola. If I can ask, are you hanging out with Samuel Clemens?

(Note: Tesla was a superstar in his day, and hung out with Mark Twain (Samuel Clemens) J.P. Morgan's daughter Anne and other celebrities of the day.)

"Yes. He's been here. He's in charge of... He's the Neil DeGrasse Tyson; the writer in charge of speaking about us.

Can we talk to Sam Clemens?

He's here.

What does he want to tell us?

(Jennifer aside) At first everything came very fast; he showed me from slowing down then sucked into the planet and the trash on the planet, and I saw the back to the future car being run on trash.

You saw a DeLorean running on trash as future technology? You mean as a methodology. Turn trash to fuel?

"Yes."

Sam, you were an excellent writer.

"He was very humbled by it."

And you were pals with Nikola.

"He channeled for him."

(To Jennifer) You don't know who Sam is, do you?

"No."

That's fine. Sam .. who greeted you when you crossed over?

"They greeted each other."

Sam greeted Tesla? And vice versa?

"Yes."

Well, it's one of those things we've talked about – our higher selves greeting our loved ones. Sam died some years before Nikola... but then Sam was there to greet Nikola?

"Yes."

Was that a shock?

"No."

What do you miss about being on the planet Sam?

He showed me a car.

You miss being a writer, or driving in a car?

Going really fast and the engineering of a car. He was a writer, I know.

But now on the flipside you can go fast can't you?

"Yes."

You miss the wind in your hair?

I'm seeing a bald guy with him. Someone else that is there that doesn't have hair.

Who are you showing her that didn't have hair?

(Note: Edison didn't have hair by the time he passed, but then neither did J.P. Morgan; I didn't think to ask.)

Sam what's the one thing you want to tell us?

"Tell people to go out and live... We waste time sitting there, just thinking, just watching things that we're supposed to do that we don't do."

That's a great quote. The two of them are amazing guys – should I tell that story guys?

(Note: I wrote a play about Mark Twain's relationship to Nikola Tesla).

"Yes." In 2020 they will help you tell it.

They will? Bye flipside people people see you later.

Jennifer; "They're all flying."

Thanks you class!

CHAPTER TWENTY

"HEALING AND HELPING OTHERS"

Nancy, Michael, Ron – Photo Courtesy of the Reagan Presidential Museum. Pete Sousa

MICHAEL JACKSON, HAWKING, SAGAN, EINSTEIN, TESLA

My questions are *in italics*, Jennifer Shaffer replies **in bold**. This was filmed on March 12th, 2019, after the screening of "Finding Neverland" on HBO (which Jennifer and I have yet to view).

Rich: Last week we interrupted Prince who had shown up with Michael Jackson. Sorry about that. What do they want to say? Is Michael here?

Jennifer: "Yes."

So Michael, you've been in the news lately.

He says, "He's happy that it's out. It's healing and it's helping others."

Anything you want me to say on your behalf? Or what do you want to say about it?

He says, "He didn't know how harmful it was. He really loved those boys, like he was ... (trying to find the words) there was a love he didn't know (how to express)... he was so separated from..."

His emotions?

He says "I meant what I said, I know they're healing, they're healing now, I know Oprah interviewed the boys and (know) how it's helping to break the cycle for everyone..." – Not only was he iconic, you know as a pop star, but he's... he didn't.. I don't know how you could say this but he's saying "This was part of his life's path."

I was going to ask him that.

He said, "Yeah."

(Note: In the book "It's a Wonderful Afterlife" a close friend did a deep hypnosis session and revealed she'd been molested by someone in her family. She said "I'm seeing that it was part of my life planning process. I'm seeing that he asked me to participate in those actions in this lifetime... and that I agreed to, or did so to help teach him the lessons in the negativity of his actions." Afterwards, she told me that 20 years of therapy had dissolved during the session.)

Prince, please help him with this if you can. So Michael, you chose this life to not only hit the heights musically but also to hit the depths?

He says, "Absolutely."

We've learned this in the research, not from those boys, not from this case or these boys... but from other people - they signed up for a lifetime to help teach others.

(Jennifer aside:) I asked him, "Is that (also) what you want to remembered by?" and he said "Yes."

So it's to help teach a lesson in overcoming negativity, overcoming trauma?

He said, "Yes." He showed me all the layers of it.

Let me ask you this question - Who's idea was this? (To have this multilayered lifetime). Your guides? Your teachers? Who came up with the idea of teaching negativity in a healing way?

"It was the environment," (to be able to do that) he says.

Let's go back to your life planning session if we can... Prince can we help him go back to his life planning session?

He says, "He has it – he says that all of it... it was everything."

So was it your teachers who suggested this? My question is, did you suggest it or your teachers, that you would teach that lesson?

He says "It was all of us, everybody agreed upon it." He goes.. he showed me something interesting. You don't have a body (back) there – when you agree upon something like this, you don't feel it, you aren't connected to it at all... that was interesting (to observe). I went to a spirit space, where you are looking at people who don't have bodies, you're looking at how things can work - it's like looking at a blueprint... sort of thing.

From an engineering perspective?

He said, "It took him becoming famous so that it would get to a point where this would be so big (and affect so many humans) that they could heal from it."

How do they heal from it? Specifically thinking of people who were traumatized by some physical act in their own life? By exposing something on a global scale - it helps people to heal?

He says, "Correct."

What's the message in your own words, that might help heal people?

He says, "Just love. Have self love. Know that it or what happened to you wasn't ... know that you didn't cause it."

You mean specifically those boys? Or everyone?

"Everyone who has been in (experienced) it," he says.

It's not that you personally caused it? Correct me if I'm wrong.

He says, "His surroundings did."

So if we're looking at it like a play and we're outside the theater, and we say "We're going to examine these things in this play, but it's going to be difficult to examine these things, but the purpose is to heal people by exposing it?

When he left the planet, he said "He was taken directly back to the planning session."

Okay. Thank you. May I ask, why were you taking that drug that knocked you out, Rohypnol?

He said, "To help him leave."

You were in a hurry to get home?

He had his bags packed, waiting.

But you wouldn't deliberate try to end it all?

He said, "No."

May I ask, was your consciousness still working while you were in that stupor state, what was your consciousness doing?

He said "He was getting ready to go." Bags packed. He showed me like a Mayflower moving truck. I just saw the fire.... you know when he caught on fire?

During the Pepsi commercial... Okay. Some did say you never quite recovered from that. If I may ask – did someone abuse you emotionally or physically? Who abused you?

He says, "His father abused him emotionally, and allowed that (other abuse) to happen by being in that industry. But as to who molested him; it felt like an uncle."

You were molested by someone close?

He says, "Yes. It was someone in the music industry – just feels like an uncle."

How old were you?

"Five" he said.

Someone in the music industry?

He said, "Yes."

But I'll guess that this "Uncle" was abused as well... the cycle has gone on for everyone. I'm not trying to mitigate it or point a finger.

He said, "He knows that."

You said you were... glad... that this documentary came out?

He says, "Yes, that was the point. He had to leave in order for it to come out – because it was so big, many people are able to heal in this way. It took someone as big as him in order to help people heal."

Okay, I think I understand. Michael thank you – I felt bad because you showed up two weeks ago and we tabled our discussion because we were talking to (a famous scientist).

He says, "It was to get in your head for our discussion now."

I haven't seen the film yet and am not looking forward to it. But I understand why it needed to be made now. Thank you for explaining that.

PART TWO: "ALL STAR SCIENCE TEAM"

Nikola Tesla – Albert Einstein - National Archives

HAWKING SAGAN EINSTEIN TESLA

Rich: Okay on to our Flipside All Star science panel – I invited four people today... Albert Einstein, I don't think we've talked to him –

Jennifer: I'm also seeing the guy with the wheelchair.

Stephen Hawking.

I forget that he doesn't need the wheelchair now, I saw him in the wheelchair and then out of it. He has bright eyes.

I asked for four people whose life stories I'm aware of - Nikola Tesla, Carl Sagan, Stephen Hawking and Albert Einstein. I want you all to weigh in on a question I have.

I just saw the Amazon forest.

Okay, that would be a question to ask, and maybe the answer is related... my question to our panel is "What is dark matter and dark energy?" They say that 70% of the Universe is some matter they don't know what it is, which is why they call it dark, and another 25% is energy they can't identify. So I'm going to start with Albert "What is dark matter and dark energy?" Or whoever wants to speak first.

"WOW!" I wish I had a pencil... he showed me like.. two.. it's so important I don't want to get it wrong, I'm seeing two holograms, one black one white, what he's saying is.. it's the energy of yourself outside of yourself.

Energy of yourself outside of yourself – or in the absence of yourself?

He says, "Like a boomerang."

Why are you showing her light and dark matter? Is that like the symbol for yin and yang?

"Yes" he said.

So is dark matter the opposite of matter? Which is to say, not anti-matter as a think, but the opposite of matter represents?

He said, "The opposite of."

So it's both at the same time, is that what you're saying?

"Yes" he said.

The words I'm using to describe what you're saying are incorrect, I get that.

It's going so fast what they're showing me –

Slow it down guys.

They're showing me trees and then the trees that are getting taken, it's creating more of that black hole more of that black matter or... the dark matter. That's where the trees were...

But in order to clarify – as an example, visually, imagine a forest of trees and then they're gone; the dark matter is the energy that is left behind of the trees who were once there?

They say, "Correct." It feels like "The trees that are not there, create the dark energy."

So you're saying the absence of energy is dark energy – it's not the opposite of it, not that it's the negative of it, but the absence of it creates a left-over imprint of hologram of its energy. To paraphrase, the absence of an object retains the qualities of the object?

He says, "Yes."

Let's go down the row. To you Mr. Hawking. Stephen – what's dark energy and dark matter?

He's showing me a chalk board – he's drawing the letter M ....

Okay. Matter...

Then... negative pi squared.

Let me repeat – M and then a left hand parenthesis...

And inside the parenthesis is negative point pi squared.

Okay, and then?

He's not done, then a right parenthesis, then times – what does the symbol for infinity look like?

The number 8 on its side.

He says, "Yes."

So he's writing M $(-.Pi2^{rd})$ x (infinity) Is this correct Albert?

"Yes" he says.

Can we restate it?

"M."

Which is matter? Is equal to..?

He says, "No. M - then a parenthesis, then negative point pi squared..."

Then a closed parenthesis times x – times the infinity symbol?

"Yes" he says.

That equals dark matter? Dark matter and dark energy – they think dark matter is 70% of the universe...

He says, "It's the absence of energy."

Stephen hold that thought for a second. Down the row to Carl Sagan our scientist poet. How would you define dark energy or what is dark energy and dark matter?

He's writing. Hold on. Um. He says, "It's light photosynthesis... buried within our electromagnetic field... argh... trying to get this right. The electromagnetic field causes all of us (to be) where we're supposed to be..."

The electromagnetic field causes everything to exist within it?

(Jennifer pauses, takes a sip of water.) He told me to take a sip because now my brain is fritzing. (To Carl) Show me again on the chalkboard? (To me) It would be nice to have a pen and piece of paper! (Jennifer listens) They just said "I don't need paper, it's a crutch..."

Just draw it out on camera – Carl's answer is that the light is using photosynthesis...

"Light.." wait. "It's not photosynthesis, but photo kinesis... not photosynthesis... light photo kinesis..."

(Note: Photo kinesis is the ability to mentally control light, electromagnetic radiation that is visible to the human eye and is emitted and absorbed in tiny "packets" called photons. Wikipedia)

You mean the energy of the light?

He says, "Yes."

Could be the etheric properties or energy of the light?

He says, "Yes. Yes. Yes. It's an invisible shield." What I'm seeing now, is, you know when they have light, when they shimmer?

It's related to that – the energy of light?

Hold on. "Yes. That energy field is in our electromagnetic field... Yes.".... (long pause)

Carl, take a deep breath.

I saw that light that's infusing our energy field... and then I saw the opposite which is out there.

He's giving an illustration of something like this; think of light and what light is and the opposite of it, or the absence of it, that's what dark energy is?

"Yes. Dark energy that's not dark."

Let me ask this; is dark energy observable from the flipside? Or can they see dark matter?

(Jennifer looks in shock.) That's ... Oh, I'm so afraid of getting it wrong. What he showed me... is... and I see this every day in my work, where when I'm accessing things from the etheric field, I'm seeing the outlines of people, coming and talking to me or talking to you...

The outlines of people etherically?

When I see the etheric – I was given this gift of seeing spirit, they showed me that, the absence of being here (in this realm) is what I'm seeing... I asked "So where do the souls go?" and they're telling me ... it's the absence of them that is dark energy.

But hang on – is dark matter and energy part of their physical realm, or is it only here, something that makes up our physical realm. Or is is both here and there?

Over there (on the flipside) is like the largest computer system conceivable.

Carl, what you're saying is, correct me if I'm wrong; that dark matter and energy are the essence of what souls are, what we're talking about is how they exist and yet don't exist.

355

He says…"Yeah. No."

Tell me Carl.

He said, "It's the abstract of our human brain waves."

You mean it's related to what consciousness is?

He says, "Correct."

So if it's accurate that consciousness is not a thing per se, but refers to a medium or a vehicle – the way water is - then dark matter is a vehicle more like an engine than a thing.

He said, "That's what they've been trying to tell us."

Okay, on down the row to Nikola Tesla. So Nikola, give us your best answer; what is dark energy and matter made up of?

He's so short! He's like the size of Napoleon.

I didn't know that. But please; explain what dark matter is. How does dark matter affect us? What is it?

He's showing me something with heaviness... wait..

You mean gravitational?

"Yes" he said.

Is that what you mean by heaviness, that it has gravitational properties?

"Yes."

So it functions like gravity does, is that correct, but includes the opposite or the absence of it?

He says, "The absence of it."

Okay, I've heard this – and it's why they know that dark matter exists, because they realized that whatever dark matter is functions like gravity but nobody knows precisely what it is .. but if no one knows what it is...

He's saying, "It's the creation of us – of what we're doing here in this existence. It's the creation of us, there's so much of it, I feel like it's a block in the pool..."

A block in a pool? Do you mean like a whirlpool?

He says, "It's a block in our minds."

So if we open ourselves up to it...

They pointed to the back of my head... they said the medulla... if we open that up... it's connected to dark matter.

(Note: The Medulla Oblongata, or the medulla, is the brain stem.)

So if we could somehow find a way to take off that filter on the Medulla, we could see dark matter? What would it look like?

They're showing me... wow. I don't know if you ever saw the film "Twilight," but do you remember when they went outside into the sun and everything and everyone's skin suddenly started to become iridescent and sparkle? It's like that. Like crystals everywhere.

Almost electromagnetic. Would it look like an electrical field?

Wow. Everything suddenly became completely quiet. Like as if I was in a vacuum of sound. Do you remember when I told you about that time I got lost in the mountains of Sedona and couldn't hear anything? Sound and everything suddenly disappeared... They're showing me that's what it would feel like ... it's not what it is... but what it isn't.

Just to be clear, it's not a negative thing to have the absence of energy - you could call it light matter, couldn't you? Is that correct?

There is something, an element that is negative about it. Because I keep asking them "Is it light?" And they keep saying "No." I'm trying not to judge it; I'm trying to find out what's negative about it...

What do they mean? Negative? Is it a word that means bad or is about the physical charge?

They're showing me battery symbols; positive and negative.

Okay, so it's about the physical charge. We live in a polarized world – it's not that it's just good or bad, but it's this yin and yang existence related to the polar magnetization.

He says, "You need both to exist."

So why is 95% of the dark matter not visible if we need both to exist?

He says, "Because it's creating all these other universes that we can't see."

If we could see the flipside, what we would see is that tiny bit of matter, where we exists, is where life exists. The rest is creating other universes.

He says, "Yes. There are so many galaxies and so many different places!"

So dark matter is like a medium or vehicle but how does it function... Does it function in the same way?

He said, "Source is dark matter."

Does it function the way energy works in our universe does, the laws of energy where it doesn't dissipate but transforms into other forms? Like energy flowing into a blackhole emerges transformed?

"Yes," he said. They're showing me our earth – showing that when things are no longer in it, then dark matter grows, gets bigger.

Who's showing you that?

Tesla.

Well thanks Nick, so if the things that are disappearing or are being destroyed are growing the amount of dark matter, you're saying its a good thing the universe is being destroyed? Just trying to follow your logic my friend.

They showed me the ice ages, how the earth transforms over time, it destroys itself through natural disasters, for example....

The earth is always transforming?

He said, "Transference."

(Note: There's a new theory about "transference" as a physics principle. "A psychologist and a physicist combine their disciplines in studying the transference as an interactive field... To unpack the notion of interactive field we describe the physics of local, causal, classical fields and directly connect them to the therapeutic encounter of the first two levels. The second two levels require discussion of nonlocal, acausal, quantum fields. In this connection, the subtle body and joint active imagination provide a physiological and symbolic experience of the interactive field." (From "On the physics and psychology of the transference as an interactive field" by Victor Mansfield J. Marvin Spiegelman 1996)

Like black holes? Is dark matter going through black holes?

"Correct" he said.

Because that's where all the other universes are?

"Yes." (Jennifer shrugs) I don't know any of this.

Who said that answer?

They all did.

Anything else you guys want to tell us about this science?

They say, "Love and have fun."

What is love in this paradigm? If you're telling us that source is dark matter than that means love is dark matter.

They say, "Yes. You have to love yourself (because) you are dark matter."

Hang on, set the concept of love aside.

"It causes wars."

Set love aside as an emotion – focus on the physical representation of it as a thing. If unconditional love is source, then dark matter is unconditional love. Is that correct or do you want to amend that?

"It has no judgment. It is unconditional love. Whatever you are is what you are."

Okay. Thanks class. That was amazing, and that was intense.

CHAPTER TWENTY ONE
"GAME NOT OVER MAN"

Bill Paxton, still from TV show "Hatfield's McCoy's"

BILL PAXTON, STEPHEN HAWKING, CARL SAGAN

Jennifer and I in our usual place, me opening the class up to whomever wants to join us.

Rich: Who do we bring forward today?

Jennifer: Bill Paxton. He's wearing a cowboy hat, has a toothpick in his mouth – wearing boots that he loves, don't know what they're made out of; I'm sure it's politically incorrect... (Jennifer listens:) Snakeskin boots? Ew.

No snakes are hurt on the flipside.

He wants to say something about his son.

James; what about him?

He says, "He's traveling or about to travel, feels like something good associated with that. Maybe you should reach out to him."

Bill cut it out – I've reached out to your whole fam damily as best I can, and haven't heard a peep out of them. Which is okay, who wants to reach out to some nutball who claims to speak to your beloved? I can't blame them; I wouldn't talk to me either.

He says, "There's going to be an opening. One of them is going to contact you. There will be an opening."

Okay. So what should I tell James?

He says, "Talk to him about Tibet and Buddhism."

Okay, sure. What do you want me to tell him? That Tibet's a cool place to go?

"Tell him that it's going to be okay, without being an asshole about it."

(Note: This is funny and bizarre at the same time. Jennifer isn't calling *me* an *a**hole*, my old friend Bill is. I am familiar with Buddhism, have been to Tibet, I know that meditation can cure many ills, mental difficulties, and there is something timeless and wonderful about the Tibetan form of Buddhism which examines the nature of reality. So – my answering with sarcasm only means, "I'll do my best.")

What's going to be ok?

He's saying, "Someone is suffering..."

Do you mean like the Tibetan concept of suffering? Stuff like that?

"Yeah."

That's the idea we go through things in life to explore them and learn from the harder things in life? Okay, I will do my best my friend.

My dad just popped in and said "right Jen?" I get so mad about him being gone. Bill thanked you.

Billy you're always welcome. Hang loose, hang tight.

He says the same for you; hang tight, hang loose, and he showed me a boat.

What boat?

That movie you're supposed to do. About a boat.

(Note: I think I know what he means, but maybe he's kidding.)

Jim (Jennifer's dad) we were going to ask you about Jennifer's first experience with spirit. What can you tell her?

He showed me something I've heard about; they left me in the car by accident with the windows rolled up – they forgot me in the car. And I overheated.

How old were you?

I was in a baby seat. They showed me I did die and came back. I remember not being able to breathe. I was around 2 years old.

Can you go to that moment aware you can't breathe? Can you be there in that moment now?

Everything is so hot.

Try to cool it down in your mind, everything's cool. Do you pass out?

Yeah.

So look around, who's with you when this occurs that alerts your folks to get back to the car?

Oh. It was my great grandmother. They just forgot I was in there. I felt like I couldn't breathe, closed my eyes, and woke up screaming. I didn't die but I almost did. I did pass out.

When you remember that, who's there to assist?

My great grandmother, on the other side; she holds me and says "Everything's going to be okay," - she did something to my heart to make me wake up crying.

Describe her to me.

She's very beautiful, dirty blond hair, this all white outfit – sometimes I see Luana like that – like a nurse outfit but not a nurse outfit. She was very peaceful; I sense that she is like my guide.

(Note: In Luana's last movie role, I had her playing a nurse in Point of Betrayal complete with a white outfit. Funny that she would appear now and then wearing that.)

Is she your guide, one of your guides?

Yeah. I didn't know that.

Does this relate to Jennifer's gift of being able to see outside her frequency?

It's because I saw them – whoever was around. They acted like it was a party; they knew I would be okay.

Who was there at this party you're seeing?

My family that wasn't born yet. Interesting. The veil was so thin.

So this is your first experience with spirit?

Yes. They're showing me they did something to my heart to make me cry. My folks told me the only reason I was alive is because I cried (and alerted them.)

Let me clarify this; it wasn't the overheating that made her adept, you're just showing her the first incident, and she would grow to get stronger and better at it?

They tap their nose – that's correct.

This relates to a conversation we had a couple of weeks ago, talking to our science all stars and asking about dark matter and energy – and someone said it was related to the medulla... back of the head, said it was the access point – and I looked it up – it's the brain stem – you pointed to where it comes up through the neck. It's the gateway. Jim step in... and any of our scientists – how do we access source while in our body? Is it related to the medulla? The brain stem? Or the pineal gland?

It's the pineal gland... it feels like a combustion – both have to work together. He says, "It's like they have to not work and work together, rewired almost."

Is the pineal gland a filter? Or a limiter?

He says, "It's an un-limiter."

So it functions like a stereo receiver?

"Correct," he says. "The frequency that gets tuned in... um... the pineal gland is like... the receiver, the filter is the medulla."

Whose idea was it to make the pineal gland a receiver? A group idea?

They're all talking at the same time. It's kind of funny – it made sense as you would want it to be through your feet and showed me a person with their feet in the air... and your body doesn't need to be working in order to access it.

Okay, is the pineal gland in every human being?

They're saying "Everybody's pineal gland is open but it's like having..." I hope I'm seeing this right. "It's like when you have a flat tire on your car doesn't work – if you have too many disbeliefs, it just doesn't work."

But let's talk about the physiology – if the pineal gland works with medulla..

He says, "Its yin and yang."

Some kids are able to communicate freely...

He says, "All children are."

So when they can't around the age of 8 is that because because their skulls harden and their reception goes down?

He says, "Both. The skull hardens and um... it's the disbelief and the parents, etc."

If you're asleep does it work easier? Does that somehow affect the pineal gland?

He says, "100 thousand percent."

During sleep the medulla is quiet, but is the pineal gland like a homing beacon?

Yes.

Okay, very good – do our science all stars want to do a follow up on this dark matter issue? One gave us a formula, one gave us images, one gave us a forest and absence of a forest...

The shadow. Right.

Anything you want to tell Jennifer to continue this conversation?

They just showed me a balloon flying up.

Who's here?

Stephen Hawking is here.

And he says "Think of a balloon?" Does he mean "a higher message?"

I'm seeing the thoughts that go up (to them on the flipside) the difference is that I have a receiver to get the thoughts to come back... (Jennifer aside:) Say it again? In the information superhighway, you're allowed (to have) messages to flow simultaneously. Like a car.

You're talking about the vehicle of dark matter? Is it dark matter you're referring to?

He said, "Yes." Thoughts go up. That alerts the people you're calling or would like to speak to, to be around.

You're answering a question I was about to ask – "How does this work so Jennifer can speak to spirit?" The answer is "the questions go up, and the answer comes down?"

He says, "It's like being on a racetrack but much faster, I have few roadblocks and no flat tires."

Let's break it down – is Stephen standing or sitting?

Standing. He has these little glasses on.

Wire rim glasses?

Yes. He's wearing a suit, and a red bowtie, a blue shirt – darker colored. Feels like a blue suit with a lighter blue... it's something like he wore when he was 19... dusted off an old college suit.

Thank you for coming in to talk to us. Question at hand is; "How Jennifer able to communicate with you? Or how are we able to communicate with people on the other side, it's like an information highway?

He stays "she stays in her lane."

That you should or shouldn't stay in your lane, or that's just her lane?

He says, "It's like I have my own lane but there 100 thousand cars swirling around everywhere." I can see the road, but I can see it's a metaphor for being able to speak to spirit.

I see; she's in the midst of all those other cars, but she has her own unique frequency that helps her?

They're showing me how much this work strengthens the pineal gland because of it.

In terms of people who don't have her gift.. who don't have the ability to speak to spirit?

It's funny, he says "It's like owning a car, think of a Fiat or something, something old or beat up in the beginning, then by learning this and doing this more and more, your energy becomes more efficient and you become more like a Ferrari." (Jennifer listens:) I was asking is it like a car getting less efficient as time goes on? And they say, "It's the opposite. The more you do it the more green lights you're going to have."

I keep hearing in this research, in terms of spirit, I hear about a shift in consciousness that's happening, and that's why we're on the planet at this point in time.

They say, "It's still only the top 1%, that are even aware of it."

Correct me if I'm wrong, how can Jennifer and I help facilitate this shift? Or can we?

"Film." Film... that's what he's saying.

What would you like to tell people on the planet that would convince them on some level that this actually is you talking?

He says "That it's backed up by science."

I heard a funny story about you the other day that Jennifer could not know the answer to this question. There was a moment in time you were on your way to a reading of a Simpson's episode – Hank Azaria was saying on the Late Show that you had suggested to them to be on the show. *You were on your way there but were running late, and one of the actors at the table read, Harry Shearer said something funny about you being late.*

He said, "It had to do with time... the concept of time."

That's correct. He said "The man has no concept of time."

(Note: This is about as mind bending a detail as I can imagine. Jennifer did not watch the Colbert show, and then neither did Hawking. What is being referred to here is the actor Hank Azaria telling a story on Colbert where he said "The funniest adlib I ever heard was from Harry Shearer" and he told that story. Remember; Hawking was not in the room when it was said – he was running late.)

How could you be aware of that?

Jennifer: Me or him?

I know your getting it from him. That's exactly what the actor Harry Shearer said.

He's saying, "The man has no concept of time."

How do you know that?

He showed me how illusionary time is.

But that sentence is exactly what Harry Shearer said. "The man has no concept of time." Tell me how Stephen put that sentence into your mind.

He showed me the word "time" and then showed me it dissipating out into the future... that's how he showed it to me. disappearing into the future... He's in my lane.

Geeze Louise, you're riding in her car and in her lane. You're in her frickin' Ferrari.

He said "She's a Lamborghini. He showed me the music outside as an example."

A frequency, yes; while you're in this car together... and music retains memory of when it was performed, right? A: I asked Jennifer a question she could not know the answer to; B: you could not know the answer to because you were not there when the joke was said Stephen. So how are you able to access what was said? Did someone tell that to you later on? Or are you able to access that time frame of that moment in time when it happened?

"Instantly," he says.

Help me with this concept... I want you to help me with this question. Are we speaking about the holographic universe?

I'll share with you the image he showed me. He showed me a disk being pulled out.

Like a DVD or CD? And each disc...

"Each disc is the Akashic record of that moment in time." That's what I (would) refer to it as.

Like slices of time? It's part of the Akashic record, but you are accessing slices of time? Packets of the moment in time?

"Yes" he says.

These slices of time exist unto themselves, so when I ask about a particular slice of time, we can access that time together, is that correct?

He says, "Absolutely."

You access it simultaneously... and people like Jennifer are able to as well?

I asked him while you were talking "Are you getting it (the information) out of Richard's head?" I'm the skeptic here and he says "no" and he showed me pulling out an old floppy disk. He's showing me tons and tons and tons of numbers and just honing in to whatever is in our lane.

So the numbers, is how the event, or how the information is stored in its frame of time?

He says, "Like Pi, down to the (specific) numbers."

In speaking of dark energy, we got a formula from someone – "Negative pi times infinity." And Pi was included. Is that what dark energy is?

"Yes" he says.

And you guys said the other day that dark energy is source? Are you saying that dark energy is consciousness?

"You have to" he says.

But if source is dark energy... that means if we're going to access slices of holographic time...

I'm seeing everything in holograms.

So even us, here in this room – we are slices of time, but let me ask you, is this idea of accessing slices of time is that the "second coming?" Is that related to understanding this kind of information as some form of epiphany that might include the concept of "a second coming?" Not from a religious perspective, but because once we realize there is not time, we can see that Jesus never left?

(Jennifer laughs) Stephen just went and got my dad. (Jim was a Mormon bishop).

That's hilarious.

My dad says, "Yes."

This is fascinating. One more time please. Past, present, future...

Oh, they're showing me the outline of a human being, when we pass away, it's like with people who have lost a limb...

Phantom limbs?

He says, "That's dark energy, what dark energy is – phantom energy of something that once existed in that space. So when people pass away it (that space) still has that energy" – that's what I see when people come in and out (of their bodies in spirit form)

You did say that the energy field is like dark energy.

I'm so glad you're filming this! I would never remember any of this. Hold on. I asked "How come I don't remember what is given

to me (during a session) and what I heard is that it negates being attached to it.

So psychologically it's a good thing - otherwise you'd be associated with every murder you've solved. Let's talk about the second coming.

My dad is laughing right now about that.

Here's my point – this whole idea that a second coming – or that Jesus is returning is related to our work. In a number of interviews, we've "brought Jesus back" because we demonstrated that Jesus never left.

"Correct" he said.

So the idea that Jesus is returning is not correct, it's that people will realize that he's never left, is that correct?

(A long pause). "Yes." (Jennifer aside:) I asked about the bad stuff. and suddenly I got an image of Saddam Hussein – who has not been in my mind for years; hear me out, (before I can protest that one man's villain is another man's hero) but that bad stuff is already happening... that's what I'm being shown, and that's forcing people to open their hearts to this, that's part of the second coming, as you've said.

The reason I asked it this way – is because I want the scientists (in our class) to look at this, and Jesus and Jim to look at this all as one piece. It has nothing to do with biblical references, that's all metaphor – it's pointing to something, but it is metaphorical. I'm referring to people feeling as if Jesus was returning as we know he's not the only avatar in the game.

"Correct." And I'm being shown that there is a big avatar soul group – he just showed me that. I asked "What's the difference between you and the rest of the humans?" and he showed me that he's aware of every avatar in his soul group.

So if someone is aware of who they were on the flipside...

"Then everything (pain and suffering) starts dissipating, then your energy field doesn't make you sick; your body can recoup (through this knowledge.)"

The reason I ask this is because it's like a lightning bolt. The idea that there is a "second coming," but if the second coming is a revelation that he never left or that we can be conscious of all of our loved ones who passed away – including but not limited to...

Jesus.

And Mary, and everyone. Sorry I didn't mean to shift away from you Stephen.

Carl Sagan just came in.

What do you want to say Carl? This is the scientist who created the music CD that traveled into deep space with Chuck Berry on it.

He's saying "Like with what I (Jennifer) do for my work, music does the same thing by being in a certain lane, like in my work. He showed me music puts people in that lane, music is like a frequency going up and up."

I've come to the realization music is identical to quantum mechanics and appears to retain the memory of the moment; so the frequency of the music also retains your experience of hearing the music. When you listen to Beethoven's 9th you're accessing all the other performances simultaneously.

He says, "And that's related to the disk (Sagan sent into space). The Akashic memory of that event."

Carl I need your help there is a scientist named Mino. He's from Japan. He was a scientist, he died and his mom wrote books bout him.

When I first see is a tree in Africa or Asia, there's a huge tree that I'm seeing... then I saw that scientist with the apple... (Newton) It has to to with time and space going back and forth?

I don't know his work; it could be about time and space. Let's ask. (He was a physicist).

Let me get this first. So you can pick an apple, the tree holds all the memories; what' I'm picking up - he's showing me one tree from two different time periods, when we are there, if we allow ourselves, we can pick up all the energy from that particular tree in that time frame, or from all the time frames.

What was Mino's work on the planet?

He says, "It was something like string theory... (Ding!). He showed me a violin... he also showed me... the guy who wrote about string theory."

Is that research important to you now?

He says, "Yes, because it leaps them into it. They go out of their mind and into it."

Is it related to time?

He says, "That there is no time. We can create everything; it's already out there, we're creating it by bringing it in – hold on. Some people don't know they can create it, they just go and let things happen, like working on a project; you have to do it and can't expect it to be done (to get the result.)"

So what kind of work do you want people to carry on?

"Mind focus," it feels like he's saying.

Anything specific related to my wife who asked about you?

He showed me her heart. He says, "She has a beautiful heart. Have her focus on where she wants to be as if its happening now. If she's in a stressful place or if she's in a space where she's stressed, have her jump out of it."

Focus on what it should be like and have her turn into that?

He says, "Yes."

What's her relation to the Pleiades?

(Jennifer aside) I'm related to the Pleiades as well. (Jennifer listens). He says, "She's part of the 7 daughters; she's like the oldest daughter."

You mean relating to the Greek myth? Or are you talking about actual daughters?

I don't know either.

So she had a lifetime in the Pleiades?

He says, "Several."

Is she visited by her friends from there?

He says, "Always."

Anything she needs to know or what's she passing along to them?

He says, "Where earth is right now; they're trying to figure it out but she's so light.... – so lighthearted, everything is like nails on a chalkboard to her... They're trying to figure out if they need to come down here."

How many *lifetimes has she had over there?*

Feels like one that was a thousand years.

Has Jennifer had any lifetimes there?

"Yes."

I've met some other Pleiadeans – I've heard there's going to be a shift in consciousness in relation to what they're doing... is that the work she's doing in her sleep?

"Yes. They want to help us save the planet."

Are they going to?

"Yes, they have to. They're checking to see if the vibration here is getting better. They want to know how they're going to acclimate."

It is getting better isn't it?

"Yes it is."

All right, thank you class, Jennifer has to run. We appreciate all your help!

*****

CHAPTER TWENTY TWO
THEY'VE ALREADY WATCHED IT

Nipsey from his YouTube page. WB Yeats (Wikimedia)

NIPSEY HUSSLE WILLIAM BUTLER YEATS DAVID BOWIE

Another day in Manhattan Beach. On the monitors in the restaurant, the news of the death of community activist and rapper, Nipsey Hussle. We begin our taping, while Jennifer looks up at the live memorial service given for him by his friend Snoop Dogg. (Calvin Broadus)

Rich: Luana opening it up to you – anything you guys want to say about the death of Nipsey?

Jennifer: (Jennifer listens) There's a connection between Prince and Nipsey – Prince says they already said... (a pause, as she listens.)

Prince what do you want to say?

(Jennifer aside) Wow. He says, "Nipsey died because of his gang relationships from a long, long time ago."

What do you want to tell us from your new perspective?

They keep saying, "They've already watched it." (The memorial service).

Anything you want me to tell Snoop on his Instagram page?

He's trying to figure out how to talk (to us). He says, "He's with God." He says, "It's much better than anyone could visualize. When he rapped... he would feel that energy when he rapped."

Prince you can help him with this form of communication. You're the best in helping him with this.

And Jimi Hendrix... is helping. All of them are standing up now, it's interesting to see. It's a class, and they're all here to help Nipsey communicate.

Nipsey, Stevie Wonder is speaking at your funeral. He just said "We're still living in a time where ego anger, jealousy is controlling our lives."

Wow. I feel like his girlfriend or wife had a dream of him and they were dancing together and he told her everything was okay.

I think she said something like that on the podium.

(Jennifer listens) He wants to say more (to us) later on.

Ok very good, thanks for stopping by. We'll continue this in the future. Thank you Luana.

She's saying "The fact that you are both in this flipside class – and your past relationship, which begin in this life in the screenwriting class, both using the art of communication... is hilarious."

My treat is that I got to meet both Jennifer and Luana in this lifetime. Two avatars of communication. Anybody else Luana?

David Bowie. Something about his wife – has a connection to Nipsey.

Is that why you're front and center? Because of his connection to your wife Iman?

"Yeah."

What would you like to say to her?

He says, "I tell her everyday that I love her."

She writes those things on Instagram; they're beautiful.

(Note: Iman's Instagram is a vestige for clever witty sayings about getting through life.)

He says, "She's a pure channel for that."

She seems like a lovely person.

He says, "I win."

You're still winning. Anyone else want to talk to us?

(Jennifer aside) My dad.

Jim what's up buddy? Someone wrote me about a dream they had about the Irish Poet William Butler Yeats. Luana can you bring him in? I think we spoke to him once briefly.

"You cut him off," he said.

(Note: Nothing quite like being chastised by someone on the flipside.)

We talked about his muse; the woman named Maude Gonne. He wrote about her incessantly, and my poetry professor told the story of Yeats startling her in an airport once, like a stalker, if I recall.

He says, "She made that up. (The relationship) It was good for the writing."

Ok. And he says "Besides; I was gay."

(Note: We don't "out" people in our work, generally. Yeats was married, had a daughter; people who are Yeats fans may be offended by hearing this, but in his defense of his using Maude Gonne as a muse for his poetry, he's arguing that he couldn't have stalked her because she's not his type. Duly noted.)

Oh, okay.

He shows me a feminine side: making fun of him stalking this woman. He didn't write about "love being a man."

May I ask, did you write the poem "The second coming" about the Great War, World War I?

He's showing me China.

How does he show you "China?"

He showed me the red dot in a flag.

Oh, you know what he's saying? That the poem was related to World War II. He wrote the poem in 1920 – he was talking about the oncoming battle of with Germany and Japan... is that it?

He says, "Yes."

Thanks William Butler. Over to David. You said you wanted me to reach out to your wife. What do you want me to say to her?

He says, "Tell her to follow... follow her heart."

Did she meet someone?

He says, "Yes." He's saying "To follow her heart; it doesn't mean she doesn't love him if he loves someone else."

Follow your heart even if it leads you to somebody else, doesn't mean you love someone less?

"Yes" he said.

Can we talk about how those communications work? Let's pretend I put this on her Instagram page, she has 1000 comments a day – how do you direct her to look at the one from you?

He says "He taps her on the shoulder."

You'll tap her to look at the text from me?

"Yes."

Does she sit at a computer when she's accessing her page?

He says "She's on her cell."

So she's in her car scrolling messages?

He said, "No, someone does it for her."

So David – give me a word that will make her realize it's from you.

He says, "Kitten."

That's your nickname for her?

That's what came through... I saw the ears... he said "It's kitten."

Something like "Kitten: David says "follow your heart because....?"

He says "Follow your heart – you do not betray the one that's in your heart."

That's great. Say, are you a writer?

"Yes, I am" he says.

That's what you wanted to tell us?

He said, "Yes."

We love short messages because we can pass along short stuff... who's next?

I'm seeing a couple of people but I need to organize it. (After a pause) Prince wants to go first.

C'mon in.

He's saying something about Dave Chapelle writing music or a show. "He's writing music." Dave feels like he's talking to Prince and he needs to know that he is.

How is he talking to him? Meditating?

Jennifer whispers something to Prince.

What? No secret conversations with the dead please.

(Jennifer protests) Let me go through my process! Okay; he showed me Dave, it feels like he's writing music... I know he's not a musician but that's what it feels like.

(Note: In an interview with screenwriter Robert Towne's mother, she said that Robert was a musician, and meant that he "writes music with his words." It's possible that's the music from Dave's mouth.)

Prince is helping?

Prince said that Dave is listening to Prince... so yes. I said "Did he see you?" He said "No, but he feels him."

Can I ask about the process? Where does he go to channel you Prince?

(Jennifer laughs) Okay. It's outside.. but like in a game room place. When he walks out of his house, it's back and to the left if you're looking at his front door. There's a man cave where they play basketball. I think it's his man cave. He also showed me Dave looking up with his wife, looking up and just thinking about him.

Is he listening to music at the same time?

He says, "No." I asked, "So what is he doing?" He said "Dave's wants to know why Prince left the planet."

We talked to you about that – should Dave read that?

He says, "Not at first." He wants me to talk to Dave about him. To talk to him..."

You should call Dave and tell him he needs to talk to Prince? Or Prince needs to talk to Dave?

I've never done that before.

Prince, you can help with this.

He said, "He'll force Dave to listen." (Jennifer listens) He said "I should talk about Prince and what Dave is thinking about... and why he keeps thinking about Prince and why he left." It will organically happen. I just heard Aretha Franklin say "I want to talk to him" and then Robin Williams – it's like a flood gates.

So if you say "someone wants to talk to you" it might be too overwhelming for them. Prince what is it you want to tell Dave Chappelle about your journey and passage?

He wants to tell Dave not to fall into the same path. I said "What, jumping off pianos?"

That's funny. Let's leave the comedy to Dave. Reach out to him.

CHAPTER TWENTY THREE:

"I UNDERSTAND YOU'RE THE PERSON I NEED TO TALK TO."

RFK: National Archives

CONVERSATION WITH ROBERT KENNEDY

Rich: Someone showed up at my apartment yesterday. We may have chatted with him before. I asked if he wanted to attend our session.

Jennifer: Abraham Lincoln?

(Note: Jennifer sees an image which is a clue to who I've invited, and if I can figure out why they put that image in her mind, we go from there. Normally, I say aloud the name of the person I want to speak with prior to our meeting and she often says "so and so is here" – the person whose name I had said aloud moments earlier. In this case, Abraham Lincoln would mean something to do with a President or Washington DC (a politician) or with Abraham himself.)

Not Lincoln but in that ballpark; the brother of a President.

Oh, Robert Kennedy. A picture of him just showed up.

Does he want to speak to me?

He says, "Yes." It's about writing. He showed me you, looking down with a bunch of writing.

Writing? You want me to write something or craft a blog about you?

Not exactly... He says, "He wants you to look something up... research... like... I'm seeing Joe DiMaggio..." (Jennifer aside:) What's going on? He's saying "It's about Marilyn Monroe's death."

Hang on. Robert showed up in my kitchen – I heard him saying "I understand you're the person I need to speak with to get a message to my children." I told him to wait until our session, to get his backstage pass from Luana to speak with Jennifer. We've chatted with Marilyn before about her journey, and she could speak with us about her death. I'm asking why he showed up in my place to get my attention?

He says, "Yeah, he knows (about talking to Marilyn) and he knows we spoke to his brother."

So what is Robert here to discuss?

He says, "It has to do with someone who is related to him."

Okay, let's focus on that. Is it that you want to pass along something to one of your children?

It feels like that's the case. Perhaps the youngest...

I don't know who they all are. But does this child share your first name?

(Note: I threw it out there, because I guessed it was his son, who had been on "The Charles Grodin" show when I worked there.)

He says, "It's a girl."

Hold on; before we get to the girl...

He said, "She's writing about it.... someone's writing about it."

Writing about what? About Marilyn, Robert?

He says, "About everybody."

About the family. Okay. Do you want me to ask the questions we normally ask? Like "Who was there to greet you on the flipside?"

Jennifer waves her hand. He says "Tell Richard to stop interrupting."

Okay. Sorry. Go ahead.

(After a pause.) Okay, follow me. He says "The secrets are in the records," and then he showed me the tapes that were taken or whatever.

Do you mean the tapes or secrets of your death or Marilyn's death?

"The secrets of Marilyn's death" he says.

Why would we care about Marilyn Monroe's death?

(Jennifer makes a face.) She just said "Stop it. Hey!"

What I mean is, of course we care about you Marilyn, and appreciate your journey, but the actual process of checking out is not that important. Once you're on the flipside, you see why things occurred. Am I wrong?

(Jennifer waves away my comment.) He says, "It has to do with those responsible for his death and her death – that she was killed and the same people are responsible."

I'm familiar with some of the accounts of her passing.

"There was a cover up" he said.

I've heard people claim her death was deliberate and people deliberately cleaned up her home, including taking a diary and pills in her possession, anything that might have been related to friends in high places.

(Note: There were reports about Marilyn speaking to Peter Lawford prior to her death, that the actor was the person who called her doctor to head to her home. It was reported in some theories that doctor cleaned up her Brentwood home (her notorious "red diary" was missing) by those who wanted to cover up the story. I try to focus on what people are telling us from the flipside, and this is the first time someone has asked (or insisted) we talk about the circumstances around someone passing. Even though it may be something that Jennifer deals with (missing persons and murders at the request of law enforcement agents who've worked with her in the past) this is a first for me.)

Maybe it's that "the truth should be out" and he's saying (or trying to say) "It should be out."

Okay. But if we can, let's talk about what happened to Robert in June 1968.

I see him going through a kitchen.

There was a young man who shot you, but forensics have said that more bullets were fired than that person had in his possession. And all of those LAPD records and photos have subsequently disappeared.

He said "Yes."

So who was behind your death? Was this fellow who is in prison for your death a pawn?

He says, "Yes."

So who was behind it?

(Jennifer listens) He says, "Another President."

Which one?

(Jennifer listens, then looks up confused). I'm seeing Lyndon B. Johnson. But it can't be him though, can it?

Let's ask Robert. Were these individuals people who worked for the CIA or who worked for him (LBJ)?

He's saying "Who worked for him."

As contract killers, is that correct?

He says "Yes."

I'm familiar with this story.

(Note: "Brothers" by David Talbot, which deals with the revelations E. Howard Hunt as to the identity of this "contract killer" who worked for the CIA and was present in a meeting in New Orleans, and was in Dallas and seen in the kitchen of the hotel in Los Angeles. That's why I asked the question. I'm aware of the case against LBJ – it's hard to fathom or believe. But I've looked into it enough (people who claimed to see him in Jack Ruby's strip club, a photo of Oswald in the same club, there's Hunt's account that Oswald was in the meeting with the CIA contract hitman, etc.) Again – I'm not trying to ask questions that bolster or deny any conspiracy theory, idea or path. I'm asking these questions because "Robert" showed up in my home and asked to speak with us.)

(Jennifer aside) I have no idea about this.

Let me ask him; are you saying that the book written by David Talbot "Brothers" is accurate?

He says "Yes." (Jennifer aside) So it is, right?

I don't know. I can say that I've read a few things and that book has the most in depth interviews. Everything I've read that he's mentioned in the has shown up somewhere else as fact.

(Jennifer aside:) That's crazy...

But let's go back to where we started. Is this the information you wanted to speak to us about, is this the "important death" or is it Marilyn Monroe's?

He says, "It's (they're) connected."

Please allow me to clarify; are you saying Marilyn was murdered by the same people who murdered you?

He says "Yes." And now he's showing me a frame – he was blamed for that. Or someone was framed as if they were involved.

Can we ask Marilyn to step forward?

Jennifer pauses: She (Marilyn) says "She didn't feel anything..." (when it happened). (Jennifer aside:) Was she on the same kind of drugs that Michael Jackson took?

Perhaps similar. I think hers were downers. (Barbiturates vs Propofol and Lorazepam) Is it important for us to ask about the manner of your death Marilyn, and if so why?

She says, "Because it needs to be put to rest."

Put the story to rest?

She says "Yes."

Robert, you showed up, caught my attention because you wanted us to focus on this by talking to Jennifer, or is this because you want us to reach out to someone in your family who is writing about this?

I'm confused; hold on. I heard "A" (first option)– but he may have meant (talking to) the daughter at first.

Well let's go through a list of your children's names... (looking up wikipedia). If you can tell us which one you want me to reach out to. (reading) Geeze; you only had 11 kids. Kathleen was the first...

What's the second? Is there a Laurie?

I see Kathleen, Joe, RFK jr., David, Courtney, Michael, Kerry Chris, Max... hang on there's more. Rory. Which one you want me to reach out to?

I think it's Rory. Rory is the one (name) that keeps coming in.

Hang on, let me look her up, as I think one is a filmmaker.

I think he gave me "Laurie" to find Rory...

It says on IMDB she is an award winning filmmaker.

He's saying "She's working on something about the era, the family in the 60's. And she needs to go deeper into this story."

Let me ask, is she making a film about you, your death or your family?

He says, "About that time period."

Quick question about RFK Jr?

He just rolled his eyes.

(Note: "Rolling his eyes" doesn't mean a disparaging comment, often is because I'm going off track or knows what I'm going to ask.)

I know he has had some trauma in his life, with his marriage and first wife... he married the actress from the show..

(Jennifer aside:) It feels like he was with her all along.

What?

He was with the actress... all along during the (his) marriage.

Okay. I think his ex-wife had some emotional, mental issues and checked herself off the planet. Might have been bi-polar or depressive.

He just laughed; "Welcome to the world of Kennedy women." He's kidding. He says "They reconciled." She just gave him a fist bump.

What message do you have for Robert Jr – he's been very vocal about the environment and has gone after the big companies that make untested, unregulated vaccines.

He says "Don't get himself killed; the Kennedys are prone to it."

(Note: Jennifer has no opinion about this information. I'm startled by it but trying to ignore my conscious thoughts. That kind of comment may seem negative, but I ask her not to filter whatever she's hearing. And I try not to filter it when I'm editing.)

Okay.. but is there a more polite way can I say it? How do you say "Don't do the work you're doing?"

He says, "He can't hear it."

Your son is a champion for ecological health, and human health. How do you feel he is doing? Is he on the right path?

"Yes" he says.

That's important to say – if there's any possible way that I can relate that "We talked to your dad and he says you're on the right path" I'll try to do so.

He says "Say whatever you can say within reason."

That's a tall order – in a reasonable conversation with someone no longer on the planet. All right – you want me to reach out to your kids and suggest they connect to you through Jennifer? So she can help them have a real time conversation with you?

He says, "Yes. You open up the conversations."

Robert's widow Ethel is friends with the godfather of my kids Charles Grodin.

He just showed me all the lines and connection you guys have.

I was not aware of that. So why did you tap me on the shoulder?

He showed me; me. (To talk to Jennifer)

Okay, that makes sense. You reached out so I could connect him to you, and hopefully his children will forge a path to him as well. Thank you.

It's funny how he showed me Abraham Lincoln first... to get to him.

Very good, thank you sir. You're always welcome to join our class discussions.

A FEW WEEKS LATER:

Okay, anyone else want to come forward?

A president again. Lincoln.

Okay, let's go with that. Abe wants to talk to us?

No, his wife.

Mary Todd Lincoln? We did talk to her briefly in another session.

Did we?

(Note: She rarely recalls what was said during a session. It's like she's on "pause" while she speaks or answers my questions.)

Yes, she talked about being placed in a sanitorium – for her issues. She told us she was a medium during her life as well, saw things in the future. But they put her in a mental institution.

"To be safe," she said.

Okay, Mrs. Lincoln. I'm surprised you would stop by, but please, what do you want to tell us?

She's going back into a history book. She's showing me a book of history.

Luana – can I ask you, is Mary Todd the next person we're supposed to talk to?

"For a brief moment," she says.

I don't mean to sound like I'm checking her I.D. – but it's unusual for someone like her to stop in unrequested or unannounced.

What she's trying to express... what she's saying is "Don't judge (it) when history gets brought up."

Okay. (Thinking it over) Does she mean because when RFK spoke with us a few weeks ago, I asked why it was important to bring up the past, or his assassination or Marilyn's murder? That it was ancient history, or "who cares?"

"Yes." She says "A lot of people care."

(Note: I'm embarrassed to realize my flippant comment "who cares about Marilyn Monroe's death?" Mary Todd Lincoln took offense to. But it serves as reminder; they're outside of time. So a tragic event that happened to them may feel like yesterday in the context of their experience. "You may consider my story ancient history, but for me it's my story, and the truth needs to be told.")

I think this is interesting – Mary Todd Lincoln came forward to protest something she heard me say a few weeks ago; "Pay attention to history because it's important." To us it's ancient history, but to them, it feels like yesterday.

She says "Yes. People care about it because it has to do with the future. Also, when you tell the truth, you rip off the band-aid or bandages."

Revisiting history in this fashion allows us to tell the truth?

I just saw slaves.

I think I get this – slavery is something that was part of our past but by addressing it, we can change our future. Because telling the truth about the past helps to change the future. Is that correct?

"Yes."

So that we don't repeat that same mistake?

She says "We always do... but then we find different ways to learn."

PART TWO

I wanted to let you know that I sent an email to Robert Kennedy's child's assistant... never heard back - but then, I wouldn't reply to me either.

(Jennifer listens) They're trying to wrap their heads around it.

Robert, do you want me to follow up on that?

"Yes."

I just have no idea how I'll get through to his daughter Rory.

You're clever. Just speak to her in a Boston accent. (Jennifer pauses:) I just went to the Cuban missile crisis. (A visual).

If I can ask Robert; "Are those people involved with Cuba (Bay of Pigs invasion) – those people involved in the planning - are those people related to deaths of you and your brother and Marilyn?"

"Yes."

Are any of those people are still on the planet?

"One is."

What's his name?

I'm seeing (that it is) someone who worked for Lyndon... and Nixon...

You mean a member of the CIA, FBI... of government?

Someone like a "Robert Mueller."

Well, he would have to be really old. What's his first name?

I'm hearing Joseph. Or Joe.

Second name?

Begins with an S... St or something. Or it feels like a Russian name... feels like Scz or Scr.

First name Joseph and his last name begins with an S?

"Yes."

(Note: It's often problematic to nail down a name. In my looking for an identity, the only person who comes close is Joseph Califano, who was involved in the Bay of Pigs in 1962, served under LBJ, then later Carter and is still alive. This is not to imply he was involved in the conspiracy; he's had a long history of notable service, (Trustee Emeritus of the JFK Center for the Performing Arts, member of the advisory council of the American Foundation for AIDS Research etc) but it is to say that he may know the identity of those involved, or has an inkling as to who might have been if asked.
https://www.archives.gov/files/research/jfk/releases/2018/198-10004-10053.pdf)

Robert, you're welcome to sit in and help us with this.

Hold on; what they're showing me is... The Cuban missile crisis, the people who were part of that also were in the military... they keep showing me that.

I understand – you're saying they were part of a government conspiracy?

At its height.

Well, I see if I can find anyone in the Kennedy, Johnson administration, who could have been alive or part of the assassinations or murders that you're spoken of. And thanks to Mary Todd for stepping in as well; the truth sets everyone free.

A mutual friend of one of Robert's children offered to send along whatever I heard "from the flipside" to a Kennedy family member. I have no idea what their reaction was. After Amelia Earhart disappeared people who claimed to "know what happened" reached out to her husband George Putnam – and in retrospect from all the research I've done, I know a couple of those medium's accounts were accurate.

It's a lot of work for them to figure out a way to tap us on the shoulder, when a person asks us to "pass this along to their children" – I can only say "I will to the best of my ability, and I hope they can hear it." In the dozen or so cases where we've done this – about report the "interview was spot on." Who am I to refuse the request? If I can, I will.

CHAPTER TWENTY FOUR
IT'S CHINATOWN JACK

Robert Towne, Edward Taylor, Jack Nicholson. (Photo by Luana Anders, private photo, All Rights Reserved)

HIRA AND ROBERT AND ED TAYLOR

Jennifer's replies are **in bold**, Robert's questions or comments *are in italics*. Nick (an old friend of Robert's) and my questions are in "parentheses." The above photo was used in the book about the film Chinatown, but Luana was not credited. Not sure where the author got it from, but their old friend Luana had this (color) print.

J is **Jennifer**, R is *Robert,* N is (Nick,) M is (Me, Richard.)

This is an experiment. We've assembled in Jennifer's office in Manhattan Beach, Nick is an old friend of both Robert and Edward Taylor, and over lunch, he mentioned that his son had passed away recently. Nick is not this person's real name, it's a pseudonym, but Robert, Edward, Hira are the real names.

(Rich M: Before we start, we should say hello to Luana first.)

Jennifer: Luana has been helping me with my group meetings. And working with Rich, I find I don't have fear.

(Nick: What does one do all day on the other side, or is there no sense of time?)

Jennifer: There's no sense of time – for me, past, present and future shows up in the same place for me. They'll show me a photo in black and white for a memory – I get information about stuff in the future.

Robert: Let me ask you about Hira or Leo...

(Note: These are two pets of Robert's. We've spoken to Hira before, and also Leo – but not with Robert in the actual room. Only he would know how accurate this information is. I knew Hira because I walked him for three years, I didn't know Leo at all.)

J: Where did you find Leo?

R: We met Leo in the South Pacific – the girls found him. He was a scrawny cat.

J: But he turned into a bigger cat, later, didn't he?

R: Yes, when he was older. (Ding!) He showed up at our bungalow on the beach and they wanted to take him home but I didn't want to – but one day I was getting up one night... all I know is I walked into the bathroom and there he was sitting on a mat – I thought, "All right, if you're that serious you're coming home with us."

J: "You saved his life."

R: I probably did.

(Rich M: That's what he's saying to Jennifer; that "You saved his life" Robert. It's a quote.)

J: He's apologizes for scratching your furniture... he had so much fun at your place, but then you moved.

R: We did move (Ding!).

J: He said "That made things even worse... the new place couldn't be touched."

R: That was true. But he did it anyway.

J: He's showing me that it was "Super fun... then they moved, but then they didn't want me to scratch things. Then I got a little older and I realized couches were to be slept on instead of scratched." He's showing me the dining room table that he slid off of.

(Rich M: I know we asked you before, but who was there to greet you when you crossed over, Leo?)

J: (Robert's dog) "Hira." He said it again.

(M: What was that like?)

J: He said "I was scared, then I was so happy. Because Hira took care of me even when he didn't like me."

Robert laughs.

J: "I knew to allow Hira to be "the best" (favorite). "Even when Hira did something wrong, the cat was blamed. We knew Hira was the best... the favorite. He says "We had an exchange; he made sure we were okay, and we made sure he was the best (favorite)."

(Rich M: When you died Leo, you told us earlier that you didn't have any pain?)

J: He said "During the last two months (there was) – he said "He wasn't in pain until the two months before he died." He says "It was only the last weeks or months he felt pain... and it wasn't that bad." (Jennifer aside) There are so many people up here who are laughing because we're talking to his pets.

R: What?

(Rich M: I'm getting that the people waiting to speak to you are upset you're not talking to your friends.)

J: I'm seeing a fellow with a checkered sports coat. He's named Sydney. (to me) Who was was the guy we talked to named Sydney?

(Rich M: Pollack. Yes, we mentioned him earlier during lunch.)

R: Sydney is here?

J: Yes, he says "He's (been) waiting to talk to you... and you're talking to Leo!" I just saw a bunch of people who were waiting to talk to Robert and I saw Sydney behind them. (Jennifer laughs)

(M: Sydney, what do you want to say to Robert or your friend Nick?)

J: Did you know someone named Marilyn? Cause I just saw Marilyn Monroe (which could be as a name reference).

(Rich M: Let's hold that for a moment because it's harder to talk to Marilyn because everyone knows of her, as an icon, but not many knew her well...)

R: I never knew her.

(N: I knew her. She was in class; Lee Strasberg's class.)

J: She said "You helped her get over being nervous."

(N: Well, I never talked to her.)

J: But she's saying that your work in class helped her with her nervousness.

(Note: This is an example of Jennifer just describing what she is getting. That "Marilyn" recalls Nick's acting in class as being effortless. She's outside of time, so it could be her accessing that memory as we speak. We've chatted with Marilyn before (about her youth, death, verifiable details) but since people have a "block" when it comes to icons, I often ask them to step out of the conversation.)

R: How is Sydney?

J: He says, "He's busy." I don't think he played golf here but he plays it a lot over there. He's wearing an old golf cap.. what was the movie.. Matt Damon was in – he's showing me that. (Later we hear that this might be Lou Towne's influence).

(Rich M: Sydney we've talked about it but not with you. How do you create a golf course over there?)

J: Any way you want to – there's a lot of people who help create it from different places.. I'm seeing also the old fashioned version of girls handing out drinks like in the olden days.

(Rich M: But how do you create it?)

J: They want to feel the dirt, the grass... and the older (the course) it is, the more you can smell that – for some golfers. Just a second – I want to make sure this is right. Someone is here you both know who played golf. (Robert's father Lou). To answer your question, Robert, "He's doing great." Sydney says "He's doing a lot of flying, doing something different." Showed me flying a plane.

R: Yeah, he flew, (pilot) yeah.

J: He's showing me going super fast – what is that, Mach 5? That's what he's showing me.

(Note: We interviewed Sydney before, I knew his son Scott died in a flight accident and we talked about that, but I didn't know the Sydney was a pilot as well until now. Mach 1 is going faster than the speed of sound, 5280 feet per second.)

R: So he's having a good time?

J: A blast.

R: Well that's wonderful

J: He's saying something about "being forgiven." He says, "Forgive me for not telling you guys about the extent of my illness or how long he had it." He's saying that um ... "I knew it (death) was coming..." Did he write something before?

(Rich M: Sydney wrote a letter to (film director) Phillip Noyce just before passing, perhaps that's it?)

J: (Sydney) He's saying, "Yes, he did." Phillip was mad about his passing.

(Rich M: Well, Phillip confirmed what you told us in our interview, Sydney, confirmed that he had written to you prior to your passing and you had replied with an apology for not being around. But Sydney, you knew Nick and Robert – is there anything you want to tell these guys?)

J: (to Nick) We had the best boat ride. (Discussed over lunch).

(N: That was Ed Taylor.)

J: Did you got out on a yacht with Sydney?

(N: No.)

J: He's showing me a yacht – in – what's the place in the South of France? Cannes.

(N: Never been to Cannes.)

(Rich M: That could be me; I was on a few boats in Cannes, maybe with Sydney. But would you ask Luana to bring forward whoever needs to talk to Nick or Robert? Person wise, we'll get to the animals in a minute.)

J: (to Nick) I know you mentioned your son – we don't have to talk about that or anything.

(N: I'm open.

What's his name?

(N: His name is Ian.)

Was there someone who got a tattoo because of him?

(N: He had something.)

Was it on his arm, do you know?

(N: I don't remember.)

He's showing me (the word) "dad" – I know you're his dad because you told me that; but he got something in honor of you as far as a tattoo goes.

(N: Oh, I have a tattoo.)

(Nick shows his shamrock tattoo.)

Do you know if he had a tattoo?

(N: I don't know.)

That's okay – that's what he's showing me... something on his arm in honor of you and it might be a shamrock.

(N: My grandson has a tattoo in honor of me.)

Is it his son?

(N: No, my daughter's.)

Give me a second as he was very specific about it. (Listens) He keeps saying it's him; he had a tattoo in honor of you. 12-21? Something about the date. Mean anything to you?

(N: My birthday is 12-3, his mother is 12-7. Oh, he died on 12-20.)

Okay, he showed me 12-21 – I was a day off. You didn't say that to me, never told me, right?

(N: Yeah.)

J: If I hear something I want to give credit where it comes from. He's really funny by the way, instead of flowers flung everywhere, he's showing me shamrocks being thrown. I know he died too soon. Was there something going on in his head, with your son? When they show me this.. did he have cancer?

(N: No... he either accidentally or on purpose took his life.)

J: I asked him did you have a crash or internal crash? He said "No." He told me he wasn't feeling well (there was) something going on mentally. (Jennifer listens) He did not take his own life on purpose.

(N: I did not believe he did – his mother did – they were giving him some heavy drugs, he sent away for some phenobarbital, and I think he went to sleep.)

J: He's saying "No, he did plan on waking up." He said he was in a lot of physical pain; his back hurt - that's not an excuse - but he's trying to show me he took the other stuff in lieu of everything else. And that he was told that mixing the two would not kill him, that he would be able to wake up. Hold on. He still wants to talk about it. He said he left no note, that there was no letter or note. He said "I would have written the best story; I would have written everything; I would have gone out with a blast! Not that way, of "going to sleep." He says "He was pissed that he didn't wake up." He's saying that it's easier for his mom to feel there had to be some reason for him to leave – (Listens) Okay, I always ask "But were

you toying with it, like playing Russian roulette?" He went like this (flips her hand back and forth) "Eh."

(N: In a different way. He had six bottles of PB...)

J: But he didn't take them all, did he?

(Note: There's no way for Jennifer to know this detail, except via Ian.)

(N: Well, we don't know over what period of time.)

J: He says "From October."

(N: They did an autopsy and they said he had enough PB to kill him or stop his heart beating.)

J: He says, "He was taking them since October."

(N: I'm at peace with that.)

J: He said "You saw him in a dream and he told you he was okay."

(N: I don't remember.)

J: He just kissed you on your forehead. He says "He loves you, said you always got him, always met him wherever he was at, and he's forever grateful."

(N: Tell him I'm grateful for knowing him and I'll see him again.)

J: "Not too soon," he said; "You have a Russian bride!"

(N: It's Robert's hour...)

J: (Holds her ear in pain) Someone just crashed this... – I just heard a high high pitch. (Listens) It's Hira again. Ouch! He said he's trying to get my attention with all these people (in the room). Is there anything around 4-16 – April 16th?

R: Who wants to know?

J: Hira is relaying a message – 4-16. I'm looking at Hira but it could be anyone here trying to give you a message. Do you have anything to do with 4-16? Might have been when you got Leo – Go ahead Robert; who do you want to talk to?

R: Is Luana there?

J: Always. She's laughing, singing; they're having a party up there. She doesn't usually show me that – she has a list of people often that she shows me; she is not like this normally. I just saw a Malaysian kid – a beautiful boy, young boy – I don't know... someone that was in Robert's movies or a movie?

R: There were two kids that ...

J: "This is it, whatever you're saying," she says.

R: There were two kids in the movie we did in South Africa – "Ask the Dust."

J: I'm feeling that one of them has (crossed over), maybe you didn't know... let me see what he has to say. I'm getting immense gratitude. So grateful that you were able to do what you did in Africa.

R: I spent time with them – I loved them.

J: One is coming through, and he's saying "Thank you so much." He might have died.. um.. in a car crash or something. But you wouldn't know this – he wants to say "Thank you, you meant so much to them."

R: I really liked them.

J: He said "Thank you, thank you." (Jennifer listens) Your dad – did he live up in Palos Verdes?

R: Yes, Rolling Hills.

J: That's him – what's his first name?

Lou.

He's like "I lived in Palos Verdes and he was a golfer."

He was a golfer.

Ah, so he was trying to come forward (earlier) with Sydney; that's the whole golfing aspect.

(Note: My phone rings. After a conversation with my wife, there's a joke about wives thinking someone is with a mistress when visiting with Jennifer instead.)

Your father is laughing about that – he says "I wish I had thought of that (excuse)."

(Robert laughs.) Well, I told him to lie; he wouldn't listen. (Laughter)

(Rich M: Back to you Lu – what is it you want to say to your buddy?)

She's still laughing along with your dad. You're saying "Lu" - and they're both named Lou. And she has Hira in her lap. She says "It's a frickin' farm up here between her cat and your pets." Okay, your dad just pulled up a chair. He says, "Everything's going to be okay, all right." That's what your dad says in between a golf swing.

R: In-between a golf swing? (Robert laughs.)

I'm asking him (how he does it) and he shows me hitting, but the ball is going over the ocean and landing in Hawaii. That's how they golf now – play however they want to play – their first hole might be one island and the next hole in another place. He showed me it twice – He said "Watch." And he showed me me how he's hitting and to get it over the ocean.

(Rich M: We've talked about this before with other people – they say "It's math – the flight of the ball, the swing of the club – it's like CGI.")

(Jennifer taps her nose to indicate "correct.") Your father just tapped his nose over and over again.

R: Let me ask you this. Can he bark?

Hira or your dad? (Laughs). Absolutely – you might hear it and turn and no one's there.

But I can't hear him now.

He's showing me that he can make you think you hear his bark (by tapping into the memory of his barking). That's him – he's showing me (that it's a pattern) – like being by the door trying to get outside. Scratching a door. I'm not getting that he did that – but there's still a pattern of what he used to do, and he still does it.

I'd love to hear him bark.

He says he'll do that but you can't discount it. But he will do it.

(Rich M: Hira put in Jennifer's mind a place in Robert's house where it's best for him to communicate with you?)

Your office.

R: In my office? It's right next to the kitchen.

There's one next to the kitchen but another on the other side of the house – an empty office.

R: It's upstairs. My wife doesn't want me to use it because it's harder to get up stairs.

He's showing me that too. I've never been to your house, but he's showing me where your offices are.

R: Hira is saying if I want to talk to him I need to go upstairs?

Let me rephrase it – you can talk to him anywhere. He was showing me your house – that office and the other office.

R: He's right about that.

He prefers talking to you outside. He says there's a nest in your backyard – a tree that has a nest, where a bird recently dropped.

R: I'm sure we've had that. What would he prefer? I can deal with wherever he liked.

Wherever your office would be. He likes being next to you. (Listens) Do you have his collar? He's showing me a tambourine – something that can be made into something musically?

R: I have a couple of his dog tags..

He says "You hid them."

R: They're in an inkwell with no ink.

He's (correcting you) saying "No; he hid them." So take them out whenever you want – if you can, put the inkwell... put it by your bed when you go to sleep, other than his portrait or the several you have.

R: I do have several.

He showed them all to me – his favorite is the photograph you took. You're holding onto him?

R: Yes.

He loves that photo.

R: I've got him...

(Jennifer interrupts) Holding him.

R: He leaped up on his hind quarters and I held him.

He loves that because that's how he wants to be remembered. He loved the weather when that was taken. He absolutely loves the cartoon or sketch...

R: Yes. That was done by a psychiatrist friend of mine. It's on a wall.

He showed it to me at lunch today – over and over again. I just didn't know what it meant. "It's on the wall but crooked," he said. He said you should use a ruler to fix it.

R: I was never able to have that level of communication with him when he was alive.

Dogs don't need you to talk, they need you to feel – other than Richard, who talked to him in a car.

(Rich M: How would you possibly know I talked to Hira in a car? Do you know what she's talking about Robert? That's the car I drove in 34 years ago, to join you on the set of "Personal Best." I was in Patty Jenkin's car – a white Mercedes and I was in the backseat with this giant creature. I would ask Hira to move over to give me room as we drove 8 hours to Oregon. I've never told anyone that.)

Her voice put him to sleep though.

R: Oh Geeze.

One of the greatest gifts is that dogs don't talk but communicate all the time – Hira knew when you were hung over, weren't feeling well, when you were mad – he'd be on alert to figure out who you were mad at, as he would feel the pressure before your were mad. He loved your cologne... some kind of musk or something?

(Rich M: Verbena. I had to go to Beverly Hills to get it.)

(Robert laughs.) I remember a day when Luisa. Wait, no, not Luisa.

"The shorter one," he said.

(Rich M: Did you hear that Robert? Hira called your first wife Julie, "the shorter one.")

R: *(My ex wife) Julie bought a house in Westwood near the Westwood Marquis. We were up the street in this house.*

He loved that street.

R: *I left the house to go somewhere and was going to head back to the hotel.*

Did he take off? He was like, "I'm f*cking out of here."

R: *He did – he took off... went down the street. He went straight to the hotel, went up the front steps and the guy who was there, a black guy... Hira greeted him. The guy opened the door for him. Hira went into the lobby, went to the elevator, they opened the door and pushed the button but Hira got off on the wrong floor.*

On the 3rd floor. Were you on the 7th?

(Note: Ding! While Robert was editing "Personal Best" he was using a hotel room as his office, and Richard Prince, his production manager and I were there every day. The 7th sounds correct, but Prince would remember.)

R: *Something like that –*

He showed me that the room was at the end of the hallway.

(Note: Absolutely correct. Ding!)

He was also hungry he said, after walking all that way.

R: *So they finally let him into the room – I thought "How the fuck did you get here?" I had no idea how he got there.*

He said his front paw hurt and he slept for a long time. He's also saying he was relieved to see you. Was there cherry pie involved?

(to me) Something you brought for him; a good dessert that you got him to get you to like you more.

(Rich M: Hira put up with me.)

(Note: I seem to recall a birthday cake for his daughter Katherine. She might have been around 3 or 4, and the cake was in the main room, and I seem to recall coming in and seeing that Hira had consumed it.)

(Jennifer to Rich M) Hira loved you. (To Robert) I didn't know any of this stuff.

(Rich M: So Luana, can we bring Eddie Taylor in?)

He's smoking – and saying "Well, if you have the time."

(N: It's about time. Edward Milton Taylor.)

R: Nick and I are eagerly waiting to talk to you Edward.

You both have told him already what to bring through.

(N: I was sitting here resenting the fact Robert was talking to his dog and not Eddie.)

Edward thinks it's fascinating; "Bitches and dogs communicate better."

(N: He never talked like that. Eddie would have left it a little more cryptic. Never mentioning dogs.)

J: Well, he did say "bitches" and I added the "dogs" part.

(M: So what did the boys want to talk to you about?)

(To Robert) Your dad just won the golf game apparently – he makes it so he wins every time. Is that fair?

Laughter.

(Rich M: Is Edward with beard or no beard?)

Clean shaven.

(Rich M: About how old does he appear?)

I got more like he comes through as 33. I'm getting 58 did he pass at 58?

(N: He's 1 year younger than me ...)

Hold on – 58 could mean May 8th or 1958. Hold on. He also showed me 76.

R: *That seems more like it –*

(Jennifer laughs) I just didn't want to believe you guys were that old.

(N: I'm 85, he's 86.)

(Jennifer holds up her clipboard where she had written "76.") I had it written down. You guys were like "The three amigos," he says. You guys did a lot of things together, like you helped each other through relationships, wives, ex wives... he thinks its funny, he finds me entertaining he thinks it's amazing you both are here. Did you guys have.. so you know, back in high school we had a journal, we'd pass between each other – he's showing me something, it's interpretation – he's showing me something passed between you guys...

(Rich M: Like a screenplay Eddie?)

Yes, he's showing me Jack Nicholson.

(Picture of Robert, and Jack From Luana's collection)

(N: I wrote a script with Eddie that he gave to Robert.)

Was Jack involved? I got shown Jack –

(N: He used to hang out at Robert's house – I was living in Robert's house when he did his first rewrite of "Bonnie and Clyde.")

J: (To Robert) You wrote that?

(N: He did a rewrite of the script... and I was in his house. He'd come out and scratch his head and say "you want to read something?" You know who was driving a jaguar up there? Luana. She had a 1958 black Jaguar convertible.)

I told my dad I wanted a black convertible Jaguar XGS with gold trim when I was 8 years old. He said "Honey you came to the Medlyns not the Marriotts."

(N: I can get you one for about 8 grand.)

I used to ride around in my Porsche convertible with Hira.

(Rich M: Luana, what were you doing driving a Jaguar?)

It was given to her. She says "I earned it." Whatever that means and she got rid of it pretty fast too. A boyfriend before the hairdresser.

(Note: We've spoken to Luana's old boyfriend Richard Alcala, who was partially the model for the hairdresser in Robert's script "Shampoo." After she broke up with Richard, she moved into Robert's living room and didn't emerge for a month. She also appeared in "Shampoo" as the receptionist. But for Jennifer to be so well versed in Luana's boyfriends, including saying "before the hairdresser" is a bit uncanny.)

Eddie is saying "what about me?" He's saying he had the best life with you guys – so much fun, out of all three of you he says he was the responsible one – very pragmatic about time.

(N: I don't remember him being insistent about anything; he was the most easy going guy about everything.)

Well, you guys saw that, but in his mind he always had an objective – He says "That's how he did it seamlessly." He's also showing me.. like three gravesites – together.

Eddie's not buried.

He showed me ashes –

(N: Didn't his ex wife put his ashes somewhere?)

R: We put his ashes in the water.

J: He's showing me throwing ashes into the water. It's a metaphor. He's saying you all three need to have your ashes mingled together.

(N: In the ocean? I'm going into a military cemetery.)

He's laughing at the notion. Hold on. (to Nick) He says "You're going to have a spectacular send off via the military – but not any time soon."

(N: I wouldn't mind.)

"He knows that," he says. He hears your thoughts. Robert – you can feel Hira here before you even go over there. you just have to ask him to be around to show you signs, maybe a sign on a tv program. Why am I being shown a tambourine again? Hira loved music he says.

He never told me!

He loved being around music – loved the loud... hold on.. the loud music.

Well I used to play Irish folk music loud.

He loved it. Who liked motorcycles?

R: Edward did.

(N: I bought his motorcycle.)

He said "You only rode it twice."

(N: I had other ones that were better.)

Someone hurt their knee on the bike.

R: Edward did.

(N: He sold me the bike because he needed money.)

J: That's what he said, you gave him over fair value and thanks you for that.

(N: I doubt it.)

(Note: Jennifer has no clue who Eddie is or was. When she reports something like "He appreciated getting more than its worth" she can't be making that up. Not easy taking compliments from the flipside.)

(M: Edward, we were talking about a boat trip you were on with Nick earlier.)

J: Oh. He's the one who said he had the "best boat ride ever," I'm sorry. Edward said that. Hold on a second. That was one of them, he also says you guys once got lost... and it got dark out there in the water. He says he drank a lot. Do you have an old compass or something?

(N: No. (a pause) Oh! I do! His widow gave me his compass. Wow. He just got me totally.)

R: Who's widow?

(N: Eddie's widow. A little box compass that his widow gave me.)

He showed me the compass that Nick has. And he said you have his compass; and that is correct.

(Rich M: Is there anything Robert has of Eddies?)

Something with a ring – I know you don't wear rings. A ring - or something that meant something.

How many years ago?

1956? Had writing on it.

(Rich M: A class ring?)

J: That's it.

(Rich M: They went to college together.)

(N: We graduated in 55.)

J: I got 56. Maybe that was his way to say you went to school together – I saw a ring with writing on it. (In answer to the question "What does Robert have of yours? The answer being "Memories). He said you have an ugly sweater. I'm not sure what that means. That was his way of showing me that time period.

(Rich M: Any messages for his widow?)

J: He showed me the middle finger. He said he doesn't blame her – she took all of it, took a lot of things from him.

(Rich M: Emotionally or stuff?)

He said don't be hard on Virgin... (her name is Virginia). She always felt something was going to go awry, she was super needy – lived in total fear. He appreciates her and is grateful – is grateful for her, he felt like she raised him.

(N: Can I tell me my son one last thing?)

J: Give me his name again.

(N: Ian.)

Ian. What would you like to say?

(N: I dedicated my autobiography to him.)

He was just trying to show me that – a book title, I thought it was something you said – he is saying he knows that; he knows... what chapter is it in?

(N: It's the introduction.)

He says there's something in the back too... he's very grateful – you put him on a pedestal. If you remember anything from today besides the compass – that if he was going to kill himself, he showed me he would have written something about it that was spectacular. He would have written the best goodbye letter. He would have left a lot more than the way he died.

(N: He was the best writer I'd seen since Robert. Thank you.)

Hira just came in and jumped on your lap, Robert.

R: On my lap?

I see both worlds the same way – both worlds are in the same room to me, I saw Hira saying "I'm not slow anymore, my front paw doesn't hurt anymore" and jumped in your lap. That's the way I see things (during these sessions). Okay he wants to remind you to put the dog tags next to your bed. When you go to sleep you, never have to say anything out loud to him.

R: So all I have to do is take the tags out of the inkwell?

Or just put the inkwell near by – it's like knowing they're close by. He said you wrapped up his ashes and put them away.

R: I did.

He says "You have to put it in writing somewhere that your and his ashes get to go to the same place." He's just very sweet, showing me how you guys were the same – intermingling. You got him and he got you – you were the most communicative owner. You over thought everything, analyzed everything, were very articulate – you even didn't like certain flooring, and were very careful with him about walking, how you used to carry him – did he have a diaper at some point?

(Rich M: Yes, he did, I was there, it was towards the last days. Robert would carry him outside.)

He's saying "I lost my dignity and you never made him feel bad. I couldn't do normal things, I wanted to be the best (companion) and you never made me feel bad. You thought it was just what you were supposed to do." And he says "Thank you." He's saying – "Even when you're thinking you were not communicating well; he didn't know that." He always felt you were communicating constantly – with the dogs and cats... (laughs) and all those people over there who want to talk to you and can't get through the door because Hira is there (in the way.)

Who wants to talk to me?

Well, your dad – and your mom too. She loves you so much. Your mom – she showed me Hira, that she's going to race Hira to get to you (when the time comes) – she says she's so proud of you. (Jennifer listens) Have you ever written music?

No.

I see music – I see you and I see music coming out.

(Rich M: If I may; I think what Helen is saying, is that Robert's words are like music?)

(Jennifer taps her nose) "Yes. They're a symphony."

(Rich M: At her funeral – his eulogy was amazing; I wish I had filmed it.)

J: She says "It was like Beethoven."

(Rich M: Your brother Roger's eulogy was also profound but your eulogy was the most eloquent I've ever heard. Is that what you mean, Helen?)

"Yes." She says. (To Robert) "You wrote her letters and that you got her. How she was raised, all the decisions she made whether to come to California from either Boston or NY, whatever she did at a young age, you got the decisions she made... having a family and changing your name..."

(Note: Jennifer has no clue of the family name change from Schwartz to Towne.)

...She knew how much you loved her and she knew how great you are, and how great you were going to be and how great you are now. And she says that she's coming back as Hira! (Laughter) Everyone wants to come back as Hira!

(Rich M: How many more minutes do we have?)

J: Eight. Robert, do you know Bill Paxton? Or that actor he knows?

(Rich M: Harry Dean Stanton. They were both in "Big Love." That's how one appears, by having the other one show up first.)

R: *I knew Harry.*

(Rich M: Harry what do you want to say about the afterlife?)

"It's not that bad. It's amazing. It's amazing once you know you're up here. Once you realize you're there. He misses being here, misses the smells, lotion on women – it's interesting how the smells can bring you back." He showed me some female putting lotion on her legs. He says "I miss that – they can recreate it (over there) – but it's not the same."

(Note: We've interviewed Harry previously. He said that Luana was there to greet him on the other side, and helped him have a "soft landing." He gave me accurate things to mention at his memorial service, and proved beyond any shadow of doubt I might have had, that he can communicate from the flipside. Even so, this paragraph above, said on the fly, is packed with verifiable details about the afterlife, and said as only Harry could have said it.)

(Rich M: Harry was in the Linda Ronstadt doc shown on CNN recently; what did you think of that Harry?)

He says "Eh, it was rough cut." (Jennifer listens) Did he play the banjo?

R: He did play the banjo.

That's the whole tambourine! I'm sorry I kept seeing the white thing.

(Rich M: That's accurate – (ding!) the tambourine body. In the documentary, Linda says she used to hear you singing those old Mexican songs, and she decided to make an album. The most successful album of Mexican music ever.)

(Jennifer laughs) He says "She ripped me off."

Robert laughs.

He said "He was naked while he was doing that, singing those tunes."

(Rich M: I believe it – but what else Harry?)

J: He showed me something – that was wrapped. Like a flag, might have to do with Buddhism too. I know he was an atheist, but he's showing me you Robert, with something purple, that's wrapped, that's stored.

(Rich M: In storage? Or a religious thing?)

Great question thank you. He says it pertains to one of your movies, maybe "Chinatown?" Yes. It has to do with Chinatown.

(Note: I'm familiar with religious relics, and the Buddhists tend to wrap up their most sacred texts in purple cloth and put them away. What Harry seems to be saying, is to "not be too precious" with the memory of the film script of "Chinatown" – to just shake off the covers or purple cloth and make it accessible to a new audience that doesn't remember the original.)

(Rich M: Does he mean the prequel to Chinatown that Robert is working on?)

Yeah. There's something – someone that's supposed to be in it that you don't want to be in it?

R: No.

He says "You need to re-invent it – to give it more life." He says "You're bored with it, and he wants you to give it more life, make it spectacular again for a newer audience... because they don't know. He's showing me glitter or sparkles... and that usually makes me think of strippers in Vegas (Note: More pizzazz?)

R: I have an odd question. About every dog I had. One was a St. Bernard mix – I called "Buddy" and the other was my very first dog who slept under my crib, named "Scrappy." She'd been run over...

"By a truck..." She had internal bleeding and she died.

R: I loved them both.

They're still there – all the dogs are still there and Hira is in charge of all the dogs you had in your life because he would have been like that here.

R: He would be.

He was in charge of the cats, total agreement on what to do and not to do.

R: That was Hira.

I don't know that but that's what the cats are saying. Hira was rather regal wasn't he?

(Rich M: Ridiculously so - he deigned to let me walk him.)

But Harry still wants to say something. He says "The Millennials need to see a new "Chinatown," with sparkles." He wants you to rethink or reinvent it to get the same impact. Eddie is showing me that compass; which is pretty cool.

N: I appreciate it more than I can express.

*****

This is about as clear a session as I can point out. Our friend "Nick" spoke to his son, who confirmed beyond any doubt he might have had, he still exists. Our friend, Ed Taylor came through and confirmed a detail only Nick would know (the compass.) Robert's dog came through and confirmed details only he would know (Hira.) It's not my opinion, belief or theory – I recorded this in its entirety. Thanks to everyone who helped us!

A still from the film "Personal Best" written and directed by Robert Towne. Caleb Deschanel in foreground, the author standing next to the Oscar award winning writer. Photo courtesy of pal Steven Vaughan.

CHAPTER TWENTY FIVE:
"NIGHT TIDE"

Dennis Hopper and Luana Anders in "Night Tide" directed by Curtis Harrington

HAWKING LUANA JESUS DENNIS HOPPER

I reveal in real time why I asked Dennis to come forward. My questions are *in italics*, Jennifer's replies are **in bold**.

Rich: Hi class. we have some members of the class we do want to talk to... quick question for Dennis Hopper.

Jennifer: Yes, he's here.

How's he look? How's he present himself?

Short hair. salt and pepper, glasses – like circles...like John Lennon glasses – looks really fit.

Hi Dennis. We've talked before...

"We have." I feel like he wants to talk about his son.

That was going to be my question. My wife saw his name today in court in Santa Monica; a woman is suing him – you want to tell Jennifer about it?

For child support?

Something like that – a payment he didn't pay, he was fined a lot of money; what do you want me to tell your son anything if I can?

He says, "Tell him not to date fucked up women." (Jennifer laughs.)

I'm not going to say that to anyone. But there is a weird odd connection. I didn't realize an old friend is the stepdad to your son, Dennis.

He says, "He just needs to put it behind him... I think just by reaching out to your friend. Dennis is saying his son doesn't read anything and it will come up again and then I saw your brother."

The one who lives in Hollywood? Jeff?

He says, "Yeah."

What about him?

There's a connection to Dennis with your brother.

Well, let's break this down. Luana, you know Dennis better than anybody.

They're smiling at each other.

Let's put it this way, we can say the word "cherry" and then say the word "Dennis" as in "taking someone's cherry."

(Jennifer aside) No way.

Yes way. Dennis was Luana's first boyfriend. She wrote a hilarious scene in a film about the incident – which I think she may have orchestrated to get the stigma of virginity out of the way.

She says, "She did. Diligently."

She wrote a funny screen in a script of hers – We've talked to Dennis on the flipside and he admitted it was accurate. But Dennis must have still had feelings for her, because he sent the largest bouquet I've ever seen – 20 feet tall – of flowers for her funeral. Jack Nicholson one that was equally huge. But in retrospect, Luana stayed in touch with Jack, but not with Dennis. What was the reason for that Dennis? What were you trying to say?

He said "I'm like trying to substitute something else that wasn't big?" He's laughing. He said "To demonstrate the love for Luana. It never went away."

You had many beautiful women and children in your life.

She showed me the consistency of it – there was no destruction of it (love).

Did you guys have a previous lifetime together?

He says, "Yes."

Can you put that in Jennifer's mind?

I'm seeing Luana in Spain, as a dancer, performer. I'm seeing him as a sailor in London – like back in 1492, there's a ship. I'm seeing pirates – I'm wondering if this a play and she was like "No." She was this beautiful dancer.. and he was this... she had dark hair, like Sophia Lorenish, just gorgeous, and they were just like kids together ... very young.

Were you guys together as lovers in that time period?

He says, "Husband and wife;" I thought it was brother and sister at first. In Spain. Barcelona. The ship has a big C on it. Like a crest... It feels like Colon – It's like Collins or Colon.

(Note: 1492? Colon? As in Cristobal Colon? (As Columbus is known in Spain) Pirates? Colon was one. I didn't ask the obvious question ("Did you know Chris?") but perhaps I will in the future.)

Were you on this ship that Jennifer is seeing, Dennis?

"Yeah. He was one of the seamen – one of the guys that worked on the ship." It feels like they were out there to discover things. Fighting against Vikings it feels like. Felt like she was from Spain.

Did you meet her during the course of your travels?

He says, "No, they lived around the corner from each other in Spain.. in Barcelona. He would go out to sea and come back."

Why did you guys choose that lifetime? What did you learn?

He said, "We knew we could entertain people."

She was an entertainer, a dancer?

"Yeah."

You met her in a club someplace?

He says, "Their families were connected."

Did you have kids?

He says, "One."

It's a slice of time 500 years ago, they focus on the time and place when we're outside of time it's all part of a dance?

He says, "And he died young, the son."

The idea that you're always connected on a journey... Luana was there something spiritual in my wife seeing Dennis' son's name today?

They showed me pinball machines - so you could ask these questions. And I feel like this girl in court was lying. I feel like she was lying and she just wanted the money.

That's what my wife felt in court as well.

(Jennifer aside) Really? You never mentioned what she thought did you? That's exactly what he said. He says, "It'll work out..." – but I asked "So why did you guys, what was the concept of love you had here?" He said, "They were both entertainers; it was something that was safe and fun."

If I can add; safe also means family, home, safety of the flipside.

He says, "Yes, correct." (Jennifer aside) I have the chills when you said that.

Luana represented home to him even though he may never have realized why. Probably why she had such a profound affect on some many of her friends.

He says, "Correct. She was that light."

The irony is that she didn't have a home here, really, bounced around to foster homes, but she was the light, the home for everyone else. Okay, who else is here?

My dad.

I quoted your dad Jim yesterday. I spent time on Quora answering questions and someone asked "How do I overcome grief?" and I quoted your dad. "Grief is only sad memories. Nostalgia is both happy and sad memories. If you can move grief to nostalgia you begin the healing process." Speaking of aliens, I've been answering questions about aliens, people who normally incarnate on another planet.

He says "Everyone's an alien."

We all are – but that's a tough concept to get across.

(Note: In terms of the research, he's saying everyone "animates" a living being – on our planet or other planets. In essence, we are "all aliens" because we all do the same thing in animating on a planet. A third of the people who seek hypnotherapists claim to have had off world experiences. (The Newton Institute) So in essence, every third person is an "alien" in that sense of the word.)

He says, "Aliens in terms of being an object of hierarchy – when you think of aliens, you immediately go to the sky, think of them as being non-human. People are afraid of them as different species – we have to get rid of the idea there is a hierarchy involved." What they're showing me is, "If you get rid of that, (that they're "foreign") they're like everyone else and don't put them on a pedestal.

Is this important to discuss?

He says, "We can – we can do that – we haven't – we focus mostly on humans..." (Jennifer aside) Half of the people I've done a session with – they talk about knowing alien cultures. They often show me consciousness getting better, the awareness that will allow that opening. Hold on... they keep coming back to the aliens; they say "You have to make the aliens not alien."

Who me? Good luck with that. So what's a word we can use instead?

They're saying, "Different life forms." "Different forms of energy." It's no different than a horse, it's just not us.

"Ghost" is the most popular term we have for people no longer on the planet, but it's inaccurate as well.

I see them all the time. Take away the word god and the world would be a happy place, don't take away god, but take away the concept of god and the world will be a happy place.

Jennifer the heretic.

Take away alien and you have the whole universe, different types of species or life forms, you take away the word Jesus and replace it with "love" – What is profound relentless unconditional love? Just use that instead of Jesus.

Who else needs to come forward?

Stephen Hawking – he shows up in his wheelchair and then walks out of it – so handsome. He's about 28, light brown hair, no glasses... hazel colored eyes.

We've talked about you recently; you talked about dark energy or matter.

So... he says, "The equations he gave us... those are (regarding) different frequencies." He's showing how each person gives off a different frequency; He says "Everybody has a mathematical equation that is a frequency – instead of a person – everybody has a frequency, every mathematical equation can determine a life form, or whatever we call it, including dark matter. We are a mathematical equation." He says "That is what we are, we bounce around negating other frequencies, that's what we do. So get rid of the word aliens and use the word frequency instead."

Is that what you want to say instead of "aliens"?

"Yes." (Jennifer aside) In my case I see people all the time who aren't on the planet.

If I can ask him, who is involved with the creation of that equation?

"The universe as a whole." He showed me a universe and how if you took out parts, they'd be fragmented.

(Note: I think he means that everything is in its place, everything has its place, it's all related, connected – that if we took one piece of it away, it would become fragmented. Like the Solar System is a system – and if one of the planets was knocked from its orbit, the entire system would fall apart.)

Let's work on this for a second..

(Jennifer aside) Here we are again! Solving another huge problem!

We like to do that – we've talked about god not being a person or thing, but being a medium or system or engine – that all people being connected is what god is.

He says, "We represent god or whatever energy that is – every single part of us, that's in existence is a frequency of god of the whole."

Okay – but if I can ask; who designed that, if anyone?

He says "We did." (Jennifer shrugs). That's weird.

(Note: Based on the previous interviews, and those in "Architecture of the Afterlife," I think he's referring to the idea that we are consciousness – that everything and everyone are connected, and somehow we "agree" to participate in this grand design, so that we are all "creating the world we exist in." That it's not someone else doing that – but we are.)

At what point did the design process begin?

He says "We being god, yes, we designed it. Just like we thought the world was flat and then it became round, the ships that arrived in the Americas, people didn't recognize as ships because they'd never seen them before, we didn't know we could send a rocket to the moon – it's analogous, once it comes into play that we can talk to people on the other side, so they can see it –

You mean it's like in quantum mechanics? In some cases the outcome doesn't occur until someone observes the process?

"Yes" he says.

When you observe something it comes into existence, according to quantum theory. If that's true – if we created whatever comes into existence, if consciousness creates matter, god, the universe, was there an architect for that concept? Someone who came or someone who came before all that occurred?

Before you said that, it made me think of what we said before, the architects were the angels and archangels of that energy.

Okay, that's a smaller group, but we have talked to some of them.

They're not here.

You mean they haven't incarnated?

It's easier for them for them to move the pieces around the game because they haven't incarnated.

So that they can't or don't discriminate based on emotion. How did the archangels come into existence?

I just saw light – this ball of light.

What is this light? The light of god or the creator or the creators?

It's a ball of light for each planet; we're all different frequencies, each planet has its own frequency... so hold on. There's always a different kind of... I just saw a ball of light, like everyone bowling, then I saw colors pop up; our energy centers, our galaxy is different than all the other galaxies. I didn't know each galaxy has the colors coming out of it – our galaxy has all of it.

And the angels are related to?

Older frequencies.

Are they better or more adept at...

No, so they show me that they have the speed of movement by thought - they don't have anything holding them back, from all the different galaxies, and they don't have to be grounded by any of them.

How many are there?

Infinite number.

So the archangels are how many?

There's 13 archangels.

Who's telling you that?

I'm not sure. There's 13 and there's thousands and trillions of angels. 13 archangels. Like 13 gods it feels like.

Who's putting that in your mind? Luana, where's this coming from?

My higher self I guess. I felt Jesus and a bunch of people.

I was going to ask an archangel to show up to help us... okay let's talk to our buddy Jesus.

He's like the conduit to the archangels... kind of their energy source. (Holds her ear). Ow! That was really painful – I sometimes get that... bam – a frequency change.

Who did that? Who changed the frequency?

I think it was Jesus' energy coming into the room.

Let's ask him a question. Were you one of those 13 archangels helping to design this process? Stay with me for this lightning round. Jesus put the answer in Jennifer's mind.

Help, I'm in a spirit sweat shop.

Jesus; 13 archangels; are you one of them? Yes or no?

He says, "No."

Satan or Lucifer. Did he actually exist or was one of those archangels? Yes or no?

I think that's why there's 12.

So you're saying he is, was or not?

It feels like it's a man made concept – something that only exists in people's minds here on the planet. There were 13, but there's 12 now.

Let's not judge it. Does he represent light and dark as an entity, or is he only a man made mental construct?

He says, "Yes. Construct."

Satan's a man made construction?

"Yes."

He comes up often – people claim he exists, that Satan represented temptation, etc – the word itself means tempter in Arabic. The fellow who "leads us into temptation" – but you're saying as humans we lead ourselves there, correct?

I should be Lucy (from Peanuts).

So this Lucifer myth?

He says, "He was an alien. Even though we need to lose that word. Another frequency."

So were the other 12 also aliens?

He says, "As I said before; they are different frequencies."

Beyond time and space; correct?

He says, "Yes."

So let's allow there's a myth that comes out of that event or story... so who came up with the 12 archangels?

12 disciples?

Don't worry about that – let's ask Jesus. Who invented the 12 or 13 archangels?

I'm getting Jesus. (Jennifer aside) That doesn't make sense.

Let's break it down – what do you mean - the frequency he exists on, is the same frequency they exist on?

I'm getting they report to him.

Okay, very good. Let's allow that Jesus is beyond our brain to comprehend.

He says, "Yes."

You're giving us incomprehensible answers dude.

He's saying "Take away my name."

An instead use the word love? So why would love...

Then he showed me a past life where the whole thing... love has caused all of our fights and wars and everything. The archangels don't have that.

Maybe we need to talk to Michael or Gabriel who we've talked to before – because Jesus isn't giving us the answer or I'm not understanding him. Why 12? Why not six?

It's not 12 as we know it. It's like saying "god."

Okay, by calling it 12 it's not a number, it's how we refer to things - it's not something you can conceive of as a number; is that correct?

He says, "Yes;" he showed me the pyramid; all the different layers of different dimensions. There's 12 that are in charge of up here (indicates higher level), and then there are more grids (below) of four and four and four and aspects of each one.

(Note: Like he's saying there's multiple layers upon layers upon layers. So each realm, each layer would have its own 12 who were in charge so to speak, but they're all manifestations of the frequencies we all share. Or something like that.)

Let me ask you this Jesus; when you stepped off the planet – were you aware of all this information, was this new or do you remember it?

He said "He just believed it – he wasn't aware of it – his awareness was, he knew, he had the same energy as the angels."

So he was aware of that?

He said "He was aware of not having any attachments to what was going on; like pain of being tortured and put on the cross."

Okay, like the pain and suffering?

He says, "He was put under."

When he was on the cross you mean?

He said, "Yeah."

(Note: There are reports in "Hacking the Afterlife" that Jesus ("Essie") has learned esoteric yoga practices, like the Six Yogas of Naropa, that put him in a state of suspended animation, or consciousness shifting outside his body. There's also claims that the "wine soaked sponge" pressed on his mouth by Roman soldiers was soaked in a stupor inducing drug.)

I talked to a couple of people who knew him after the Crucifixion.

I did as well, I guess.

Right, you recalled being his daughter Sarah. But one was an apostle or James. He talked to an apostle who you knew as James. His description of you was that he saw you in the cave after the crucifixion and you were recuperating from injuries. was that correct?

He says, "Yes." (Jennifer aside) Funny, he showed me Jon Snow.

(Note: That's a reference to Jon Snow being killed during the season finale of "Game of Thrones" – and he's dead for all intent and purpose, but through incantations comes back to life with a gasp.)

Well this friend saw you recuperating in a cave.. saw you after the crucifixion.

It's like there's no time in space – everyone that has had experiences with him, on some level we all have, this group in ongoing, and this other group is ongoing - their souls – each group has all these different people, they can pass through one person and see the same information from another's perspective, even though that other person would not understand it.

Yes. And some people who existed before you lived – when asking them questions, they claim to have known you, even if they weren't alive at the time you were alive. The way people in councils sometimes claim to know me or have met me – even though they're outside of time.

Your dog Sam.

Yes! One council member claimed to know me through my dog, Sam who died 40 years ago! Whaaat? How can that be Jesus?

He says "Frequencies – that's why everyone loves your voice." (My audible versions of my books.)

Do you mean they hear the voice of god? Or dog?

Oh brother. So now he's showing me how people travel, we call it a "Merkabah."

(Note: It's an ancient Hebrew word that means vehicle, or etheric vehicle – and has come to mean form constants in new age circles.)

That's a vehicle – is that what you're seeing?

It's an etheric vehicle.

Someone's consciousness might see this object as a bike, race car: What kind of Merkabah do you travel in? A Mercury sedan?

Ha. My Saturn.

Stephen Hawking; I didn't mean to abandon you – "alien are not aliens." That's what you wanted to say?

He said, "Yes. And when you say get rid of the terminology – tell them to not lose god."

Okay, I'll tell them, Stephen Hawking told us to get rid of god – and Jesus backed him up. I think it's a funny idea that I ask council members if they know me during my sessions with people not under hypnosis.

Just to see if you're famous.

Ha. Yes! Once I asked two council members and one said "Yes, I've know your, and the other one said "Hope, never heard of you."

I think it's because the people have read your books and then their council knows of you.

But that's the wild thing – I had just met this person who had never read any of my books. I think it's just they're outside of time.

Exactly.

They run into a council member over there... and they laugh about it. "Hey, have you met this Martini goofball?"

It's the vortexes that circle all of the energy centers that ... Hold on. I'm still trying to figure out the answer about the number 12. I'm being shown so many many different things...

Maybe it's like a form constant – or that there's some part of nature that divides everything by 3. 12 is divisible by three.

That's what I see, yeah, I saw three groups of four.

And when we talk bout the "holy trinity"... also divisible by 3. Let's follow this; we know that the spirit part of "Father, Son and Spirit" was pneuma – or breath. Later it was spirare in Latin – which also means to breathe. So "father: creator, Son: creation: and the breath that animates humans – or consciousness if we go back to the original meaning of word. So what is consciousness?

He says, "The mind."

It's the thing that animates us – if god is the father the whole universe, the son is the human, the thing that animates us is the breath. The Holy trinity has always been a multiple of 12.

That's it; you got it.

The reason there are 12 is because they have their own fiefdom – but who designed the game?

I keep getting we are the designers. I see <u>us</u> in this restaurant from an aerial view.

Was there a beginning to this game design or an end?

What my brain sees – is my favorite quote from William Blake about the grain of sand; it's infinite, the levels the degrees where you soul evolves, taking in all the of the things that you don't have zero judgment; people can't wrap their heads around it – there is no endgame, there would be no universe if we didn't keep creating the world – we're on this planet, we have to do a better job to keep us in creation.

(Note: The quote by Blake is: "To see a world in a grain of sand, And a heaven in a wildflower, Hold infinity in the palm of your hand, And eternity in an hour. A robin redbreast in a cage, Puts all heaven in a rage. A dove-house filled with doves and pigeons, Shudders hell through all its regions.")

Let's ask Jesus one last question – are you guys helping us ask these questions?

He says, "Yes, exactly."

Is there going to be a giant reboot of the planet?

He says, "There already is a reboot. They need to bring their awareness up to get more help, there is a way to be quicker." (Get help quicker)

You want me to write about it the history of the universe in a blog?

He says, "No. There's going to be like subheadings, and there might be 12."

I love that they say there's no number they're referring to when they say 12. Sounds Buddhist, like the concept of "emptiness."

They say "There's no way we can comprehend it."

We can't help it because people have been running around with fingers in our face about numbers since we got on the planet.

Numbers are so sacred; we truly are mathematical equations of the best kind.

Should we give credit to Stephen for that?

I said it!

Elegant and eloquent – we'll give Jennifer credit for saying it... while she was talking to Stephen Hawking! Thanks class!

Another wild conversation between Jennifer, Luana, our class on the flipside. Mind bending to say the least, but consistent with the other interviews.

CHAPTER TWENTY SIX:

"BUNCH OF HOCKEY PUCKS"

DONALD J. RICKLES

During an interview with the radio show host George Noory ("Coast to Coast") I asked him if there was "anyone on the flipside" that he wanted me to interview. I filmed this interview in January, haven't been on the show since, to let him know we did as requested.

My questions are *in italics,* Jennifer's answers are **in bold.**

Rich: So we have one other guest we invited today. Anyone want to pop in and show Jennifer where that person is?

Jennifer: Robin Williams popped in and wants to know why he doesn't get called on.

Well, that makes sense as the next person we're going to speak with shares his frequency. Someone Robin knows, that's why I asked for his help with us reaching out to this person.

You asked Robin for help bringing this person forward? That's interesting. I think I have it. Do I know this person?

In a way, yes.

Richard Pryor. That was my guess.

(Note: I know this sounds like "What's My Line?" I usually ask prior to the session for this person to "come forward" and she guesses who it might be. She almost always gets it on the third try, and sometime, much to my chagrin, on the first try. In this case, I try to help her; we had a conversation with Frank Sinatra in a previous session.)

We don't have to guess. Let's ask our friend Frank. You know who I'm talking about. He's the only Frank in our group. He's friends with Frank, was in the film "Toy Story..."

(Jennifer laughs.) I know who you're talking about.. I'm hearing Donald. Don?

That's correct.

I have him in my head. Don Rickles? I still don't know who he is.

Better that you don't – the questions that I ask will make sense to me alone. Let's ask Luana (Anders, our moderator on the flipside) Is he here? Donald J. Rickles?

"Yes."

Don, what's you're opinion of our class?

He says "Groovy."

(Note: I call it a class because they started referring themselves as a class. I've never heard Jennifer use the term "Groovy.")

Your wife's name is...

He said, "Barbara." (Jennifer aside) Now I know who he is! He showed me his face, that short guy – he reminds me of Joe Pesci!

(Ding! His wife's name is Barbara) Martin Scorsese is quoted as saying "Don was a great actor who made everyone cry with laughter." What do you want to tell us?

He says, "Have fun and go outside."

Who was there to greet you when you crossed over?

Who's the guy... not Richard Pryor... Sammy Davis Jr.

What was that like? How did you see him?

He's laughing, saying they "flipped a coin" – They're laughing like – "you lost."

Like you flipped a coin and you lost?

He says, "And then here you are."

On the flipside. Let me ask a silly question - when you see Sammy does he appear to you with both eyes intact?

It's a hologram so it's different. You see him with his real eyes.

Sorry, I know it's a weird question.

He was showing me something different, his face had the outline but not the density.

Don, what do you miss about being on the planet?

He says "Benny Hill."

He hasn't been on in a while. But I get the reference even if Jennifer doesn't.

He says "He misses the smells." Whew. Like he was showing me the smell of dirt, he says "I love cigars that thick smell of smoke, and he missed the scents of everything."

Did you smoke cigars?

He said "He gave those up a long time ago.. then he showed me George Burns...

Okay, so have you been hanging out with him?

He says, "And Sammy and a bunch of others."

Frank?

"A lot" he says.

Tell us about your friend, Frank?

I asked him is Frank fun? He said "Fun? Frank? Not." He says that Frank is showing him around.

Like where, what does he show him? Like other planets? Other realms? Or just around our planet?

"Just around the planet." And when he said that, they showed me artwork. Their standing in museums around the globe.

Hang on, you and Frank are hanging out in museums?

He says, "It's like they're learning about things."

So tell us. Let's say you and Frank go to a museum. Is it real or imaginary?

He says, "Real. A lot of people are around them."

And they can't see you? So like you and Frank could be standing in front of the Mona Lisa, but no one can see you there? When you're with Frank, it's like the two of you, old friends, hanging out? What museums have you visited?

He said, "Istanbul."

Okay, very good, you picked one country I've never been to.

(Jennifer taps her nose to signify "yes") He went like this... tapped his nose. They know you haven't been there – I don't know why they thought that was... funny. Okay, they're showing me a place you have been; The Met.

So walk us into the Met – what's it like from your perspective? Are you both walking?

He says, "Flying... through the doors."

Fast?

He said, "In an instant. It's instantaneous."

(Note: We've heard this from other folks – when asked "What's different about being over there?" People often reply "Well, you can fly for one." They say that it's the "speed of thought.")

What painting would you go to see?

He says, "It's whatever they focus on their energy on."

Would Frank pick it or would you pick it?

Don says, "He'd pick it but Frank wouldn't want to see it."

Would you go to see the Renoirs on the second floor for example?

He says, "Then they'd go from The Met, think of another painting... and then go to Paris."

So you'd think of one of the Renoirs in The Met, and then think of another Renoir and suddenly fly to the Tuileries for example, is that right?

"Correct" he says,

Are you showing Frank or is Frank showing you?

He says "They're just hanging out..."

Let me ask, when you stand in front of a painting, Jennifer and I have talked about this – but it's like a slice of time. And by examining that slice of time when the painting was painted, can you step back in time and go to when it was created? Is it like going to a movie?

"We all don't have Jennifer's gift" he said.

So you're just looking?

Hold on. He's showing me that they can get a book that talks about the painting and its creation and read it really fast.

That's an unusual way to visit museums.

He said, "You can go back in time and see the artists... and go back to where and when it was being painted... within reason."

Have you done that, Don?

He said, "No."

But you could?

"Yes."

Okay, who put the idea in George Noory's mind that I should talk to you?

He said, "Luana."

Why? Why'd you pick Don?

"Because he (George) needs to lighten up – he's showing me his assistant." (Tom, one of his stressed out producers that Jennifer met.)

I was talking to George on the air, I offered that we could talk to anyone on the flipside. At first he said "I don't want to say their name" so I said pick someone you want to talk to if you could and he said "Don Rickles." Luana, did you put that name in George's head.

She says, "Yes."

Did he ever meet Don or is he just a fan?

He says, "He did meet him. Twice. In Vegas."

Was George a young guy?

"When he was in his 40's."

So when they met... did they speak to each other, or did he just come and see you? Or are you aware of meeting him?

He says, "They knew the same people – "

Don, what do you want me to tell George?

Tell him "There's no room up here."

Ha! Okay. I'm sure he'll be glad to hear that.

He says "Tell George to stop worrying about his heart."

Any message you want to give to your wife Barbara?

Jennifer smiles, laughs. He says "Tell her to stop spending all my money!"

That's funny. What else is she going to do with it?

He's kidding about that. He says he misses her very very much.

(Note: He said it twice. I had looked up Barbara's Instagram account prior to this session and knew he had a dog named "Chauncy.")

You had a friend named "Chauncy." You want to put who that is in Jennifer's mind?

He's showing me a giraffe? I know it's an animal.

It is, but he dresses up in different outfits...

Does he dress like a monkey?

(Note: I've seen pics on social media that Don and his wife posted of their dog in different hilarious outfits.)

Yes, he dresses up in different costumes – hilarious. Anything you want to say to Chauncy?

He says, "He's been fed to much." He showed me the dog getting bigger.

C'mon Robin, I'm asking about Don's dog – you want to weigh in with a punch line?

He's like "I don't know! It's not my dog!" Don says "I talk to my dog." He says "the dog actually sees him – he barks up in the corner; I try to tiptoe in and he catches me. (Jennifer listens) And the dog also misses him too – he knows he's gone... he's becoming more vocal (about it)."

Just Chauncy or other animals see him?

He says, "Just Chauncy."

That's funny, Sherry dreamed our cat called out to her – our son dreamt that the bird was angry he didn't hear him... is it that our animals speaking to us via their frequency in our dreams?

"Yes."

(Note: In "Backstage Pass" I include an interview with Robert Towne's dog Hira.)

What are the animals trying to tell us Don? Besides "save the planet?"

He's says, "To slow down – they're trying to tell us to just breathe, stop running around, that's why there are so many anxious animals around watching us run around."

I would think it would be something to do with...

"Waking us up" he says.

So Don, if you're suddenly aware the cow you're eating is saying "Hey! Don't eat me" it would be hard to finish your burger?

He says, "Yes."

As I said on George's show, some might consider our world as the circus, some people are performing in it, some better at being in the audience, some are good at stunts, some bad, some want to just play, have fun and get in the mud; when they go home on the flipside, it's great to be back home but it's also fun to be in the mud here on Earth.

Literally that's what Don was showing me --- getting into the dirt (when showing me smells). I felt he felt like he was giving me smells from baseball; was he in a movie about baseball? He was giving me smells of popcorn, hot dogs..

That's the thing he misses? Do you want to apologize to all the hockey pucks worldwide?

He said, "No."

I heard that he called Frank a hockey puck, and they became the best of friends...

Frank showed up when you said that.

Here's a question; Frank performed at Bush's inaugural and Don did a routine. But a Reagan's inaugural, Frank insisted Don do the show but not rehearse. Why was that?

He said, "Security."

What do you mean?

He said, "Don was trying to get into the theater, but he couldn't get past the security."

That's funny.

They have so much fun over there. They all get to hang out together. I said "You guys have no responsibilities!" and they

showed me how they help all the heads of the planet. I forgot that they constantly help us.

How does Don look to you, your mind's eye?

Thinning hair, with a combover. At about age 28. The knowledge came much later.. he has the playfulness of a 4 year old.

Don, what do you regret about your journey?

He says, "Not doing more." I asked him "To help with the planet?" And he said "Yeah people in general." He says "He got comfortable... (and) he got tugged by people..."

I think he worked a lot. Well, I guess we can wrap it up – we want to say goodbye to everyone and thank them for helping us; thanks Robin, Frank, Don and Luana.

They just keep making the show more spectacular. Luana is just bringing us up to speed.

I gotta go; bye class! Thanks everyone!

****

I once met producer (Laugh-In) George Schlatter. My friend Charles Grodin sent me over to his office as he was looking for someone to ghost write his memoirs. He was on the fence about doing that – so many great and funny stories about people no longer on the planet as well as people still on the planet. He told me stories about Don and Frank and about what it was like in Vegas in those days, and the amount of laughter they all had together. It felt like someone tapping into another era, and I hope one day he decides to write that book. But some part of me thinks that it was easier to talk to Don and Frank because I met someone who loved them both dearly.

CHAPTER TWENTY SEVEN:
CUB FANS EVERYWHERE

Ron Kunde in the Cubs organization

RON KUNDE FORMER CUB, PRINCE, MICHAEL NEWTON AN AKASHIC LIBRARIAN and NELSON MANDELA

Some folks have complained that we "only speak to celebrities. In this case, I chose was a former Cub that was a family friend, Ron Kunde. I can verify a number of details with Ron because I knew him well – one of my brother's best friends.

My question are *in italics*, Jennifer Shaffer's replies are **in bold.**

Rich: Okay class, we've only got a half hour – what's up, who wants to come forward. Luana, we're turning this discussion over to you.

(Note: Our class moderator)

Jennifer: Luana says she talked to you this morning, gave you a baseball player, someone who played sports?

I was writing an essay about how you create sports on the flipside this morning.

You were?

Yeah. What baseball player is this?

At first she showed me someone I would recognize; Joe DiMaggio. But it's your friend, the one who played major league baseball.

I have only one. Ron. What do you want to tell us?

He said, "Tell your brother "hello."

Okay. Ron I may have asked you this before; who was three to greet you?

He's showing me his mom.

(Note: In this research, about two thirds of our "conscious energy" is not on the planet, is always "back home" and hence why during near death events sometimes people see loved ones who are "still on the planet.")

Can you show Jennifer how you did cross over?

I'm feeling suffocating; it was like an accident.

It was related to his career.

He says, he was "Playing baseball and having a heart attack."

Correct. He was playing softball on a local league, hit a home run and died crossing home plate.

He showed me.

One of the last photos of Ron playing softball

Ron lets talk about something I find unusual – your dad had already crossed before you, but when you crossed over you saw your mom – what about your dad?

It feels like he was a chief or some kind. That's what he's showing me.

He could have helped coach Ron – or maybe that was a nickname; Chief.

It might not be his dad, but someone else who was with him.

Before he died, Ron's dad was operated on for an illness, and they screwed it up. The hospital made mistakes, and it so happened our mutual friend was a nurse the ER, and without knowing the connection, told me they had screwed up this operation. When I heard that Ron's father had been operated on, I passed it on to my brother who passed it on to Ron.

It felt like they cut too much.

They mistakenly cut something. I told my brother...

Jennifer taps her nose as if to say "He's agreeing with you."

What happened – and eventually Ron won ten million from the hospital.

He says, "For negligence."

That's right. How many years did you die after your father?

It feels like around five.

But I'm reflecting how that money came through for your family.

He says, "He has a son."

That's correct. (Kevin) What, if anything do you want me to tell him?

"Go after it" he says.

Are you talking about this research, or just in life?

"Yeah."

I can tell you Ron, when the Cubs won the World Series we were all talking about you.

He says, "You should have seen it up here."

Let me ask about that; did you see fans or old cubs rooting for them?

"Everyone" he said.

Was that a quid pro quo – like "If the cubs win then we elect Trump?"

He says "That's actually really funny."

Accurate?

He's just .. he says "There's no comparison."

What would you like me to tell my brother Rob?

He says, "Tell him... to stop being blocked. He still has a lot of good years left."

Like "Overcome your fears, reach for the stars, have more fun?"

He says, "Yes. Okay. I'm just saying..." He says, "We're all rooting for your brother up here. They all love him the way they did back there."

Who's they? There are number of his friends on the flipside.

I'm getting four or five.

There's Joe Brizzolara and a few others; any message for Robbie?

They're showing me something with the car on the side? Like a fender bender? (Jennifer gestures as if the side of the car was damaged.)

His wife did have an accident recently. (Ding!)

They are all laughing about it...

They're laughing about her car accident?

He says, "Yes, (to them) it was funny." They're saying "She needs to get her eyes checked... but they say definitely "It wasn't her fault."

That's wild. I'll let him know.

He says, "It's (a) small (thing) not to worry about it..." I feel like Rob has been writing and stopped it. He feels like he has a block. He says, 'Tell him to talk to him me more; they'll pull in musicians to help him."

(Note: Rob is an amazing guitarist and he does play music, so "writing" may refer to his guitar playing. "Tell Rob to reach out to his friends on the flipside more.")

Ronnie we had so much fun with you on the planet.

He's saying "He hit it out of the park." Did he used to chew tobacco?

I don't think so – some players did.

He's showing me like a place, like there was a joint you used to go to – like an old ice cream stand.

Could have been the ice cream stand at the ballpark uptown in Northbrook. Little Louies? The night he died he had a long conversation with my brother about how much he loved him... and at the funeral, his wife said...

He said, "He needed to hear that."

That's right. And my brother told you how much he loves you as well.

He said, "Yes."

What about that conversation, why did it occur?

He says "He just knew he was leaving."

You summed it up for him; but then why did you leave early?

He says "It was the right time to go."

Are you coming back soon?

"Not without you." (Jennifer smiles.)

Very funny. Not without your peeps. You had a heart murmur – why did you choose a life with that and be an athlete at the same time?

He says "He couldn't have one without the other – he's showing me that if you have previous lives getting to that point they all add up to a future lifetime. He says "He's making his heart stronger."

For a future life?

He says, "Yes."

(Note: We've heard this before, from the "outside of time" perspective, a person can see "all of their lifetimes" as a series of performances on stage, and how each performance affects or relates to the other ones. People report a choice of a lifetime with addiction for example, so in a future life they can be a doctor to help heal people with that issue.)

Thanks Ronnie!

Some of Ronnie's baseball cards. Forever a Cub.

****

So Luana, does anyone else want to jump the line.?

I'm getting chills so bad. My dad just gave me a big kiss, said "I love you." Prince came forward.

What's he want to say?

It's about your music. He says "You should change the ending to the song you were writing last week."

Okay, I was – and I know what he's talking about.

"The third one... the ending is too low and it should be higher."

I think he means louder... or do you mean the voice is bad?

No, it's ... did you play ukulele on it?

Almost. I thought about it. It's a guitar song and I can fix that.

He said "It will synthesize better."

Thanks buddy – song advice form the flipside.

(Note: This isn't the first time he's mentioned a song of mine, and how I should fix it.)

(Jennifer aside) I can't make this up. (Listens) I asked if he wanted to be my date to see Jennifer Lopez perform tomorrow and he said "Yeah – why not?"

Julian Lennon reached out the other day and I told him how Prince told us that somehow Julian had influenced Eric Clapton to play "Purple Rain" as an encore at his show. Was that accurate?

He says "Yes, 1000 percent."

How'd you do that? Did you talk to Julian's higher self up there?

He showed me "Road maps." I don't know. You mean John or his son Julian?

Julian. But let's ask John – did Julian get my email about this topic?

He said, "Yeah."

Did he understand it? Did it freak him out?

He says "Not really" – he showed me the white feather again, whatever that means. John said "He believes in that."

Okay, I get that – I told Julian if there's anything we can do to help the white feather foundation we would. I told him we talked to the purple one, Prince... Okay Luana, anybody else? Who else wants to chat?

Morton.

Hello Michael! (our nickname for Michael Newton, who's "Journey Of Souls" launched me into the flipside.) I have a couple of questions for you; first, how are you doing?

"Fine," he says. He says "He's very happy with what you're doing – he's showing me where we sat before (in the restaurant, and how you've shortened it (the process of speaking to councils)."

Well, let me ask you about that – talking directly to councils as I do in my other books.

He's showing me the energy of that... whatever's happening is healing... it brings their frequency back to that time period; they get more connected. He says "We're always connected, but your awareness gets more connected."

Because their awareness is with their higher selves?

He says, "They're spring boarding for them – it's helping (the people who see the councils) with their grief."

I find it interesting to talk to councils and ask them questions about where they're from.

He said, "A thousand galaxies."

This one woman was holding the hand of a council member who was from another planet – and was kind of freaked by holding his claw. Is this method, or this line of questioning okay with you – or is there anything I should add or subtract?

He said "Ask the person their earliest childhood memory here."

You mean memory of talking to spirit or conscious memory?

He says, "Just conscious memory. Because it (the memory) will turn into something."

I used to ask that question often "What's your first conscious memory?"

He says, "Some people need that, it helps them get more comfortable."

I know that your former student Paul Aurand has been working with scientists, some from the University of Virginia, helping some recall near death events and demonstrating how hypnotherapy can be used by science to access memory.

He says "That's pretty amazing." He also says "You're going to be teaching your method."

The Martini Institute? That's a funny idea.

I'd join.

I've spoken to some people trained by the Newton Institute about the kinds of sessions they're allowed to teach...

He says, "Rules need to be thrown out the window." I just felt my dad say "Michael is the good Samaritan – he's still doing research for the greater good."

I don't think these therapists want to step on any toes.

"There are no toes," he says.

Very funny.

****

Okay, let me ask about a session I did the other day with a woman over skype. I walked her in to visit with her council – she wasn't under hypnosis at all, but she could clearly see her council members and interview them. And when I asked her guide "Trixie" a seven foot tall Amazon, if she wanted her to see anything else, she took us to this Akashic library. Your father Jim took us to an Akashic library before – maybe he can help me unpack this. Instead of seeing "books" she saw them as tennis balls sized lights. Like energetic swirling lights.

That's how lights attract lights – our whole existence is light.

Her guide was showing her this library, she was seeing them not as books, but literally as light. Your dad Jim showed us a book once, and showed us that it was energy – or etheric – and at some point as I thought we were through, I asked if her guide wanted to have her see anything else and the guide walked us over to a librarian. She described this little guy about 5 feet tall – looked a bit like Danny DeVito; but a million years old with an eternally young face.

I just got an image of Yoda.

Okay. Funny, she did say he was a Yoda like person – when we asked for his name, he told us "Huey."

They were saying "Yoda, like the essence of Yoda." (Jennifer aside) I asked is it because of how he looked and they said "No."

Are you asking him directly?

(Jennifer aside) I don't know.

Let's ask Luana to bring him forward.

He's here.

(Note: Again – this is not "a person I know" per se, as we'll see in this interview. He's someone who says he's like a "regional director" for Akashic libraries. I "met him" during a two hour session with a woman back east who wanted to speak to her council and guides. Her guide introduced this fellow to me, and now, Luana has brought him into our class.)

He told me he was really busy over there and didn't have time to wait for this woman's questions. He also told us to call him maestro instead of Huey. Can we talk to you Maestro, or are you busy?

They have him blocked in. She put him in my head...

Let me ask you a question.

(Jennifer aside) Is this someone you knew?

No.

Was he a council guy?

No, he was a guy in a library – went to a council and he was the detour after.

He's morphing into various different – he morphs into different looks from what I'm getting. Whatever it is... whoever it is..

My first question; "What's up dude?"

He showed me us talk... talking and stacks of infinite records a mile high... "that's what's up."

Are you the only Akashic librarian or one of many?

He said, "Source." He showed me being him and shooting out thousands of him in different lights – you know when they show someone running and there's an echo of each image?

Multiple images?

He, if I'm getting this right – he said "Source." He says "Our soul is like the ocean," we've talked about that... each wave is a different person. That's him.

So you are the source librarian – people see different variations of you in their Akashic libraries?

He's saying it again; "Source." (Jennifer asks) He's God?

Let's clarify that.

He says "You see what you want to see."

Well we've learned in these sessions that God is not a person, per se, but more like a medium or a nexus?

That's what he showed me; like everyone is a light and everyone is connected. Everything that's on earth, all the different layers of the planet.

I know this is a complex conversation...

(Jennifer aside, joking) Let me take my gum out of my mouth..

Have you always been the librarian or did you become the librarian?

Jennifer smiles. He said, "He became his own librarian." He showed me coming from other galaxies, being a part of someone else's world. He says "He became his own "God" here – his own librarian..." It's funny, I was shown the Mormon church, because they talk about "being your own God" in the afterlife.

Yes, I'm aware of that mythology. But instead of the term God or deity, let's use the word librarian as it's easier... you came from another realm originally?

He says, "Yes."

How many years ago?

He says, "It's not years, but ten millions of years, square root of pi – kind of answer."

Was that in a realm that anyone is aware of on this planet?

He says, "Yes."

They are not in our universe, but in another realm?

He says, (Another realm) "That's connected."

In terms of levels, what level would that be?

He says, "It's like we are the power source for the other galaxies."

Okay... your universe is the source of all the other universes?

"It's complicated," he says.

Just trying to clarify. We've spoken to people from higher realms, and have had conversations with people like Jennifer who recall being on the 5th or 7th level – So, correct if I'm wrong – you lived in another realm, give us like a level...

"Eleven" he said.

That just gives us and idea, are you still in touch with people from there?

"Yes." He says "He needs a lot of people he needs an army he's the source for them – (Jennifer aside) I'm like "Are we the power source for him and his universes and I'm getting "Yes."

(Note: This seems to refer to a previous conversation where we learned that dark matter or dark energy is the source of matter in other universes; discussed in a chapter with scientists later.)

But you're the librarian for all libraries?

"No." He says "There are a lot of libraries."

So the other libraries that you're not in charge of, others are in charge of?

He said, "Yes."

How many libraries are you in charge of?

He's saying, "It's like you take the population of Tokyo and you multiply that by a billion – it's infinite."

Everybody in our realm?

He said, "No."

Are you the librarian for everyone on earth? Just clarifying.

"Yes" he said.

And some other places...

He says, "We're connected to all of that – he's in charge of all of that."

In my interview with you, you said the books of our past lives are not about history.

He says, "No."

You said they were about fear – the times we conquered fear.

"Yes. It's the opposite of fear," he says.

Explain that to Jennifer – so the books that are in our Akashic library are about love?

He said, "Yes."

Conquering your fear, not just overcoming... the records that we retain are about how I overcame fear in a previous lifetime?

He says, "Yes, that's why past life regressions help."

So what is love?

He says, "Love is the heart center, he showed me it's connected to everything; oceans, seas, the earth."

We're connected heart wise, but all things? The ocean, an object, a table?

"Yes" he said.

On a quantum level – things don't come into existence until we choose to observe them according to quantum mechanics.

He's saying, "It's like the boat theory – will natives first saw people on ships, they didn't know what they were. They didn't come into existence until they knew."

Does that apply to everything?

"Yes."

What do you want to tell us maestro?

He says, "To stop fearing the unknown. The more that you love, the more that opens you up, heart wise, the more knowledge comes to you."

Are you talking about the law of attraction in terms of money?

"It's energy, it's how you disperse it" he says.

So why did you choose to show up to this guide during this session. She wanted me to meet you – why?

He says, "It should be in your books, the discussions we've had. "

It will be.

(Jennifer aside) He's smoking a cigar. A Cuban cigar.

How long have you been smoking Cubans?

He says "100,000 years." (Jennifer aside; I know they weren't invented yet.)

Did they exist prior to being on the planet?

He says, "Everything did."

Cigars existed?

He says, "When we open ourselves up we reveal things that have always existed, we get things. Somebody was really lucky getting a cigar, someone lucky, getting Microsoft."

You're saying those things existed, but our conscious awareness of them does not – until it does, and then inventions are made? Is there something you want to show us so we can become billionaires.

(Note: My questions may sound flippant, but when I meet someone like this, an intellect that is hard for me to keep up with, I try to throw a few curve balls if I can.)

He showed me your heart center.

So tell me how can people access Akashic libraries?

He showed me lying down – he showed me meditation. If you don't judge anything you can get anything. If you're not fearful of things coming in – it's very challenging to not judge what you see or hear.

Should people focus on you in their meditation to go to the Akashic records of their many lifetimes?

He said, "No. They should focus on their hearts."

What's a question for their heart? To say "I'd like to visit my library?"

He says, "Another way to say it is "I'd like to visit who I am elsewhere.""

Is there a better word than Akashic?

He says, "Using the word library helps everyone get there."

How about heart library? Library of my heart?

He says, "That's what it is but – if you want people to get there, you can't use that word – they might think it's something else." (Jennifer laughs) He says "You shouldn't change it from Akashic because people have finally understood it; it's taken thousands of years to get people to hear it – even if they're not religious." I say energy centers, Chakras... Akashic means heart.

I think in Sanskrit it means etheric or "invisible."

But it means "heart."

But Maestro, can you show Jennifer something?

He says, "He doesn't like being called Maestro. He says use light."

That's too hard to use in a sentence... Mr. Light... and try not to interrupt me Huey when I'm asking you a question. (said jokingly)

He says, "Speak for yourself." (Jennifer laughs)

Here's my point...

He's answering your question before you can ask it; saying "He had a bodyguard, he was speaking to his front line."

This woman's guide was amazing, her name is Trixie but she's this 7 foot tall Amazon with a sense of humor. It was wild, she said "I want you to meet someone before we leave here." This woman saw her library as tennis balls, glowing lights – fractals. I asked you if these were books – the fractals are books... is that correct?

He says, "Yes."

You said calling them "Akashic books" is the right term –

He showed me something being pressurized, they're... since there's no time in space, it's a record of time where you are.

Okay; like a packet in time? Who creates them?

He says, "Our higher self does – that's how we get out of this lifetime – we have several outs."

We create the packets?

"Yes" he says.

How many does a person have?

He says, "Thousands. They are not all just one lifetime. Everything making up one big shape – love, hatred, all these things, loss, that all becomes fractals - eventually they become cohesive and turn into "your books." (One's akashic library).

(Note: What he's saying is that these "fractals" that follow us around, some people see geometric shapes while under hypnosis, some see them in the light of day – they are our "Akashic records" that function as "portable hard drives" for our development. What makes this unusual is this is the first I've heard that these "fractals" are what we see when we visit Akashic libraries.)

When Jennifer and I went with her dad we were looking at books ... energetic etheric books – but are they all our fractals, just ours, or are we seeing other peoples?

He says, "We are seeing.. we are all one, it's the universe's library, it's all of us..."

But my question is – let's say during a deep hypnosis session, we are visiting the library with my guide and I say I'd like to visit someone else's records. Are we allowed to do that?

He said, "Yes; everything's connected you can see whoever you want – everything that's affected them."

So what's in the books functions like a URL or a link?

"Yes" he said.

I'm aware that the brain is similar – perhaps the brain doesn't actually store memories – but let's say an engram might store a link that refers to the "off site" portable hard drives that retain the memory of an experience. I tap you on the leg and a pathway goes to your brain.. the theory is that we don't store information there but offsite?

"Yes." He showed me that.

So we have our own personal cloud, each of us, and the cloud is our fractals filled with memories from all of our lifetimes?

"Yes."

And the engrams in our brains serve as a link?

He says, "Yes. It also comes back thought – as well - both ways. If we're feeling something here we get information coming from there, maybe not our past lives but something else."

Let me ask this, if it's possible to access other people's past lives..

He says, "We're in the bandwidth." It's like me (Jennifer the medium) thinking someone is going to die – it's a frequency I'm translating.

It's a question – can people remember or access other people's past lives? Or are they remembering their own individual lives?

"Yes."

Like somebody they were connected to, a brother, etc...

He says, "They may not get their own past lives, but will pick up on other people's past life – the way that I energetically pick up on past events."

Well, that's the argument that scientists use to argue that past lives don't exist.

They showed me something interesting, the memories we get from other people's past lives don't affect us... that ones we pick up on.

But people under deep hypnosis..

He says, "While under hypnosis they can't get other people's experiences."

One example was a session I was doing with a fellow who recalled being tarred and feathered. After a few moments, he realized that he was empathizing with the kid that he was looking at back in the 18th century – a kid who had been tarred and feathered. And he was one of the perpetrators.

He said, "Each one is traumatizing." (The viewer and the experiencer).

My point is how to differentiate when someone might be remembering previous lifetimes or if they're experiencing someone else's.

They just showed me being in the matrix and being fluid – a lot of people pick up energies from other people. When I work on a case, I have to check if I'm looking from the point of view of the perpetrator or a victim.

Okay, thank you Mr. Librarian.

It's one of his people – he's able to talk through people.

What does that mean?

He has a medium up there – he or she or whatever is talking through someone there right now...

My question is – why? Why are you talking to us?

He's showing me you. Because your research is helping a lot of people and there's a buzz up there about it.

One last question – I asked if you ever met anyone from the planet who impressed you over there, someone in the library, and it was someone from our class. I asked Jennifer if he'd reincarnated – he had said "Yes," and Jennifer recognized who his reincarnation is on the planet.

He said "James Dean."

Yes.

(Note: We interviewed James Dean and I asked if he was thinking of coming back and he named someone that I am friends with his best friend. So after the session, I texted the friend and asked "Hey, your pal so and so – has anyone ever told him he was the reincarnation of someone?" And he wrote back **"James Dean. All the time."** When I spoke to him, he detailed all the times in their friendship he'd heard people tell this fellow he was the reincarnation of James Dean. And we heard the same from "James Dean" himself (or what appears to be himself.) And in this case, I'm asking the librarian to confirm this detail.)

That's who it was... this woman, I've never met her before, in her session she's quoting the librarian as saying that he saw James Dean in the library, and I had asked him during the session "Was that true about him reincarnating into this friend of my friend? and he said "Yes, everything you heard about it is true." Mind bending. Anyways, thanks for answering our questions; it's not easy everyone has a lot of questions, and we're like kindergartners.

He says "Well, sometimes you learn from kindergartners."

Okay, thank you sir. I know Jennifer has to leave, but Luana is there anyone else we need to talk to today?

Jennifer listens, then makes a face.

Don't judge it. What?

Nelson Mandela. At first I thought it was Arthur Ashe for a second... don't judge me!

Nelson, welcome - because we spoke to Arthur a few weeks ago – but I think we asked Nelson a question or two before – can you sit down and talk to us? What's he want to say?

I think there's an anniversary coming up. (Note: It was on June 20th that he addressed US; June 22nd the UN; his birthday is July 18th)

Nelson what do you want to say to us?

He's showing me you – in my mind's eye, saying "You're correct about the planet. There's layers of it. I see layers going down at once."

What do you mean by that sir?

He says, "They're helping the planet from up there like we're trying to help it from here."

So the layers are you guys helping and us trying to help...

He's showing me like a room full of people on cell phones not paying attention.

What's a way for us to break through that?

He says, "Your books."

What can I say to them that will help?

"Science" he says.

What can we say on your behalf in your words, your heart that will convince people this is you speaking?

I hope I'm getting this right.. "Peace is when the amazon forest is full of life."

Okay.

He's saying, "Full of life." He's showing me all the trees, all the animals. "When we take away the amazon we take away the peace of the two different kingdoms – between man and nature - and it makes it so unbalanced that things start happening (natural disasters) like a shark attack, things getting disrupted."

What can we do to get people to pay attention to the planet in a different fashion?

He's showing me you on a picket line with a sign.

What's the sign say?

"Green peace."

Two words or one word? Greenpeace is an entity.

He says, "No. Two words."

So two words "Green Peace." We need your help reaching out to people who should we reach out to? which of your friends would be receptive to your message?

(Jennifer aside) This is so weird. I'm not going to judge it. He's showing me Puerto Rico. Something in Puerto Rico – I'm thinking "Why Puerto Rico?" I don't know.

Hold on – let's break it down – I asked "Which of your friends.. and you showed her Puerto Rico; does that mean Lyn Manuel Miranda?

He said, "Yes."

I get it.

(Jennifer aside) I don't know how.

He put it your head to go to my head; Lyn is from Puerto Rico; he was recently there with Hamilton... are you saying he should do a play about you?

He said, "It's already in the works."

(Note: "Already in the works" could mean "it's being planned up here on this side of the curtain.")

Okay, that's someone to reach out... so you want me to tell him "We were speaking to Nelson Mandela and he told me to reach out to you and tell you there's a play you're going to do about him." Which will convince him that this is actually you speaking... and the message he wanted us to pass along is that he wants you to help save the planet through Green Peace."

He said, "Yes."

Okay, who else?

"To Sting."

Do you know Sting, Mr. Mandela? Did you meet him?

He showed me Sting and Bono – I think he's saying "They've thought about what's going on in terms of the Amazon."

What message to Sting could I pass along knowing it's coming to you?

He says, "That's he spoke to him recently."

Since crossing over?

"Yes."

In a dream? Or a song?

Just like this – us talking. He was getting a message.

So Sting had a dream or a message recently?

He showed me everyone getting the same message at the same time...

Okay, so everyone is getting this same message we are, Sting is getting a message, and Bono is getting a message? I'll do my best to reach out to them.

He's showing me cleaning up the oceans, how dense the salt is in the ocean, we should be cleaning that up. Making clean energy.

So your top three are Bono, Sting and Lyn Manuel Miranda?

"Yes." He says "They're all getting messages, they're planning it everywhere, they're all getting the same message."

so what's the best way for others to participate and help?

He's saying "Think tanks. Like minded groups."

What about President Obama? Should I reach out to him?

(Shakes her head). He's showing me there's almost not way to get through.

Well Nelson's a big name – if he can get the message through, he'll get it. Not from me, but from someone else.

He says, "He'll come in later."

What about your pal Oprah?

I was shown an image of Oprah and her dogs; super happy... that kind of pure happiness. Yes, absolutely; reach out to her.

Look, the people who are aware of my work, aware of Jennifer's work – the ones who have experienced speaking to their loved ones on the flipside know that we're not making this up. I'm happy to pass it along. May I ask you some of our mundane questions about your journey, Nelson? Who was there to greet you when you crossed over?

He says, "His mother."

Okay, who are you hanging out with now?

He showed me some of the members of our class. He's showing me Luana, for example.

We've had quite a gathering of people in this so called class, from Abe Lincoln to Martin Luther king... What do you think of what we're doing, this connection to our class?

He said, "Amazing. Amazing." He showed me Morton again, (Michael Newton) how they're leaning how to talk to people here, and we're in turn getting people to open up their minds so they can do it.

I was thinking of friends of mine who are from South Africa who might help you...

"You should talk to them, definitely," he says.

I'll do my best. That's cool. So you're hanging out with people in our class? What do you miss about being on the planet?

He's showing me tangible, touching. He says, "Holding people. The sand in my toes. The feeling of people – Hugging. Physical touch, water between my feet, sand at the beach, clean water."

I can almost hear you saying "clean water" in your accent. Are you planning on coming back soon?

He says, "Part of him is already (back) here."

Okay, where?

"The Amazon."

As a male or female?

He's saying "A male." He showed me a guy with a spear – I asked "Like are you spearing fish?" He said "No."

Do you mean like an indigenous native?

"Yes. That's it."

What country?

He says, "Peru."

Why did you choose that lifetime?

He says, "I wanted to feel the dirt." What he's saying is that he can feel all what this person is feeling, so he's understanding firsthand that there's no fish, the animals are dying in the forest.

What percentage of your energy is in this guy?

"Thirty" He says.

(Note: Michael Newton would ask people "how much or your conscious energy was in your lifetime?" I noticed that the number was usually between 20 and 40% or "about a third" or our conscious energy. Two thirds of that energy is "always" back home.)

He's showing me "It feels like 100% of his energy to the person that he is incarnated in, but that person is not aware of it.. maybe like 10% is aware.

Is he aware in his dreams? Does he sometimes recall your life?

He says, "Yes."

Which does he remember more of; the pain or the later adulation?

He showed me a flag – he says, "that's a symbol of being free."

So in a dream he might remember being you?

He says, "No, he doesn't see him but he comes through in a different way..." (Jennifer aside) I just saw something... I was just shown that in the dream state we get to go within our soul group to experience other versions of ourselves; we get to see through their eyes what they're doing.

Actually, I was writing about this morning.

(Jennifer aside) Really?

I was writing about how we spend a third of our lives asleep – cats sleep 14 to 18 hours a day – nature doesn't make mistakes, so why would nature create a creature that sleeps 2/3rds of its life? Unless somehow we have it reversed; while we are asleep, our etheric bodies are doing all kinds of things.

"Correct" he said.

We sleep a third of our lives, we have other activities while we are asleep. Is that what you're saying?

He says, "Yes. Nature doesn't make mistakes; we do."

Nelson any last words?

(Jennifer holds up two fingers.)

Peace?

He says, "Green peace."

Thank you sir!

CHAPTER TWENTY EIGHT:
GODS OF ROCK AND ROLL PHYSICS

Ma Durga, 8 armed deity.   Tom Petty; 2 armed American deity.

TOM PETTY AND FLIPSIDE TEACHER MA DURGA

Rich: Who wants to talk to us? We had an earthquake last week and bees are acting weird – who wants to talk to us about this? Luana you want to bring us a Queen Bee?

Jennifer: It's almost like she's bringing someone in whom we've met before. I saw a vision I've seen before of someone with all these arms.

I remember her.

(Jennifer aside) I don't.

She was your father's teacher in a class we went to visit in deep space. Is that correct? I forget her name.

She says, "Yes!"

(Note: In a previous session, when Jennifer first began to access her father on the flipside, I asked him what he was doing and he said "attending class." We asked him to "take us there" and he described a giant auditorium in deep space, where this 8 armed teacher was teaching the class advanced astrophysics. I interviewed the teacher briefly.)

Does she have a name?

It sounds like Zander but spelled with an X.

Thank you for showing up... shall we call you Madame X?

"Yes."

Describe her to me; what do you see?

She's really tall she has this huge cloak, this wrap that covers everything, like what a king would wear. Only it's green and velvet and beautiful.

Does she have hair?

Yeah but it's all up – in a weird upwards do... (Jennifer gestures above her head.) It's colored like a prism when light shines on it, it has different colors.

How about her eyes?

She only has one eye I think...

What about her arms?

She has them, but then she has lots of other arms back there.

Eight?

She says, "Yes."

You're a teacher of astrophysics correct?

She says, "Yes." Hold on. It's almost like she's a Hindu goddess.

(I looked her up; searched for "8 armed Hindu Goddess") The reference I got is Durga – who is the mother of Ganesh! She's the only 8 armed Hindu deity I can find.

I'm getting that. "She's related to Ganesh."

Ganesh was part elephant and part human (his mother had 8 arms). But let's ask her; each arm represents insight or knowledge?

She says, "Wisdom, Yes. And the number 8 is equal to infinity... "

Right; the symbol for infinity is the number 8 on its side. Each arm...

She said, "Represents something symbolic."

So you manifested in this way so people who are Hindu would know who you are?

She would show herself to them – she's showing me a certain way with her back turned towards me – when I'm looking down I see all these lights (students in class depicted as lights).

Do those lights represent students in your class?

Yes; including my dad.

You were brought in by Luana to talk to us about bees on earth?

She showed me the bees getting so hot – it's not a temperature thing but a frequency thing... I was shown like their so much static they can't stay here.

(Note: Although smart meters are reportedly less harmful than cell phone towers, farmers and beekeepers have posted videos online claiming the meters killed nearby trees or bees. http://www.ncsl.org/research/energy/regulating-and-encouraging-smart-grid-technologies.aspx This came to mind as I wrote this sentence.)

Do earthquakes disrupt the bees' frequency?

She said, "Yes. Like when a car goes down and releases a lot of energy, "It's like their spirits are evaporating in their bodies."

People have observed them going in circles after quakes – they've lost their way?

"They were already gone," it feels like.

So the quake destroyed their ability to move?

She says, "Yes. They couldn't acclimate. Some (solar) flares interrupt human behavior."

Do you mean solar flares?

She's saying "Yes, that what causes it. Climate change is causing the epicenter of the earth to get super hot."

Well something else to worry about. Earlier we were talking about the work of Charles Darwin.

I was expressing something I learned from a session with Darwin's great great great great granddaughter. As we were talking he came through and gave me information that only her family knows... It had to do with a child that was illegitimate, that was African that was sick, that passed away.

He told us that his wife wrote much of the book "Origin of the Species." He said, "His original intent was to write about how do we know what we are?" He was going to call it "Origin of the Spirit." It was supposed to be about the origins of spirit, how we evolved, as he was talking he showed me his relative I was speaking to and them as himself... as if a pile of sand was going into her and then coming back out.

He was showing me that "We're the same DNA, we're the same cluster." He said "You don't know where you are." I replied, "Yes, I do, I'm at the Rose Cafe in Venice California." And he said "No, you don't really know where you are."

And all of a sudden, it was like going into the vortex. It's happened to me twice before, once in Sedona, and the other in Peru, when everything becomes quiet, and all of a sudden I saw all the other dimensions going along at the same time.

And he said "You think you're here; but you're not." He asked "Do you ever see yourself in your dream state?" And I saw myself as a chubby little Swedish boy. It was like the rug was pulled out from under me.

He said "Why do you think you can't go into past, present and future? (It's) because you're not really here, you're a blip on the screen, a place on the sand..." He reiterated the title was supposed to be "Origins of Spirit."

Okay, let's get back to Madame X, the eight armed teacher.

(Jennifer aside) Do you know where we left off?

You explained to us why the bees are dying off.

She says, "It's like humans having cancer; bees don't get cancer but they can't sustain staying in their body – people think that cancer is a form of combustion in your body..."

So instead of bees getting cancer they're dying? By this disruption of equilibrium?

She's telling me "It goes back to the sun flares; some flares affect us because they're massive, it takes quakes to affect bees."

So what do you want to talk to us about?

"The epicenter" she said.

The planet is getting hot? The core is getting hot?

It's like lava...showing me something with lava.

(Note: There's predictions flying around about Yellowstone being on the top of a volcano that will eventually erupt. Also, I've heard the theory that solar flares precipitate earthquakes on Earth.)

Whenever I go to the epicenter, I get shown myself in the core. I'm trying to understand what they're saying. From what I understand, this is my interpretation, "It's that our core is not being grounded, everything is frenetically off balance, when you're that small, like a bee it can't survive that disruption. For them the only option is to say "I'm out of here.""

They're showing me a memory of my past life where I couldn't save the children I was supposed to help... (Jennifer asks:) what does this have to do in this dimension now? I'm hearing "We have to be kinder to our planet. Which we know if we aren't kinder to our planet, the planet feels that we aren't acclimating and puts it out there. They are showing me a bunch of things, people rising up, people already feel like they're out of sorts, that's why they're leaving, like we're the most dense dimension we're in..."

Are you saying that the collapse of the bee colonies, for whatever reason, is related to humans committing suicide?

She says, "It's related to our atmosphere; we can counterbalance it by having more trees. The oxygen from the trees make everything more grounded."

Well, trees retain carbon – they release oxygen. We've heard this; if you plant a trillion trees you can save the planet.

(Jennifer aside) I don't know any of this on a scientific level.

I had a conversation with a tree the other day and he said "Be kind."

And that's what they're saying now; "Be kind."

What do you want to tell your followers in India?

She said, "Stop smoking." I saw a whole group of people smoking.

That may be related to pollution.

She says, "They stopped believing, something about them "not believing.""" I'm being shown that a lot of people in India do what they're supposed to do because they're supposed to do it, but there's not the creative energy you get when you have faith in something."

Well faith in something, or blind belief can causes wars; you're saying that people in India are no longer connected to spirit?

She says, "Yes."

Thank you. Anyone else want to come forward?

Tom Petty came to me yesterday and he just showed up again today.

What's up, Tom?

He says, "He wants to talk to you." He has a daughter?

(Note: If Jennifer had read up on Tom, she'd know he has two. But this is her way of translating what she's saying and shows she's not bringing an agenda to this conversation.)

I think they're litigating his estate.

He says, "He wants you to pass along a message." Something about her allowing people, something like... allowing... "that not everyone is good..." no, hold on...

Let's see if we can unpack it. Are you talking about her (someone advising her)?

He says, "Yes."

There's a problem or issue with them?

"Yes" he says.

Tom. Really? C'mon man. I'm not going to get in between the family and their (people who advise them). First, please tell us what can I say that will make your daughter(s) realize this is you – some object perhaps that only she would know that you gave her?

(Jennifer listens.) It feels like a car. Or a belt.

Let's start with the belt. What's it look like?

It's a belt buckle. I just saw rhinestones... or diamonds.

Is there a design?

He says, "She'll know." When he says that.... he's showing me something with a car too – and then this sparkly belt buckle. Might have diamonds on it.

That he gave to her or willed to her? Was it gifted?

He says, "He gifted to her."

How many years ago?

He says, "12 years ago – or she was 12 at the time. Felt like the buckle was from 1972... He gave it to her when she was 12?"

(Note: Jennifer just reports what she sees. She got the number 12 – and then is trying to understand what it could mean. I have no clue, but ask for clarification.)

That's when you gave her a belt buckle, when she was a kid?

He says, "Yes." I think she may have found it lately.

(Note: It often happens that Jennifer is trying to translate an image she gets, and then when I ask her a follow up question, gets another image – which may or may not go with the question I asked. They're outside of time, and sometimes they answer my questions out of order. From what I can gather is that there is a belt buckle, that someone knows about it – and when it's found, they'll say "Oh right. I forgot about that belt buckle." It happens often with Jennifer's reports.)

And there's a car you gave to her or she owns?

He says, "He willed her the car."

What color is it?

It looks like my dad's car; red with fins on it... he had a 1957... it looks like a Cadillac convertible, it's a classic car. What was the car Tesla sent to space?

I think it was a red Tesla that went to space.

But it might have looked like it.

(Note: Again, she got the idea of a car, then saw the Tesla tribute to David Bowie, a car that Elon Musk sent towards Mars in honor of David's song. So it may be a metaphor, or may literally be a classic convertible.)

Could be – but it was a convertible?

He said, "Yes."

Based on these two things you want her to realize that this is you?

"Yes."

What are you saying? They need to find someone to help them mediate this? Or resolve it? Is that what you're saying Tom?

(Note: It's not my theory, opinion or belief that life goes on. I've been filming people claiming that to be the case for over a decade. It appears that's what he's trying to tell us in my opinion to reach out and give them some advice. For the record, I did, I have no idea if they took that advice.)

"Yes."

So you're saying she needs her to talk to Jennifer so she can talk to you, is that correct?

"She needs to talk to you. Yes." That's what he said.

Honestly, I can't call up a person and say "Hey, I need you to call Tom's family because he told us... etc."

You can write a post that says it.

Okay, Tom. (I did and passed along his recommendations.) Anything else you want to say Tom?

He says "Thank you." (Jennifer aside) I know not to judge it, he showed up yesterday... and he showed you and I asked "What do I need to do?"

That was an odd conversation. Geeze, Mr. Wilbury, have a sense of humor over there why don't ya?

They totally do – I just give you the wackadoodle information that I get.

(Note: I passed along this information. I know their litigation was settled but I have no clue as to why. Glad that's behind them.)

Anything else Luana?

She says "Thank you."

How does she look (to you)?

She looks to me like she's very proper, wearing a white scarf, very pulled together... she blows you a kiss. I feel like.. they're very loving towards you today... I'm asking "Is that me or them?"

What am I doing that's different?

They keep encouraging you because what you're doing is dimension changing; they showed me the dimensions and you're making people understand them in an easier way... and you're staying true to your truth. All of them are kind of shaken up about it. They're tripping about you on the other side.

"I'd like to accept the Oscar for being the flipside expert guy."

(To me) I feel like we're both doing what we're supposed to be doing. Who picks this job of talking to the afterlife?

We've been doing this five years now.. and it's wild.

They're saying, "You need to know how much they love you."

If you love me so damned much how about some Lottery numbers?

"4, 7, 6, 21, 52, 78." How many do you need?

I don't think any go up that high... What's the mega number?

"42."

Maybe someone reading or hearing this will win and donate me some cash. Whatever. Luana, you and used to be able to do this really well.

(Note: Luana and I had the uncanny ability to guess roulette numbers over the phone. If I was in Vegas, she'd call and give me winning roulette numbers and vice versa when she was there. We both won every time.)

They're showing me that <u>I'm your lottery</u>.

Thanks class!

CHAPTER TWENTY NINE
PLANNING OUR NEXT LIFETIME

Cass Elliot, Wikipedia

CASS ELLIOT, JESUS

As usual, something sparked my attention prior to our meeting. I had seen a film that starred "Mama" Cass Elliot, and knew the my longtime agent Joel Gotler had been pals with her. He's read this chapter, and says they never had a romantic relationship, were just friends, but for the most part, this account is accurate.

Rich: Hi class. Well, I saw two documentaries this weekend...

Jennifer: "One was boring," they said.

One was "Echo in the Canyon" a concert masquerading as a documentary; Jakob Dylan interviewing all the original bands from Laurel Canyon.

They're saying "We should do that about the other side."

We should interview people on the flipside the way Jakob Dylan interviewed people? That's a good idea. Then I went to see that documentary about David Crosby, "Remember My Name."

I got that it was more about his drugs.

That's right, his heroin addiction. So class, what did you guys think of that?

Roger Ebert just showed up. (Jennifer aside) I know you don't like him.

(Note: Roger gave my film "Limit Up" a "thumbs way down.")

I have no beef with Roger now, I'm always glad to see him. Thumbs up dude.

He just gave me the chills. He says "It's going to hit more people because of the addiction – it was hidden, something hidden about it – people didn't know how bad it was – he (Crosby) played Russian roulette every single time... (he did drugs).

After seeing the film, I sent him a note on social media. In the note, I mentioned Crosby's girlfriend Christine Hinton who died at 21.

When you said her name, Christine, I got an image of all these robots. She's 21, so I don't know why they showed me this – they showed me red lipsticked girls from the Robert Palmer video "Addicted to Love." That's what showed up, but I don't know where this is going.

You mean like a groupie thing?

Yeah; but they're all robots.

Are you saying Christine was more like a groupie?

No. I think there were too many groupies that got in the way. The robots represent the groupies, it's like he (Crosby) feels bad because he feels responsible for her death – they had a fight, she was crying, and went to meet someone...

They didn't mention that in the film, but makes sense.

She said she caught him several times (with groupies) – I know the crash wasn't her fault... hold on. I saw a tree... and she's showing me it *was* her fault. Something about (it being) her fault.

In the film, they showed a news report, a horrific crash.

She says "No one did a toxicology report on her."

So it may have been drug related? Well, either way, she died in a car accident, I think it was in Marin.

She showed me something with a tree. Felt like a tree lined street, a street like Laurel canyon – curves in the road.

My point was that she's still with him, and I think she was with him every step of the way – but I don't know if she was as in love with him as he seemed to be with her.

It's timeless. This (relationship) has been going on for awhile, they keep trying to get it right. Remember when we spoke to Junior Seau and he told us that every lifetime we're trying to chase the other lifetime when it didn't work, to make it work? She's saying "They almost had it – I felt like she was told not to go but she did."

On the other hand, his music wouldn't have happened without her loss.

Which will then catapult him in the next life... hold on. Because he'll want to do more music, that angst will be there so they have a better shot at it (next time around.)

He seems pretty driven in terms of music; it appears it's the only thing that keeps him going. He's lost all his friends because he's a pain in the ass. I was thinking about Cass Elliot who appears in the film. Luana, do you want to bring Cass in?

I don't know who that is. She's really tall isn't she?

Well she may be over there. Does she seem tall or big?

Maybe I saw someone looking up at her. She may have been big here – She showed me that girl from "The Mamas and Papas."

That's correct. (Ding!) That's her.

What? It is? I don't know anything about them, or "The Mamas and Papas" but that's what I got from her. She was in that band?

Yes, Cass Elliot. Funny she would show you the band – she is that band.

She's very much different over there... now.

How to you perceive her there?

Flamboyant, like with peacock feathers; if she was wearing an outfit it would be with peacock feathers, sunglasses, crazy hair – "A lot taller over there," she says.

(Note: The image in Wikipedia is her in peacock feathers, which I've never seen until uploading it for the book.)

Well, you appeared in three movies this weekend Cass; in "Once Upon a Time in Hollywood," "Echo in the Canyon" and "Remember My Name." David Crosby talks about you with great affection.

Feels like he was a father figure to her.

They were close friends.

She says "Everyone was jealous of their relationship... they all thought..." She says "She for sure wanted to sleep with him."

He said in the film "No one loved her the way she wanted to be loved."

She says "That's correct." She was like "I don't care, I wanted to sleep with him anyway." It might have been daddy issues – Was he older than her?

He is now... she was much bigger, like a big person.

She's showing me she's not big anymore. She's funny. She showed me "I look like the girl in Mamas and Papas..." and she was that person!

Michele Phillips is the other female member, I met her on that boat trip. She's still on the planet, the other girl from the band. In Echo in the Canyon she reveals she had affairs with a lot of folks – and says "I really enjoyed myself in the 60's!" But I didn't know how Cass had died, and Crosby implies it was heroin. My agent Joel knew Cass.

She said "He was a lovely fellow... but he can be a pill."

(Laughing). I'm sure he's a pill to more people than me.

(Note: I've known Joel for a long time, never a pill to me, she's being sarcastic.)

"That will change," she said.

Okay, Cass, thanks for the note of confidence.

It feels like they she was in love with him when she was young.

You want to talk about that, Cass? Why did you check out so early?

"To get a new body," she says (laughing.)

Cass, who was there to greet you when you crossed over?

Her cat or dog at first... then her grandmother... on her dad's side. She was there to greet her. She's telling me she had thyroid issues, there was something wrong with her heart; that's why she gained all the weight – it felt more like (it was) alcohol that killed her.

I don't know – Crosby implied it was heroin.

She said "You could say that." (Jennifer aside) I asked her "Was it heroin?" and she showed me a bunch of things – "Wrong place, wrong time, wrong drugs," she said.

Who are you hanging out with over there?

"Jimi. (Hendrix) We're planning our next lifetime."

Who else?

She said "Luana. That's why she's here." (Jennifer aside) Oh. That's interesting. She showed me 7 different groups of lights – she showed me something profound... but just said "If you keep talking it won't be." (I zip my lip) She showed me (packets of light) all the musicians hang out together, then all the (people from the) medical field hang out together, all the industrial people, all the business minded people, all the great minds... they're together.

And scientists?

Yes. There's a philanthropy group which includes the scientists – she's showing me 7 groups and there are subgroups.

7 groups? Are they in our class or just in general?

I'm hearing "It's related to seven dimensions." I'm asking "But can't you cross back and forth between dimensions?" They're telling me "You have to have a pass for one that takes you to different ones." They're saying "The class in and of itself has a lot of ones within these groups; Stephen Hawking, Carl Jung and then

our musicians, so you (Jennifer and Rich) have passes... that's funny – like the title of our book is "Backstage Pass!" You have (to have) a pass depending where you want to go. At this moment, they all have the intention of talking to you, so they're (all here) together. But they're saying your idea to interview them over there is brilliant!

(Note: A lot to unpack in this answer. To paraphrase, "there are multiple dimensions." Some have noted different realms during their near death experiences, some have noted them during deep hypnosis sessions. In her session with Scott De Tamble, Jennifer saw herself on the "7th realm" coming down to "work on the 5th realm" and reported that we exist "in the third realm." This is the first time we've heard anything about "having a pass" to access them. Not sure who doles out the passes (we know it's Luana to get into this class) but interesting to hear.)

So you prefer hanging out with your groups over there?

She says, "It's way more powerful hanging out together."

But some claim they exist on the flipside by themselves, so why do those hang out alone?

She says, "Because they may irritate (the others) and piss people off. So you avoid being in your group, then you realize you miss them and go back."

(Note: This sounds more like a Cass Elliott answer than something from Jennifer. First I've heard of people "going off by themselves" to avoid interacting with their "soul group." But makes sense.)

What dimension would you prefer to hang out in?

She said, "The spiritual dimension."

Flying around?

From what I'm getting, I don't know if I'm interpreting this correctly; but "the top one," without a sense of hierarchy. I asked Luana "Where do you go?" and she showed me different dimensions, she showed me that's the highest one (the "spiritual one") – you get access and you are suddenly there, it's not like you have to go anywhere to get there... but the most fun though, the

dimension that is the most fun for her is the one with musicians and actors she says... I'm asking "What would you call that group?" "The Entertainment Group" she says. She says, "We help people to have memories."

(Note: That's also funny because that was the name of the company the man who produced our films, Jonathan Krane called his first company. "The Blake Edwards Entertainment Group" then later, MCEG. (Entertainment Group)

(The Ptolemaic system. Ptolemy, a 1st century Roman author, drew this map of the "heavens." From University of Oregon.edu)

How so?

She says, "When you use music as part of your memory, when the memory is about music, so like when you see your first concert, or you hear a song that jogs a memory, it tags you to whoever you were during that point in time."

Like frequencies in music? The same frequencies stimulate the frequency of the memory?

She's saying "Like you piano playing on the Millennium cruise boat created a music memory for many."

One of our classmates, Penny Marshall was there.

480

She says, "She's over there, yes."

(Note: An unusual reference. She's referring to me being invited to "play the piano" on a cruise ship by the head of New Line Cinema for the 2k event. When I heard about this floating party, I sent a joke fax to the head of the company, Bob Shaye, saying I was "available to play piano." I was surprised when he invited for two legs of the cruise. However, when I arrived on the ship, some people I knew were shocked, mocking me; "What the hell are you doing here?" as if I'd interloped on an A-list party. Luana's friend Francis Coppola said "Why is it whenever I go to great party, you're always there?" (Luana and I had spent 8 years going to their home for Thanksgiving). As I walked away from these guffaws, I heard Luana's voice in my head "This is why you're here. To turn those opinions around." Various celebs had me accompany them as they sang or danced; Penny Marshall had me play "Hello Dolly" while she changed the words, Francis had me act in a play he directed, Phillip Noyce and I met a 125 year old woman in Dominica; I scattered some of Luana's ashes in whatever port we sailed to. No idea if I changed any opinions, but this is the reference.)

Anything you want to tell your friends, Cass? What should I tell Joel?

She said, "Tell him – to get seeing glasses."

You mean better reading glasses?

She's saying, "Not glass - but glasses to see things etherically."

All he's got to do is read this book.

She's saying "He can't hear people either, he can't hear anything from the flipside – but he means well." She says he's going to help you. He needs to be.. "You are prodding him and he feels that if he opens himself up to this research, he's going to miss a lot of people – like the guy who told us that it's too hard to realize there is an afterlife because how sad it made him feel."

Yes, that was Harry Dean Stanton. Said he was an atheist because the alternative was too painful. So it's too painful for Joel to open up this door?

Jennifer taps her nose. (for "yes!")

Cass, what is one thing can I tell Joel?

She's showing me a drink. I don't think he drinks any more.

You mean some health drink?

I'm trying to get something from back there – I'm trying not to judge it... hang on!

Okay.

She says "She loved being lost with him." I don't know what that means.

You mean physically, like being in a car?

I asked that – she said "He'll know what that means."

(Note: I asked him. He said they were just friends – so perhaps she means "lost in the miasma of music and Los Angeles.")

Okay. Who else wants to talk...

Oh. Billy. (Paxton). Earlier, we were talking about Texas and getting guns and cowboys... might as well show up.

As I was driving over Bill is the person who popped into my head.

He's telling me about a birthday of his wife – might be a big one, like 60? Give me his last name again, sorry.

Paxton. His wife is Louise.

"Like Thelma and Louise," he said. I think she might have had a big birthday... but he says "He was there." She may have felt him brush by her. He says "She looks better than she's ever looked; he's like "Yeah, I still love her."

Has she looked at the letter or film I sent her? (I sent her a transcript of all of our chats and the film "Talking to Bill Paxton")

He says, "She put it aside, she wasn't ready." She has a hard time believing he's around. He's showing me like shouting at her that he's there.

Anything you want me to pass along?

He said, "Something with her tooth needs to get checked."

How do I pass that along to her?

I just saw Tyler Henry the (Hollywood) medium. I think Tyler's going to read her. I think it will inspire her to go back to what you told her.

Is that what you wanted to tell us?

He says, "Yes. She's going to go back and look at the letter."

She may reach out at some point in the future?

He says, "After a reading." Why do I keep getting shown my friend Dr. Drew? Dr. Drew and you – doing a show or something – like a late night show.

Could be the thing we've done – that 15 minute interview, where I walk Dr. Drew into the flipside on YouTube.

That's it.

(Note: That's on MartiniZone.com on YouTube. I went on Dr. Drew's wife's radio program, and asked Dr. Drew if he wanted to "take a walk into the flipside" with me. He didn't believe in an afterlife, but in 15 minutes we were accessing a past life (that I was able to forensically verify) and a visit to his council, that was similar to other people's trips to their councils, and is reproduced in the book "Architecture of the Afterlife." But the clip is online.)

So what does he mean, he wants me to repost that?

"Repost on your blog about it" he said.

Okay, I can do that I'll give you credit for it Bill.

And Luana she just went like this (stepped in front of him) She wants credit too. I actually asked her to help me with my "Wine and Spirits" group on Monday; it was the best; I got a standing ovation; they were like "Oh my gosh!" Our class helped make me feel comfortable.

Good job guys.

And she watched the movie "Once Upon a Time in Hollywood with me" and she showed me that too.

What did she think about that film?

Luana said "Boring... but fascinating." She said it was more fun watching people in the audience trying to figure out if was okay watching a film about the Manson murders.

Okay, but what made you think of that? Is there someone associated with that film that you want us to talk to?

(Note: Luana was invited up to the house where the Manson murders took place along with her close friend Robert Towne. Both of them passed on the invite. Luana had dated a hairdresser in Gene Shacove's salon, a fellow named Richard Alcalla (mentioned in an earlier book) so she was familiar with Jay Sebring, one of the people killed by Manson's followers. I had thought about interviewing Jay, but she wanted to talk about someone else.)

I'm seeing Jimi Hendrix again. Was he in that film?

No. But hang on, let's unpack this. You're seeing Jimi Hendrix. That's probably a reference to the Monterey Pop festival where Luana drove with Harry Dean Stanton and Fred Roos to see Jimi. It just so happens that fifteen minutes ago I wrote an email to Fred about the budget of her film, as a studio is interested.

"That's it." She had to go through that to get to this.

She wants to talk about Fred who was with her at the Hendrix show; an hour ago I got an email from the studio asking what the budget of our film should be. Luana? What should it be?

I heard her say "It's priceless...."

It is, but everyone can weigh in. Question is not what I can make it for, what should I tell the studio?

She says "Tell them (a number) and they'll give you (a number).

Tell them one number and they'll give me part of that?

She says "They're going to scramble it in your head between those numbers."

Did I unpack that correctly? Jimi Hendrix leads to Fred? Because Luana knows that you don't know what Fred Roos looks like, so she gave you a reference point instead.

She's saying, "Right."

I'd like to ask about the session I did the other day where we spoke to Jesus on both days. Anything you want to weigh in on my conversation?

They said "It was amazing." They showed me it was limitless. They showed me you breaking the velvet rope. That's a good name for a chapter.

(Note: That's the name of the chapter in "Architecture of the Afterlife.")

One council told me to be cautious, I replied that the people who aren't supposed to understand it will not. In the same breath she said "They're telling me "You're the bridge. What you're doing is bridging the different realms.

Luana is saying "Jennifer is the cell tower; you're the bridge. You provide comfort. I can't take away people's grief or sadness the way that you do; you actually help people with their grief."

I got that advice from your dad; turn grief to nostalgia, lest we forget. So my conversations with Jesus were accurate?

They were, but they're like "Rich, what do you think?" I'm a skeptic too, but they showed me how exhausting it is when we doubt what they're saying. They're saying "we can reserve so much energy if you would just fly with us."

Is there anything I missed in the conversation?

They showed me you hearing it correctly.

Okay, Luana, who else wants to come through?

Thank you Billy.

I think it's cool that I heard his name and then you saw him.

I just know not to negate; he always comes through as such a funny, bright person. It was a great entrance, talking about guns in Texas, and he was like "Yo, let's just get after it...?

What about our Junior Seau/Paul Allen/Dave Duerson film?

Remember the hockey player I said who came forward to tell me he died from CTE? Try to connect it to someone who is a doctor who is dealing with this.

You mean like scientists dealing with CTE. I should reach out to them?

"Privately – a couple of times," they said. Why am I getting Jack Nicholson? Luana says you need to call him.

It was wild, Jack showed up in one of my non hypnosis sessions. I was talking to someone on the flipside, a council member and I asked "Are you familiar with my work?" And he said "Yes, through Jack." And I asked "Jack who?" And she said "Jack Nicholson." This woman has not read any of my books, her council member was telling her that he was aware of my work by connecting to the "higher consciousness" of Jack. Let's ask Luana; was this correct?

She says "Yes."

The only way I can explain is that Jack's higher self and you were in touch with this fellow; is that correct?

Hold on... I'm talking to Luana...

How is it that Jack's higher self is aware of my work?

I got "Hot Lips" (Sally Kellerman) and all the people you're connected to.

It was odd, I met this woman at a screening, she invited me for coffee, I helped her access her dad on the flipside, we visited her council – she's never read any of my books – and as I had her access her council, this lead council guy said "Tell him I know of his work through Jack. He'll know who I mean."

She's saying "It is definitely Jack." She wants you to talk to him about it.

And how would I do that?

She says, "Call him." She said "He has nothing else to do, remind him of the letters (that he wrote to Luana when they were young actors in class) and tell him there's something else Luana wanted to give him. (Jennifer aside) I just want to make sure I'm getting this right. They're making fun of me. She's saying, "He's afraid of talking about the flipside, it reminds him more of his character in the Shining." She says "By talking to him about it, you're going to soften his eventual landing on the flipside, when he finally returns home – Like Luana did for Harry Dean by showing up with that car."

What's the sentence I should say? "Luana wanted me to reach out to jack and I need to talk to him about something?"

She says, "Yes, the assistant will think she's alive."

(Note: I did call him, and the assistant *did* think she was alive, asking me to *spell her name*. Jack called me back, we had a ten minute chat about Luana, about the film, and he confirmed something that Harry Dean Stanton told me to tell him. It's not something public, something private, that only Jack would know. I told him what Harry had said and Jack said "He's right." Not something I could have known, something that Jennifer could have known – but Harry did. It doesn't make it any easier to lose close friends, but it can give us solace to realize they aren't very far away.)

Luana Anders photo of Jack on the way to acting class. (All Rights Reserved)

Jack's got some of Luana's ashes up there in his home. Is this call going to help him?

I think he may be worried about his legacy as well.

He's privately, quietly helped so many of his friends.

But nobody knows. Maybe it's telling the Luana and Jack story and all those in between. They're showing me he'll be excited about it. All those back stories – like Luana and the hairdresser story.

Well, I'm doing my best to get her story right.

She showed me coins flying into the air

What's that mean?

The money doesn't matter. You're already famous up there. Just be creative with the story. And then Amelia popped in.

Well I'll make the Amelia story after that, as it will open that door.

I have to run. Bye class!

We love you.

CHAPTER THIRTY:
THEY'VE BEEN WAITING

Pere La Chaise cemetery in Paris. Author's photo.

ANTHONY BOURDAIN, BILL PAXTON, PRINCE, ANDY KAUFMAN, GARRY SHANDLING

In the last book, Anthony Bourdain came through loud and clear and gave us notes on just about everything – how to reach out to his opera singing daughter (didn't know he had one), what kind of food I should put in my diet to help my health (string beans) and an antidote for depression; (meditation.) He's funny, charming, and always has something to add to our discussions.

Here we are at another session at Fishbar in Manhattan Beach. My questions are in italics, Jennifer's replies are in bold.

So class, who wants to talk? Luana?

She has like a whole list of things; she did this her papers. (Pretends to be straightening out a stack). "They've been waiting."

Can we ask Anthony Bourdain a question?

He's here; wearing jeans, blazer and a shirt, smoking a cigarette.

I read your interview with a medium and Dr. Medhus on ChannelingErik.com, anything you want to add or correct about that?

He said that *we* helped him be able to do that. He said that right off the bat.

In terms of slowing your energy down, what's the formula? How many degrees do you need to slow down?

He said "You mean like a recipe?"

Is slow the right word?

He said "s l o wwww..."

Are you half the speed up there? Two times? More?

"Yes, it's just different." He said "It's like being on the freeway instead of a road. And on this side, we're on the dirt road. He showed me a freeway, a regular road, a dirt road; different types of paths."

So do you slow yourself down by half? Or two thirds?

"It depends on the person; what's going on in their head."

Like with your friends, or Asia Argento; how much do you slow yourself down to talk to her?

He says "She's not aware of him... he's been trying to – to everything to reach out to her."

Anything we can do?

"Give her the book," he said.

In your interview on Channeling Erik you said you met God, speaking as if he was an individual.

Anthony is smiling.

My question is, was that a metaphor or a physical person that you met?

He's showing me that it almost felt like a hub. He says "Like a frequency hub, like an electrical outlet and other frequencies come from that and we all make up the one."

Okay, so the idea of who or what God is - it's like a medium... like water or oil?

He showed me *me*.

Well, you are the medium. But I mean like paint is a medium for color.

Jennifer taps her nose as it say "that's it."

From what I understand you were talking to a medium, Veronica Drake, Eric Medhus and his mom Dr. Elisa Medhus, and in the interview they quoted you saying that you'd "Met god and he was hilarious."

He was laughing before you asked the question – I asked him "Did you see yourself?" He said that he did.

You're looking at the source or the medium of everything. He did say that in the article, "Everyone is connected."

He showed me like the base of a power switch; he showed me that spot... it's interesting.. I saw him moving with tons of glass, you know how in the film The Matrix, how everything moves together in slow motion?

The bullet effect?

Those are the speeds I'm seeing. It's the same things in multiple dimensions...

So speed is like time?

When you asked that, I was triggered to ask "Is that (visual) speed?" He says "We create speed and time here."

In our dimension?

"Yes. It's all at once there."

(Note: Meaning once we are "outside of time" on the flipside, we can observe things in "all dimensions at once." I.E. We can observe all of our lifetimes.)

What do you want to talk about Anthony? You're the great interviewer.

He's fascinated about how to communicate with this side, and he's trying to reach her...

Asia?

Did she have a fall recently? He showed me her stumbling.

Maybe he's referring to her being sued by some friend of hers.

He said "She'll get up, she'll be unscathed." It was like he showed me her getting up and wiping off her arms. He says "That's part of her charm." He's showing me that she would throw things, she'd break things.

Anthony's interview of Asia in her home gives a sense of who she is; a complicated person.

He says "and I'm not?" He says he was the one who complicated things...

But compared to her?

"She's a comet. Ten thousand trillion times a comet..."

Anyone else need to stop by?

My dad.

Hi Jim. Ask how's your class in astronomy with the 8 armed teacher?

(Note: She makes another appearance a year later, at the end of this book.)

When you put it like that... he says he's learning so much; there's so much to learn.

Like what?

Like how to travel. He showed me orbs... how to travel... between dimensions. That's interesting. I was wondering why you see faces in orbs, it's like an imprint.

Are you talking about orbs you see in photos? My understanding is that they're fractals that retain all the information of your previous lifetimes.

He says "That's true."

But why do they have different sizes?

And colors. Because of your lifetimes.

So bigger the orb, it has more information? Is it true they pick up gunk? Because in my first deep hypnosis session, I visited that classroom where they were cleaning the fractals or orbs.

My dad says "Yes. They get gunk like cars." My dad loved cars.

Like cars pick up engine oil?

If I'm seeing this right, wow, they pick up gunk because of what we're doing with the earth... the way we're traveling whatever is happening, cutting trees, killing oxygen... causes gunk to form on them.

Okay. But in terms of these orbs... can you show Jennifer one of these orbs Jim? Let's look inside.

He showed me like a pathway, you don't feel like you're in that...

You mean opening up an orb would be like opening up a top and you look inside and see a pathway?

It's like a convertible inside.

Do they contain the emotions of previous lifetimes? One person I interviewed said they saw a holograph of themselves.

That's what I saw before... when I ask to see someone's health – I see the hologram of the person. Their past present and future.

Does she see the perfected person?

Yes.

Is that a construct created by your imagination, or by the soul itself?

I would also see their etheric self, even when their self here was horrible.

Anthony who would you like to interview? Is there someone you want to interview on our behalf? Someone you're curious about.

I'm seeing Aretha again.

What do you want to know from Aretha?

Jennifer laughs. This is so fun. The best movie is in my head; Prince just came by, then Bill Paxton, and then Aretha came in; her voice is just so amazing. She has this perfume, it smells good. (Jennifer listens) Now she's showing me you playing guitar – like last Tuesday, you were playing?

I was.

She's trying to help you.

I was playing the original version of "The house of the rising sun."

(Note: It's on CDBaby.com under "Richard Martini").

Prince helped as well.

That's funny. It sounds weird to say it, but I'd be lying if I didn't report that I did "feel assistance" while playing it. Just noting that I did feel something.

You have not told me that – so for her to come through and tell me that –

You're right. I never told you that I perform or play anything. I don't think you've ever seen me play.

I saw piano and guitar...

That's accurate. Billy, we saw you sneak by.

He's jokingly waving Aretha away, as if she's "old news."

I was talking about you on the set the other day..

He said it was fun.

I was talking to someone of you... I spoke to Renee Zellweger.

He said "Tell her I said hi."

Okay, Prince you snuck in?

Billy is like, "That's it?"

Well Prince snuck in – I saw that they put out some new songs for you... your thoughts on the new material?

He says "Time doesn't matter – but it does." Jennifer aside: I asked "Do you guys miss time?" They said, "No."

What do you miss Prince?

He showed me the female body. He's trying to joke around. He says, "He misses being famous..." then laughs.

So on the flipside you're not famous, just another soul?

"Yes."

But people who run into you are aware of your talent?

"Yes, all the lights that you see; you see them all together, you hang out with people who have the same frequency."

That's why you hang out with musicians for example?

"That's why there are so many in this class... and actors."

All part of the same healing light of the universe?

Jennifer aside "I asked him what color he was radiating; purple?"

We asked him that before; that day he said red. What does he look like now?

I'm seeing orange. I didn't know we asked him, I was just kidding. It's like the more you know, the higher the frequency is.

That's a good question for Anthony to ask Prince, Robin or Bill. I think we started talking to you fellows a couple of years ago.

Bill said "Like three."

I would guess your knowledge is exponential compared to what we've learned... It was Michael Newton who turned us onto this concept or radiating colors.

You mean Morton.

(Note: When Michael Newton showed up the first time, Jennifer said "Morton is here." I said "Who's that?" She said "The guy you did the documentary about." Since then Michael Newton refers to himself as Morton when he shows up.)

Yes, Morton; he said it was a reflection of how you're feeling at that moment – someone who is purple could radiate a different color depending how their journey or path is...

That's why they can't lie.

You've said that before. But in terms of communicating with us – we've only progressed so much in the past 3 years, but you guys must grow in knowledge exponentially on the flipside. Is that accurate?

"Not all are affected in the same way. There are so many different people." By the way Rich, they're telling me you are famous over there.

That's funny. But let me ask Prince; when you're called upon by Luana to come forward – as we've heard "the light goes on that the class is happening," and people just show up... do you look forward to this, what's your feeling about being in this communication class?

He says "It's a lot of fun, because we (Jennifer and I) don't discount what they say." Jennifer aside; you taught me that, "Don't judge it, don't discount any of it."

(Note: Sometimes Jennifer will see an obscure image that does not make any sense to her, but I suggest she not "judge whatever comes in." It's funny to hear this from these folks, people often tell us that it's frustrating their loved ones don't believe they still exist.)

A bit like the Garry Shandling reply, when he told us that he was "golfing" on the flipside. I asked him quite seriously how he did that, to construct the courses from his experience or imagination, and I asked him specifically "How many holes do you play, is it like 36 holes?" And he said "No, two. The tees are far apart."

He's here.

How are you doing Garry? I understand Judd Apatow is making another film based on your diaries.

Garry says "He wants him to do it."

You guys were very close friends, correct?

He says, "Yeah, he's excited about it."

(Note: In "Backstage Pass to the Flipside" Jennifer interviewed Garry about his tempestuous relationship with his former manager Brad Grey. Brad passed away at 59, not long after Garry died – so we took the opportunity to chat with him.)

Rich: I want to ask about a couple about Brad Grey.

Jennifer: I don't know who that is.

Garry, would you tell Jennifer who that is?

"They were friends when they were young, best friends, felt like they were together."

(Ding!) Brad was Garry's manager and knew each other from their early days. Then Garry got really successful so did Brad but then something happened.

"A divorce."

Brad's around he can pipe in.

What's his last name?

Grey. They did have a divorce of sorts.

"Yes, they split up."

It was over finances... money.

He's saying "It was very stupid. It was big and that's what made it so stupid."

It was battle.

"It took a huge battle; nine years."

Sounds like it; it wound up in court. Garry had to testify...

"About how Brad mismanaged it."

Garry won big sum of money.... but lost because it took a toll on his life and heart and everything else.

"It killed him." He said "It killed him."

Well you're not dead now are you Garry? No!

He said "Try using that joke on the other side."

Okay, I will. So listen, Garry you helped a lot of writers, you helped make careers, when are you going to start helping me?

"I already am," he said.

You helped Judd Apatow have a successful career and a life.

I don't know who that is.

He's written and directed a bunch of films... Directed the film about him.. The "40 year old virgin."

I loved that movie..

Judd said Garry helped him write or rewrite it, is that correct Garry?

He said "A third of it."

In the film, they all spoke of how much you helped other people, other comedians; you're aware of that correct?

"Yes."

Garry what's your view of Buddhism now... in the film that Judd directed, called "The Zen Diaries of Garry Shandling" you talked about detachment.

"It didn't work" he said. He's laughing and said.... "He held that hot stone."

Luana can fill you in, detachment is great if it means to let go of anger, fear, stress, all the emotions you don't want to have, but you stay connected to love. It doesn't mean to detach yourself from love or positive emotion, because that's why we're on the planet.

Some people don't want to do all that.

I also noticed our classmate Gilda is in the news, her documentary "Love Gilda" is out and its fun to see her make people laugh again.

The person that is in the film is channeling her – whoever is putting it together...

You mean Amy Poehler? She's the host of the show.

She's telling me that she's basically channeling her; then I saw Jim Carrey who did that for that comedian, what's his name.

Andy Kaufman? Wow, okay, I spoke to Jim one night about Andy because his sister moved into the home across the street from my parent's home in Northbrook. Is Andy Kaufman available?

He's hanging out with Robin Williams at the moment.

So Andy, when I was in high school, I came across that guy "Tony the Healer" the healer that you went to see when you were ill. It must have been startling for you to realize the guy was a faker.

"Yes, he was."

Why did you choose to check out so early in this lifetime? Or was that an exit point?

"Yes."

Who was there to greet you when you crossed over?

"It was a lot of people..." it felt like it was his sister... if she's still on the planet, it could have been somebody that was like her.

You're saying it felt like a sister?

It might have been a twin that died in childbirth.

Okay. Since you've been over there, what's been your experience?

He's made everyone laugh.

You were famous for making fun of the joke or bit itself.

He's showing me that he channeled somebody else. A comedian. Someone from the 1920's...

Who?

Buster Keaton comes to mind.

Andy, are you going to come back soon?

He says "He helps comedians." He showed me Amy Schumer.

Are you helping them with the kind of comedy you used to do – avante garde? Or just general creative tips?

He showed me Amy looking at a scene and then seeing something in the corner, "looking outside the box."

Okay, very good. Class, any questions for Andy? Luana?

They're dancing.

Andy, Luana, who's making you laugh?

I don't know why, but I got shown Tom Petty. Have we talked to Tom?

Indeed we have. He gave us the name of the book "Backstage Pass to the Flipside." Tom are you making Luana laugh?

"They all are."

All right Luana any parting words? Should we mention (the current President?)

She showed him tripping over his tie. They showed me (a Supreme Court Justice) with devil horns and a pitchfork. They're saying "It's all about disrupting the norm to get people involved. It's that same frequency. There's an inner revolution without the violence that's going to go on."

Who said that?

All of them did.

Okay, Jennifer has to go. Thanks class! Catch you on the... you know.

CHAPTER THIRTY ONE:
NOT GONE, JUST NOT HERE

The Botticcini altar piece of Mary's ascension

AMELIA JESUS DR. HELEN WAMBACH

Another visit to Manhattan Beach.

Rich: Welcome back from your trip to Boston. Who needs to come forward and talk to us?

Jennifer: Amelia Earhart and Luana.

What do you want to say Amelia?

It's like she has... a book. It feels like it's her aviation booklet with all the flights, she's going back to... going back to this particular time, like her flight plan. She's showing me Japan... it's something that has to do with what happened to her. Something happened back then that set things in motion for her.

(Note: US Marine Robert Wallack found her briefcase on Saipan in 1944. She may be referring to the paperwork inside.)

Which resulted in the outcome for her final flight?

She says, "Yes."

Is this an event that took place in the 1930's?

She says, "1927. There may have been some instance in 1927 that affected the later flight."

I'll have to look into that. Maybe it's about the League of Nations.

(Note: That's a tough one. Amelia doesn't make history until 1928 when she flies in the back of a plane from Newfoundland to Britain. It was Lindbergh who made the first flight in 1927. In 1927 she was teaching English to Syrian and Chinese refugees in Boston.)

There is a mission right now with famed explorer Bob Ballard searching the Pacific for your plane.

She just rolled her eyes.

They claim they found a skull from 1940, claim it might be yours.

She showed me that it is the skull of a fisherman, someone with a spear.

That's who the skull is?

"Yes." She's saying something about you looking something up.

I was referring to the League of Nations; they had a rule that the Japanese couldn't build deep water ports in their mandated islands. That was one of the issues the US wanted to learn about. Part of her "spy mission" might have been to demonstrate that was happening.

She says, "Correct to all of that."

The reason they arrested her was for being a spy but the cameras were reportedly never used..

She showed me one camera that had some footage... but it got washed away.

I had heard that she buried one camera.

(Note: As reported in a book by South African journalist Oliver Knaggs who interviewed the Queen of Mili atoll who claimed they watched her bury a "metal box" after she landed.)

She showed me instead lines of Morse code. I felt like she was lost because of that.

(Ding!) That's correct; they were communicating with her via Morse code but she was responding by voice.

(Note: According to historian Elgen Long, whom I interviewed while working on the film "Amelia," he said his research showed 90% of all communications from the US Coast Guard ship Itasca were Morse Code, and only one reply came from her in Morse Code.)

She says, "But there is some element of her not wanting to get caught."

I read in her book "Last Flight" that she didn't know Morse code.

She says, "But Fred Noonan did."

Well, in her book, she said the both of them didn't know it.

She's making fun of it. She's showing that it's like me studying French – he knew the basics.

There was a problem with her using Morse Code?

She's saying, "It has something to do with her not wanted to get caught."

Did she deliberately miss Howland Island?

She says, "Yes. She did."

Hang on. She deliberately missed it?

"Yes" she said.

Why?

She says, "To circle back..."

Well... she knows she didn't have enough gas to circle back... but had enough gas to turn left and head for the Gilbert Islands even though she wound up in the Marshalls. Maybe that's what she's showing you – turning back by turning left. There was a theory she deliberately missed Howland so they would come looking for her.

"Yes" she said.

That's correct?

She says, "Partially."

It seems like it was so terribly screwed up.

(Jennifer aside) If you think you're going to die why would you miss an island?

Well, reports show she was running low on gas. However, the manifest shows that she had more gas than initially thought – so maybe she knew she had enough gas to get to the Gilberts. Maybe saying she was running out of gas was part of the mission. Plan B was to land in the Gilberts on a friendly isle. However, perhaps due to an error in navigation, she was already 200 miles NW of Howland. So when she turned, she made it to Mili Atoll in the Marshalls; not the Gilberts.

She says, "That's why she deliberately missed it..." Hold on. She said "She didn't care (about the mission) she had to get as far away as possible from where she was, (to find a place to land) she didn't care about missing it (Howland), she had to go further and she didn't want to be caught (by the Japanese)." I felt like it was going backwards... but it was her "last exit," I think. Was it like 26 miles away from where she was supposed to land? They showed me Catalina. Like it was that far away. (From where she was supposed to land at the Gilberts to Mili Atoll.)

Could be. It's about 100 miles north of the Gilberts. (However, I noticed the Saipan and Catalina look nearly identical in size.) She missed the Gilberts and landed the Electra on Mili atoll... where it wasn't destroyed, the brakes broke, they took her all the way to Jaluit with the plane. From there taken by seaplane to Saipan where eyewitnesses saw her brought ashore. The plane was towed, the plane was in a hangar. When she got to Saipan, she was seen coming ashore by people I interviewed. I have people who saw her do that. I'm pretty aware that's what happened – she didn't want to be captured.

(Jennifer aside) She was on the plane with Fred?

Yes. Both were seen coming ashore.

(Jennifer listens). She says, "He was really sick."

I think he was more physically hurt than her. The man who treated his wounds (in Jaluit, Bilimon Amaron) said "She was okay, but he was badly hurt from the landing."

I'm getting he was really sick with his stomach... and that "He was executed because he said *he* was the only spy."

Okay. Let me repeat that for clarity. They assumed Fred was the spy because of his military background. Also they didn't suspect her, a woman to be in charge of anything. And then, in terms of sacrificing himself, Fred said he was the spy so they would spare Amelia – and he was executed for being the spy. Is that correct?

She says, "Yes."

Well that lines up with the research. Thank you. So what else are you here to tell us this Amelia?

She said, "Because they have it wrong."

You mean the National Geographic show. What can I do to make it right?

There's something about the whole.. it feels like 1927, something you'll find out that will make more sense what her flight path was... (and the mission).

An incident with you or with the Japanese?

She says, "With her."

Okay. I'll look that up.

"Yes" she said.

Something happened in 1927 that's related to why you did the mission?

She says, "Yes."

I'd guess it had to do with the League of Nations?

She says, "Yes. But it was super secret." She showed me the guy with the cigar.

FDR?

She says "She loved Eleanor so much."

That would make sense with her doing this favor for FDR... if she loved Eleanor she was willing to do it.

She says, "Yes. They assured her safety – but they changed the path of the flight."

(Ding!) That's correct. After her crash in Hawaii, they changed the flight path to go from East to West, to West to East.

She said, "She and Eleanor shared a lot of secrets."

(Note: We've covered Amelia and Eleanor both preferring women in the book "Hacking the Afterlife." Amelia "came out" via three different mediums who answered the same questions as to "who she was in love with, and whether it was a painter." I already knew the painter was a woman, and Amelia, ever the pioneer she was, has reported that she was in love with this woman, and she and her husband George Putnam had an open (yet secret from the public) marriage. They were so good at keeping that secret that this will be news to some reading this sentence. I ask the following as a way of saying "It was written.")

But this was meant to be wasn't it?

She said, "But not if they're going to get it wrong now."

There's nothing I can do about that.

She says, "You can. They have documents that will back this up."

The only way to get this right is if you can help me get this story told.

Something about 3 months ago – you talked to Amelia about 3 months ago? She says, "There's a technical plan or set of plans about where she went."

Okay, thanks Amelia.

(Note: "Hacking the Afterlife" includes three hours of interviews with Amelia Earhart via multiple mediums, where she proves beyond any shadow of doubt that it's her by revealing new information about her death that I was not aware of, was not in the research, but later turned out to 100% accurate. I won't go into those details here, but suffice to say, when Amelia "speaks through" Jennifer, I do my best to follow up on whatever she says. Including what she says above. Stay tuned.)

INTERVIEW WITH DR. HELEN WAMBACH

Luana, should we talk to Dr. Wambach?

Jennifer "Yes." (Jennifer aside;) I don't know who that is.

(Note: Jennifer has no idea who Dr. Wambach is, or was. Everything about to be said is not coming from Jennifer's mind or subconscious.)

It's okay, I do. So Dr. Wambach...

She showed me Helen Keller.

I think because her first name is Helen. She wants me to call her that instead of Doctor Wambach. So Helen, what's up? Why did this fellow send me your tapes?

She says "Because she told him to." She's showing me that your research and her research; it's like side by side – you take it to a different path – she's saying by studying her method, she will teach you another way how to do the same things... She says you're very lovely.

Well thanks, Helen.

Um. The way we discussed it with Morton; she says, "His work is similar to what she used to do."

(Note: "Morton" is Jennifer's nickname for Michael Newton; when he first appeared during a session Jennifer said "Morton is here." I asked who she meant, and she said, "You know, the guy you made a documentary about.")

That's accurate. Helen's work predated his by a decade.

She's saying, "40 years ago – she showed me like a loop and another loop will open up for you. She's showing me the guides and who we talk to now, but she's suggesting that there are more people to talk to."

On other levels?

She showed me one person for each continent sort of thing. She said, "You're already doing it. Like when you're interviewing Jesus, or Buddha." She's telling me there's like 11.

Avatars, like when we spoke to the fellow who identified himself as "the librarian" in that library. He told us then he was in charge of "all libraries" I might be aware of. We talked to The Librarian who said he wasn't in charge of all of them, just the ones that you would know. I'm assuming that's what they mean by "higher" or "more people to speak with."

She said, "Yes."

Let's go back to Helen. Who was there to greet you when you crossed over?

Her dad it felt like. Did she have two husbands? I feel like she had two loves - one love that she had when she was younger. She's showing me that she took care of her mom.

What do you miss about being on the planet?

She's feeling her skin – like touching her... wrists.

Do you miss tactile things?

She says, "Yeah. That and being smarter than everyone else."

That's funny. So over there you're just as smart instead of being smarter. Who are you hanging out with on the other side?

She says, "This class, the group of people we're speaking with... she's showing me they're having a blast. She's showing me dancing with Robin Williams, although in this visual he kind of looks like Mrs. Doubtfire."

Helen, when did you join the class?

She says "A month ago when that guy contacted you."

Okay, very good. So what are you doing over there besides dancing with Robin Williams?

She says "Enjoying myself – (during her lifetime) she was so concerned about the other side... She says, "All I wanted to do was study it and now I'm on the other side..." She says "She didn't have any fun during her lifetime – now she's making up for it." She says "I am traveling, and we are doing everything!"

I was wondering if you have run into any of your clients?

She says, "All of them."

Were there stories accurate?

She says, "They take it deeper over here."

So was the reincarnation of President Buchanan one of your clients?

She's saying, "Yes, in that context of the research, yes." She says "The President wasn't my client – but in that context, yes."

(Note: In the thousands of cases she did with people under hypnosis, she said there was only one who recalled a previous lifetime of any notoriety, and that was after recalling 9 other lifetimes that were fairly mundane. In this case, the person had access to a number of details about Buchanan's life she was able to look up.)

I was curious if you run into people you worked with... how does that work? Do they seek you out?

Jennifer aside: I asked her do you help people over there? And she said "If asked, yes, but she doesn't seek out people... but if they ask her for help yes." What's Morton's name?

Michael Newton.

(Note: If Jennifer was trying to convince me that Michael Newton was in the room, the least she could do is remember his name.)

Helen, what's your impression of him?

"A bit stuffy," she said.

Do you consider yourself colleagues?

"Oh yes." She said "Master minds without the minds."

That's funny and very clever. Anything you want me to pass along to your fans or friends?

She's saying something about a Joshua...or someone with a Jay name.

How about this guy who sent me the tapes?

She says, "Thank him for listening."

From what I gather, he helped you sell your tapes, and pointed out that he always paid the estate even after you were gone – I know you're not concerned with your estate.

She says, "Or lack thereof – as you know; we don't do it for money."

(Note: Another funny line. She's saying people who study consciousness or past life memories aren't in it "for the money." Truer words never spoken.)

Anything you want to express to this fellow?

She said, "Tell him I'm so grateful. He was so kind – when he was there or not there. She's telling me "He put his own hardships aside for her.." – She said something like the children love him – or something about children who love him. She said something about children loving him. She said, "He was like a son to her."

I'll pass that along. This is more of a medical question, in your book "Reliving Past Lives" you mentioned an autistic child who was one of your patients. and how you helped them to access...

Jennifer aside: I keep getting Cody Lee over and lover.

(Note: Jennifer is friends with the mother of Cody Lee, the autistic singer who is currently on the America's Got Talent showcase.)

But in your book, you recount how the child refused to participate. Your therapy was to just let her sit by herself, and you'd "send thoughts to her."

She's telling me "She got all the information."

But eventually the child picked up a toy telephone and spoke to you directly – no one knew she could speak, but she recalled her previous lifetime where she read and wrote. It was as if she was refusing to participate in this new one. Have you run into her?

She's saying "Last week, but it's not a week, over there." She's saying "Before she (this girl) came to the planet they planned everything; it's like one big experience that is happening simultaneously."

You're saying this child planned this lifetime of autism?

Absolutely – she says "Going back to before it happened – she was acknowledging you."

I understand. It's what we've spoken of in the past, about the life planning session. I think that's important to pass along. What we perceive as difficulty may have been planned in advance.

"Yes." She's got more. "If you knew everything was planned or chartered, would you do better or worse? That depends on the person."

You're pointing out that not everyone should hear that these things were planned in advance, so they can learn the lessons on their own? I heard this recently during a session; "don't squeeze the chrysalis."

"Correct."

So that the butterfly finds its own way to learn or emerge into knowledge.

She says, "Right."

Let me ask you this Helen; even though this lifetime might have been chosen in advance...

I just got Michael Jackson.

(Note: This isn't a random image tossed into Jennifer's mind. In our in depth interview with Michael, he spoke of planning out his lifetime to include the ups and downs. That on one hand he was going to share his musical talents with the planet so that everyone would embrace him, and at the same time experience being abused as a child by a relative, carrying that on to abusing other children, so that people who are in the closet about that can come into the light. Not something I would have constructed or offered as an observation; it was his – but I understand it in the context of people claiming that we all plan our lifetimes in advance. We improvise along the way, we have free will to screw up, or change our minds, but in general, we've agreed to participate in the fashion chosen.)

But there is improvisation involved, people can change the paradigm?

She says, "Yes, we all have free will." She just showed me in my office where I help people change the path they had chosen.

(Note: Meaning, they seek out the advice of a medium like Jennifer and by realizing their loved ones still exist, are able to set aside profound grief or sadness to continue to live their lives as planned.)

Are our higher selves giving out Jennifer's office number? How is it that we are able to navigate chance?

She says, "There are thousands of coincidences that occur..." (Jennifer aside) Recently a family of 5 came to my office, I hadn't seen them in years, we discussed all the coincidences occurred that

brought them back to me. Including the five of them sitting in the airport talking about me, when I suddenly appeared on the television monitor in front of them ("Below Deck" airport talk show). It took so much work and coincidence for them to get together that night and then have me appear in front of them at same time.

What else does Helen want to tell us?

She showed me tying up everything with a string, those files, the CDs of her sessions.

You want me to make to write about your appearing in my life as a chapter in a book or something bigger?

She says, "Later on." She says "You can't do everything... but go to the ending, the last part of the audio tapes. There's something there you need to listen to."

That part of your talk will have something in there that's a directive for me?

She said, "Yes. I just got "81..." I don't know if that's how old she was when she passed.

(Note: She was 61 when she passed on. It's likely giving me an edit point to listen to the tape at the 81 minute mark.)

So it's not for this book – but maybe sometime in the future?

She says, "Yes."

Dr. Helen Wambach

So I have these tapes from Dr. Wambach. The fellow who sold them on her behalf saw some of my posts on social media about her research, and sent me the original tapes of her sessions. They're eight hours long and demonstrate her technique. Basically, Dr. Wambach was a clinical psychologist helping soldiers with PTSD after the Vietnam war. During these sessions, they started recalling past lives.

Helen devised a scientific study to examine what they were saying. To avoid bias, she did group sessions (not one on one) offered them various time frames to "remember previous lifetimes" (not directing them to any particular one.) She then asked a series of questions about what they saw or experienced. The questions were designed to corroborate known historical records of the eras that they recalled.

In her study, she dismissed those who seemed to be "imagining" (about 1%) and focused on the answers of people who could recall "types of food consumed, types of cutlery, the construction materials for homes, the materials used for clothing." The reason for that is those are known quantities. People know when the fork went from two prongs to three, three to four – and people in general aren't going to focus on those minute details in more sensational memories. But by forcing them to focus on the mundane, Dr. Wambach was able to get solid research.

In her book "Reliving Past Lives" and "Life Before Life" she recounts these 2000 cases. Some talk about "choosing their lifetime" and report that 50% of the cases recalled "switching sexes" in their memories of different lifetimes. She noted that there was "no case" where a person recalled "entering the womb of the mother" prior to the six month.

I met Michael Newton and began my research in 2008. Michael's career spanned the 60's up to the 2ks, and Dr. Wambach's research was in the 1970's. She published ten years before he did (with Bantam). However, their results are identical in the sense that people could explore why they chose to incarnate, how they chose to incarnate and the process in general. Michael Newton's work focuses on the "Life between Lives" information – while Dr. Wambach's focuses on the "past life" memories, as well as how the brain filters out information that it doesn't need to survive.

She noted that it appeared that the brain was receiving "more information than we are aware of" and offered that perhaps the "right brain" was the open conduit, while the left brain was the "hyper vigilant filter" that kept out information that wasn't necessary for survival. In that sense, her idea mirrors what Dr. Bruce Greyson talks about in his "Is Consciousness Produced by the Brain?" talk on YouTube (reproduced in "It's a Wonderful Afterlife") where he offers that there appear to be "filters" on the brain that when altered, or the brain is dying, allow people to access this information.

I find in fascinating that both Dr. Wambach and Dr. Greyson are speaking of the same filters – although his research is from medical cases in the UK where Alzheimer's patients have died, and the hospice care workers reported 70% had spontaneous memories of their lives just prior to death "as if the filters had died along with the brains." Dr. Wambach used hypnosis to come to the same conclusion that there are filters in the brain that keep out information that isn't useful to our navigation of the planet.

I have made digital copies of her tapes, and when the time is right, I'll put out something so that people can use her technique and her questions to see if they can reproduce her results. When that happens, I'll report it on my various websites and social media. Stay tuned.

CHAPTER THIRTY TWO:

EASY RIDERS

Luana and Peter in Easy Rider.

Around Peter Fonda's passing, "Easy Rider" played at my local cinema in Santa Monica, the "Aero." After the screening, I met three young folks who had never seen the film. I asked their opinion: "It's so timely, it really speaks to what's going on in the country now."

For those who haven't seen "Easy Rider" in awhile, it's about **prejudice,** it's about **judging people** for the way they look, it's about realizing that we **talk about freedom** in a way that we think is settled law - and that it isn't on many levels. With the rise of fascism in the country, or misplaced xenophobia, the film speaks directly to those issues in a way that is startling.

A still from Easy Rider; Peter and Jack

My comments are in italics, Jennifer's replies in bold.

Rich: Hi Jennifer. I did have a couple of people I wanted to talk to and Luana, I don't how important they are to talk to. I'll leave it up to you.

Jennifer: She says "They're a 9 out of 10 for whatever research you're doing."

(Note: Jennifer doesn't know who I've invited, but in terms of how Luana views this next guest; "He's a "9 out of 10.")

Let's start with the 9. This is someone Luana worked with and knew.

And is related to Jack Nicholson.

Yes. (Ding!) This is someone who recently moved to the flipside.

And is also friends with our class member from "Big Love."

Harry Dean Stanton? Okay, I didn't know that. I was quoting Harry yesterday.

Harry Dean (back right) along with costars Jack Nicholson, Randy Quaid, Freddie Forrest
Luana appeared in films or TV shows with all of them

(Note: Six Degrees of Luana. Harry Dean, at the funeral of his close friend Warren Oates, "told an anecdote of his comrade's encouragement when a mutual scene from Peter Fonda's "92 degrees in the Shade" was near the brink of collapse." (*Medium.com*) Peter Fonda, whom Jennifer has no clue I'm talking about, is telling us from the flipside he and Harry Dean were friends.)

Harry showed me a flower.

Okay there is something that Luana and Jack were involved in that this person I am calling forward was part of. Does he want to come and speak with us?

He says, "He doesn't know how. He didn't know how to communicate when he was here."

Well, Luana can help him. Is he ready to talk to us?

I saw Anthony Bourdain.

(Note: When Anthony died, Peter was filmed (YouTube) saying "I was so sorry to hear that. I really liked him. It's so sad." I don't know if they met, or he was just a fan, but now they can chat. The topic of suicide comes up in a few minutes.)

Then I saw the karate guy – from Kung Fu.

David Carradine. Indeed, he looked a bit like him. Let's put him in the chair. Can we bring him forward?

Marlon Brando just sat in the chair, I thought that was funny.

Sorry Marlon, it's not your turn; we'll talk to you later. (We have talked to him, earlier. Another actor known for motorcycles that friends of Luana knew.) So this person is an actor. Luana there is a movie you did with this guy and someone else in our class.

She's showing me that room where everyone met each other?

Jack Nicholson with his former acting teacher Jeff Corey

(Note: Jennifer is referring to Jeff Corey's "classroom" where Luana met Jack Nicholson, Sally Kellerman, Roger Corman and other close friends – all actors who worked for Roger in films. Peter's career began as Jack and Luana's did – working in Roger Corman movies. We have spoken to Marlon before - about how one of his chairs wound up in his next door neighbor Jack Nicholson's home, and how Marlon's *"unedited will"* fell out of the chair.)

Her acting class. Yes, he was there around that time. He's in a movie with Luana. Luana, show her what this guest did in this movie.

I saw him driving... (or)... on a motorcycle?

Focus on that motorcycle if you can. What color is it? You guys, show her the motorcycle from the movie.

I'm seeing white... which doesn't make any sense.

And some red and blue – I can't believe you don't know this movie but it demonstrates how I've not spoken to or helped you in any way. Luana appeared in a movie with Dennis...

(Interrupts) Hopper!

Correct. The guy in our interview chair passed over a few weeks ago. You never saw their movie?

I'm sorry. Is it called "Freedom" or something about freedom?

Close. "Easy Rider."

(Jennifer makes a face) Never saw it.

Well, it is a film about freedom. That's fine – you don't know who starred in Easy Rider, do you? His name is Peter Fonda.

(Note: Indeed, having seen the latest 4K print after this interview, there's a speech at the end that Jack Nicholson gives Dennis saying **"They don't fear your hair. They fear what you represent; freedom."** Peter starred, Luana played his girlfriend in the commune, Jack played the lawyer, Dennis directed it, cowrote it with Peter who produced the film.)

Is that Jane Fonda's dad?

Ask him. Peter, what's your relation to Jane?

He says, "Brother and sister." (Jennifer frowns)

Don't be disappointed; it just shows you have not been prepped.

Sorry. I would not have known.

Luana is this the 9 out of ten person?

She says, "Yes." (Jennifer aside:) Did he have throat cancer? I felt his throat.

Could have been...possibly.

(Note: Yes, the throat area; Peter died of lung cancer.)

"It went through his whole body," he says.

So Peter, that reply shows that you can converse with us. Tell me, how does he appear to you?

They're saying "She didn't (even) know who she was talking to!" That's what they're saying. I kept seeing James Dean, but I didn't think that he might represent the motorcycle. He (Peter) has this wavy hair, and looks.. well, you already described David Carradine.

A tall thin guy. Let's invite Dennis to join us as well.

They're all there.

Peter, who was there to greet you when you crossed over?

He says, "His mother."

Peter with family, with his wife, Peter's mom; Frances Seymour Brokaw. She reportedly was bi-polar, and when hearing they were going to divorce, took her own life. Reportedly, Peter wasn't told what happened for five years after the event.

She's short, like tiny – I saw Jane's face in hers, something somewhere in her looks - felt like she died 30 years ago or something. Felt like she had something wrong with her brain... her heart... I saw pills.

(Note: His mother, Frances Brokaw was petite compared to husband Henry. She died in 1950, so if the comment "she died 30 years ago" is enough to stop a person from reading on, as I'm fond of saying, *"Now's the time to get off this bus."* Jennifer is reporting - and her feeling was that it was "30 years ago" when it was 70. People on the flipside give images that represent events, like "pills" for "suicide." I don't know if she was taking pills for her condition, but it's been widely reported she was manic depressive or bi-polar which may have led to her suicide.)

What was that like to see your mother again?

He says "Bliss... and questions." He had so many questions, a script of unanswered (ones).. a list of questions; she left too early." She said to him "It was going to be okay," and then his dogs came to him (on the flipside.)

Peter, have you had a chance to see your father?

He says, "Yeah, but he was in the back."

(Note: "Staying back" is often reported when people aren't sure what the reception to seeing them will be like. Again, Jennifer has no idea who his father is.)

Is he able to converse with you or is he still working out his journey?

He says "They missed levels." I don't know what the levels are.

(Note: In this context, it may be that something prevented them from greeting each other at first.)

So he's not conversing?

He says, "He's in a different place (mentally), trying to think about how to come back."

(Note: This is in the "flipside" research as well, people under deep hypnosis talking about the process of planning their return, gearing up so to speak, to make that return.)

Peter, your mom was there to greet you, but she left the planet in a startling way – did you talk about that with her? Did she explain why that happened?

Was there a sudden impact to her chest, like a force?

(Note: Having done a number of these with Jennifer, I've heard from her before that "sudden impact" may refer to as a "sudden or unexpected passing" – like it wasn't expected or planned. She may be seeing the gunshot that Peter speaks of in a few minutes. But in the case of his mother, Frances, it was a few days after hearing of her impending divorce that she committed suicide.)

Well, in a way. But Peter, she was the first person to greet you – have you since conversed with your dad?

He says, "Yeah."

After your mom passed away, you had an incident that happened when you were 10 or 11 years old.

(Jennifer, after a pause) He says, "He saw her."

What happened to you that you saw her?

He showed me being angry and couldn't breathe.

It's been reported there was an accident, but I don't know if it was purposeful or not.

He's saying "He had a near death experience." (Jennifer aside:) Did he have a near death experience?

Do you want to show Jennifer what happened?

"It was a gun" he said.

That's correct. (Ding!) Was that an accident or on purpose?

He says "He was out of his mind, it was both – the safety wasn't on."

So it was an accident that you shot yourself?

He's showing me the bullet went straight through him... (gestures to her body).

But then you saw your mom?

"Yes." He shows me crying and just loving her and understanding everything she went through all the sadness she went through.

And then you came back?

He says "He felt like he was ten years older after that."

(Note: I'm familiar with accounts of near death experiences, having interviewed a number of people who've had them as well via IANDS.org (International Association for Near Death Studies) From a biography of Peter: "In his 1998 memoir, "Don't Tell Dad," he chronicled his difficult, distant relationship with his famous father. Describing Henry's role in John Ford's Fort Apache (1948) as "an unsmiling, bitter, strict hard-ass..." when asked about his father, he'd say "Have you seen the film?" Born in New York, he and Jane were sent to live with an aunt and uncle in Nebraska following the suicide of their mother, Frances Ford Seymour, in 1950, when Peter was 10. On his 11th birthday, he accidentally shot himself in the stomach and nearly died. Years later, he told John Lennon, during an LSD session, that "I know what it's like to be dead", a phrase which ended up becoming part of the lyrics for the Beatles' song She Said, She Said. https://www.theguardian.com/film/2019/aug/17/peter-fonda-obituary)

When they talk about Peter's life, they include this anecdote; John Lennon had dropped LSD, and Peter was whispering in his ear "I know what it's like to be dead." It creeped John out, but he put it in a song "She said, She said." However, what Peter was saying was accurate; he had a near death event, and "knew what it was like to be dead" because he saw his mother. Is that right, Peter?

He says, "Correct."

What was it like to see Luana on the flipside and where did you see her?

They were backstage for that concert – do you remember the car ride to that concert we spoke of?

(Note: She's referring to the Harry Dean Stanton story of how Luana had built upon the memory of their trip to the Monterey Pop Festival in 1967.)

But this time he was already backstage with her at the concert – some type of concert.

Let's ask; was it the Monterey Pop concert?

They're saying "Yeah."

Well, why not? Once you can construct or create a CGI of the Monterey Pop festival why not use it again to bring in other friends? So Peter, at some point after you stepped into the flipside, you found yourself backstage at Monterey Pop festival?

He says, "Yeah. It was like...in a grassy area. I saw (Luana) blowing bubbles."

Besides Luana, who did you see?

Robert Kennedy? I don't know why he showed me him.

Well, it was 1967; he might have been there. Maybe to remind us of the time period. Were you a fan of his?

Peter says "He disliked the war..." -- Something about how "He hated the war," but Peter says "He didn't trust the government at all."

When you see Luana, she's blowing bubbles; what's she wearing?

He says, "Like in a 60's dress, with a headband, hair down, playing a tambourine."

You recognized her as Luana, correct?

"Yeah, but it felt like it was *that* moment in time – that it existed then." He says "He knew it wasn't a memory though."

How did you know it wasn't a memory?

He says, "Because of the landscape, it wasn't tangible." He showed me that scene (in the film) "Twilight," when they go out in the sun...

An unusual landscape?

He says, "He thought he was on the best acid trip of his life."

Who did you see at the festival?

He said, "Jimi Hendrix."

When did you see Dennis?

He says, "A little later, he was coming back, towards the back of a stage... to the side, looked like Dennis was there controlling things on the stage – something backstage."

Dennis Hopper and Brian Jones, Monterey Pop Festival

(Note: While I haven't found any photos of Peter at the festival, Dennis was there with Rolling Stone's founding member Brian Jones. From "Michael Bloomfield: If you Love these blues" (Backbeat Publishing 2000) "Our first job was the movie score for "the Trip." We went to LA to record it, that's where we met Dennis Hopper and Peter Fonda. they were always in the studio with us, and Jack Nicholson was involved in that. Then, after the film score, we played the Monterey Pop Festival. (as "Electric Flag"))

How was that reunion?

He said, "Quick."

(Note: She said "Quick" before I could finish the question.)

He said, "When he walked away, that's when I realized more what was going on... seeing Dennis, that was the defining moment when he knew he was on the flipside."

Peter, I know your daughter – can you put that in Jennifer's mind? Bridget Fonda; she worked with Bill Paxton.

Bridget Fonda from my film "You Can't Hurry Love" (Vestron)

He says, "Yes." He says "He goes and sees her in her dreams. Two days after he passed she had like a full apparition, like she saw him."

Anything you want to tell her?

Something to do with paperwork, "Dot your i's cross your t's" – almost feels like property issues. He wants to say "Dot your i's and cross your t's." Tell her "Everything's going to be okay." He says "She remembers the dream, but she's discounting it. He wants her to know that he was there in that dream state with her."

Were you friendly with Bridget's husband?

He says "Of course; anyone that can handle Bridget..." He's very funny.

She's married to Danny Elfman, the composer.

(Jennifer aside: From "Oingo Boingo?")

Yes, and many film scores. So Peter, were you close to Danny?

He says "Of course he is..." (A pause) (Jennifer aside:) something about his shoes... something about him "Doing what he wants to do and not what others want him to do." Like "get bigger shoes" as a metaphor.

Like "Don't let others define you?"

He says, "Yes."

Because he wants to compose bigger scores or do something else?

He says, "Like something else completely – and he should."

What about Bridget? How is she doing?

He says, "Her children are older now... but... She's really busy with her family."

She's kind of retired from acting, but I did put her in her first speaking role in a film.

He's saying "You gave her the confidence."

I don't know about that.. but Luana was in it too – isn't that odd Peter? What's odd is that it never came up – never discussed. I Luana was hilarious in "You Can't Hurry Love" and Bridget was a bit nervous at first.

(Note: I saw Easy Rider at 14, perhaps saw it a dozen times since. When I went to USC film school ten years later, I met Luana and we were together for 20 years. Through her, I met everyone she knew on the film, from Punky Brewster's dad (Virgil Frye shoes a horse) to assistant editor Henry Jaglom, to studio producer Bert Schneider, to Jack, Dennis, Peter (at the 25th reunion) to Karen Black. Luana once dated Dennis, so I knew all the details when I cast Bridget in my film "You Can't Hurry Love." Luana plays a mom in the film, and Bridget is the love interest. But for some reason, I never connected that Luana and Bridget's dad had done "Easy" Rider together.)

He says "Luana helped her."

(Ding!) She did; Luana showed the film to her pal Francis Coppola, and he cast her in Godfather part Three.

Is she the one with blue eyes?

Yeah, terrific actor, did a film with Bill Paxton, who called me and said "I finally got to work with Bridget." Bill was going to star in "You Can't Hurry Love" with Bridget and Luana – but enough about me – Peter back to you, what do you miss about being on the planet if anything?

He says, "The food."

(Note: It's a common refrain. People claim to be able recreate many things on the flipside as a mental construct - from playing golf to riding horses, but it's harder to construct the actual taste of things, or tangible things like touch.)

Anything you want me to tell your sister Jane?

Jennifer laughs. He says "Tell her it's not scary up here."

What's that mean?

He says, "That it's not scary up there! She's afraid of death."

She thinks it's all going to end? Well let's bring your mom here for a second... I forget her first name.. (Frances). Let's ask her a question; mom what do you want to say to your daughter Jane?

He said, "Take your time; there's no rush."

(Note: There's an iconic scene in "Easy Rider" shot in the cemetery in New Orleans, where everyone was improvising an acid trip. In Peter's scene, he holds onto a statue and refers to it as his mother, telling her he hated her for "leaving so soon." She's with him on the flipside, so I wanted her to come forward and remind us of that fact.)

Peter?

He says "Time doesn't exist up there."

Peter, do you remember your last moments on the planet? Was Jane with you?

"Yeah." He said, "He looked up and said he saw their mom." He says "At first I was nervous... and then she just... he saw these beautiful lights."

Were you smiling?

He says, "He was, but at first he was terrified."

What were your last words here, first words on the flipside?

I'm not getting the right interpretation, but something like "I'll see you soon... at lunch." Something like that.

Meaning?

Like "There's not going to be any time between the next time I see you."

Okay, it'll feel like a few minutes later when they see each other again - like "lunch." Anything you want me to tell her to focus on? Have you tried to visit her?

Jennifer laughs, rolls her eyes. He is so funny. He says "She's felt him. Definitely felt him around her." He says, "She can smell him, there's a certain scent." (Jennifer aside: I'm asked "Is she going to miss you?" and he laughed and said "no.")

Jane Fonda, Wikipedia. Advocate/actor

Peter can we bring your dad forward? I don't think Jennifer knows who your dad is. Luana is that possible to bring him?

(Jennifer shrugs; she does not.) What's his name?

Henry... or Hank.

Was he a director or a producer or something?

Kind of. Right business.

Why did he just show me the show Chips? With Erik Estrada?

(Note: This is an odd reference, and I had no idea if Henry knew Erik. However, they did "Midway" together, where Henry was an officer, and Erik a young sailor.)

Who was there to greet you when you crossed over?

He's showing me a horse.

Was this your horse? Did you work with this horse? Or did you own this?

Henry Fonda, "My Darling Clementine" 1946

He said, "Owned it. It was like a racing horse." He said, "He had a lot of them." I was getting the color gray. He says, "He owned him when he was young or his family did."

You had a long career and Jennifer is not aware of it... but I am.

He's showing me... the theater (plays).... and movies.

That's correct. He was an actor – let me ask you Henry; what was your favorite role?

(Note: According to his Broadway Theater Credits, he did 18 shows on Broadway starting in 1929 and 125 feature films, nominated for two Oscars ("12 Angry Men" and "Grapes of Wrath," he won for "On Golden Pond")

There's a lot of them that he just showed me. One with Robert Redford.

Robert Redford giving Henry Fond an Oscar

(Note: While it's not widely known, Robert Redford's career began with an appearance with Henry Fonda: "Redford, began his TV career at 22 with a small part in the NBC drama "The Last Gunfight" with Henry Fonda. (LA Times. "Robert Redford the TV kid.") Also Robert Redford presented Fonda an honorary Oscar in 1981.)

Is there one with a lot of men... ("12 Angry Men" was one film he was nominated for.) Did he play in a movie where he was the President?

Yes, it was called "Fail Safe."

(Tapping her nose) That's the one.

(Note: I know when Jennifer is tapping her nose, she's doing it to say "yes." "Fail Safe" was made in 1964, directed by Sydney Lumet. Fonda plays a President in the middle of an accidental nuclear attack.

"American planes are sent to deliver a nuclear attack on Moscow, but it's a mistake due to an electrical malfunction. Can all-out war be averted?" It's currently got a 95% rating at Rotten Tomatoes)

You were also in "The Grapes of Wrath," directed by John Ford, written by John Steinbeck. It was an iconic film; your dialog about the era is the one they usually quote. It was an amazing performance (nominated for Oscar). I know when Jennifer looks you up she'll see how many films she's seen you in.

(Jennifer shrugs) I'm sorry.

That's fine – really, that's great; it shows that you haven't thought or heard of any of this in advance.

Fonda in "Grapes of Wrath"

He says "He felt that Grapes of Wrath was a different kind of story telling; he felt it wasn't acting."

Indeed. And "Fail Safe" was low budget, shot on a confined set, like a stage play; Henry was brilliant in it.

I'm sorry, but he keeps showing me this guy from Chips... Erik Estrada?

Okay, who is showing her Erik Estrada and why?

Luana.

Lu, why are you showing her Erik? We know you guys you don't drop random references. Is there some connection with Peter and Erik?

(Jennifer aside:) Maybe it's about Peter.

Erik Estrada on Twitter

Well; both played motorcycles guys... Peter, they had a new 4K version of Easy Rider a few weeks ago at at Radio City Music Hall, were you aware of it?

Peter leading the way

He said, "They were all there. He loved it, he loved to be celebrated and remembered."

If I may ask, why is that important?

He says, "Because that celebration connects them to here, more – people start thinking about them and then they can "work their magic." (i.e. connecting to them)

About Erik Estrada, do you want us to say something for him?

They're saying "You're going to connect it in some way."

Okay. I'll try. Thank you Peter for stopping by.

(Note: Indeed, there is a link between Henry, Peter and Erik. Erik worked on on the film "Midway" with Peter's father Henry, then later in life, after "Chips" and "Easy Rider" made both Erik and Peter "America's motorcycle actors" he and Peter were the co-chairs of the 2000 March of Dimes Motorcycle Ride in Shreveport. "American Motorcyclist Oct 2000" They've also both hosted the Hollywood Christmas Parade.)

*****

"**She Said, She said**" by Lennon/McCartney (John changed the gender of the person speaking to him which changes the tone of the story.)

"She said, "I know what it's like to be dead
I know what it is to be sad"
And she's making me feel like I've never been born.
I said "Who put all those things in your hair?
Things that make me feel like I'm sad...
And you're making me feel like I've never been born.

She said "You don't understand what I said."
I said "No no no you're wrong,
When I was a boy, everything was right.
Everything was right.
I said "Even though you know what you know
I know that I'm ready to leave
'Cause you're making me feel like I've never been born."

Peter had a near death experience when he was a young boy, so in this party, where John says he met Peter for the first time they were reportedly "tripping on LSD" and Peter says, "I know what it's like to be dead," and John replied "You're making me feel like I've never been born." John reported later this was the genesis of the song, that it was "creepy to have this American actor repeating this phrase."

Aside from the "well, they were both tripping, what do you expect?" Peter had a near death experience when he was shot in the stomach at the age of 12. As noted above, he "saw his mother" (who had died earlier) during his near death event. (Paul McCartney saw his mother, and wrote "Let It Be" as a result.) John had lost his mother at an early age as well. "I know what it's like to be dead" is a literal statement; Peter did.

John's reply is "You're freaking me out" not because he didn't want to hear it, but because he understood it. If that's accurate, then he was "making him feel as if I've never been born" because "birth" is a relative thing if consciousness continues. Not born. Not dead.

John goes on to say "I'm ready to leave" (he could have said "go," as it would have rhymed with "know") – but instead says "I'm ready to leave," (as in "leave the planet") if that is the case – that if between lives we experience joy and unconditional love, and it's a place we "return to" then "what's the bloody point of being here and suffering?"

"When I was a boy everything was right" he sings – that is, before the loss of his mother, and before Beatlemania. He then says "Even though you know what you know; (that life goes on) I know that I'm ready to leave (this lifetime) 'Cause you're making me feel like I've never been born."

It may be a stretch, but that's what came to me while listening to the song recently – and what I'm saying is relative to what they've said since crossing over. My two cents.

CHAPTER THIRTY THREE:

OUR LIBRARIAN LUANA

Luana by Monte Hellman

Filmed at Fishbar in Manhattan Beach. My questions are in *italics*, Jennifer's replies are in **bold**.

Richard: Hi Jennifer; our buddy Robert Towne called me yesterday and asked me a couple of questions. He was worried because he said he couldn't find the Hira discussions we've had.

Jennifer: I was going to say that – when you said his name, the first impression I got was about... what's his name?

Hira.

My first impression from Hira was that Robert is or was thinking about getting a new dog. That's the impression I got. (Robert says he's not) But he's showing me that Robert was so heartbroken over Hira, I don't know if he can bring himself to get another one.

Can we bring him forward?

(Nods) He's here.

Hello Hira. How are you?

He says "Awesome!"

Hira, what are you doing these days?

He says "The food is quite tasty up there."

Okay – I understand that. Food and taste are a mental construct so we have to create them over there... So Hira you've been in Robert's mind recently. Put it in Jennifer's mind as to why.

It's about a movie. He is thinking about or thought about making a movie.

I know Jennifer doesn't know what movie Robert is working on, but I do. Do you want to put it in her mind Hira? A movie that you were involved in making?

I saw and image of you with a bullhorn.

Oh that's funny. But I'm referring to something else.

(Note: I didn't realize it until I transcribed the interview that the only movie that he could be referring to is "Personal Best" where I spent a bunch of my time on set using a bullhorn. I drove Hira personally to the set in Eugene Oregon. My job was to wrangle the extras – and it was daily with a bullhorn. Jennifer would not, could not be aware of that but Hira is.)

He's showing me like it's a remake... like there's a movie he's trying to remake – like 1, 2, 3... (sequels included).

Yes, that's correct. Hira; what do you want to tell Robert?

He showed me to not condense it but make it more open (she expands her arms wide) and to not lose his mind over it... opening up and expanding instead of trying to keep it to one audience. (I assume he means "not for cineastes but for everyone.")

(Note: Since then we got the same kind of note from Robert's pal Harry Dean Stanton in another chapter.)

A wider storyline? I invited Robert to hire me as an ombudsman.

(Jennifer aside) I think he will.

Okay, I'll tell him "Hira told me to tell you to hire me." But Hira; I need to hear it in your voice. Is this supposed to happen?

They're all rolling their eyes (over there), like "of course this is part of the journey; they're showing how it's all connected." They're talking about "Luana's screenplay about their acting class, that story with Robert and Jack."

That's right – she wrote "Real Feelings." (Story of the Jeff Corey acting class, Fred Roos producing.) Hira is it possible for you to show up to see Robert or to connect with him?

He says, "Yes."

What's the best method for him or someone to connect (with a pet on the flipside)?

He showed me Robert lying down, looking up at the sky outside.

On the grass?

He's looking up into the sky... why am I smelling cigar smoke? I don't think Robert smokes.

He used to. Cigars or cigarillos, I forget.

Hira is remembering that.

Or it could be Eddie Taylor – he liked to smoke cigars if I remember.

He's here. (Edward)

Okay, what's he saying or what does he want to say?

He's saying "Don't smoke cigars, Robert." (Jennifer aside:) It's so weird there's a lot of people up there trying to help... but Hira in particular showed up before you said his name. He's showing me that look, Robert lying with his head back, looking up.

Eddie; you want to add anything? To connect Robert needs to look up with his head back?

I see that his eyes are open – not closed. Then I saw like a blue bird, a hummingbird... or something.

What's that mean?

I don't know.

Maybe if he sees a bird he'll know he's connected?

Hira is telling me... when Hira was sick Robert would lie down with him in the grass and just look up, just lie with him. I feel like that's where he got his inspiration... It may have been just a memory of his, before he was sick, but he showed me doing that again; that will give him that same inspiration and then some.

Hira, Robert told me a story about you and some animals on Catalina. You want to show her that?

First thing I saw was a buffalo.

(Pause). OMG. Fuck me. That's it!

(Note: Robert and I were chatting about Hira on Catalina, and he told me this story about Hira and some buffalo that were on the island.)

There's one in particular he's showing me.

That is it but there was more than one... I didn't know buffalo were over on Catalina; I was only there once with Luana.

Hira is showing me he loved them (the buffalo), he felt like he was just as big and strong as they were – in his mind, being as big as a horse.

Robert told me that Hira went over a pissed on a buffalo chip. Why'd you do that Hira? To upset them?

(Jennifer laughs). He said "He was scared shitless." He said, "I was scared shitless, even then I knew Robert couldn't protect me. And they (the buffalo) got really mad (at first) and then... they started laughing. They didn't chase him – they didn't bother him – He's showing me they were laughing. He said "I was scared shitless."

Think how funny that is; Hira telling us a story from his pov when I just heard it from Robert's point of view. I will tell him that Hira. I'll email this to him.

"You gotta tell him that." (Jennifer aside:) And that you never mentioned buffalo.

That's right. I did not mention buffalo; that's awesome! Anything from you Eddie?

He says he's not happy with the new title of this new project (whatever it is.)

The Chinatown prequel?

"Yes." I don't know... He says "It's infringing on something...." (Listens). Wait, Hira is coming back. He showed me a little mouse, then he showed the buffalo looking at him like he was a little mouse. He says "It was like that – I was scared shitless and they were like we're not going to bother with that (little mouse). Hira said "I knew Robert couldn't protect me" (from them) but Hira walked away like "try to come after me."

So to clarify; to connect with you or Eddie, Robert should lay down somewhere – the grass or maybe a lounge chair. Look up at the sky, look at the clouds, remember being on Catalina, meditate on that. Is that right Hira? So he can connect with you?

He'll make it evident (that he is).

He'll put it in Robert's mind?

"He's too much in his head," he said. Tell him to do whatever he used to do when Hira was sick.

Hira had a prostate problem he couldn't walk and Robert used to literally carry him outside even while he was still on the phone. But something like that? Imagine you and him together and just look up into the sky and you'll be there?

"Yes."

*****

PART TWO

ROBIN WILLIAMS, THE ALPHA AND OMEGA

Hi class. Luana; who wants to talk to us?

Robin Williams is like "pick me!" He just wants to make it into this book.

You're in every chapter dude – "love love" – I can't burp without saying "love love."

(Jennifer listens) He says, "You need to tell people we're helping from the other side; we're really really putting focus in helping people."

Do you mean their relatives are trying to reach them?

It almost feels like... "Energy is their currency and cash is our currency, right?" He says, "Whatever you focus your attention on you'll get more of that... you'll be pounded with more of it." Like if I focus on the energy I'll get more of it. I'm seeing this intersection of light.

You guys are trying to help loved ones to speak to people over here? Or everyone who thinks of you? I'm just trying to figure out what you're saying Robin.

(Jennifer makes a face while I speak) He's looking at you, like "Are you done yet?" He says "Family first, loved ones. But then all of us are one, what we already feel, it's like a balance trying to get an equilibrium." He showed having the best tap water in the world... it's so clear over there. He's saying "If you think of water over here as crystal clear and over here on this side, the veil is thinning, so the water is moving back and forth, the consciousness is moving back and forth. He's showing me the energy within everybody, we all have it, we can all connect to people on both sides. He's saying we don't because people aren't paying attention, or are picking up on everyone else's energy.

How can we help them to focus?

He's saying "To be still once a day; check in with yourself."

But you were never still Mr. Williams.

He says, "And why do you think I'm learning this over there?"

It's also what Anthony Bourdain told us; meditation, being still. That's a way to connect to the other side. What should they think about when they're meditating?

He says, "Think of "What are they doing to help the planet?" Ask for images. Ask for sense smells, or visuals to receive suggestions on how help the planet. I just asked about a group of ants that I accidentally killed today and I wondered "Oh no, what have I done?" And they showed me something you said awhile ago, Robin just drew a circle – they just "swish!" Come right back into their next lifetime."

So we should be meditating on how to help the planet? Was that accurate what I heard, plant a trillion trees?

He says, "And then some, yes."

Thank you Robin – who else is here?

My dad is coming forward ...

Hi Jim. Okay Robin, sorry, we need this chair.

Robin said "Love love" the way he used to say "Nanu nanu."

Hmm, is that what "nanu nanu" means? Love love?

My dad is laughing. I'll tell you about a dream first, he told me to mention this. I was in this dream, and he appeared in the room, and at first it was like "Oh wow, there's my dad" and I could feel his arm. But then I thought "I can't tell him that he's not alive or he'll disappear, I want to spend as much time as I can. I didn't want to say anything because I didn't want to lose him, I was like "I have to believe or else I'll lose him!" And I started to cry and I said "Dad, do you know you're not alive?" The second I said that he started to disappear. The second I don't believe in something... with anything, with love...

Okay, this is for your dad. Jim, correct me if I'm wrong, but it's also people have a dream where they see their loved one, they say "Oh my God, you're dead!" But they are doing the shift in focus, because of their fear. What was the point of the dream what else is she worried about Jim?

That's funny. He put me in a room by myself and everything... going away – I'm worried...

(Guessing) That you're going to wake up and not be able to talk to the flipside?

Yeah!

Well, that would be great! No more arguments! No more having to translate for the flipside!

My dad is laughing. Sometimes people want love advice and I give it to them, but then realize they shouldn't have heard it.

Jim, what is it she needs to hear about this?

He showed me all the dimensions landing at the same time. Everything I've said happens at different time periods.

Ask your dad to step in to say if you're on the right path or to tell her "it's not supposed to be known."

I've been learning that too. I just have to believe - that's the whole purpose. Trust that what comes to me is supposed to come to me for whatever reason.

I had an odd dream last night. Luana? Can you help with this?

She says, "Yes." She's wearing purple, her hair is in a ponytail.

Our friend Robert was in this complicated dream. There was a movie set, with real people being the real folks in the prison set – others were actors acting like prisoners. I heard Robert say "There are three people in the school of Roman Napkin."

A scroll made up of Roman napkins? That's what I got.

Luana, what are we talking about here? I think I have an idea, but wanted to hear it from you.

Feels like one of the big mysteries.

What's a big mystery?

Like that big chest... what's it called? The Ark of the Covenant... Nights of the Templar?

That's correct. (Ding!) Who's showing this to you?

(Jennifer listens) Jesus.

That's who I was thinking of with reference to the word "napkin." School of Roman napkin; I searched that, found the word in Latin. "Sudarium" is this word I've never heard but it means...

A cloth.

(Ding!) It does. Someone posted a question on Quora: "What do I think of the Sudarium of Oviedo?" That's the face cloth that was supposedly on the face of Jesus in the cave, the shroud made its way to Turin, but the face cloth went to Oviedo, Spain.

I got the "Coat of Many Colors."

You mean the Bible story of Joseph's coat?

He said, "Yes."

Jesus? Why did you show her that? Is that because Joseph's coat was a rainbow coat?

He said "Yes."

Was Joseph's coat a meditation of rainbow color? So this is a reference to "Rainbow body" or how a person can meditate and create a rainbow light?

He says, "Yes."

Wow. Glad I can unpack this. We've talked about this – but again, did the rainbow light create the shroud?

"Yes" he said.

Reportedly the Sudarium was the face cloth – both had blood on them, which proves that whoever was under them was alive, because you don't bleed when you're dead. Discovery Channel had people prove the shroud and the Sudarium came from the same cloth.

(Note: "The Shroud of Turin and the Sudarium of Oviedo "almost certainly covered the cadaver of the same person." This is the conclusion from an investigation that has compared the two relics using forensics and geometry. The research was done by Dr. Juan Manuel Miñarro, a professor at the University of Seville." Aleteia Archives 2016).

I got shown movies like "Angels and Demons" or "The Davinci Code" from that writer Dan Brown.

In the dream, Robert said "School of Roman napkins" and we get to this. Weird. Like the term "Vanum populatum." I didn't know what it meant, six months later I heard it means "annihilate vanity." Jesus, you want to weight in? Its your shroud.

Why do I feel like his body was replaced? I was shown a body being replaced.

You mean was Jesus switched out?

Yeah.

Are you saying he was switched out on the cross or later?

(Note: The Qur'an makes the claim that the man on the cross was a double, and that Jesus was switched out. However, that's not what she's saying.)

Or in the tomb.

I think you're seeing when they moved his body – from one cave to another one. Because they would have found a body if it was switched out. Did I tell you about Joanna? I did a session with a close friend of mine.

I'm getting "She was like Jesus' sister."

The Tongerlo Last Supper, by Leonardo da Vinci and his studio. Courtesy of the Sheen Center.

Well, she remembered being very close to him (the chapter in "Architecture of the Afterlife" "Witness to the Crucifixion") remembered her name, Joanna, her family – everything. She was so close to him that at the crucifixion she saw herself standing between Mary and Magdalene. I had never heard of Joanna, but when I looked her up, biblical scholars say she was very close to Jesus. So the story as we know it, is that you were on the cross, survived, are you saying at some point they switched the body so there was a dead guy?

It almost feels like he was outside of himself.

Okay, but let's explore this. Was that because of his experience with esoteric yogas (that we've heard before) where he shifted his consciousness away from his body? Let's ask him what happened. Walk us through it, you're on the cross, then what happens?

Somebody gave him something to withstand the pain.

A drug?

Like belladonna.

I've heard that story, ("Mystery of the Jesus Papers" NBC) that perhaps the sponge they stuck up to your face was filled with a drug to knock you out. But afterwards, you're off the cross, you're in a cave, alive, the shroud is around you. There's this Roman napkin on your face, you've been covered with aloe and myrrh brought in by Joseph of Arimathea... and then you have this rainbow body experience which creates the image on the shroud. Is that correct?

He says "He was healed."

Taken to another cave and healed? How long were you in that cave?

Feels like six weeks. Feels like he was threatened by being there.

That would make sense; if they found you, there would be hell to pay. So then you escaped?

"Yes" he said.

We've heard you went off to France to pick up your wife?

He says, "Yeah." (Jennifer aside) What does the bible say about this?

Well, none of this. But eventually, after the crucifixion, after the cave incidents, he goes to Galilee, about 60 miles away, some see him, don't believe they're seeing him. Sees the pals of his, Thomas doubts him, pokes his holes, then he eats, drinks and sleeps with his apostles. Not something someone etheric or in an energy body might do. And then according to the "Acts of Thomas," he takes Thomas do the docks and sells him to a slave trader, then walks on water, he then reportedly leaves for France to pick the Magdalene up. Takes about a year, with his three kids, daughter Sarah, heads back to his stomping grounds in Kashmir, traveling with his mother Mary who dies somewhere in Pakistan, and lives out his days as "Yuz Asaf" ("Bodhisattva") in Kashmir. Jesus, please, correct me if any of this account is wrong.

(Note: It's a funny paragraph, I know that I'm using leading questions, but Jennifer has always corrected me in the past whenever I say something inaccurate. In this case, her non interruption doesn't mean I'm correct, but it does mean to me that I'm not inaccurate.)

He's showing me his feet – the only thing that was wrong.

Did his feet have holes in them? Must have been hard to walk.

He says, "Whatever they put on him to heal him, they put that on his feet as well and helped to heal his feet."

Everyone has told us your hands were not nailed but tied.

"Yeah" he said.

But your feet were nailed?

He says, "Yes."

The stone cast of your feet in Kashmir (of "Yuz Asaf") shows a guy who had holes in his feet?

He says, "Yeah. He had holes in his feet and not his hands." I just saw you in a charter carrier, saying "I'm going to take all you guys on!"

(Note: I don't know what Jennifer means by "charter carrier" but I'm assuming something like 'I'll be burnt at the stake.' "Charter carrier" as an excursion means "persons who acquire the use of a motor bus to travel together as a group." A bus full of heretics?)

So Luana, is there anything else, anyone else we need to talk to in class. Not to kick our friend Jesus to the curb, sorry dude.

(Jennifer wipes away a tear). It makes me really emotional just seeing him how bad they tortured him.

He was a courageous fellow.

He showed me that it was temporary and then he made a circle. (Meaning, he used his hand to show how he shifted his consciousness away from his body, and then came back to it.) You can see why people would get upset with our conversation.

So Luana who wants to chat with us?

She says, "Prince." He says he loved Dave Chappelle's tribute to him in his new Netflix show. That's why Mork came back in. Robin said, "Love love."

Okay, Jennifer has to run. Thanks everyone!

CHAPTER THIRTY FOUR:

MAMBA OUT

Kobe Bryant visiting pals in Italy. Private collection.

Kobe Bean Bryant

Jennifer and I are in our usual booth at Fishbar in Manhattan Beach. It's been a few weeks since Kobe Bryant, his daughter Gianna and their friends all died in a helicopter crash. I thought of a novel way to conduct an interview with Kobe. I had met him when he first arrived in LA, as I'm friends with former Laker Manager and his wife, Mitch and Claire Kupchak. I've known Claire since she was a student at USC, I filmed their wedding in San Antonio. Mitch introduced me to Kobe when he first came to Los Angeles, and he was a polite, tall teenager who became a legend.

I'm aware of how much interviewing someone who was famous might seem problematic – what don't we know about him? But in this case, I knew he spoke Italian fluently because he grew up there. I happen to speak Italian and thought of a different way for us to interview someone on the flipside. I would ask questions in Italian, and ask him to put the answers in Jennifer's mind.

Prior to the session, I was trying to think of anyone who might know Kobe, and Junior Seau popped into my mind; "Dude. What about me?"

Rich: Hi class, we missed you since Jennifer was on vacation. Is there anyone who needs to jump in first?

Jennifer: Did you ask for Junior Seau to be here?

Yes. I did. (Ding!)

He wants us to expand on something and I don't know what he means by that.

Perhaps expand more in this interview. Is that correct Junior?

"Yes." (Jennifer aside) The other day, I asked him to help me with my workout. He showed up and then everyone showed up – including my instructor's mom. I forgot by asking for help, it opens up the floodgates.

We have someone tangentially related to Junior, which is why Junior is here; he's going to help us.

Oh. Kobe Bryant.

That's correct. (Ding!) On the way here I asked if he was available.

"Yes."

Kobe, is it okay to speak to you?

"Yes." (Jennifer aside) He just showed me the person that I knew that worked for the Lakers and said "You know he really liked you."

Kobe, how are you able to reach out to Jennifer?

He showed me Luana.

But how did Luana approach you? How did that work?

She talked to him about Jack Nicholson.

Oh, okay, that makes sense. Jack and Kobe were friends.

I didn't know that – I knew he was there all the time.

Jack gave a rare interview, where he said that Kobe was like family to him. And one of Jack's kids posted a video of him on her page, saying she had been "crying all day." So yes, of course, I didn't think of it, but Jack's friendship with Luana would be a connection.

(Note: Luana and Jack were bike messengers at MGM. Luana was in an acting class and one day saw Jack beating the shit out of his bike. Luana suggested he might use that anger on stage and invited him to her class with Jeff Corey. He remained a loyal friend throughout her life, and at her funeral sent a 20 foot high bouquet.)

He also showed me the guy with a raspy voice. The one who owned an island?

Marlon? Well, he lived next door to Jack. That would be an interesting person to run into on the flipside.

He says, "It was."

Can we talk to you about your crossing over?

He says, "A little bit yeah."

Who was there to greet you on the other side?

He says, "His grandmother on his dad's side. Her hands were very soft," he said. He said he was in shock obviously, at first he was looking for his daughter ... (He's showing me) Trying to... hold on. (Listens) He said "He did something to hold onto her, to try to shield her from the impact."

I'm sorry. Does she want to speak to us as well?

She's there, he said "He normally tries to keep her out of the media."

Of course, and I don't want to be intrusive. The only question I would ask her, is if you are aware of previous lifetime with your dad?

"Yes."

Could you show that to Jennifer?

The Bryants in Italy on Vacation

It felt like they were in France in a horse carriage together, very fancy. There were these very nice, big horses and they were in a carriage and it was very cold outside. It felt very cold.

If you don't mind me asking, Gianna, what was it like for you to cross over?

She's said "It was like... it was scary (at first) until it happened – but then, like going into a blissful state at first, blissful is not the right word, just kind of a state of being..." She says "She didn't see her dad right away and then it happened, and (then) she saw him." And then there were these exchanges between them, if I'm getting this right, exchanges between them of a kind of understanding or knowing this was going to happen – like remembering "Oh yeah that was supposed to happen." They didn't know if it was going to be a car accident or some other kind of incident, but that type of energy of knowing."

(Note: I wouldn't presume to know why these events occur, but I can report that what is being said here is consistent with other reports of sudden passing. One example, at the funeral of Olympic wrestler Dave Shultz, his father Phillip recalled during his eulogy that when Dave was five years old, he came to him and asked if "He could keep a secret." His father said "Sure," and Dave said "Dad, I visited my council, these old men with white hair. And they said I could come here to teach a lesson in love. But I won't be here very long." Phillip said he forgot about the interview until his son was killed.)

Are you saying that this was part of the journey for both of you and after crossing over you became aware of that?

He said, "Yes." (Jennifer aside) He's showing his wife Vanessa. He's say something about the connection between the three of them. As if, "They have had lifetimes together before, but so have Vanessa and Gianna." (Jennifer aside) I'm asking about their journey... I feel like he's saying "There was also a tremendous connection between Vanessa and Gianna, as strong as the one with Kobe. Just a tremendous love between them and she will feel that loss equally."

Do you mean the love her mom had for Gianna?

"Yes." She showed me they had similar past lives; Vanessa will miss her daughter just as much as her husband.

I'm sorry to bring the topic up. They were connected on a deeper spiritual level in some way? Previous lifetimes together?

He says, "Yes."

Kobe, what do you want to say to your family or friends?

He says, "That we're not in any pain. That we have a lot of company."

Who's with you? Relatives?

He says, "Yes." Like a cousin... but also people in sports. He showed me... Junior Seau is here...

(Note: I'm not aware of any connection here between the two of them, but on the flipside, people report that people with the "same frequency" often hang out together. Junior is likely helping him communicate.)

So when you crossed over, your grandmother was there at first, then you started to see people you know that passed away or their higher selves?

He says, "He saw his cousin." Something about his cousin.

(Note: His cousin might be the father of one of Kobe's cousins, John Cox IV. His grandfather, John Cox II died at the age of 68 in 2011.

Another cousin is basketball, Laker veteran Cedric Ceballos, (born in Maui). In a follow up interview, we might learn who this cousin is.)

Kobe with his cousin John Cox (Private photo)

Have you seen anyone we might know, from our class for example?

He says "He saw Michael Jackson."

Oh? That must have been unusual.

It was like (he said) "What are you doing here? Why are you here?" Michael is the one who told him "It gets easier."

So Kobe, what are you doing over there now that you've been there for awhile?

He said, "Playing basketball," he said. "And baseball."

So who do you play with? Is it one on one, or is it with a team?

He says, "It's infinite. They play around the universe." He says "He's playing with different versions of himself."

(Note: We've heard variations of this from numerous people, that on the flipside, we are able to "construct" playing fields, games, environment. Golf is often reported, and the math involved in taking a shot that travels from one part of the planet to another.)

Do you mean one on one with younger versions of yourself? Or do you mean the people who show up to play against you are playing with different versions of yourself?

He says, "Different versions."

So when people see you, they see you as when they knew you – Kobe with hair, Kobe without hair?

He says, "Yes." (Jennifer aside) It's so interesting... You're you – people that come up to you, see you the way they used to see you, but they are getting the information of how they saw you. Kobe is observing how different people saw him at different times of his life. It's like "Oh wow, he sees me differently."

Anyone that we might know that you have played with?

This is going to be hard for me to identify people.

Maybe a number?

He shows me Michael Jordan's number. (23).

Have you played one on one with Michael's higher self?

He says, "Yeah."

And who wins those matches?

Kobe says "He does!" (Jennifer laughs).

That's funny. We've talked to people about how they construct a playing field - Junior explained it's like playing the Madden video game times ten, each person who plays brings the memory of their own stadium who participates. But are you saying it's not entire teams, they don't do squads but just with a few players one on one?

He says "Yeah, it's more like that, what you (just) said." I was asking him, like "You play one on one with yourself?'

Let me ask this; in the one on one games with Michael Jordan's higher self, does he think he's winning?

He says, "Always."

(Laughter) So he may think he won and you may think you won – we have to allow that's possible in this mental construct. No one loses.

He's saying "The difference is that he's completely up there, but Michael Jordan is not."

That's funny – so you can pass right through him? Or go around him more easily?

He says, "Likewise. Yes."

You and I met once, maybe Luana can put that in your mind.

He said "It was in 1996."

That's right. (Ding!) It was at a screening through a mutual friend – Mitch Kupchak, who was the assistant to Jerry West at the time. Later the General Manager of the Lakers. Mitch's wife and I were pals and I filmed their wedding. Now I want to shift gears for a minute Kobe. I'm going to ask you a question in Italian and try to put the answer into Jennifer's mind and she'll respond in English. Okay?

He said, "Okay."

"Quando pensi di italia, cosa pensi? Cosa pensi de la tua vita in Italia? Cosa ti manca? Cibo? Amore?" (When you think of Italy, what do you think of? In terms of your life in Italy, what do you miss? Food? Love?)

(Jennifer listens) It's hard to express. He says "You're asking him something about "What do you love?" and he's having a hard time focusing on what he misses.

Quando pensi di Italia, cosa pensi? Cosa ti manca? ("When you think of Italy, what do you think about? What do you miss?")

He's showing me a car, a race car.

Quale macchina? Ferrari? Lamborghini?

He says "Ferrari."

Okay! That's a good answer.

(Jennifer, to me) What did you ask him?

I asked him "What do you miss about Italy?" and he showed you a Ferrari. If you're trying to think of an image that represents Italy, that's a pretty good one.

(Jennifer aside) That's so funny.

"Allora, quando sei arrivato a la prossima posta – quando sei morto, cosa successo? ("So then, when you arrived in the next place, when you were dead, what happened?")

He said, "It dropped" or "he dropped." He says.. (Listens) I don't know if I should repeat the question to him in English, because that's what I normally do...

I don't think you need to repeat it. (The helicopter did indeed drop.) This is just an experiment; Quando sei morto cosa hai pensato? ("When you died, what were you thinking about?")

He's showing me, his family. He's showing me like the people in his family, his wife. I'm seeing like an aerial view of them being out on the Laker floor when he got an award.

Okay, that would make sense. I asked "When you crossed over, what were your thoughts or what were you thinking about?" And he said his family (and perhaps the game of basketball associated with his family.) Che cosa vuoi dire a tua moglie? ("What would you like to say to your wife?")

He's showing me riding a bike.. and he's carrying something on a bike. Like ice cream.

"Questo e un memoria? Luana poi aiutarmi?" ("Is this a memory? Luana can you help us?")

I felt ice .. wet; he's showing me ice cream or weather conditions - I'm not sure.

Okay. "Voi dire ghiaccio or gelato? Quale?" (Okay, do you want to say "ice" or "ice cream?")

The other one, not "gelato."

"Ghiaccio?" (A pause, realizing something) "Vuoi dire quando vuoi parlare con la tua moglie dare un senso di freddo come ghiaccio?" (Ice? Do you want to say that when you want to speak to your wife you give her a sensation of cold, or a chill, like ice?")

(Jennifer quickly taps her nose, before I can ask the question) "Yes," he's saying "Whatever you're saying is correct."

He's saying "When I want my wife to know I'm around her I give her the chills, the sense of ice going down one's back!" Wow. That's why I asked "ice or ice cream?"

(Note: That's pretty cool. I understood what he was trying to show us – I asked how he was able to talk to his wife, he responded with a vison of ice cream, then a vision of ice on a person's back; I asked if he was referring to giving his wife a chill, and he said "yes" before I could even ask the question. It's part of what Jennifer and I have learned before. To connect to someone, say their name, ask your questions. "When you hear the answer before you can ask the question you'll know you have a connection."

Then he just showed me Gina Seau – when Junior's wife came here for a session and spoke to Junior.

"Voi che faciamo un interview insieme con tua moglie?"

He said "Si."

I asked him if he wanted us to do an interview with his wife Vanessa and he said "Yes."

(Jennifer, amazed) Wow. He also showed me my clients down in Orange County, as if by confirmation that I should be doing that in the future.

Cool! I just wanted to prove this was possible to interview someone on the flipside in another language.

There was never a language barrier; it's always been what they tap in my mind.

Let me ask this; "Luana, senti. Cosa pensi di questo forma? Va bene or no?"

She says "Non." (Jennifer shrugs).

Okay, we'll proceed in English. I asked her in Italian "If this was a cool way to go, to continue our interview in Italian, and she said...

She said "No."

Kobe, you're saying it would be cool to put Jennifer together with Vanessa to speak with you directly?

He said "It's too soon. There are too many people grabbing at her at the moment." But when it's supposed to; it will literally fall into my lap kind of thing.

It's funny, I often think "Oh, I've got to film that to help people who are suffering!" but I'll guess some prefer a private conversation with their loved ones. So you and Jennifer and Vanessa should meet up sometime without me. Thanks for your help Junior; Kobe, Junior has been trying to help us cure CTE by showing up in our sessions.

He says, "Everyone knows about it up there."

It helps people here to understand not only can we talk to our relatives, but we can ask and get answers to important questions about how to help cure diseases, or how we can help the planet. Kobe, what do you want to tell your fans?

He says, "To love every precious moment. To breathe it all in. Don't waste time hating. Don't waste time hating or (any) unnecessary roughness."

One of your fans, Snoop went after Gayle King for asking an inappropriate question to a female athlete. We've spoken to a number of people who on the flipside including Michael Jackson about their journey and how discussing the negatives things of their lifetime can help people back here. Can you give us any insight into the incident between you and the girl in Colorado?

He says, "It was a mistake."

A misunderstanding of intent?

He says "Yes, but it doesn't matter..." Let me see if I'm getting this right.. he's saying "It's like one drunk driver hitting another drunk driver."

You mean you had a perspective of what was happening, she had a perspective of something different, both learned lessons when they crashed into one another?

He says, "Yes, but it doesn't matter because you were both still drunk."

Does it help anyone to talk about this?

He said "Not right now."

I just want us to reach beyond that, as we've heard in our classroom discussions that by discussing trauma, whatever it is, that it can heal people by discussing it?

He says, "Do it when... do it before... before it gets out."

Correct the mistake before others hear about it?

He says, "Before it gets out. It's not that it was a mistake." He's saying "Instead of what happened (in this incident) to her, (with the media trauma afterwards) to be the bold one who comes out and says "Hey this is what happened."

But I'm talking about a bigger issue. We've spoken to people who have been abused, experienced trauma; people talk about it here so they can help others release some of that trauma. We understand it's not a matter of asking for forgiveness, you signed up for your lifetime, everyone signs up for theirs. What was the lesson or benefit from this incident if anything?

He says "For him, it was to make him hunker down and focus with his family."

So you're saying the incident had value for everyone?

He says, "Yes, in a lot of different ways."

Anything you want to say to Mitch Kupchak or Shaq?

He showed me Mitch losing his hair. He says "He shouldn't have left the Lakers."

But hang on Kobe, but it seems you were you responsible for him leaving the Lakers because you replaced Mitch with your agent.

He says, "Yes he was, (responsible)."

So why did you do that have your agent replace Mitch?

He said, "He was being greedy."

Okay. That's pretty straightforward. Hang on, do you mean yourself or Mitch?

He said "I was the greedy one."

Not that I can pass this along to Mitch because no one is going to believe we talked to you anyway. Anything else you want to say brother? I shouldn't call you brother, sorry. My habit.

He thought that was funny. How do you say brother in Italian?

Fratello.

He's laughing. He says "I've learned how intricate our hearts are and how we are connected. How we love... and how connected we (all) are."

Is your dad on the planet or over there?

(Jennifer listens) I think he's still here...

(Note: He is, he's a year older than me.)

His dad was also a basketball player.

Kobe is saying that he knows Michael Jordan's father who has passed and is over there.

Can we bring him forward?

(Jennifer shakes her head) They're saying "He's not allowed to cross the velvet rope."

That's funny. We probably have to make a reservation. Well, what can his father tell you to say to Michael on his behalf? Can we ask him that?

He says "Tell Michael he's living his life the right way. And not to ever look back."

This is coming from Michael Jordan's dad?

He says, "Yeah."

Anything else you want to tell your friends and family Kobe?

He says "He'll be there on the 24th."

The 24th?

He said, "His memorial at the Staples Center."

Sorry, I forgot. Of course. Okay, very good Jennifer is a resource for you and she can help you connect to her family.

He said he was at my ("Wine and Spirits") event last night, checking it out.

What's your opinion of what we're doing?

He said, "It was confusing at first, but great for everyone else (who connected with family members). It's a gift, he's saying "It's her basketball." (Referring to Jennifer's ability to connect with the flipside)."

Thanks Kobe, Gianna. Luana thanks for helping, we appreciate it; it's a lot of work but what the hell, why not? We love you all.

Let's end on that note. Not gone. Just not here.

I decided to conduct this interview in a language I knew that Kobe understood but that Jennifer did not. As mentioned, it's like opening a door, and getting used to how to communicate. In the coming weeks, perhaps we'll revisit having a chat with him if he's so inclined. We've found that once we've had them in the classroom, they show up often when we're interviewing someone else. We ask "So who are you hanging out with over there?" and they'll often reply with the name of someone we've interviewed. Sometimes I take that opportunity to ask new questions and get newer information. It's wild, but it literally is like "having a cellphone to the flipside."

Martini Out.

AFTERWORD

"NEW LANGE SYNE"

Jennifer Shaffer   Luana Anders by Monte Hellman

LUANA ANDERS   PETER TOWNSEND

This session seemed to be a more fitting ending to this journey into the architecture of the afterlife.

It's a bridge between this book and the other ongoing interviews between myself, Jennifer Shaffer and Luana Anders on the flipside. Earlier in the week Jennifer and I did a session where I was asking for people to "come forward" so we could interview them. Jennifer said *"Is Pete Townsend alive?"* I asked why. She said, **"Luana is mentioning his name."**

I pointed out that the lead singer for "The Who" is still alive, and while we do have "higher selves" that are accessible while we are on the planet, it would be a bit unusual for him to show up specifically to speak with us. Instead of pursuing why or who this was, I asked other questions about who I was interested in speaking with.

Then later that night, I was at a Christmas party with an old friend, Bill, someone who knew Luana well and had written scripts with her. He said "I often pass by her old house and think of her." I said "Well, you can access anyone, including her. Just imagine her sitting across from you – imagine being able to hold her hands. Can you do that?" My friend looked into the distance and said "Okay."

I said "Now ask her something you don't know the answer to. Ask her "Who was there to greet you when you crossed over?" My friend paused and said **"She said "Peter."**

I didn't ask who that was – I was just demonstrating how easy it was to access the other side. But when I was transcribing the session with Jennifer earlier in the day, the name Peter jumped out at me. Peter Townsend.

So I looked up Peter Townsend online, and found a photograph. I want to say that I felt instantly "that's him" – but I tried to set that aside. "It could be him" is what I allowed, and did some research about this fellow. On the way to Jennifer's office, and old friend of Luana's, screenwriter Robert Towne called and I said "Oh, by the way, when I ask you "Who is Pete Townsend, who comes to mind?"

He said "The RAF pilot."

I thought, "Wow, yes, of course, he was famous to members of Luana's generation, like her friend on the phone, and the singer from The Who would be a more likely reference for me." I asked him why he said that, and he said "That's who came to mind."

I thanked him for reminding me who it was I wanted to speak with via Jennifer. It had slipped my mind – but now it was clearly in the forefront. The following was recorded a few minutes later. For those familiar with "Backstage Pass to the Flipside," my old friend Luana Anders conducts the class, and Jennifer the medium gives me whatever visual or aural replies that she gets from Luana on the flipside.

My comments are *in italics,* Jennifer's replies are **in bold.**

Rich: Hello class. Hi Luana.

Jennifer: Hello.

How was your New Year's, Luana?

"Exhausting," she says.

Why?

She says, "Everyone thinks of the new decade – when they're holding onto the old one. This is the new decade," she's saying that

they were "All trying very hard to have people leave things in the past. Stop thinking about the past."

Stop reminiscing on New Year's? Good luck with that.

She says, "What it does, by thinking of the future, is it creates a bounce of energy, more new energy. Whereas the old energy keeps people mired in the past."

New Lange Syne instead of Old Lang Syne?

She says, "Yes." Luana is tapping her nose. (Jennifer aside) I don't know what that means.

(Note: Jennifer is tapping her nose because that's what she's getting from Luana who is saying "correct" by showing herself tapping her nose. But in the same sentence, Jennifer reveals that she doesn't know what Luana means by doing so – or what I meant by the obscure sentence "Should old acquaintance be forgot?" should be "Old Acquaintances are never forgotten, they're new again." At least that's what I was trying to say.)

"For old acquaintance to be new and always brought to mind?"

(Recognizing the tune) Oh, right. It will help the planet. Yes.

I was talking to Luana's old friend Bill and I was doing a demonstration at his Christmas part of how simple it is to speak to people on the other side. So I told him to ask her "Who was there to greet her when she crossed over" and he said "Pete." And I don't know a Pete.

I saw her cat.

Yes, I think we've talked about that before. But the first person was the question – what about this Pete fellow?

That's what she says. It's accurate that he was there. I think he's a father figure, or like a family figure, perhaps a grandfather; I'm seeing someone holding her hand and walking her over there.

(Note: This is an example of interpreting imagery. Jennifer sees someone holding a child's hand and walking them into the flipside;

may be a family figure, a father, or grandfather – a metaphor for a family member helping someone to cross over.)

Let's talk about this Pete.

"Pete Townsend."

Why'd you say that?

I don't know.

It's the same name we heard from her a week ago, but I didn't say it. Can we talk to Pete Townsend?

"He's here." (Jennifer aside) Is he dead? The lead singer for The Who?

No. There are more than one Pete Townsend apparently. Try not to judge it. Can we talk to this Pete?

He said, "Yes."

What's he look like?

This guy is shorter... he's very handsome. He's a Brit.

(Note: This Pete Townsend wasn't short, but is shorter than the lead singer for The Who. Lunch shows up, so we pause the conversation. After lunch, we invite him again.)

You're still there. Hello. Mr. Pete.

He's saying "It took long enough!" He has a bit of a temper. (Jennifer aside) But there is no time over there!

Luana, what's the purpose of bringing Pete to speak with us? Is he an old friend of yours?

She says "You can say that." From a long time ago.

Did you ever meet him in this lifetime?

She's showing me going in and out of consciousness when she had cancer. Saw him them. She said she talked to you about a dream she had.

This same guy? I don't remember the dream.

She says, "It's similar to your classroom dream. Like a future person for me."

(Note: Luana is referring to a dream I had where I was in a classroom and seeing her in it. At the time I had no context for how I could be seeing a younger version of her in a classroom that I clearly recognized as her.)

Pete let's ask some questions. Do you mind?

"Open book" he says. "No put intended."

Show Jennifer a lifetime where you and Luana met before?

I'm seeing London. "It's been many lifetimes."

What year are you accessing?

He said, "1813."

Were you a man or woman at the time?

Everything "switched" when you said that – (like a flash of visuals) He was a woman.

And Luana? Was she a man or woman?

They're laughing. "A woman too…" (Jennifer aside) It felt like they were in a brothel or something.

Where in London?

He says, "Kensington." I keep wanting to go to Knightsbridge.

(Note: Kensington is three minutes from Knightsbridge. In 1813, Charlotte Hayes was a successful brothel owner who kept luxurious brothels near Knightsbridge in St. James. She's listed in the "Harris List Of Covent Garden Ladies" (wikipedia) and owned brothels in and around Covent Garden. According to research, 50K women out of 1 million residents worked in the trade at the turn of the 18th century. If one wanted to, they could ask Luana and Peter for more elaborate descriptions, names, etc during that era).

Pete is the person I looked up yesterday, is that who you are?

He says, "A part of him, yes."

(Note: This is a common answer. "A part of him" refers to the idea that we bring about a third of our conscious energy to any lifetime. (People report between 20 and 40% most often). When I ask people questions about their journey, they're often very precise in their answers. So asking "were you this person in a past life?" they often reply "well, part of me was." In this case, I looked up "Peter Townsend" and the first person who came up with this famous RAF pilot who was a war hero in Britain, then made special assistant to the King, eventually fell in love with Princess Margaret but wasn't allowed to marry her. He subsequently married, had a number of children, and lived happily ever after. He passed in 1995 a year before Luana's passing in 1996.)

Peter Townsend; Norwegian archives; family Instagram photo.

Show Jennifer what you did during your life.

He says, "He was in the military... And he was shot."

Was he shot at or literally shot?

He says, "Both. All of it. He keeps showing me a plane. He was a pilot. He's showing me Hitler."

(Ding ding ding!) Yes, the Peter Townsend I looked up yesterday was a pilot who fought against Hitler. You were known for that.

"He's also showing me fighting against the Japanese as well."

I'll have to look that up.

(Note: I did. Peter Townsend was posted in Singapore in 1936 through 1939. He fought valiantly in WWII in the Battle of Britain; was shot at and shot down, losing a big toe to shrapnel.)

Was he like an agent or military intelligence?

Could be.

That's why Amelia Earhart showed up earlier.

(Note: For fans of "Hacking the Afterlife" we speak extensively with Amelia about her life and journey and her arrest by the Japanese for being "a spy" and her incarceration and death in Saipan (where parts of her body and her plane still reside).

I feel like he was like Indiana Jones.

(Note: News footage of him from the news reels of the era show him as a dashing man in uniform and pith helmet helping various cultures and people in South Africa.)

Something about the gold rush? Mining. Something exciting – treasures, it has to do with finding treasures of the planet.

Peter you had a relationship with someone. Can you show that to Jennifer?

Like an actress.

Someone in England.

Was she in the royal family?

Yes.

I saw Queen Elizabeth but I don't think it's her. Her daughter? Sister?

Princess Margaret was the daughter of Queen Elizabeth and a sister to Elizabeth II. (To Jennifer) Did you see the show "The Crown?"

Yes, (Margaret) she's a brunette.

Do you remember that episode about the military guy she was in love with that they decided to send away and keep it apart?

(Jennifer's eyes go wide). Wow!

That was his story.

He says, "It's true. This is him."

(Note: An episode of the Netflix show "The Crown" detailed the events around the relationship between Margaret and Peter Townsend. The Crown wasn't interested in seeing them together, so they sent him away to South Africa. I've been working with Jennifer for five years proving that we can access the flipside and interview people who've crossed over and get forensically accurate details from them. See "Backstage Pass to the Flipside: Talking to the Afterlife with Jennifer Shaffer.")

Luana, was that weird to see Peter when you crossed over?

She says "She knew people who knew him. Various friends..." (Jennifer aside) I'm seeing the Beatles."

(Note: Luana met the Beatles in 1965 in Los Angeles after their Hollywood Bowl performance, where she was invited to a party to meet them. She also was close friends with British actor Michael Gough.)

I'm thinking of a friend of Luana's that she starred on Broadway with; Michael Gough.

(Jennifer aside) That makes sense.

I was researching how Luana might have known this RAF pilot, I found that Michael Gough and Peter Townsend appeared on the same BBC show in the 60's. Peter, did you meet Mick?

"Many times" he says. "When we were young and ruthless."

Funny way to put it. Mick was a young actor working in the theater back then, correct?

Michael Gough – private collection.

Let me ask Mick Gough a question; do you have any message for your lovely wife Henrietta?

(Jennifer lets out a long sigh.) He just showed me the woman from the Sound of Music.

Julie Andrews. (Guessing at the metaphor) Was that the kind of love you had for her?

"Corny, but yes."

Luana and Mick on Broadway 30 years apart. She was billed as Margo Anders in "The Fighting Cock" in 1959 and finding him backstage in "Breaking the Code" in 1987. Corny buy why not?

Luana, recently a number of your friends have mentioned you to me.

She showing me talking to her friends and having them reach out to you – but it's to remind you (that) she's always around.

Peter, what do you want to tell us?

(Jennifer aside) It's so odd that in my past three public readings, everyone had an aviator in the session. It's a theme I shouldn't ignore.

Let's ask our class; what's up with all the flying references?

They're saying "We are pilots. We're already flying – a lot of flying references, but we're already flying, there's no physical plane around us."

A metaphor for flying at the speed of thought?

(Jennifer taps her nose.) It was for you to be able to reference it (this way).

If I had asked Luana about Peter early on, I never would have made this connection. Two days ago I asked my mentor and old boss Robert Towne, "Did you hear of Peter Townsend?" He said "Yeah; the RAF pilot." Not what I expected but it's a generational thing.

I only know the guy from the band, "The Who!"

Me too. That must have been a little odd Luana, when you saw him on the flipside?

How old was Luana when all that was going on with Peter and all that went on?

It was in the late 50's early 60's as her acting career blossomed.

They showed me (how) everyone nearly connected, all those people in England, nearby - but not connecting.

Did you know of Peter during your life? Or did you ever meet him in person?

She's reminding me that she said "no" already.

573

Are you part of the same soul group?

"We all are. And we are all pilots in a way."

(Note: When exploring Jennifer's fear of water, or flying over water, we accessed her past life memory of being a fighter pilot and crashing into the ocean. "Soul group" is a reference to Michael Newton's work where he found that his clients claimed in-between lives we have groups (or classmates) where we incarnate together, depending on the lessons required.)

Personally, I'm not a fan of flying. Just saying.

She says, "Yes, we're part of the same soul group, we all have different ways of having fun, some people have different ideas of how to have fun, or (ways they) got out of being here..." She's showing me like having a parachute on. I'm asking her "Why a parachute?" She's says "I don't need a parachute – since I'm already flying."

Anything Peter wants to say to family or friends?

He says, "I'm always with them."

Thank you Peter.

(Note: I had a second person I wanted to speak with, and had just thought of them when I noticed Jennifer holding her ear in pain. It's something I've seen her do; she mentions the shift in energy in the room being painful when someone shows up with a strong energy or frequency.)

Did you have a shift in tone there?

(Nods) It hurt.

I asked someone else to come forward.

Warn me next time, would you?

Sorry. My wife Sherry had a vision of someone last night – she was meditating on healing our son who has a bad cough and she said she meditated this person into the room.

Was it a deity? One of the Gods for Tibetans?

(Ding!) Yes. She was emanating a color.

Blue?

Green.

Sorry – I can see that color now and it felt like a Tibetan deity.

Luana can we interview this Tibetan deity briefly?

(Jennifer aside) It's also somebody that I've seen – only she was blue, clothed (in a cloak) with all the (multiple) arms.

Is this the same person or a version of that person?

It's the same (being). Same energy, yeah.

(Note: When interviewing her father, he took us to a classroom in deep space, to an advanced class in astrophysics; when the teacher appeared, she was radiating a blue light and had multiple arms. We've spoken to her on a few occasions.)

Can I ask some questions? How did Sherry manifest you?

She says, "She thought of the highest level of healing."

When Sherry described you, I said "Oh, you talked to Tara?" Sherry said "No, not Tara." But is that a name to refer to you as?

She says, "It's like using the word "God.""

Sherry saw her specifically as someone with wings – show Jennifer how you appeared.

Feels like an avatar from the Avatar movie – glowing skin, iridescent. Radiance. Unique eyes.

Almond shaped?

Yeah, dark in color.

Sherry saw this avatar do something – can you show Jennifer what it is you did?

She put colors into his forehead. Like a bright, yellowish tint.

(Ding!) That's correct. She saw it as a jewel.

That's what I'm seeing – how it's being pushed in – not what is being pushed in.

Sherry saw it as an emerald being put into his forehead.

They showed me an association... like a heating pad, cooling down the brain. Like using its heat to break (the fever) it down.

Was that for heat or for healing?

She says, "Healing. It's energy that came from Sherry."

That healing energy was then manifested as an emerald and pushed into his forehead?

She says, "They were helping Sherry at the same time."

Once the healing light enters, then what happens?

She says, "It breaks up and goes into the whole body, disperses or injecting energy to where there is hurt – where his cough is.." I can see it in his chest. "He slept for a long time after it."

He did. But is the energy like water?

She says, "Yes, like raindrops sprinkled inside his body."

(Note: I ask because when our daughter was 4 she talked about being a doctor in Tibet and how she helped people – she said she would "turn on the tap of healing light" and then "sprinkle the drops around the home and the person's body." She described how she "sprinkled" energetic healing light like water, and the energy heals the person.)

Does this make people better?

She says, "Yes." They said "Sherry was the fertilizer – the catalyst. But a lot don't believe it is possible – so belief is important for the outcome. She was the catalyst in that ... knew it existed on a consciousness level."

She said that she didn't know if it happened or was a dream.

She's saying "It did happen, absolutely – that's why her hands got so warm."

Tara are you associated with Sherry, Luana or just the whole process?

It's like seeing the Archangel Michael for someone else; (the manifestation is) available to everyone, it's associated to everyone that believes he or she exists.

Shall I put this at the end of the Architecture book or Backstage Pass?

She says, "Both. Like you have to know the power of prayer, that prayer works. But you can mix it up with visualizing it going in."

To paraphrase, one could think of Jesus or Tara, or their mother, or a famous scientist and get the same results?

She says, "Yes; all the same feeling of light energies."

Will you meet us all on the flipside, Tara?

She says, "No, here. Whenever you bring these concepts to light, the more it vibrates up and we feel it."

Will there be more people seeing you as a result of this research or is this something that's been going on for eons?

She says "She's been doing it for gazillions of years."

Are we helping to open this up to people by doing this research?

She says, "Yes, with your words, printing it – like Sanskrit – different texts have it (the same information)."

I was in a Nepalese restaurant today, I saw a poster of green Tara – and spoke to the woman who owned the restaurant, whose name is Tara. It turns out we met on a bus in 1996 in Brooklyn, on a Tibetan holiday, where we shared a ride to a monastery in Woodstock.

(Jennifer laughs) Of course you did.

Okay guys. Thanks Tara. Thanks Luana. Thanks Peter Townsend... famous RAF pilot – everything worked out the way it was supposed to – I guess you weren't supposed to marry crazy Margaret.

He said "She wasn't crazy; she changed the rules, they're changing now."

Peter do you have any relatives we need to reach out to?

He says, "Yeah, you'll have to dig it (them) up."

(Note: I have.)

Anything else you want to mention Peter?

He says, "It was well worth it. And then some." He says he "Just wishes he could have enjoyed it" (when he was here).

Thanks for stopping by.

I got an image of a circle inside of a triangle... like we've come full circle.

That you would know Luana, and we could have this conversation 30 years after her passing... must have been a little startling. It is for me.

She says, "It was an easy landing; they knew the same people (but) just had never met."

Awesome.

She says, "To the moon and back we love you all! Bye!"

****

I end this book with this uplifting chapter. This research began with Luana, and this book ends with her giving us new information. Not about death or who we were – or about reminiscing about previous lifetimes. (**Auld Lange Syne becomes New Lange Syne**). We learned something new about our old friend Luana, we learned something new about how to ask our healing avatars for help.

The *architecture of the afterlife* shows that our loved ones are much closer than we imagine they are.

I've also been editing "Architecture of the Afterlife: The Flipside Code" while finishing this one. Both reference each other. For more in depth interviews with "councils" and "guides" mentioned here, I recommend picking up "Architecture of the Afterlife" as a companion piece to this one. They kind of dovetail each other.

Robin Williams gets the last word:

"Love Love."

ACKNOWLEDGEMENTS

ABOUT JENNIFER SHAFFER

With husband Fred

Jennifer Shaffer is a world-renowned Psychic Medium. Her cases have been profiled on 20/20, Buzzfeed, Dr. Phil, and Oxygen. Jennifer donates her time to law enforcement and families of victims, by assisting with criminal cases and helping find answers. She is the Co-Founder, VP & Law Enforcement Case Expert for Impartial Witness, a strategic artificial intelligence software platform designing partnerships between law enforcement and the intuitive network. Jennifer founded the JS Intuitive Investigations Academy and also teaches an intuitive investigations development course for various skill levels. She is the subject of two bestselling books by Richard Martini "Backstage Pass to the Flipside" and has a private practice in Manhattan Beach.

Author, Speaker and Intuitive Spiritual Teacher, Vice President and Law Enforcement Case Expert for Beneficial Intelligence Syndicate. Impartial Witness Case Expert Through BIS for Law Enforcement, FBI Officials and The Intuitive Investigation Alliances and Academy. Advisory Board Member for FOHVAMP Families of Homicide Victims and Missing Persons.

Jennifer has been seen on CBS Television, HLN on CNN, FOX, Free Form on ABC and she just had an appearance on BRAVO. Her heart is with her JS Investigation Alliances where there is a collaboration of Intuitives that donate their time to families and law enforcement for unresolved homicides and missing person cases.

Jennifer's JS Intuitive Investigations Academy will serve as a platform and safe place for individuals to learn about investigations. She will be mentoring those who want to learn about their own abilities while working on investigations. Jennifer was recently asked to serve as an Advisory Board Member for FOHVAMP, an organization that helps Families of Homicide Victims and Missing Persons. Evidential Intuitive Medium Jennifer Shaffer Sees, Hears, and Feels those Spirits who have Crossed Over.

Jennifer is a "Translator of Spirit." She is a Clairvoyant Medium, Medical Intuitive, Intuitive Investigator and Profiler. Her investigation cases have recently been featured on "20/20" and "Dr. Phil," and she has also been a reoccurring guest on the "Ricki Lake" show. Jennifer is clairvoyant, clairaudient and clairsentient which means being blessed with sight, hearing and feeling from the spiritual world that both enlightens and brings comfort. Jennifer receives guidance that gives you confirmation of past events, informs you of the future, brings clarity to issues, and messages from your departed loved ones. Spirit wants to help by giving powerful insights from the other side.

She can be reached at JenniferShaffer.com

FROM RICHARD MARTINI "A THOUSAND THANKS"

First and foremost, thanks to Jennifer. I bow to your skills as a medium, a medical intuitive, as someone who helps people heal. We've had many laughs during our sessions; there's nothing quite like hearing something profound and being able to laugh about it. To her pal Michelle for the **bold faced type** idea.

A shout out to Scott De Tamble, lightbetweenlives.com, to Michael Newton, thank you for your work and your research. Thanks to George Noory, his Coast to Coast and "Beyond Belief" crew at Gaia.com. To Joel Gotler, literary maven, to those on Quora who correct my posts and weigh in on my far out postings

But most of all, a special thanks to Luana whom I met *40 years ago*! To think she would have such a profound influence on me in life and after is really wild. I appreciate her relentless patience, her ability to herd cats – the members of our class. Thanks to all those in attendance; Robin, David, Prince, Michael, Julian, John, Jim, Jimi, another Jim, George, Tom, Rance, Billy, Harry Dean, Cis, Randal, Harry, Robert, Edward, Craig, Sydney, Howard, Roger, Gene, Ray, Anthony, Kate, Uncle C, Rig, Paul T, Craig O, Billy M, Mom, Dad.

Thanks to those who've generously donated towards the research: Mary Fesler, Chris Rawls, Julie Harmeyer, Tash Govender, Diana Takata, Don Thompson, Alex Broskey, Savarna Wiley, Robert

Thurman, Carin Levee, Chris Monaghan, John Wylie, Daniel Kearney, Maureen Johanson, Bill Dale, Eric Harrington, Lisa Yesse, Tamara Guion-Yagy, Lynette Hilton, John and Lucy Tibayan, Jon Burhham.

Luana Anders outside of time

Dedicated to my wife Sherry, daughter Olivia and son RJ – I love you! *Thanks for choosing me.*

Richard Martini is a journalist, author and award-winning filmmaker. Boston University, USC Film School, Master of Professional Writing. He's written and/or directed 8 theatrical features including "You Can't Hurry Love," "Limit Up," and "Cannes Man." He wrote for Variety, Premiere and Inc.com, documentaries include "White City/Windy City – Sister Cities" "Journey Into Tibet with Robert Thurman" and "Tibetan Refugee." His books; "Flipside: A Tourist's Guide on How to Navigate the Afterlife" "It's a Wonderful Afterlife Volume 1 and 2" and "Hacking the Afterlife" are available at all online outlets. The documentaries "Flipside: A Journey Into the Afterlife" and "Talking to Bill Paxton" are available on Gaia.com "Architecture of the Afterlife: The Flipside Code" is on all outlets. For further info: RichMartini.com or MartiniZone.com

www.ingramcontent.com/pod-product-compliance
Lightning Source LLC
Chambersburg PA
CBHW071113080526
44587CB00013B/1323